W9-BDZ-168

AN
IDEOLOGY
IN
POWER

DK265
W58

AN IDEOLOGY IN POWER

Reflections on the Russian Revolution

BERTRAM D. WOLFE

Introduction by Leonard Schapiro

𝔰𝔡

STEIN AND DAY/*Publishers*/New York

FEB 2 1 1978

174017

Copyright © 1969 Bertram D. Wolfe
Library of Congress Catalog Card No. 68-31612
All rights reserved

Published simultaneously in Canada by Saunders of Toronto Ltd.
Designed by Bernard Schleifer
Printed in the United States of America

Published in conjunction with the Hoover Institution
on War, Revolution, and Peace of Stanford University

Stein and Day/*Publishers*/7 East 48 Street, New York, N.Y. 10017
SBN 8128-1204-2

CONTENTS

FOREWORD

It is a great privilege for me to figure in one of Bertram D. Wolfe's books—even as an interloper in a foreword. For those who, like myself, have ventured into the field of the history of the Soviet Communist party know full well how much we owe to *Three Who Made a Revolution*. It was literally the first attempt in any language to sift out of oblivion, after forty years or more, the tangled facts of a period of party history over which Soviet historians prefer to draw a veil. Indeed, Mr. Khrushchev was right when he once remarked that "historians are dangerous people. They are capable of upsetting everything." I suspect he was thinking of Mr. Wolfe!

The author of the present work, however, is much more than a historian of the party or, at any rate, much more courageous and venturesome than the usual run of historians. For he does not hesitate to apply his detailed knowledge of history to present-day analysis. I suppose we all do a bit of current analysis now and again but we are usually only too happy if it is decently forgotten when once it has served its ephemeral purpose. Not so Mr. Wolfe. Here he offers us a current analysis over twenty-five years without alteration. I hope all his readers will do like myself—rush off to see how often they can catch him out in his predictions, to which we now, with the benefit of hindsight, know the answers. They will, like myself, be time and again agreeably disappointed for the plain fact is that Mr. Wolfe was nearly always right. For him this should offer the satisfaction of knowing that he has done what so few other analysts of the Soviet scene have ventured to do. For his readers, I hope, it will offer convincing evidence that there is a basic rightness about the method of analysis which he adopts.

This basic rightness, as I see it, consists in the fact that Mr. Wolfe has mastered the essential nature of a totalitarian society. He does not, as so many analysts do, apply criteria of judgment to Soviet politics which may be valid when applied to, say, Switzerland, or to the British Labour Party, but are meaningless for anyone who knows what the Soviet system of totalitarian party control is like. And so this collection of essays and articles assumes a unity in spite of its anthological nature—it becomes a kind of handbook of totalitarian behaviour in its various aspects, both internal and external. The literature of totalitarianism is still small and incomplete and such an addition to it can only be welcomed.

One final word, Bertram Wolfe is not only concerned to analyze, he also offers sombre advice on the conclusions which should be drawn by those responsible for Western policy from analysis of the past. This is the point at which Mr. Wolfe's record of accurate prediction becomes a good deal more than an agreeable parlor game. For if it is the case—and his readers can judge for themselves—that he has been able by his analysis of a number of vital questions to foresee the trend of political developments in the Soviet Union and the communist orbit, it follows beyond a peradventure that we can only ignore his advice for the future at our peril.

LEONARD SCHAPIRO

London School of Economics and Political Science

PART I

The Ideology:
From Marxism to
Marxism-Leninism

I MARXISM AND THE RUSSIAN REVOLUTION*

Historically, Marxism is an offshoot of the idea of Revolution, an idea comparatively new in history. The idea was born in the last quarter of the eighteenth century and has dominated much of the thinking of the nineteenth and twentieth.

Contrary to what Marxism in all it varieties holds, the idea of revolution arose unexpectedly, unplanned, unthought of, taking its leading actors by surprise, creating for itself an explanation and an ideology or a complex of conflicting ideological fragments only after the fact.

Some would locate the starting point of the idea in North America in 1776. But the inherited English freedoms and physical sources of liberty in America were already the matter of European utopian dreams long before Franklin arrived in Paris or Lafayette came to the rebellious colonies and before the celebrated "self-evident truths" of the Declaration of Independence were proclaimed to mankind. The freedoms of the English colonies from the outset and the social conditions of a continent where unoccupied land seemed limitless, poverty no longer a God-ordained state, and careers were open to talents without limitations of estate or caste—these, and not national independence, were what made the New World seem *new* to Europe.[1]

Moreover, the American was never a proper revolution to capture the imagination by scenes of unforgettable drama. At best it was a revolution *manqué*. It had no fascinating engine in the public square that by mere force of gravity could make men shorter by a head; no emotion-choked reign of terror to chew up rich and poor, men and women, young and old, and finally devour the revolution's own children; no dramatic extermination of generals and factions during the revolution; no sequel of purge and Thermidor and Bonapartism. It did not dream of beginning the world afresh with a new calendar and history starting with *the year one*. At its end, impenitent Loyalists went off freely to Halifax; leaders of American

---

*This chapter is derived from an address delivered on October 8, 1967 (see note 43).

1. For a study of the idea of revolution see Hannah Arendt, *On Revolution*, New York, 1963.

"factions," Jefferson, Hamilton, Adams, Daniel Shays, lived out their lives to die a natural death, a death most unnatural for French or Russian revolutionaries.

Even the War between the States, the bloodiest in military history up to its time, was not a proper civil war: as the stillness descended upon Appomattox, the voice of General Grant could be heard saying to the Confederate cavalry "Keep your horses, boys, you'll need them for the spring planting," while the leaders of the rebellion, Jefferson Davis and Robert E. Lee, were to live out the remainder of their lives in peace and die in bed.

Not in the Marxian but in a narrow and literal sense there was an economic connection between the American War for Independence and the Revolution in France. The French monarch had been so generous in his aid to the American colonists that at our revolution's end his treasury was empty and the monarchy bankrupt. Not the rise of a new social class nor dire poverty in France, but a bankrupt treasury in a prospering land opened, unexpectedly to all, a period of revolutions.

In 1787 the king of this powerful, prospering country called together an Assembly of Notables to listen to a shocking report of royal bankruptcy and to approve suggested reforms whose main purpose would be to tax the notables who had not been taxed before, in order to replenish the empty coffers of their king. The nobles had no more far-reaching intention than that of defending their privileges against these incursions and of finding fault with Calonne for permitting the greatest treasury on the continent to go bankrupt. But their year-long resistance to the finance minister's plans was the first in a series of revolutions which, in retrospect, are lumped together as the Great French Revolution. It was this *révolte nobiliaire* and not some action of the petty, insignificant, and un-self-confident industrial bourgeoisie of France that opened what Marxists and Marxist-Leninists, and many historians along with them, persist in calling "the bourgeois revolution." If by bourgeoisie is meant a "rising social class" begotten by industrial capitalism, its wealth largely invested in industry and the employment of industrial labor, with its values derived from "capitalism," with a special and distinct "relationship to the forces of production," and a distinct more or less uniform psychology and will, such a class nowhere appears upon the scene throughout the great drama. Neither initiator nor actor nor chorus, it did not "come to power," nor displace another "ruling class," nor substitute its values for the prevailing ones, either during the revolution or at its end, nor gain substantial benefits from it, nor win from it free room for industrial development.

The chief beneficiaries of the Revolution were the new and expanded bureaucracy; the landed proprietary groups that got the *biens nationaux* at bargain prices; and the peasants. Then Napoleon, Jacobin child of the

Revolution, established a new nobility, requiring a landed endowment of anyone he raised to the peerage and forbidding him or his heirs to alienate the land except in exchange for other lands. The old values that gave more prestige to land than to trade and industry continued to prevail in France after the Revolution was over and after Napoleon's fall from power. The enormously expanded bureaucracy continued to be the real ruler of France all through the nineteenth century and into the second half of the twentieth, through volatile periods of French political life when ministries and governments changed so frequently that, were it not for the stable rule of the bureaucracy, France would have been in a state of perpetual chaos. As to the third beneficiary of the Revolution, the peasant, his acquisition of a family farm left him without the need or urge to crowd into the cities so that French industrialization was delayed by the lack of a free-floating labor reserve.

Beyond that, I must leave it to the Marxists of various stripes to torture the image of the independent peasant, owner of his land and implements and the product of his toil, into some semblance of a "bourgeoisie." I leave, too, to the self-appointed spokesmen of the proletariat the task of falsely flattering the bourgeoisie by calling the Rights of Man and the all too slow widening of democratic suffrage and parliamentarism "bourgeois freedoms." I can only think that their purpose is not so much to exalt the bourgeoisie as to belittle the freedoms.

Far from opening up a period of rapid industrialization, the French Revolution left French industry feeble, backward, and confined by all sorts of limitations inherited from the Empire. French industry remained stagnant, French banking investment remained limited to loans to governments and speculation in currencies for well over a half century after the "bourgeois" revolution. The long period of economic stagnation was broken only in the sixties when Isaac Péreire introduced the first industrial investment bank, the Crédit Mobilier. Then an upsurge of industrialization began, not under "bourgeois" auspices, but under the auspices of a group of bankers and entrepreneurs who were ideological followers of the utopian socialist Saint-Simon.

Thus it took fervent adherents of a socialist creed to weaken somewhat, and then only partially, the dominion of the aristocratic proprietary and *rentier* tradition which felt that to invest in commerce—and still more so in industry—was to lose one's ease and dignity.

"THE DREAM OF REASON"

The year-long resistance of the nobles compelled the monarch to convoke an Estates-General, a time-honored device of bankrupt monarchs, but one which had not had to be used since 1610. Naïvely, the king made the democratic gesture of asking the people of France for advice on how the Estates-General should be constituted. It was this, and not the growth of a new rising class with a new ideology, that opened the floodgates to a spate of ever more sweeping proposals.

Inditers of addresses to the king and of proclamations and editorials in new provincial and urban journals; orators in a flowering of clubs and meetings, assemblies, *communes, parlements,* and accidental mobs; new baked pamphleteers; authors of resolutions and *cahiers de doléances;* obscure provincial lawyers and journalists who had never had an audience or a voice in political life—all of them might have taken as their common device: "I know nothing about it, therefore I can speak freely." One has only to hearken to this confusion of voices, and ponder these shiny new proposals for making the world afresh, to realize that they were anything but the voice of political experience or the expression of the interests of any estate or "social class," least of all of the careful calculations of the *bon bourgeois.*

The stream of suggestions grew in number and fury like a spring flood. The *révolte nobiliaire* "taught the Third Estate the language, tactics, and gallantry of opposition." And, once the floodgates were open, each suggestion overreached its predecessor. "What this interpretation restores," as the historian George Taylor observes, "is the sense of an unplanned, unpremeditated revolution that in many and startling ways exceeded the aims expressed in the *cahiers de doléances.*" [2]

Thus an essential feature of a revolution is that it gains in unplanned momentum and constantly overreaches itself until it takes the form of the idea that the world can be swept clean of all that exists, all that time, experience, tradition, custom, habit, law and the slow organic growth of society have engendered and "history can begin anew." Nothing at that moment is to be examined for the purposes of improving or reforming it, correcting some specific abuse or some obsolescent feature. That would not be revolution but "reformism," and there are no more abusive epithets in a revolutionary's vocabulary than the words *reformist* or *reformism.* What a revolution needs, Marx wrote on the eve of the upheavals of 1848, was "destruction and dissolution" and "the forcible overthrow of all existing conditions." In the space made clean and empty by the iron broom of revolution, a totally new world would be created. Thus the day comes, as it did on September 22, 1792, when the very calendar is scrapped and time itself begins anew with the First Day of the Year

---

2. George V. Taylor, "Non-capitalist Wealth and the Origins of the French Revolution," *American Historical Review,* Jan. 1967, pp. 469-96. Compare the vivid image of Alexander Herzen, written after a close-up view of the revolutions of 1848 in Paris: "the tousled improvizations of revolution."

One of the New World in creation. At this point man becomes as God, and replaces the old God in the temple by enshrining there his own Reason to be worshiped. And, as the Devil reminded Ivan Karamazov, "There is no law for God . . . all things are permitted, and that's the end of it." With that "all things are permitted," the history of contemporary nihilism begins. It is fulfilled in the terror of the French Revolution; in the attempt to exterminate whole classes of the population and the blood-purges of the Russian Revolution; in the crematoriums of Hitler's Germany and projected European revolution. Said Talleyrand of the French Revolution, "It was made by builders of theories for an imaginary world." According to Robespierre, it was accomplished "by putting into laws the moral truths culled from the philosophers." To these striking formulae we need only add the wry comment of the artist, Goya: "The dream of reason produces monsters."

THE MYTH OF THE BOURGEOIS REVOLUTION

In historical terms, then, Marxism may be defined as an elaborate misunderstanding of the French Revolution, of the role of "classes," and of the very nature of revolution. Marx took as his initial axioms—self-evident truths that seemed to him in no need of proof. The first axiom holds that a revolution begins as a consequence of a social transformation of society and takes on overt political form only when a new class has grown ripe enough to challenge an old "ruling class," take power itself, and make over the world in its image. But we have seen how unexpectedly revolutions come, how they take their initiators and principal actors by surprise, how they create their ideologies in torrents only after the fact, and how these ideologies compete, displace each other, overreach themselves, until society, which cannot live forever at fever heat and under perpetual tension, disorder, and confusion, welcomes a subsidence of excitement and a relapse into quiet, even if order is brought about by the same guillotine that symbolized the culmination of disorder, even if order is brought about by a Bonaparte or a Stalin, even if the new despot coninues and enlarges disorder from above but no longer demands or permits that it arise from below.

Marx's second axiom took it for granted that the French Revolution could be meaningfully defined as a *bourgeois revolution*, its ideological dreams and nightmares described as *bourgeois ideologies*, and its driving force and victor could be termed *the revolutionary bourgeoisie*. Each of these "axioms" dissolves in the face of empirical examination of the events, the leaders, the roles, the ideas, and the actions of the revolution. The same dogmas were taken for granted and given yet cruder formulation by the Marxist epigones and notably by Russian Marxists of all schools. Russian worshippers of the poetry of the machine and of technology might look to Germany as the model to follow, as Germany had looked to England, and as later many lands, including Bolshevik Russia, would look to America. But however far behind the French economy might be, when it came to revolution, France was the land to follow. In the workshop of French history there was a mode for every taste: 1789, 1793 and 1794, 1799, 1804, 1830, 1848, 1870 and 1871. The France they dreamed of and lived by was a France seen through the prism of the writings of Marx, more real to them than the France of history.

Almost every figure on the Russian political stage wore a costume tailored in Paris. Tsarism was the *ancien régime*. Vyshnegradskii, Witte, and Stolypin were the Turgot, Calonne, and Necker. Lenin was a Jacobin—his opponents said this to denounce him, and he repeated it after them with pride. He was a Russian Robespierre—on this too both he and his opponents agreed. And he was as well a Russian Blanqui. In a gentler mood, he called his rivals Girondins or the Swamp; when harsher, Cavaignacs.[3] Trotsky dramatized himself as the Marat of the Revolution, later as it Carnot. To the sailors of Kronstadt, whose hands were stained with the blood of their officers, he said in the summer of 1917 that they were "the flower of the Revolution" and their deeds would be copied all over Russia until every public square would be adorned by a replica of that famous French invention "which makes the enemies of the people shorter by a head." Trotsky and Stalin in their debates hurled at each other the epithet "Bonapartist." Stalin's regime Trotsky branded as "Thermidor." When Tsereteli in 1917 proposed to disarm the Bolshevik Red Guard lest they overthrow the Provisional Government, and Lieber supported him (Mensheviks both), from his seat another Menshevik leader, Martov, hurled the epithet *versalets!* (Versaillist).[4]

As the French revolutionaries had donned imaginary togas and fancied themselves ancient Romans, so Russian revolutionaries sought to reenact the scenes and roles of revolutionary France. Much ink would be spilled, and in the end much blood, to determine Russia's place on the French revolutionary calendar (was she on the eve of her 1789 or 1793, her 1848, or her 1870?). The soviets were pictured by Lenin as enlarged replicas of

3. General Cavaignac, Minister of War in the French Provisional Government set up by the uprising of February 1848, put down the uprising of the Paris workingmen in June of the same year. Lenin applied the epithet now to the generals of the army, now to the Kadets, now to Kerensky. Characteristically, he expected his readers to know who Cavaignac was, and since polemics were largely addressed by intellectuals to each other and not to the workers or peasants, his readers, living in the same French dream as he, knew.

4. Versailles had been the headquarters of the Republican government of France that attempted to disarm the National Guard of Paris in 1870. Resistance to the disarming was the beginning of the uprising of the Paris Commune.

the "Paris Commune type of state." [5] After the Bolsheviks took power, the ink and blood would be poured out in combat with the ghosts of "Bonapartism" and "Thermidor" while the real problems were those arising out of an entirely new formation, totalitarianism, which had no exemplar in French revolutionary history.

In justice to the Marxists it should be said that they were not alone in their use of the formulae, "bourgeois revolution" and "revolutionary bourgeoisie." Whole generations of historians, most of them non-Marxist or only tenuously Marxist in outlook, took the same terms for granted. But recently, particularly in the last decade, the French Revolution has been undergoing a far-reaching re-examination. In France itself, and in England and the United States, historians have been questioning this vocabulary of social history and interpretation, and with devoted scholarship and freedom from preconceptions, have been examining the tax rolls, the banking records, provincial and municipal archives, the composition of committees, of delegations to assemblies, the actual records of investment in land, in annuities, in venal offices, the records of ownership of land, the histories of great families, the texts of *cahiers de doléances* and a host of similar materials. Their work has reopened questions long considered settled, questions that are economic, social, political, and intellectual. Recently a battle has been raging in the usually somnolent pages of the *American Historical Review* between historians engaged in this work of empirical re-examination and those who would cling to the old terms "bourgeois revolution" and "revolutionary bourgeoisie" even if they have to stretch the terms to the point where *bourgeoisie* no longer means a definite class with a definite relation to the forces of production and a definite degree of participation in the starting of the revolution, the inspiring of its ideological fantasies and programs, and the guiding of its results.

A brilliant summary of the labor of re-examination that has been accomplished thus far appears in the article by George V. Taylor, "Noncapitalist Wealth and the Origins of the French Revolution," cited above. Professor Taylor, like Alfred Cobban in his *Social Interpretation of the French Revolution* (Cambridge, England, 1964) finds that "the phrase, *bourgeois revolution*, incorporates a self-confirming system of deception [and] acts as a standard for selecting, interpreting, and arranging evidence, and because of this the research usually ends by confirming

5. Actually the Paris Commune was an emergency city government, while the soviets of 1905 (imitated in 1917) were an emergency general-strike committee. Marx's final verdict on the Paris Commune, written in a letter to Domela Nieuwenhuis on February 22, 1881,   said: "The Commune was merely the rising of a town under exceptional circumstances; the majority of the Commune was in no sense socialist nor could it be. With a small amount of common sense, they could have reached a compromise with Versailles." Lenin read this letter when he was preparing *State and Revolution* but studiously ignored it.

assumptions that creep in with the terminology." After reviewing the entire re-examination, and much of the argument of the opposing school, Professor Taylor concludes his many-faceted, closely reasoned study with these words:

The phrases, *bourgeois revolution* and *revolutionary bourgeoisie*, with their inherent deceptions, will have to go, and others must be found to convey with precision and veracity the realities of social history.

The conclusions of these historians who have thus been reopening a long "closed" question will come as no surprise to those of us who, having questioned the dogma that the Russian Revolution was a proletarian revolution, were then driven to re-examine the French Revolution as to its supposed bourgeois character. But the devotion, thoroughness, and precision with which these scholars have been going about their task of re-examination merit the gratitude of all who take seriously the field of social history.

FROM ABBE SIEYES TO KARL MARX

When the King of France asked for suggestions on the composition of the Estates-General, Abbé Sieyès was ready with an answer which, if it clarified nothing, had a ring to it that echoed down the corridors of time and, over half a century later, evoked in the mind of Karl Marx one of the core ideas of his own doctrine:

What is the Third Estate?—asked Sieyès, and answered—Everything. What has it been hitherto? Nothing. What does it desire to be? Something.

The misunderstanding concerning the Third Estate began with the Third itself. The First Estate represented the clergy, the Second the nobility, the Third the towns. Since a walled town is a *bourg*, all the inhabitants thereof, whether noblemen, clergy, *noblesse de robe* and other purchasers of high office, *rentiers*, owners of urban property, merchants, bankers, industrialists, artisans, lumpenproletariat, unemployed, or beggars, all may be denominated *bourgeois*. Immediately it came together the Third Estate passed a decree claiming to represent "ninety-six per cent of the nation" and constituted themselves as a "national assembly" qualified to represent the "will of the people." They demanded double representation and a vote by head in place of the traditional vote by estates, which would give them a majority in any vote; then they invited clergy and nobility to join their Assembly. When the king ordered them to meet separately, the other two estates left the hall, but the Third sat tight. "You have heard His Majesty's orders," admonished the master of ceremonies. "Know you," answered a thunderous voice, "that nothing but the bayonet will avail to disperse the commoners of France." The mild king said, "Well, let them stay," and directed the other two estates to join the "National Assembly." Ironically, the first champion of the Third Estate was an Abbé, and the voice that rang out on their behalf was the voice of le comte de Mirabeau, while the group of *proprietaires* as a whole "furnished eighty-seven per cent of the Third Estate's deputies to the Estates-General" and provided it with its leadership.[6]

Thus the second stage of the French Revolution began, along with the legend of "the bourgeois revolution" and the "revolutionary bourgeoisie." The legend that the Third Estate represented the people of France was a convenient political fiction, like Lenin's fiction that whenever the Party speaks, it is the proletariat that is speaking. Moreover, for a people who for several centuries had been juridically distinguished as to privileges and duties by membership in juridical estates, it was natural to imagine that men think, act, and feel, as "classes."

In 1843 when Karl Marx went with his new bride to Paris to become co-editor of a journal, he was still anticommunist. But the smell of revolution in the Paris air transformed him completely. Within six months, he had lost his job, been thrust thereby into the "intellectual proletariat," fallen in love with Paris redolent with revolutionary memories and socialist theories, and found his true vocation. He became possessed by the idea that a new Great French Revolution impended that would somehow fulfill the large ideological fantasies which the first had left unfulfilled. When next the Gallic Cock should crow, sleepy Germany too would awaken and take her place, not merely in the revolutionary procession but at its head.

If the "revolutionary" bourgeoisie had left its promises unfulfilled in the "bourgeois" revolution, where, Marx asked, was the class that would fulfill them? And where the nation best fitted to lead beyond the political revolution to the social revolution? He found his answers in two logically untenable but psychologically understandable non sequiturs. With the words of the Abbé Sieyès echoing in his ears, he asked: "Where is the class bold enough to cry out the defiant challenge: *I am nothing, I must become everything?* [7] And he answered:

---

6. The figures and a detailed analysis of the real nature of the Third Estate can be found in Taylor, *op cit.,* and in his sources.

7. Marx's rhetoric was better than the anti-climactic pronouncement of Sieyès, wherefore it went straight into the closing line of the chorus of *The International:* "We have been naught, we shall be all."

One must admit that the German proletariat is the *theoretician* of Europe, as the English proletariat is its *national economist* and the French proletariat its *politician*. One must admit that Germany has just as much a classical vocation for the *social* revolution as it has political incapacity. . . . Only in socialism can a philosophical people find its corresponding practice, hence only in the proletariat the active element in its liberation.

Two non sequiturs, but in them was contained the central core of Marxian doctrine. It would become Marxism-Leninism when in the place of the German proletariat Lenin put the Russian.

LENIN'S MARXISM

The term, Marxism-Leninism was never used by Lenin himself, but is the hallmark of the successor ideology. Only upon his death did his orphaned lieutenants design it as a cloak to cover the fact that there was no Lenin among them and as a way of claiming continuity with him through the collective possession of his doctrine, thus establishing the basis for an apostolic succession: Marx, Engels, Lenin, Stalin, Khrushchev, Brezhnev . . . X.

The struggle for the mantle of the apostolic succession between Leon Trotsky, organizer of the seizure of power and of the Red Army, and Joseph Stalin, made by Lenin the master of the Leninist political machine, was a struggle to the death. Trotsky was organically inacapable of building a party machine of his own or using his power lever, the army; but Stalin made deadly use of his power lever, the party machine. Except for Zinoviev, the other lieutenants did not dream of taking Lenin's place, nor count as serious contenders; yet all of them perished in the struggle for the succession. As differences grew on matters for which Lenin had had, or had left no clear solution, his leading lieutenants disputed with each other as to which of their proposed solutions was the most truly Leninist, but all the contenders agreed on the same general definition of Leninism as "the only Marxism of the period of imperialism, proletarian revolution, and the construction of socialism." To this they added Lenin's own claim that in the Bolshevik faction he had built "a party of a new type,"—as indeed it was insofar as it could be considered a party. Though the problems Lenin's successors faced have changed constantly and their attempted solutions and very outlook have departed from Lenin's views, their definition of Leninism has survived unaltered.

In the *Theses of the Central Committee on the Fiftieth Anniversary of the October Revolution* the nature of Leninism and the relation of Lenin to Marx are defined as follows:

The Bolshevik Party, a proletarian party of a new type, emerged and gained strength in the course of the class struggle on the firm foundation of Marxism-Leninism. . . . Under the new conditions brought into being by the epoch of imperialism, Lenin creatively developed Marxism, raising it to a new higher stage. His theory of the socialist revolution was one of the greatest contributions to scientific communism. . . . Drawing upon the teachings of Marx and Engels, he produced solutions to key theoretical and practical problems of the building of socialism and communism. . . . Leninism is the eternal source of revolutionary thinking and revolutionary action. The name of Lenin has become the symbol of the new world.

In the eyes of orthodox Marxists, the great heresy of the closing decade of the nineteenth century was the heresy of "Revisionism," a heresy born of the pronouncement of Edouard Bernstein, Engels's literary executor, to the effect that Marxism was a brilliant analysis of the political and economic structure of capitalist society in Marx's own day, but since his death in 1883 new conditions had developed not foreseen or experienced by him so that a fresh look at society and the tactics of the socialist movement was needed. Though Lenin was· one of the angriest denouncers of Bernstein's "revisionism," it is clear that Lenin's "creative development of Marxism under the new conditions of the epoch of imperialism" is itself such a "revision." Let me add lest I appear to be siding with Mao Tse-tung in a current controversy, that Mao's revision of Marxism leaves even less of the richness and complexity of the original doctrine intact than does Lenin's or Stalin's or Khrushchev's. Indeed, Lenin, Trotsky, Stalin and their epigones all belong to that order of "terrible simplifiers" that Burckhardt foresaw for our century, while Mao and his disciples from Lin Piao to Mao's wife and public voice are more terrible simplifiers still.

In any case it is clear from the Fiftieth Anniversary Theses as it is from everything published nowadays in Russian "theoretical organs" that while Lenin is cited endlessly, and as a rule irrelevantly, and in China Mao Tse-tung is cited *ad nauseam*, in both lands Marx is hardly quoted at all. His name is receding into the distance along with the comparatively peaceful and stable days of the world he knew. When it is invoked it is as a warrant of the "scientific certitude" of victory, as an act of residual piety, or as the sonorous opening for the litany of the apostolic succession.

But this was not always so, for Lenin accounted himself an orthodox Marxist, at times the only orthodox Marxist on the face of the earth. In his *Philosophical Notebooks*, written during the First World War only for his own eyes, he gravely set it down that "after a half century, not a single Marxist has understood Marx!" It is clear that he allowed for one exception, else how could he judge that the others had misunderstood?

He read and reread the works of Marx and Engels, treating the two as a single sacred person every utterance of whom was equally "scientific," i.e. infallible, and of equal probative value. At every turn and in every controversy, "Ilyich consulted Marx," looking for helpful suggestions and for quotations with which to crush his opponents. In so vast a body of writing set down for changing situations and in varying moods, one could find a quotation for almost anything, so that his opponents had their authoritative quotations, too. Yet Lenin devoutly believed that the whole body of writing of his two-headed oracle made up a single, monolithic structure. In *Materialism and Empirio-criticism* Lenin wrote:

In this philosophy of Marxism cast from a single block of steel, you cannot eliminate a single substantial premise, a single essential part, without deviating from objective truth, without falling into the hands of bourgeois-reactionary falsehood.[8]

An actual count reveals that Lenin quotes Engels far more often than Marx and that the quotations from Marx come almost entirely from a single period that begins as the storms of 1848 were brewing and ends when Marx belatedly became aware of their subsiding, in the late summer of 1850. This is the most violent period of Marx's writing. The ebbing of the storm should have been obvious by 1849, but for a year and a half Marx kept trying to bring back the lightning by making a noise like thunder. This is the period of his exaltation of Blanqui, the latter's "class dictatorship of the proletariat" and "revolution in permanence", the period of Marx's hymns to "terror" and "the fist," of his praise of "so-called popular excesses, the people's revenge against hated individuals or public buildings," and his urging that the Communists should not discourage but encourage and seek to take leadership over such acts of mob violence. This was the Marx Lenin loved to quote; for belief in the efficacy of voluntarism, revolutionary violence, terror, and "street justice," along with belief in Blanqui's élitist conspiratorial attempts to seize power and, from the heights of power, to seek the approval and stir the revolutionary activity of the masses—all these were to become constituent parts of Lenin's Marxism, and the Marxism-Leninism of his successors.

But in September 1850, Marx and Engels broke with the Communist League whose *Manifesto* and *Circular Letters* Marx and Engels (actually Marx) had been drafting. Instead of acknowledging error and correcting it, Marx broke with his followers for remaining faithful to his tactics and outlook of the three years preceding the break. He wrote off "naked will

8. Lenin, *Sochineniia*, Vol. XIV, p. 312. References to Lenin's *Collected Works* (hereafter referred to as *Lenin*) are to the Fourth Russian Edition, unless otherwise noted.

as the driving force of revolution, instead of the real facts of the situation." Thereupon Marx began his major lifelong task: to study "the real facts of the situation" in order to prove that a social revolution would flow inevitably not from the impassioned will and superhuman energy of revolutionary voluntarists, but from the "law of motion" inherent in capitalism. At this point the schizoid rift between the sense of fatalism and the exaltation of the revolutionary will became complete—as complete as the irreducible revolutionary passion in Marx's temperament could permit it to become.

From this "riper," or later, Marx-the-inevitabilist, burrowing his mole's way through the tomes and statistical reports in the British Museum and devising "objective proofs" and "objective measurements" to determine when the "crisis of capitalism" would "mature" and bring about the "expropriation of the expropriators," Lenin found little to use. His quotations from Marx pick up in volume again when, after the fall of the Paris Commune in 1871, Marx glorified the Commune he had opposed in 1870. But when ten years later Marx reviewed and rejected this interpretation of the Commune, as we have noted, Lenin looked at this Marx with wilfully unseeing eyes.[9]

Marx's increasing recourse to determinism and inevitabilism Lenin simply translated into the "scientific" guarantee of the inevitable victory of socialism. But to use Marxism as a computer for the calculating of the moment of ripeness of a given country for social revolution went against Lenin's spirit, for the "given country" in his case was backward Russia which at best seemed to promise by this method of calculation only a "bourgeois revolution." Still less did Lenin permit himself to recognize that Engels, freed at Marx's death from the spell of Marx's titanic will, proceeded to develop the determinist, measure-of-ripeness side of Marxism to its logical extreme, especially in the last half decade of his life in the articles collectively intended as a political testament.[10]

That Lenin's uncritical admiration of Engels was not a mere tactical maneuver in his feuds with other socialists is proved by passages in his letters to Inessa Armand not intended for other eyes. Because of the intimate nature of their relationship, he could not silence her with abusive epithets when she disagreed with him but had to explain himself. Inessa, it seems, noted important differences between Engels's pacifism and defensism for Germany in the event of a two-front war with Russia and France and Lenin's defeatism for his own country, and between Engels's growing determinism and passive waiting until the time should be "ripe" and the socialists have a majority in the Reichstag and in the

9. On this see the writer's "The Paris Commune, An Ambiguous Revolution," in *Marxism: 100 Years in the Life of a Doctrine*, New York, 1965.
10. See *Marxism: 100 Years in the Life of a Doctrine*, pp. 83-101 and 219-229.

army before his party should take power and Lenin's ardent and impatient voluntarism. I have not seen her letters which the Marx-Engels Institute keeps under seal, but in a number of answers written by Lenin to Inessa in the last three months of 1916 and the first three of 1917, he defends Engels against her strictures.

Engels was right [he says in one of them]. In my time I have been pained to see many accusations charging Engels with opportunism, and my attitude is sceptical in the extreme. . . . Try, say I, just once to prove that Engels was wrong!! You will never be able to.

In another letter he writes:

I am still "in love" with Marx and Engels and will not tolerate in silence any slander againt them. No, these are real people! From them we must learn. From *this* ground we must not depart.

And in yet another:

Engels the father of passive radicalism? Not true! Not at all. This you will never be able to show.[11]

Inessa Armand seems to have done her homework, and her unpublished letters were apparently well founded. Moreover, from the very outset, Engels brought to the famous partnership a far less stormy temperament and a much greater inclination to "science rather than utopia" and to inevitabilist determinism rather than voluntarism. As early as the autumn of 1850, as soon as Marx and he had sobered up from their apocalyptic illusions of 1848, Engels published a warning on the "premature" seizure of power in a backward country not "ripe" for socialism, a warning that reads as if it might have been addressed to the Lenin of 1917. At any rate, his socialist opponents were constantly quoting this to Lenin, his rage being greater since he was incapable of repudiating Engels.

The reproach of Engels as echoed by Lenin's contemporaries during his rule would trouble him to the end. The last theoretical article he ever wrote, published in January, 1923, just before paralysis silenced forever tongue and pen, was a final attempt to answer the reproach that he had seized power in a country unripe for socialism in the name of a class insufficiently advanced in culture and organization to exercise power.[12] Ostensibly he was answering the semi-Bolshevik Sukhanov, but Sukhanov

11. See my "Lenin and Inessa Armand," in *Slavic Review*, March 1963; *Encounter*, February 1964; or in my book of profiles, *Strange Communists I Have Known*, New York, 1965; London, 1966.

12. "O nashei revoliutsii," *Lenin*, Vol. 33, pp. 436-439.

was only enlarging upon the words of Engels written almost three-quarters of a century before:

The worst thing that can befall a leader of an extreme party is to be forced to take power in an epoch when the movement is not yet ripe for the rule of the class he represents, nor for the carrying out of the measures which the rule of that class would demand. What he *is able* to do does not depend upon his will but upon the level that the conflict between the various classes has reached, and upon the degree of development of the material conditions of existence, on which at any given moment the level of development of class antagonisms rests. What he *ought* to do and his party expects of him doesn't depend upon his will either, nor upon the then degree of development of the class struggle. He is bound by the doctrines and demands that he has been advancing. . . . Thus necessarily he finds himself facing an insoluble dilemma: what he is *able* to do contradicts his entire previous activity, his principles, and the direct interests of his party; and what he *ought* to do he cannot realize. In a word, he is forced to represent not his party nor his class, but the class for whose rule the movement is ripe. In the interests of the movement itself he must realize the interests of a class that is alien to him, and put off his own class with phrases and promises and the assertion that the interests [he is actually realizing] are their interests. Whoever gets himself into this twisted position is irretrievably lost.[13]

Since this was written more than a century ago, Engels could have no presentiment that the "class" whose interests Lenin would come to represent would be Djilas's "new class," the party-state bureaucracy.[14]

THE SINGULAR INVENTIONS OF V. I. LENIN

The problem of dating the Russian revolution on the French revolutionary calendar caused no end of controversy and for Lenin an intense internal struggle, until he contrived to reconcile his will to power with the "orthodox" pronouncement of his masters, Plekhanov and Axelrod, that Russia was too backward for a proletarian-socialist and ripe only for a bourgeois-democratic revolution. This required an alliance with and support to the "revolutionary bourgeoisie" in their struggle to take power and establish a "bourgeois democracy." Lenin propagated this view with his usual dogmatic energy, yet in his heart he could not reconcile himself to it. The bourgeoisie, he held with contempt, was not a consistently revolutionary class (and on reflection one must agree with him). They were no fighters, not bold enough, nor courageous enough, nor ruthless

13. *Marx-Engel Werke*, Vol. VII, pp. 400-401.
14. Or perhaps, as Wittfogel has suggested, Marx and Engels thrust out of their consciousness the awareness that the nationalization of all industry and agriculture would necessarily lead to the development of such a bureaucratic "ruling class." On this see Wittfogel, *Oriental Despotism*, Chapter IX.

enough to see "their own" revolution through to the end. They would be ready to compromise, to strike a miserable bargain and sell out their proletarian supporters.

Of course Lenin did not trust the proletariat to be consistently revolutionary either. (And again we must agree with him.) This leaves as "consistently revolutionary" only self-chosen individuals like Lenin and special groups and detachments of extremists that at one time or another cooperated with him. Indeed, he measured their revolutionary consistency by the extent to which they did cooperate with him, and to all of them he applied his formula that the central question of all alliances and confrontations was *Kto kogo?* (Who whom?) Miraculously, the formula translates to perfection. Lenin bade his followers put now one verb now another between the two prounouns, to wit: Who *uses* whom? Who *gets the better of* whom? Who *vanquishes* whom? Who *destroys* whom? —or any other polite or impolite verb that the reader may wish to supply.

There is the case of the Kronstadt sailors, anarcho-Bolsheviks, impatient, turbulent men. They began their epic deeds in February 1917 by thrusting some of their officers under the ice. They marched in Lenin's demonstrations fully armed, bearing banners with any slogan Lenin thought up; they were the trigger happy men in trucks and armored cars who shot at shop windows and passers-by during the abortive July uprising; they provided some detachments and two destroyers and the battleship *Aurora* that fired the terrifying blank shell during the October coup; they were used by Lenin as a bludgeon when he threatened his Central Committee that he "would resign and go to the sailors" if they outvoted him; they supplied shock troops for the ensuing civil war. But when the war was won and the sailors of Kronstadt demanded that he implement some of the promises he had made to the Russian people, then he and his lieutenants outlawed them, took their fortress by storm over the ice, and executed their leaders both Communist and Anarchist, thus giving a tragic answer to the question of *Kto kogo?* [15]

Other such alliances in which extremist groups marched together with Lenin were the Maximalists and Socialist-Revolutionary terrorists in the *exes* (revolutionary holdups) of 1906 and 1907; and the Left Socialist Revolutionaries who entered his Council of Commissars on December 1, 1917. There the Commissar of Justice Steinberg tried in vain to dilute Lenin's dictatorship with some considerations of ethics and justice. Early in March 1918 the S. R.'s walked out on the issue of Brest Litovsk, then were provoked into an uprising, and crushed by the Cheka.

The temporary alliance with the anarchists in 1917 unfolds a similar

15. The reader who knows no Russian may want to know how Lenin's celebrated formula is pronounced. The *g* in *ogo* is pronounced like a *v* so that *Kto kogo* is pronounced Kto kavó. The unaccented *o* here as frequently, sounds like a short *a*.

story. Anarchists of various varieties marched together with Lenin, attracted by his emphasis on those parts of his program for subverting the Provisional Government that seemed to have been borrowed from their arsenal. The Bakunist-Kropotkinist school found encouragement in his picture of the Soviets as a federation of communes modeled on the Paris Commune; the anarcho-syndicalists were won by his calls for workers' control and union management of industry and peasant seizure of the land; while all shadings found sustenance in his attacks on the war and the government, his slogan of *All Power to the Soviets*, when he meant *All Power to the Bolshevik Party*, and his declared intention to set up a government that would begin to "wither away" on the first day of its existence.[16] But Lenin's first acts after taking power were disillusioning, for now their anarchic impulses were not useful but troublesome to his new government. The setting up of the Council of Peoples Commissars and the Cheka, the abolition of freedom of the press, the attack on the right to strike, the setting up of a Supreme Economic Council to run industry, the proclamation that anarcho-syndicalism was a bourgeois and counterrevolutionary deviation—all these developments made it only too clear that the man who seemed almost an anarchist while overthrowing a government, was at the opposite pole where his own power was concerned, more ruthless, more efficient, more ambitious to embrace every aspect of life than any tsar. The anarchists fought rearguard actions side by side with the Kronstadt sailors, with Makhno in the Ukraine, with the green peasants in Tambov. Thereafter they were silenced by the Bolshevik government's ownership and monopoly of all newspapers, meeting halls, and printing plants, and their voices were stifled in isolator cells and concentration camps, by firing squad or pistol shot in the base of the brain in the cellar of the Lubyanka.

If this was Lenin's attitude toward organized detachments that had fought by his side, his attitude toward accidental street gatherings, mobs, and the unorganized masses generally, was to encourage their outbursts of violence and vengeance, although he found their wrath too short-lived to be dependable. On October 10, two weeks before his coup, he acknowledged that the masses had become weary and apathetic. Four months after he seized power he complained that "the revolutionary enthusiasm of the masses which sustains their state of tension and gives them the strength to apply merciless terror to the suppression of demoralizing elements doesn't last long. . . . Dictatorship is iron rule, boldly revolutionary, swift and merciless in the suppression alike of exploiters and hooligans. But our rule . . . is often more like jelly than like iron." He was through with reliance on the masses for merciless, systematic terror, and turned

16. On this see "The Anarchists in the Russian Revolution," by Paul Avrich, *Russian Review*, October, 1967, Stanford, pp. 341-350.

the task over to the newly created Cheka, the Extraordinary Commission for the Suppression of Counterrevolution, Speculation, and Sabotage.

The question of Russia's ripeness only for a "bourgeois democratic revolution" was more complicated for Lenin than the inconstancy of the masses or the impermanence of the various alliances he entered into. If the central question of alliances was *who uses whom?* the central question of revolution was *who gets power?* If it was to be a bourgeois revolution, the bourgeoisie would get power: thus they would be using him, not he them.

From 1898 to 1905 his lips and pen repeated the formula of orthodoxy, but his spirit wrestled with the problem of who then would be using whom. When he went abroad in 1900 for a pilgrimage to Plekhanov and Axelrod, both sensed this ambiguity. "We turn our face to the liberals," Plekhanov said, "you turn your behind." [17] Yet so dutiful was Lenin in retailing their formula to opponents and followers that it led him to utter a prophetic warning to Trotsky: "Whoever attempts to achieve socialism by any other route than that of political democracy will inevitably arrive at the most absurd and reactionary conclusions, both political and economic." [18] It must be said that history has borne out the truth of this prophecy as it has a matching prophecy made about the same time by Leon Trotsky concerning Lenin's centralized and dictatorial party machine:

The organization of the party will take the place of the party itself; the central committee will take the place of the organization and finally the dictator will take the place of the central committee.

Both forebodings were fulfilled to the letter. In 1917 when they joined forces for the seizure of power, the two men amnestied each other's errors. Trotsky accepted Lenin's party machine; Lenin Trotsky's impatient formula for skipping the "bourgeois" democratic revolution in favor of a proletarian dictatorship in permanence. An undemocratic party machine to make an undemocratic revolution—from such a mating what other progeny could spring but a permanent single-party dictatorship?

During the upheavals of 1905 Lenin was still wrestling with the prescription that the revolution had to be bourgeois and democratic. At the same time he was issuing such horrendous slogans that his opponents told him he would "frighten off" the bourgeoisie. That gave him a unique idea for reconciling the appearance of orthodoxy with the impatience of his will to power.

The bourgeoisie, he answered his critics, could not be trusted to carry

17. *Correspondence of G. V. Plekhanov and P. B. Axelrod,* Vol. I, p. 270.
18. *Lenin,* Vol. 9, p. 14.

out their own revolution anyhow. They would compromise, make deals with the throne, settle for a limited monarchy, desert when the going got rough. Well then, good riddance!

Those who really understand the role of the peasantry in the victorious Russian revolution would not dream of saying that the sweep of the revolution would be diminished if the bourgeoisie deserted it. For, as a matter of fact, the Russian revolution will assume its real sweep, will really assume the widest revolutionary sweep possible in the epoch of bourgeois-democratic revolution only when the bourgeoisie deserts it and when the masses of the peasantry come out as active revolutionaries side by side with the proletariat. The proletariat must carry out to the end the democratic revolution, and in this unite to itself the mass of the peasantry in order to crush the autocracy by force and paralyze the instability of the bourgeoisie.[19]

In short, a bourgeois revolution without the bourgeoisie! Who but Lenin could have thought that up? The peasantry would serve as an *ersatz* "bourgeoisie," and "the democratic dictatorship of the proletariat and the peasantry" would serve as a substitute for "bourgeois democracy." Who but Lenin could have thought that one up, either?

Having invented a bourgeois revolution without the bourgeoisie and a democratic revolution without democracy, there was one more innovation for Lenin to make: a proletarian revolution without the proletariat. Actually, he had been working on this since 1902. "Cut off from the influence of Social Democracy," Lenin wrote in his first signed article for *Iskra*, "the workingmen's movement becomes petty and inevitably bourgeois." That single sentence was enough to finish off the entire existentialist class theory of Marx. With his usual methodical hammering home of his views, Lenin expanded it in article after article, then into that classic formulation of Leninism, *What's to be Done?* If "consciousness" comes not from the instincts and experience of the working class but only "from outside," if its bearers and formulators are "by their social position educated representatives of the possessing classes, the intelligentsia," then such a classless elite of "professional revolutionaries" might seize power, not as Marx thought, where the economy was most advanced and the working class most numerous, organized and cultured, but just as easily, nay more easily, where the economy was backward and the workingmen neither a majority nor mature nor conscious nor organized, and where the political organization of all parties was rudimentary. Not ripeness is all as Marx had thought, but readiness is all. This line of thought runs back not to Marx but to Babeuf, Buonarroti, Blanqui, Pestel, Bakunin, Nechaev, Tkachev, and Chernyshevsky.

19. *Lenin,* Vol. 9, p. 81.

Such a classless elite as Lenin contemplated, since it was "the vanguard of the proletariat" by self-selection and definition, could seize power through nationalist uprisings in colonial lands or at the head of peasant armies. It would be possible for restless students, ambitious officers, politicians out of power, and nondescript guerrilla bands to seize power in the name of the proletariat in lands where the proletariat was in its infancy or represented only in the rudimentary form of artisans and craftsmen or plantation workers and serfs, and modern industry was virtually non-existent. Such proletarian power could come out of the mouth of the guns of peasant armies. Thus Ho Chi-minh and Mao Tse-tung could found their "proletarian regimes" in lands not yet "ripe for capitalism" but by definition ripe for socialist or communist power or, more precisely, for single party dictatorships where the single party, though it speaks of socialism, may be nothing more than a dictator's praetorian guard.

When it became apparent to Lenin that the workingmen of Western Europe were rejecting communism, at the Third Congress of the Comintern he turned his face to the East and spelled out the implications of his elitist doctrine for the nationalist revolutionaries of Asia and Africa. Indeed, it is only Hitler and Mussolini in Europe, and in Asia and Africa nationalists become heads of states, that would imitate certain aspects of Bolshevism. What they imitated was not Soviets or "workers' rule," but one-party government, an elitist ruling caste, and personal dictatorship. Thus was completed the transformation of Marxism into Marxism-Leninism. Lenin's successors from Stalin to Brezhnev have in varying ways applied this doctrine to Nasser, Nkrumah, Sekou Touré, Ben Bella, Sukarno, Ho Chi-minh, and Mao Tse-tung. Support for "wars of liberation" is the Siamese twin of the slogan of "peaceful coexistence," particularly if the leader of the war proclaims himself dictator in the name of socialism or communism, backs Russia's proposals in the United Nations, or plays the dangerous game of *kto kogo* by seeking arms and "technicians" in Moscow.[20]

However far this may be from Marx's conceptions, there is a kind of *valenki* (or homespun) wisdom in Lenin's paradoxical bourgeois revolution without the bourgeoisie and his substitution of an elite one-party dictatorship for proletarian rule. How else could he strive for his own revolution and his own power in a backward and overwhelmingly peasant land, where even demography spoke against proletarian dictatorship?

In 1917, when the tsarist regime collapsed unexpectedly to itself and to Lenin and to the demoralized, "slothful, and unfit for combat" (Trot-

---

20. For a more complete treatment of Lenin's vanguard theory see my essay, "A Party of a New Type," in *The Comintern—Historical Highlights*, Drachkovitch and Lazitch, Editors, New York, 1966, pp. 20-44.

sky's words) [21] garrison of the capital, when a company of soldiers impulsively disobeyed a command to fire on a demonstration, and a few "well-aimed stray bullets" felled some officers, it was fear of punishment for their unexpected violation of army discipline that made the peasants in uniform fear to return to their barracks, caused them to try to call out other regiments, or seek to mingle with the crowds, and give up their arms. The same fear made them turn to the Duma, the spokesmen of unfamiliar parties, and the Soviet, in a search for justifications, protection from punishment, and larger meanings for their impulsive act of mutiny. All these things they got in full measure. After a moment of fear and hesitation, society gave them celebration and glorification, and gave them to understand that they were the victorious heroes of the century-long, forlorn struggle that tiny bands of intellectuals had waged for freedom.[22]

It was Lenin, irreconcilable enemy of the spontaneous and elemental *stikhia*, who understood most clearly that in this gray mass, with its fear of punishment for indiscipline, its desire to avoid transfer to the front, its disorderly use of its weapons, its new-found glorification, its unrest, uncertainty, inexperience, and vulnerability to plausible demagogic slogans, was the dynamite to blow up the infirm foundations of the Provisional Government.

Lenin wrote of the *dvoevlastie*, the dual power of Provisional Government and Soviet, but actually, in 1917 and 1918, both before and after Lenin's minuscule party seized the telephone and telegraph office, the bank, the Winter Palace, and other symbols of centralized rule, the real power lay in this third, the only real force, the gray mass of the *stikhia* with guns in their hands and a profound uncertainty as to what use to put them to. Unlike the Soviet of 1905, the Soviet of 1917, along with delegates from the factories, contained also soldiers' deputies. In that lay its superiority over the Duma and the Provisional Government.

---

21. Trotsky had just received an offer of support from a machine gun regiment. He found that "the machine guns were not in working condition and the soldiers had become lazy and were also completely unfit to fight." The quotation is from his remarks in a gathering of various persons active in the October coup, meeting together to match memories and try to pin down the details of the October days as they actually occurred. The meeting took place on November 7, 1920, in Moscow, was recorded stenographically, and printed in *Proletarskaia Revoliutsia*, No. 10, Moscow, 1922, the cited remark being on p. 66. A French translation is now available in the Fiftieth Anniversary number of *Est & Ouest*, Paris, 1-31 Octobre, 1967, with the cited remark on p. 15.

22. V. B. Stankevich, *Vospominaniia* 1914-1919 g., Berlin, 1920, pp. 70-77. "The well-aimed stray bullets" is a phrase used by Colonel Stankevitch in his vivid description of the confused panic among the men who had mutinied and the moment of fear and hesitation among the leaders of political life and even the most popular and radical of the officers. For a more extensive treatment of this subject see my remarks at the fiftieth anniversary discussion of the Russian Revolution held at Harvard University, published under the editorship of Richard Pipes in *Revolutionary Russia*, Cambridge, Mass., 1968, and the chapter entitled "The Triple Power: The Role of the Barracks and the Streets" on pp. 138–149 of the present volume.

"A revolution," wrote Mussolini, "is an idea with bayonets." Or as Mao put it more nakedly: "Power comes out of the barrel of a gun." Both of them had learned from Lenin, who knew instantly that if he could link up even for a brief moment of history those guns with his ideas, or at least alienate these peasants-in-uniform from their superiors and their habit of obedience long enough to neutralize them on the day of his *coup*, then the coveted power might be his. After that there would be time enough for the renewal of his battle with the *stikhia* to "transform it from a revolutionary mass into a captive mass," a transformation that Merle Fainsod has called "one of the most poignant of totalitarian achievements." Lenin was not abandoning his war to "organize everything," merely furthering it by first disorganizing everything in order to open for himself the road to power. Out of this dual process he might not be able to make a proletarian revolution or a socialist revolution, but it would not be a bourgeois revolution either.

What then would it be? Out of the past seems to come once more the voice of Friedrich Engels, this time telling Vera Zasulich how tricky a revolution can be when the "conditions work against" those making it:

The people who boasted that they had *made* the revolution always found out the next day that they did not know what they were doing, that the revolution *made* by them was not at all like the revolution they wanted to make.[23]

LENIN DEFINES DICTATORSHIP

When we get power [Lenin wrote in 1916] we will establish a dictatorship of the proletariat. . . . Dictatorship is the rule of a part of society over the whole of society, and, moreover, a rule basing itself directly on force.

After two years in power, he summed up his rule in one grim sentence: "Dictatorship is a harsh, heavy, and even bloody word." And on October 10, 1920, rounding out his third year, he bade his opponents remember:

The scientific concept of dictatorship means neither more nor less than unlimited power, resting directly on force, not limited by anything, not restricted by any laws nor any absolute rules. Nothing else but that.

This formulation is beautiful in its clarity, for the first step in the

23. Letter to Vera Zasulich, April 23, 1885. Engels wrote it in French, but it has been published so far only in a German translation, in *Werke*, Vol. 36, p. 303, and a Russian translation in *Perepiska K. Marska i F. Engelsa s russkimi politicheskimi deyateliami*, Moscow, 1947, p. 251. The German translation seems to be from the Russian and not from the original letter.

establishment of totalitarian power is the destruction of all the restraints that, even in an autocracy, tend to limit power: the restraints of religion, morals, traditions, institutions, constitutions written or unwritten, laws, customs, private conscience, public opinion—in short, anything and everything that may place any limits on power and any restrictions upon an attempt to atomize and remake a people. The history of all totalitarian regimes[24] has proved the rightness of Lenin's "scientific" definition.

Lenin moved naturally from his dictatorial regime inside the Bolshevik party to dictatorship over the land in which his party ruled. Except for his strange utopian dreams of the period when he was writing *State and Revolution*, there is nothing in Lenin's basic writings to suggest that he ever thought the proletariat itself capable of dictating or ruling. From the outset he showed distrust of all social orders of society. To his distrust of court and gentry natural in a revolutionist of his temper, his distrust of the "bourgeoisie" and of liberals and democrats, which tended to distinguish him from the Mensheviks, and his distrust of the peasantry as property-minded because they wanted to own the land they tilled and dispose of the product of their own labor, Lenin alone among socialists added distrust of the working class and of the rank and file and local and district organs of his party. His dictatorship was correspondingly wide and deep in its scope.

The spontaneous development of the workers' movement [he had written at the beginning of his career as a "Leninist"] leads to . . . the ideological enslavement of the workers to the bourgeoisie. . . . Therefore, the question: what is to be done to bring to the workers political knowledge? cannot be answered by "go to the workers,". . . . The Social Democrats must *go into all classes of the population* . . . direct all manifestations of this all-sided struggle, to be able "to dictate a positive program of action" alike to rebellious students, to dissatisfied zemstvo figures, discontented members of the dissenting religious sects, indignant schoolteachers, and so on.[25]

Thus, what Lenin was aiming at in 1917 was nothing less than a dictatorship over the proletariat through its self-appointed vanguard, and, through the proletariat as "the most advanced and revolutionary class in

24. It seems to me that only three regimes can properly be termed totalitarian: the Russia of Lenin and his successors, Hitler's Germany, and Mao Tse-tung's China. Neither Mussolini nor Franco, to mention two regimes frequently called totalitarian, could afford to destroy millions of their people to atomize society. Neither tried to make his power coextensive with all the concerns and activities of society. As for Mussolini, though he coined the word *totalitarismo* and gave us our first working definition of the term, he left extant such institutions as the King, the General Staff, and the Church, which helps to account for the speedy disappearance from power of him and his regime at the first reverse in war.

25. For elaboration of these views of Lenin, sources, context, and analyses of their meaning, see my "A Party of a New Type," in *The Comintern: Historical Highlights,* edited by Milorad Drachkovitch and Branko Lazitch, New York, 1966.

society," over the entire population. Quite literally he proposed to do in 1917 what he had first outlined in 1902: "go into all classes of the population . . . direct all manifestations of this all-sided struggle, dictate a positive program of action alike to rebellious students, dissatisfied zemstvo figures, discontented members of the dissenting religious sects, indignant schoolteachers, and so on." *Dictate a positive program of action to every class of society*—that is what he and his successors have done for fifty years. In this sense, too, their dictatorship has been total.

That "dictate" was never merely metaphorical Lenin made clear quite early while still an editor of *Iskra*. To his colleagues he wrote this memorandum: "We should show every kindness to the peasantry but not yield an inch in our maximum program. . . . If the peasants don't accept socialism when the dictatorship comes, we should say to them, *It's no use wasting words when you've got to use force.*" On the margin Vera Zasulich wrote: "Upon millions of people? Just you try!" When Lenin came to power, that is just what he tried.

For more than three years of his four-year rule he tried force, until the disappearance of agricultural goods and the uprisings in Kronstadt and Tambov forced him to retreat. But his "best disciple" returned to the attack: with fire and sword, force and famine, concentration camp and firing squad, against millions of peasants, he drove them, minus their hastily slaughtered livestock, into the new serfdom of the collective farms. And Stalin's successors seem determined to continue the system of collectivized agriculture though their agricultural statistics proclaim the fact that in meat, milk, butter, eggs, fruit, and vegetables, with nothing but a hoe, a spade, a watering can, a bent back, and the joy of knowing that they are working for themselves—on 3.3 per cent of the arable land of Russia the self-same peasants produce 34 per cent of these products on their private parcels.[26]

For all Lenin's distrust of the "petty-bourgeois spontaneity" of the masses, it was they and not his little band of professional revolutionaries who in 1905 shook the foundations of autocracy and in 1917 overthrew the Tsar. Lenin saw then that the role of his professional revolutionaries was not to prepare a revolution but to prepare to take advantage of an upheaval which, like the French revolution, took all the principal actors by surprise, astonishing the victors no less than the vanquished. His *apparat* proved to be a machine not for making revolution but for seizing power once the revolution had been made, and power lay in the barracks and the street. So unexpected to Lenin was the fall of the Tsar that as late as January 20, 1917, he told a youth audience in Zurich that he did not expect his generation to live to see the revolution, a privilege re-

26. See *Bulletin of the Institute for the Study of the Soviet Union*, Munich, September, 1968, pp. 31-32; *Est & Ouest*, Paris, January, 1969, pp. 11-15.

served for theirs. And no less unexpected to him was the freedom accorded him by the Provisional Government. He expected to be arrested when his train pulled into the Finland Station on April 3, but he was greeted instead by brass bands, honor guards, searchlights sweeping the midnight sky, a bouquet of flowers, and an armored car to take him to Kseshinskaya's Palace.

"Mir schwindelt—my head spins!" he said to Leon Trotsky as they waited in the wings in the early morning of October 25. And in 1918, to console his followers for the "delay" in the revolution in the West, he confided in a moment of frankness:

To foretell when a revolution will ripen, to promise that it will come tomorrow, is to deceive. You remember, particularly those of you who have lived through both Russian Revolutions, which of you could have asserted in 1904 that in two months a hundred thousand Petersburg workers would go to the Winter Palace and open a great revolution? And remember, how could we in December 1916 assert that in two months, within a few days, the tsarist monarchy would be overthrown?[27]

When the Tsar fell and power was nominally in the hands of the Council of Ministers of "the freest war-time government in the world," when the masses, worn out by the babel of conflicting voices, unfulfilled expectations and unsolved problems, were relapsing into apathy,[28] and the government had lost its support in the army after the Kornilov fiasco, then Lenin's party and its scratched-together, miserably armed detachments were sufficient, under Lenin's unremitting pressure, to forestall both the Soviet Congress that was to meet on the morrow of their coup and the Constituent Assembly. Lenin had his way even against the judgment of the majority of his Central Committee, and with his so-called "Soviet Government," he faced not only the Constitutional Convention

27. *Lenin,* Vol. 27, p. 442.
28. When members of his Central Committee insisted that a mass uprising was now impossible because the masses had become passive and indifferent, Lenin did not deny their apathy but explained it: "The absenteeism and indifference of the masses may be explained by the fact that the masses have grown weary of words and resolutions." (Minutes of the Central Committee Meeting of October 10/23, 1917). Lenin's coup did not need an uprising of the masses any more than the coups envisaged by Babeuf, Buonarroti, Blanqui, and Tkachev. The flood of words and resolutions that had wearied the masses greatly increased in volume after Lenin took power. This deluge of decrees, he said later, "played a big role as propaganda." (See *Lenin,* Vol. XXIX, pp. 185-86, where he speaks of "hundreds" of such unrealizable decrees.) If apathy breeds dictatorship, dictatorship in its turn breeds apathy, a dilemma neither Lenin nor his successors have been able to solve. Today as in Lenin's day the headlines in Pravda are largely exhortations to greater "voluntary" activity in fulfilling the will of the leaders and the needs of the state, exhortations to work harder, to produce more, to waste less, to take better care of machines, to improve the quality of the goods, to raise per capita productivity, to be grateful to the party and the state, to compete with each other in "socialist competition," to fulfill the plan "ahead of time." Even to party whips this unendingly repetitive exhortation makes dull reading.

but the Soviets as well with a *fait accompli*. Thus did Lenin seize power not in a land "ripe for socialism" but in a land ripe for seizing power. Afterward he said in astonishment, "it was as easy as lifting up a feather." [29]

DREAM OF UTOPIA

During July 1917, a few months before he made his coup, a strange thing happened to Lenin in a succession of hideouts. The Bolshevik-Anarchist attempt to probe the ground with the bayonet in early July had ended in failure, and the Government had gotten wind of the fact that he was receiving money from the German General Staff. "Won't they shoot us now?" he asked Leon Trotsky, who apparently knew nothing of the German help.[30] Uncertain how much the Government had learned, Lenin thought it best to go into hiding while Trotsky courted arrest and trial.

Enforced leisure in scenes remote from the day to day struggle gave Lenin time to meditate on the world he would bring into being on taking power. He was secure in his hideouts, in the home of Alliluyev, hidden in a haystack on the marshy shore of a lake, then in the cozy safety of the home of the Police Chief of Helsinki in Finland. A long suppressed side of his nature came to the surface as he dreamed of the cloud-cuckoo land he would create when he could sweep away the old and build the world anew.

Since 1916 he had been under the spell of something Bukharin had written. Bukharin had spoken of "a general attack [of the proletariat] on the ruling bandits in which they destroy the state organization of the bourgeoisie" and free society from the crushing weight of the modern superstate Leviathan; then "production will be directed by *society* and not by the state." Lenin had been as much taken by Bukharin's fierce image of the smashing of the state as by his gentle dream of the beginning of stateless freedom. It was not like Lenin to think thus, yet now the vision of a stateless society took possession of him. In his hideout, buttressed by a handful of quotations from Marx and a much greater number from Engels, he wrote his own version of the dream. He spoke of "a magic means of getting the toilers, the poor, to share in the day-to-day work of governing," of "setting up a state apparatus of ten or twenty million people," of making that administration so simple that "every laborer or kitchen cook [kukharka]" could master it.[31]

29. *Lenin*, Vol. 27, p. 76.

30. Leon Trotsky, *The History of the Russian Revolution*, Vol. II, p. 93, Ann Arbor, 1960.

31. From the first work he drafted in his hideout, "Can the Bolsheviks Retain State Power?" *Lenin*, Vol. 26, pp. 87-88.

His imagination continued to soar as he proclaimed an unwonted and unlimited faith in the spontaneous creative power of the masses and outlined his unlimited promises in a little book to be known as *State and Revolution*. There had always been in Lenin a recessive strain of an insurrectionary anarchist, until then held firmly in check by the authoritarian, centralist, dictatorial strain that had dominated his spirit since 1902.[32] But now, in the sheltered remoteness of his hideouts, he meditated on Bukharin's little book, recalled the hitherto repressed but no less sacred quotations from Marx and Engels, and built his daydream utopia. If he deceived the masses with his simplified slogans and sweeping promises, if he took in Anarchists, Left Socialist-Revolutionaries, and many of his own intellectual followers by this dream, I cannot help but think that for a brief moment he persuaded himself as well.

Nothing in the resultant *State and Revolution* fits into the pattern of the orthodox Leninism that runs from *What's To Be Done?*, begun in the autumn of 1901, to the *April Theses*, begun on the train headed for the Finland Station, nor into the pattern of the steps he would take beginning on the morning of October 25, 1917, to consolidate the power he had seized during the night. But there had been a young Lenin once who dreamed of freedom and who "bore a passionate love" for his master, Plechanov. He had stifled the dream as he had the great love, and sought to remake his spirit according to his blueprint of what a revolutionary should be. The model for his blueprint was the "rigorist," Rakhmetov, from Chernyshevsky's novel, the title of which he had borrowed for his own key work, *What's To Be Done?* Like Rakhmetov he would harden his spirit by sleeping on nails, stifle the love within his breast, school himself "to regard all persons without sentiment and keep a stone in one's sling," stop listening "too often" to his favorite music ("It makes you want to stroke people's heads, but you mustn't stroke any one's head, you might get your hand bitten off, you have to hit people over the head").[33]

In *State and Revolution* there is no party to command and centralize all direction and control, no submissive mass to carry out the party's orders. In this Utopia it is the masses who are in command. An unwonted Lenin expressed complete faith in the soundness of their spontaneous reactions, their elemental moods and instincts. There is no need of *edinonachalie* or one-man rule, such as he was to advocate after a year or so of attempting to rule over mass chaos.

32. On the influence of the Bukharin work in recalling to his mind the anarchist strain in the writings of Marx and Engels, see Lenin's letter to Kollontay of February 17, 1917; also *Leninskii Sbornik*, Vol. 2, p. 284, and the article on *State and Revolution* by Robert Daniels in *The American and East European Review*, February, 1953, pp. 22-43.

33. On Lenin's retooling of his own spirit according to his new blueprint, see my character study of Lenin in *Marxism in the Modern World*, Milorad Drachkovitch, Editor, Stanford, 1965, pp. 47-89.

ɔrkers, having conquered political power, will break up the old bu-
.ucratic apparatus, shatter it to its very foundations until not one stone
is left standing upon another; and they will replace it with a new one consisting of these same workingmen and employees, *against* whose transformation into bureaucrats measures will be taken at once . . . 1) not only elec-
tivity but also subjection to recall at any time; 2) wages no higher than
that of a workingman; 3) immediate going over to a situation in which *all*
in turn will become "bureaucrats" and for that reason *no one* can become
a "bureaucrat." [34]

There was to be no standing army, no police, no bureaucracy, no
hierarchy, justice would be dispensed on the spot by the revolutionary
instinct of any accidental crowd that gathered at the scene of a crime
(Lenin called it "trial by the street," in America we call it lynch law).
Affairs of state would be so simplified that from the beginning they
could be handled by any one who knew how to read and write and perform simple operations in arithmetic, and later they would become simple
enough to be mastered by any female cook [kukharka]. Such is Utopia
in this un-Leninist Leninist classic.

FROM DREAM TO NIGHTMARE

Once in power, the dream of a utopia where the masses were free and
managed everything on their own initiative was converted overnight from
dream to nightmare. On November 18, Lenin called upon the people to
"show initiative" by "arresting and handing over to revolutionary tribunals" all guilty of sabotage, opposition, or concealing of supplies. The
street would be the judge. Then, in a draft article, with unconscious irony
entitled "How to Organize Competition," Lenin called on each village,
town, and commune to show "initiative and inventiveness" in devising
ways of "cleansing the Russian land of all noxious insects, scoundrel fleas,
bedbug rich." (Such epithets deprive men of their humanity and make
inhuman treatment of them more "natural".)

In one place they will put into prison a dozen rich men, a dozen scoundrels,
a half dozen workers who shirk on the job. . . . In another, set them to
cleaning outside toilets. In a third give them yellow tickets [prostitutes' identity cards] after a term in prison . . . so that the entire people can act as
overseers over them. . . . In a fourth, they will shoot on the spot one out
of every ten guilty of sloth. . . . The more varied, the better . . . for only
practice can work out the best measures and means of struggle.

Within another three weeks, his faith in the masses even for vengeance

34. *Lenin*, Vol. 25, p. 452.

had ebbed away and he invented the Extraordinary Commission or Cheka. On January 27, 1918, he demanded that the entire working class be conscripted for the terror. Workers who did not want to join in the hunt against "speculators" must be "forced to under threat of deprivation of their bread cards."

Regiments and workshops that do not accurately set up the required number of detachments [*accurately* is a typical word for this pedantry of terror] will be deprived of bread cards and subject to revolutionary measures of persuasion and punishment. . . . Speculators caught with the goods . . . will be shot on the spot. . . . The same punishment for members of the detachments convicted of bad faith.

Capital punishment for crimes against property was abolished in Tsarist Russia. As a socialist, Lenin himself had voted for the abolition of capital punishment for all crimes in 1910 at the Copenhagen Congress of the Socialist International. But now he restored the death penalty even for "bagmen," peasants who brought grain or vegetables in bags on their backs to trade for things made in the city. "As long as we don't apply terror, shooting on the spot," he said on January 14, 1918, "we won't get anywhere."

When the Civil War ended, in January 1920, the death penalty was abolished, but it was restored in May. It was not abolished again until 1947, then once more restored in 1950. Under Khrushchev the death penalty was imposed with great publicity for "exceptionally serious economic crimes," including looting and embezzling of state and public property [private property is not that sacred], counterfeiting, speculating in foreign goods and currencies, cheating on a large scale, and for "repeated" crimes against state property. Under Brezhnev capital punishment for crimes against property seems not to be strictly enforced, but it has not been repealed. As the philosophy professor, George Kline, has observed:

To take a man's life because he has taken the state's property is a practice that cannot be morally justified in terms of *any* ethical position that recognizes the non-instrumental worth or intrinsic dignity of the human person.[35]

When the twentieth century opened, men were sure that capital punishment for crimes against property and torture to extract confessions had been abolished for good in all civilized lands. What then shall we think of the regime Lenin set up and his successors continue?

Il n'y a que le provisoire qui dure. Doubtless Lenin did not intend his

35. George L. Kline, "Economic Crime and Punishment," *Survey*, October, 1965, pp. 67-72.

application of terror to chaos to be more than temporary. But the terror outlasted him and his successors have guarded this part of their heritage. The *che* in Cheka signifies "extraordinary" or "temporary," but with ever changing names and initials, GPU, OGPU, NKVD, MVD, KGB, the secret police has swelled up and become ubiquitous, spying on Communists no less than on noncommunists, spying on each other and on the army, planting agents in every embassy, getting reports from *dvorniks* in every apartment house, seeking to ferret out economic crimes, thought crimes, and all the galaxy of crimes that "socialist legality" can think of. A recent informed estimate puts the number of the secret police at approximately a million. They themselves, and the people of Russia, recognize the continuity in all the changing initials by still using the term *chekist*.

LENIN'S DEATHBED DOUBTS

As he lay dying, Lenin began to have second thoughts on his proud "scientific" definition of dictatorship as unlimited power, resting directly on force unrestrained by any limits, ethical, legal, or traditional. Surely force should not be used by Communists in their discussion with each other. Anxiously, he said to Bukharin in one of the latter's last visits to him, "Let no blood flow among us."

And the peasants? Did he remember the words of Vera Zasulich as he dictated now his article, "On Cooperation," in the scant four to fifteen minutes per day allowed to him by his doctors? One cannot use force to bring the peasants to socialism, he decided, nor did the NEP need to be reversed. What they needed was more industrial goods for the peasants in exchange for their own products, better equipment, general literacy, and genuine cooperatives that would attract the entire peasantry, and indeed the entire population. The NEP, plus cooperatives, plus culture [36]—would carry the peasant, and carry Russia, from state capitalism to socialism.

On January 4 and January 6, 1923, he dictated in two fifteen minute sessions his "On Cooperation." [37] He recognized that he was shifting from the use of power ("we don't need more power, we have enough of it") and "political struggle" to "cultural work" and "civilized, i.e. European, cooperatives." "We are forced," he dictated in words that must

36. Lenin was obsessed now by the fact that he had seized power in a backward land. All his articles dictated during this last illness returned again and again to the lack of culture of the Communist administrators and of the masses. In "On Cooperation" he said: "Complete cooperative organization is impossible without an entire cultural revolution. For us the political and social overturn has proved to be a predecessor of the cultural overturn, that cultural revolution which we nevertheless must now face."

37. *Lenin,* Vol. 33, pp. 427-431.

have taken much travail to come to, *"We are forced to admit a radical change in our entire view of socialism."*

In introducing the NEP, we forgot to think about cooperatives. . . . the only task that really remains for us (in connection with the NEP and because of the NEP) is to organize the population in cooperative societies. When the greatest possible part of the population is organized in cooperatives, socialism automatically achieves its aim. . . . Now we have the right to say that the simple growth of cooperation is identical with the growth of socialism. . . . Before us remain two main tasks. The one is to completely transform our apparatus which is worthless. . . . the other is cultural work among the peasants . . . with the economic aim of their learning cooperation.

Not force, Lenin sought to explain to those in whom earlier he had so often inculcated the idea of force as the sovereign means, not force but patience and simplicity and generosity were needed. The means must be *"the simplest, easiest, most acceptable to the peasant."* It had cost hundreds of millions of rubles to bring capitalism into being. In the same way, "we too must give extraordinary support to the system we are trying to bring into being, the system of cooperatives." He spoke of financial aid, help to cooperative marketing in which "the really great masses of the population take part," tax aid, bank loans, subsidies, bonuses, more culture on the part of the Communists to fit them to foster more culture in the peasantry, financial assistance against bad harvests and famines, and "a number of other economic, financial, and banking privileges."

NEP is adjustable to the level of most ordinary peasants and does not make any excessive demands of him. But it will take a whole historical epoch, in the best case one or two decades, to get the entire population through the NEP into the habit of reading books, the ability to be a cultured trader, which means a good cooperator . . . and to give the assistance that will produce a civilized cooperator.

The work was published with great fanfare in *Pravda*. But neither Trotsky, nor Kamenev, nor Zinoviev, nor Piatakov, nor Stalin accepted the solemn injunction. And when Bukharin sought to enjoin this attitude toward the peasantry upon Stalin, it cost him his good name and his life. Whether Lenin would have come to these thoughts without the close attendance and three warnings from the Angel of Death we do not know. What would have come of following Lenin's behest we can only guess. But one thing is clear: forty years of Stalin's way of forced collectivization and its continuance by his successors has produced an unending state of crisis in Russian agriculture, while the petty incentive remedies proposed from time to time do not touch the heart of the problem then created nor give signs of solving it.

Lenin longed to be able to address one more congress of his party to communicate his belated doubts on the value of unrestricted and unlimited force as the great solver of all problems. It was not only on the peasantry that he wanted to speak, but on the way force was beginning to corrode the inner life of his party itself. He had just learned that Orjonikidze, a Georgian carrying with him plenary powers as representative of the Central Committee, had bullied the two leading Georgian Communists, Mdivani and Makharadze, in a discussion on the problem of the extent of Georgian Communist autonomy, and had struck Mdivani a blow in his face. Then General Secretary Stalin and Cheka Chief Dzerzshinsky had "investigated" and sustained Orjonikidze. To Mdivani and Makharadze Lenin wrote, with a copy for Trotsky whom he begged to take up the case on his behalf: "I am heart and soul behind you. . . . Orjonikidze's brutalities and the connivance of Stalin and Dzerzhinsky have outraged me. On your behalf I am preparing notes and a speech."

The speech could never be delivered; Trotsky, for reasons he has never been able to make clear, refused to take the case. As for Stalin, whom Lenin in his last days sought to have removed from the dangerous post of General Secretary, he went on to flesh out Lenin's "scientific definition" with a nightmarish content, untrammelled by the moral impedimenta that Lenin carried with him from the more humane age and social layer into which he had been born. It was Joseph Stalin who showed what naked force "not limited by anything" could really amount to. Now indeed, "the dream of reason was to beget monsters," at the thought of which even Stalin's closest accomplices still shudder. Stalin went on to complete the atomization of society that Lenin had begun; to finish off the last vestiges of independence of such organizations as the trade unions and the various bodies of writers; to break up the silent solidarity of the village, wipe out the independent peasantry, and agglomerate the separate atoms into the new serfdom of the kolkhoz; further to intensify speedup and piece work in the factory along with Stakhanovism, fixity on the job, and the addition to the classic Russian body-soul-and passport of a new document, the workbook. None of these repel Stalin's successors, indeed, they regard this part of their heritage with pride and build upon it.

But many of Lenin's lieutenants who were contemporaries of Stalin were shocked by his ruthless exploitation of worker and peasant for the "primitive accumulation" of capital funds for forced industrialization. As Stalin became aware of the disagreement inside the ruling party, he spread the blood purge into the party that Lenin had built, until it too was completely atomized. With every purge of a leader came the purge of a retinue, those who admired him, those who had served under him, those whose fortunes had been advanced by him, those related to him by friendship or blood. More Communists were killed on the orders of Joseph Stalin in time of peace than all the anti-Communist governments, armies, police, and courts had executed during civil war, white terror, and the suppression of communist uprisings. If Hitler could number his communist dead in tens of thousands, Stalin could number them in hundreds of thousands.

The bloody stain spread through the army, disgracing it as no other army in history when 70 per cent of all its high officer staff from the rank of colonel up to general and marshall were declared to have been "traitors in the service of foreign enemy powers" and were executed. A social mobility of sorts was promoted by decimating whole strata of party secretaries, managers, technicians, engineers, planners, and even statisticians (all of which doesn't prevent some denizens of ivory towers from asking solemnly whether Stalin wasn't "necessary for the industrialization and defense of Russia?"). The purge culminated in a purge of the purgers, prosecutors, judges, executioners, even chiefs of the secret police and their subordinates. And just before death claimed the despot he was busy planning a new widespread purge beginning with the most reputable doctors in Russia serving the health of the top rulers in the Kremlin. For this reason, when he lay dying, he himself was without an experienced doctor.

If one were to say that Stalin was necessary to the total atomization of the Russian people, there would be some truth in it, though how much of the nightmare arose from the vengeful and paranoid nature of an aging tyrant and how much was "rational" from the standpoint of atomization for totalitarian rule is impossible to say. What is certain is that at the time of his death, even the closest circle of his lieutenants and his own family had lost members in the purges while the rest feared for their lives.

REGIME OF PERMANENT ILLEGITIMACY

As the survivors engaged in a muted struggle for the succession and did away with Beria in good Stalinist fashion, they gave pledges to each other that no secret police or praetorian guard would ever again be permitted to make a shambles of the party. Yet such is the alluring nature of total power, and such their heritage from Lenin and Stalin, that they have done nothing to institutionalize their pledge so as to safeguard their country from the possible rise to leadership of another "mad dictator."

Since Stalin's death, his lieutenants have been wrestling with his ghost, destalinizing, rehabilitating some of his victims, partially restalinizing, as they strive to determine the proper size for the ghost, a problem that remains insoluble. They cannot write him too large lest they remind people of their own complicity in his crimes and lest he continue to dwarf them all, rendering them too small to succeed him. Yet they cannot write him too small either; for from him they inherit their own power, the atomized society over which they rule, the conquests he made during World War II, the totally subjugated peasantry and proletariat, the monopoly of the means of communication, the legend of an infallible party possessing an infallible doctrine. Moreover, through him runs the apostolic succession and their very claim to rule over a great nation.

A strange infallibility this, for they themselves have testified that the infallible doctrine and party structure gave them five years of a Lenin so soft in the head that he surrounded himself with traitors, all of them able to fool the great genius. He was followed by twenty-five or thirty years during which the party and country were ruled by a dictator increasingly paranoid who unjustly and capriciously calumniated and killed countless loyal and wise comrades. Then came ten years of the rule of a lout who proved to be a feckless adventurer and a hair-brained schemer. What does that make of the first fifty years of Communist rule?

Elsewhere [38] I have ventured to formulate a "law of diminishing dictators," not merely because Stalin seemed to me to be of smaller stature than Lenin, and Khrushchev smaller than Stalin (as Brezhnev seems smaller than Khrushchev), but because there is something in the nature of Lenin's epigones and their dictatorship that causes them to exclude from their entourage men of independent mind, or original and critical intelligence, in favor of unquestioning supporters, eager executors, courtiers and sycophants.

To be sure, there is always the possiblity of surprises. The man who seems smallish while dwarfed by the Infallible-in-power, once he succeeds to unrestrained power himself over one-sixth of the earth, more than two hundred million people, the world's largest army, orbital bombs, and rockets that can hit Venus and the moon may grow into his job in ways that may surprise his entourage. Absolute power, unrestrained by any institutional checks or moral code or any surrounding critical voices, tends to unhinge the mind. And always there is that sickness that affects all tyrants—they cannot trust their friends.

When, fifty years ago, the Tsar of All the Russias renounced his throne for himself and his son, the ancient monarchical hereditary legitimacy was ruptured. The Provisional Government that succeeded was of doubtful legitimacy but possessed the grace—the only significant grace in a government arising out of revolution—to regard itself as *provisional* or *pre-legitimate*, and to recognize as its highest political task that of founding

---

38. In a paper presented ten years ago at St. Anthony's College, Oxford, *The Durability of Despotism in the Soviet System*. See below, pp. 181–199.

a new legitimacy through a constitutional convention. When Lenin forestalled the Soviet Congress, presenting it with a dictatorship of his party
as a *fait accompli*, then dispersed the Constituent Assembly by force of
arms, Russia remained without a legitimate government. Lenin as we
have seen formulated this view himself with admirable clarity when he
described his dictatorship as

nothing more nor less than unrestricted power, not limited by anything, not
restrained by any laws, nor by any absolute rules, resting directly on force,
that, and nothing else but that.

Having rejected all limitations, constitutional, legal, traditional, or
moral, having taken power by force and held it by force, having deliber-
ately forestalled or dispersed any possible source of a new legitimacy,
Lenin had openly proclaimed a dictatorship that should last until the
apocalypse, the coming of "complete Communism." This consummation
he devoutly believed before he took power, or so he wrote in the bemused
pages of *State and Revolution*, was a blessed event that would come with
astonishing celerity. The revolution would spread to the ends of the
earth. The state would "begin to wither away" on the day he took
power, and state affairs would become so simple that they would provide
"a magic means of getting the toilers and the poor to share in the day-to-
day work of governing," beginning with "a state apparatus of ten or
twenty million people" in which none would be bureaucrats for all would
be mastering the affairs formerly reserved for the bureaucracy. In time
those affairs would become so simple that every *kukharka* could master
them.

But what withered away on the grim morrow of power was not the
state but the very idea of the withering away of the state. With the one-
party state that Lenin founded, he strove, and Stalin strove more successfully, to embrace every aspect of social and individual life, until the
party and its state became, or sought to become, co-extensive with society,
thereby swelling to totality. In place of every cook becoming master of
affairs of state, the state became master of the affairs of every cook.
Gradually, the apocalypse of "complete communism" was pushed into
an ever remoter future, becoming a part of eschatology, the "science of
the last things." Until then, an unending succession of present generations
are to be sacrificed to that ever receding future, which means that each
present generation will continue to be discontented with its lot and in
need of continued dictatorship.

For such a regime, even after half a century of continued existence,
no legitimacy is possible. It may well continue to endure indefinitely, for
it rules over an atomized society and possesses a total monopoly of the

means of livelihood of its subjects, a total monopoly of power over them, and a total monopoly of the means of communication and public expression of thought.

To disarm its critics, Lenin early developed four devices of semantic confusion to supplement his honestly held belief that his party was entitled to absolute and total power because it possessed an infallible scientific doctrine which told men what *History* wanted them to do, be, and become. The first device is the confusing of the proletariat with the people. The second is the confusing of the Party with the proletariat. The third is the confusing of the *apparat* or Party machine with the Party. The fourth is the confusing of a tiny oligarchy, or a single V*ozhd* or Leader or Boss, with the Party machine. Thus when the Vozhd speaks, the Party leadership has spoken. When the Party leadership has spoken, the Party has spoken. When the Party, vanguard of the proletariat, has spoken, the proletariat has spoken. When the proletariat has spoken, the people have spoken. And insofar as the Russian Party manages to retain leadership of the International Communist Movement and "All Progressive Forces," the peoples of the world have spoken. As for the totalitarian state it is merely the most all-embracing of the transmission belts of the totalitarian Party.

All of these semantic inventions are to be credited to Lenin. As La Rochefoucauld called hypocrisy the tribute that vice pays to virtue, so we may recognize these subterfuges as the tribute that dictatorship pays to democracy, man's will to be free and to control his rulers. These inventions have grown stale and unprofitable after fifty years of repetition, but Lenin's heirs do not dare dispense with them lest their world come tumbling down.

As we probe these fictions they dissolve before our eyes. The Soviet Government is no Government by Soviets, for all decisions are made elsewhere, in Party councils. The Party is no party, for party means a part. Where there are no contending parties and no groupings on principles allowed within the single party, life dies out in it.

Where then shall legitimacy lodge? There is no provision in statutes or constitutions for a personal leader, yet an infallible doctrine in the long run requires a single infallible interpreter. If there are a number of conflicting interpretations, the doctrine itself loses its certainty and its "scientific" and infallible character. The people, being voiceless and denied independent organization, may look with sympathy on one or another of the contending factions, and pluralism will break out in the *monolith*. The word monolith is well chosen for it is the single block of granite that marks the spot where political life lies entombed under the weight of total dictatorship.

When a leader dies, who shall name his successor? Not the Soviets, for they have been drained of life; not the people, for they have no voice; not the Central Committee for it has been replaced by the Politburo or Presidium, and that in turn by the Secretariat. Only "a handful of politicians, a clique," as Rosa Luxemburg put it, remains to proclaim its "collective leadership," concealing its rivalries and internal differences until a new Infallible emerges to proclaim his former collective associates to be antiparty or opponents of all the sound and wholesome policies that the party in its wisdom is adopting.

From her cell in prison in the summer of 1918, Rosa Luxemburg admonished Lenin with friendly intention in these words:

Freedom for the supporters of the government alone, freedom only for members of one party—that is no freedom at all. Freedom is always and exclusively freedom for the one who thinks differently. All that is wholesome and purifying in political freedom depends upon this essential characteristic, and its effectiveness vanishes when freedom becomes a special privilege.

With the suppression of political life in the land as a whole, life in the Soviets must also grow more and more crippled. Without general elections, without unrestricted freedom of press and assembly, without a free struggle of opinion, life will die out in every institution. . . . A few dozen leaders will direct and rule . . . an elite of the working class will be invited from time to time to meetings to applaud the speeches of the leaders and unanimously approve resolutions . . . not a dictatorship of the proletariat but a dictatorship of a handful of politicians, a clique. . . . Such conditions must inevitably cause a brutalization of public life. . . .[39]

How grimly history has confirmed her prophecy! What she could not foresee was that it would be Lenin himself who would destroy the internal life of his party by prohibiting under pain of expulsion serious groupings for the discussion of differences. Or that his General Secretary would kill more members of his Party than all its enemies put together.

The vision of purpose that once inspired this dictatorial structure began to erode the moment Lenin found himself in possession of the levers of power. But the basic ideology of Marxism-Leninism was structural in character. Organization, centralization, the monopoly of economic power, political power and spiritual power, permanent dictatorship, force unrestrained by anything, these were the substance of Lenin's dreams from 1902 onward. He completed the edifice of dictatorship not under the impact of civil war but after the civil war was safely over when, at the Tenth Congress of his Party, he pushed through the provision prohibiting groupings for internal party discussion.

Like despotic structures in general this totalitarian structure has built-in staying powers. Given the "law of diminishing dictatorships," given too the muted discontents and weariness and boredom with fifty

39. Rosa Luxemburg, *The Russian Revolution*, Ann Arbor, 1961, pp. 69-78.

years of ever less vivid repetition of the semantic fictions we have noted, there is no way of telling how long this structural system will endure. But at the end of fifty years it is clear that within it inheres no independent public life, no true legitimacy, nor any intention of seeking it by a free discussion and free vote of the people subject to its rule, or a free functioning of the "public bodies" imposed by the party and state upon an atomized, yet over-organized people.

"Yes, the dictatorship of a single party!" said Lenin in 1919. "We stand on this, and from this ground we cannot move." [40]

"The Communist Party has been, is, and will be, the only master of the minds, the only expresser of the thoughts and hopes, the only leader and organizer of the people," said Pravda on the fortieth anniversary of the seizure of power by Lenin. And the First Secretary of the Armenian Party Central Committee added the fitting commentary: "Only ignoramuses (for I do not speak now of outright enemies) could maintain that there might exist some other force besides the party . . . some other force than the party leadership, that could express the will of the Soviet people." [41]

All through the self-congratulatory editorials of the fiftieth jubilee year, Pravda rang the monotonous changes on the same theme in such formulae as "The Communist Party is the mind, the conscience, and the will of the Soviet people."

In this formula is expressed the durable core of what has been misnamed the "Soviet" system. What I said of it ten years ago at Oxford, I am afraid must still be said today:

As long as collective leadership does not determinedly broaden itself instead of narrowing; as long as it does not openly treat itself as pre-legitimate in the sense of aiming to replace itself by a broader, non-dictatorial organization of power; as long as power itself does not flow down into the basic units of the Party (where it did not inhere even in Lenin's day); and as long as it does not then overflow the party dikes and spill over into self-organizing corporate bodies, independent of party, police, and state; as long as there do not develop organs and arenas of organization and expression free of party controls; as long, finally, as there develop no organized, independent, institutionalized checks upon the flow of power to the top, not a mere slowing but an actual reversal of the whole trend of totalitarianism—there is no reason to regard any directory or collective leadership as more than an interregnum between dictators, and at each dictator's death there will be no legitimacy to provide a lawful succession.

And at the moment of this writing I cannot imagine any faction in the

---

40. Lenin, Vol. 24, p. 423, Speech to the All-Russian Congress of Education Workers, July 31, 1919.
41. Literaturnaya Gazeta, December 28, 1957.

Communist Party that would make as its program and purpose the devolution of power to the limbs and parts of the body politic, or a genuine attempt to establish a new democratic legitimacy. Nor can I presently imagine a set of circumstances that might engender such a faction or tendency.

—January 1968 [42]

42. Presented orally on October 9, 1967 as the opening paper in a conference on fifty years of the Russian Revolution organized by the Hoover Institution of Stanford University. Written in its present form in January, 1968, for publication in the proceedings of that conference, edited by Milorad Drachkovitch and published by the Pennsylvania State University Press under the title, *Fifty Years of Communism*.

II BACKWARDNESS AND INDUSTRIALIZATION IN RUSSIAN HISTORY AND THOUGHT *

> When all other countries are crisscrossed by railroads and are able rapidly to concentrate and to shift their armed forces, Russia must necessarily be able to do the same. It is difficult, it is expensive, but, alas, inevitable. . . . With regard to railroads, as in many other things, we are particularly fortunate; we did not have to expend energy on experiments and strain our imagination; we can and shall reap the fruits of others' labor.
> —A. S. Khomiakov

Historically, most Russian critics of their country's condition, particularly Marxists and liberal Westernizers, held in varying degrees four propositions: (1) their country was backward; (2) while the West was advancing in seven-league boots, Russia remained stagnant; (3) her progress was blocked by removable obstacles; (4) once these were removed, Russia would follow the path already traversed by the West, although on this fourth proposition all who longed for a shortcut entertained reservations, their favorite shortcut running through the peasant "commune."

But what was this West which Russia was predestined to follow? When Russian intellectuals looked for an industrial model, West meant the England of the industrial revolution. Or Germany, which had followed England's example and was beginning to overtake her. When they concerned themselves with political obstacles to "modernization," West meant France, the France of a century of uprisings, barricades, *coups d'état*, the France in which the great broom of revolution had swept away the *ancien régime* in one dramatic decade, and with it, supposedly, all hindrances to progress.

To be sure there was a catch. If all that was needed to unleash economic progress was a "Great French Revolution," why did the French economy limp so haltingly behind those of England and Germany?

There being no political answer to this question in their formulae, it

---

* A chapter of a work in progress first published separately in the *Slavic Review*, June 1967.

was better not to ask it. Nor to ask whether the year of the Terror, with its 40,000 victims, was necessary to progress. Better to glorify the "Great Revolution" than to question its methods or its outcome.

COPYING THE PARIS STYLES

French insurrectionary spirit and verbal audacity captured the imagination of the powerless Russian intelligentsia. Since in old Russia one could only dream, and since in dreams one is not responsible for consequences, there was no reason to put prosaic limits on their dreams. In the midst of oppression, the intelligentsia developed their ideals in freedom . . . freedom from reality, from practical activity, from roots in society, from tentativeness, shading or self-questioning, from any limits on speculation and asseveration. "In all things I go to the uttermost extreme; my life long I have never been acquainted with moderation," wrote Dostoevsky. His words could serve as the device of most of the intelligentsia. And, in a different fashion, of the peasantry as well.

Liberals might prefer the ordered progress of England. But the Autocracy, as extreme as the revolutionaries, left little room for autonomous liberalism. One school of Social Democrats, of which Axelrod was an example, because of their concern for the *self*-activity of the working class, looked to Germany's great mass organizations and German Social Democracy as its model. But *self*-activity was the last thing which either Lenin or the government wanted of the working class. The ideologues of the Autocracy and the ideologues of Bolshevism alike felt that it was their mission to be the guardians of, and do the thinking for, the popular classes. If "spontaneous" is normally a good word in our vocabulary, it was an evil one in the vocabulary of both Tsarism and Bolshevism. Nay more, *spontaneity* was a thing of evil to the greater part of the entire spectrum of Russian thought. *Stikhiinost*, which means both elementality and spontaneity, suggests the stormy, uncontrollable, unpredictable character of the elements. The thin layer of the Russian intelligentsia and the bureaucracy alike tended to fear and oppose it, seeking to contain or channel it into the ways of order, direction, and "consciousness." In moments of illumination the Russian intelligentsia felt that it was suspended over an abyss which at any moment might open and swallow it. Pressed down from above, sucked down from below, many nineteenth-century revolutionary intellectuals appealed to Tsar and nobles and to their fellow intellectuals to transform Russia by a planned revolution from above lest they and all they valued be wiped out in an elemental storm arising in the depths. In the twentieth century Gorky often admonished Lenin not to stir "the dark people" to deeds of violence and blood. Our word, spontaneity, has no such stormy reverberations.[1]

UNILINEAR PATH TO THE FUTURE

Whether "following the path taken by the West" meant the political-social revolution of France or the Industrial Revolution of England, the underlying proposition that there was a single unilinear path for all lands moving from "backwardness" to "modernity" does not bear examination. According to this theory, there is but one line of progress along which all nations are marching at various points and at various speeds. The *locus classicus* for this widely held nineteenth-century view—at least for Marxists—is a passage in Marx's Introduction to the first edition of *Das Kapital*, where he acknowledges that he has "used England as the chief illustration in the development of my theoretical ideas" but admonishes his countrymen not to shrug off his conclusions as inapplicable to them:

De te fabula narratur. . . . The country that is more developed only shows to the less developed the image of its own future.

More scrupulous than the dogmatists he was to beget, more troubled by the recalcitrance and complexity of history, Marx had reservations concerning the universality of this unilinear picture. If he suggested that feudalism was pregnant with the "modern bourgeois" order, and capitalism with the "socialist" mode of production, he did not, like so many of his latter-day disciples, see "feudalism" in every land where there were latifundia and bondsmen or peons. Insofar as his schemata were unilinear, they pictured feudalism, where it existed, as destined to be ended by the despoiling of the small proprietor so that the latter would be "thrown on the labor market." But this pattern did not obtain everywhere, nor at all times in history. In his well-known listing of "progressive epochs in the economic formation of society," he included not only "the feudal and modern bourgeois modes of production" (which were steps in his inevitable march to socialism), but also the "ancient" and "Asiatic" modes.[2]

---

1. An excellent study of the meaning for Russian socialist thought of *stikhiinost* and its supposed opposite, *soznatelnost,* is in Leopold H. Haimson, *The Russian Marxists and the Origins of Bolshevism,* Cambridge, 1955.

2. *Zur Kritik der Politischen Oekonomie,* Stuttgart, 1921, p. LVI. the passage reads:

> In broad outlines Asiatic, ancient, feudal, and modern bourgeois modes of production can be designated as progressive epochs in the economic formation of society. The bourgeois relations of production are the last antagonistic form of the social process of production . . . ; at the same time, the productive forces developing in the womb of bourgeois society create

Like "Asiatic despotism" with its long ages of persistence of the same basic structure ("millennial slumber"), Russia, too, troubled the simplicities of Marx's formulae. His schema had been derived from his study of the social and economic history of England, where the Enclosures and the Industrial Revolution despoiled the tillers of the soil, separated the artisans from their ownership of their own means of production and turned them into propertyless "proletarians." Though this process "has taken place in a radical way so far only in England," Marx never doubted that "all the countries of Western Europe will go through the same development." [3]

But of Russia he was not so certain. On the one hand Russia was "semi-Asiatic." Marx here was not talking geography but institutional structure. Russia had known prolonged and universal bondage, but not feudalism. Her supercentralized "oriental despotism" was built on the foundation of a dispersed and backward agriculture and village handicraft in isolated and powerless villages, each self-sufficient, and each lacking connection with the others, in their economy, in awareness of common interests, or in the physical connection of a network of roads. Moreover, those villages possessed their peculiar institution, the *obshchina*, with its communal title to the land that it partitioned and repartitioned, its communal dictation of the methods of agriculture, its power over the freedom of movement of the villagers, and its collective responsibility to the State. Was this only a negative phenomenon, a source of despotism and stagnation? Or was it also true, as the *narodniki* believed, that the "communal village" fostered unconscious socialist feelings and relationships and might enable "the Russian people to find for their fatherland a path of development different from that which Western Europe has followed and is following?" [4]

---

the material conditions for the solution of that antagonism. This social formation brings, therefore, to a close the prehistory of human society.

Professor Wittfogel has suggested in his *Oriental Despotism* that Marx's "progressive" epochs here do not constitute a *developmental* scheme, but rather a *typological listing* of "antagonistic" societies. This is no doubt so. However, a total reading of Marx's work makes it clear that he frequently made a mental switch from "typology" to "inevitable succession," at least when he was thinking of three of these types, namely, feudalism, capitalism, and socialism. When the peasants and artisans are "expropriated" and thrown on the labor market, feudalism "leads into" the bourgeois order. And the bourgeois order, by its very nature, is pregnant with the seeds of the socialist order. Thus the passage from *Zur Kritik* quoted above begins with typology, but ends with the idea of "pregnancy," with its strong suggestion of inevitability.

3. Quoted by Marx from the first French edition of his own *Das Kapital*, in a letter written in 1877 to *Otechestvennie Zapiski*. This letter, in the original French, is in *Ausgewaehlte Briefe*, Berlin, 1954, pp. 365-68, and in Russian translation in *Perepiska K. Marska i F. Engelsa s russkimi politicheskimi deiateliami*, Moscow, 1957, pp. 177-80 (hereafter referred to as *Perepiska*).

4. *Ausgewaehlte Briefe*, p. 366, where the sentence is quoted in Russian from a review by N. Mikhailovsky entitled, "Karl Marx before the Tribunal of Mr. Zhukovsky."

To answer this question Marx studied Russian as did Engels. They read all they could lay hold of by way of official reports and controversial literature. Yet, to the end of his days, Marx's voice faltered when he tried to answer. For he and Engels were ambivalent concerning the "class nature" of the Russian State, the meaning of the communal village in general, and the Russian village in particular. On the one hand, as Engels put it succinctly in his *Anti-Duehring*, it was clear to them that "the ancient communes, where they continued to exist, have for thousands of years formed the basis of the most barbarous form of state Oriental despotism, from India to Russia." [5]

On the other hand, particularly Marx was more than a little seduced by the *narodnik* idealization of the "socialist spirit" of the *obshchina*. Would "the revolution," anti-Tsarist in Russia, socialist in Europe, take place before the *obshchina* had too far disintegrated? Or would the Russian peasants be fated "first to transform their communal property into private property," [6] then be expropriated and turned into proletarians on the English (and "inevitable" West European) model? If the second occurred, which seemed likely unless "the revolution" came quickly, Russia would be "giving up the best chance which history has ever given to any people, and would suffer all the fated vicissitudes of the capitalist regime." [7]

The alternatives thus posed by Marx were false, since the basic feature of the *obshchina*, which caused the government to enforce its existence and even continue it after the Emancipation, was the obligatory collective responsibility of the village for recruits, redemption payments, and taxes. [8] But the fact that Marx, unlike his Russian disciples who called themselves Marxists, should have raised the possibility of these alternatives showed that he was not as dogmatic as they concerning a fated unilinear path for

---

5. *Anti-Duehring*, New York, n.d., printed in Moscow for International Publishers, p. 206.

6. *Perepiska*, p. 42, in a letter to Vera Zasulich.

7. *Ausgewaehlte Briefe*, p. 268.

8. Though Vera Zasulich, when she wrote her letter to Marx, still believed that the *obshchina* might serve as a short cut to socialism, her letter speaks of the necessity of first "freeing it from excessive taxes, redemption payments and police arbitrariness." (*Perepiska*, p. 240) Marx did not touch these points in his answer. Cf. Karpovich: "The prevailing opinion among the authorities tends to view the most characteristic features of the rural commune in modern times as a product of comparatively late historical development. . . . The periodic redivision of the land arose in the eighteenth century, likewise the strip system and the compulsory course of husbandry." (Bowden, Karpovich and Usher, *Economic History of Europe Since 1750*, New York, 1937, pp. 296-97. The sections on Russia are by Professor Karpovich.) (Ibid., p. 600.) Florinsky writes: "The Emancipation Acts of 1861, granting personal freedom to the former serfs, created at the same time a highly complicated system of economic and legal relationships which amounted, in the last resort, to the establishment of a new bondage for the new 'free' tiller of the soil, his bondage to the land commune.

Russia, on the model of his schemata in *Das Kapital*. For Marx, not only was Russia's past different, but its present—tentatively—was open.

In his letter to the Russian journal, *Otechestvenniie Zapiski*, written in November 1877, Marx still left this troubling question unanswered. Moreover, he warned his Russian readers not to take the schemata drawn up by him for Western Europe as "a historico-philosophical theory of the general march imposed by fate on all peoples regardless of the historical circumstances in which they find themselves." He instanced the case of the ancient Roman peasants, expropriated and turned not into wage-workers, but into the "idle mob" of the Roman proletariat, to show that often "strikingly analogous events, taking place in different historic surroundings, bring about totally different results." [9]

That he could give such a warning shows the superiority of Marx to those who call themselves Marxists. But of course, there were limits to how far he would allow that history was open, for in the next breath he made it clear that if the *obshchina* should much further disintegrate, Russia too must enter on the same and single path on which the West European lands were, inexorably in his opinion, following England.

Two years before Marx died, Vera Zasulich once more besought him to fit the Russian village into the schemata of *Das Kapital*, and settle the "life and death" question of Russia's destiny. Again he hesitated, then, after a number of discarded drafts, replied with curt brevity that his book had spoken of the historical inevitability of the English road only "in the lands of Western Europe. . . . Hence the analysis present in *Capital* does not give any conclusions either for or against" a special fate for Russia's peculiar institution.[10]

At the very moment when Marx was wrestling with these thin and indecisive drafts, a writer in *Narodnaya Volya*, without benefit of Marxist orthodoxy, was working out a more realistic conception of the nature of the Russian State and its relation to agriculture and industry than Marx and Engels or Plekhanov and Lenin were to formulate. The State, said the anonymous author in a series of articles published in 1880, is not an

---

Established primarily for fiscal reasons—in order to secure the collection of redemption payments imposed on the liberated serfs in exchange for the parcels of land transferred to them on their emancipation—the land commune became one of the chief obstacles to the economic development of the country. Not only did it prevent any improvement in agriculture, but it also greatly hindered the formation of a permanent class of hired labor, of a town proletariat, which is one of the indispensable conditions of industrial progress. . . . It was not until the shock of the Russo-Japanese War and the terrible agrarian disturbances which followed it that the Government [under Stolypin] undertook a radical reform [of the communal village]. (*The End of the Russian Empire*, New York, 1931, p. 15.)

9. *Ausgewaehlte Briefe*, p. 371.

10. *Perepiska*, pp. 241-42.

executive committee of any ruling class or combination of ruling classes but in fact an independent organization, hierarchical, disciplined, and despotic, based upon brutal police power and the absorption of most of the population's income by heavy exactions.

"Our State owns half of Russia as its private property, and more than half of the peasants are tenants on its lands." Political and economic power are inextricably interwoven in its fabric. In addition to being the greatest landowner, it is also "the greatest capitalist force in the country." It has set up much of Russian industry, put up a tariff wall so high that the most backward industry could survive and make a profit. "A whole series of feudal prerogatives have been created for those who own the mines. For centuries, the people of the Urals have been handed over like slaves to the capitalists.

"The building of railroads in Russia provides a spectacle that is unique in the world; they are all built with the cash of the peasants and of the State which, for no apparent reason, hands out hundreds of millions to various business men. . . . The kopeks of the peasants flow into the pockets of stockbrokers and shareholders from the Treasury of the State. Russia is in its stage of primary [or primitive] accumulation in which wealth comes less from production than from more or less outright pillage."

The State is an autonomous organization, the only autonomous organization in Russia, and it "would hold the people in economic and political slavery even if there were no privileged class in existence." [11]

THE PLURALISM OF HISTORY

Today historians have come to recognize the pluralism inherent in the variousness of the human spirit, the uniqueness of each country's history, each epoch, and social scene. But, as often happens when the specialist is having second thoughts, the doctrine of unilinear development lives on, simplified, vulgarized, all-pervasive, in journalism and popular thought. Today the communists apply Marx's unilinear doctrine concerning Western Europe not only to Russia—even as it follows a path manifestly so different from England's—but also to Asia and Africa.

Thus in their comments on the Chinese revolution, both communist

11. The articles which are here summarized are programmatic. Their main formulator was presumably N. Morozov, but they represent the views of the little circle of leaders of the group that published them. I have followed the summary by Franco Venturi in *Roots of Revolution*, New York, 1960, pp. 667-68. They are excerpted from *Narodnaya Volya*, Nos. I, II, and III, 1880, which were reprinted in *Literatura partii 'Narodnoi Voli,'* Moscow, 1906. See also L. Tikhomirov, *La Russie politique et sociale*, Paris, 1886, p. 206.

and noncommunist writers have spoken of traditional China's land system as "feudal," *feudal* having become in modern journalism not a precise term for a definite system of relationships but a mere pejorative for any noncapitalist or nonsocialist landowning system. It is more than doubtful that a Chinese feudalism ever existed at any time. In any case, one of the essential prerequisites for such a system, namely primogeniture, was abolished in China in the Third Century before Christ! It was the consequent lack of "strong property" which prevented the landowners and tillers of China from setting up a counterweight against centralized bureaucratic despotism. The resultant subdivision of the land and the pressure of population upon it made not the large landed estate but the "pocket handkerchief farm" the key agrarian problem of early twentieth-century China. If there are good reasons for not calling Russian bondage "feudal," there are still better ones for not using the term in connection with China.

Because of the uniqueness of each country's history, when nations borrow from each other—and in the age of world wars and world communications such borrowing has become well-nigh universal—what is borrowed suffers a change as it is transplanted.

To take a familiar example, how different is America's Congress from Britain's Parliament whose offspring it is. How different from these two—and from each other—are the French Chamber, the German Reichstag, the Russian Duma. How remote from these are their offspring, the parliaments of the new nations of Asia and Africa. Until at last, the very word "parliament" seems to be stretched beyond the breaking point when it is made to cover Franco's Cortes and Sukarno's handpicked council, or when a meeting of the Supreme Soviet is headlined by our press as a "session of the Soviet Parliament." But quite frequently, a borrowed institution may alter, even profoundly, the course of the life stream into which it enters. Yet even more profoundly is it transformed by the life of which it becomes a part.

THE TRANSPLANTING OF IDEAS

Not institutions alone, but ideas and doctrines suffer a radical change on transplantation. Most of Russia's nineteenth-century ideas were imported from the West as in the eighteenth century Peter imported techniques and institutions. But what was taken and what ignored or rejected from the variegated Western intellectual scene, and how these ideas were utilized, held, and built into all-embracing systems or exclusive means of salvation, were things characteristic of the borrower rather than the source.

Ideas tended to be borrowed without the long history that begot them, without any of the qualifications, shadings, offsets, interplay with opposing and contrary ideas, characteristic of the more pluralistic West. The borrowed ideas were made characteristically Russian in that they quite literally possessed those who thought to possess them. Each doctrine in its turn tended to become mutually exclusive of its predecessor, and all-embracing. One lived by the *ism* of the moment and felt moral scorn for those who had not seen the light. "I become terrible," wrote Belinsky in a moment of penetrating lucidity, "when I get some mystical absurdity or other into my head." Fichte, Schelling, Hegel, Feuerbach, Marx, Darwin, to mention only a few, each in turn possessed Belinsky utterly. Westernism itself, as Chaadaiev showed, could become a peculiarly un-western religious tenet. Even "scientism" became a quasi-religious creed. "When a member of the Russian intelligentsia became a Darwinist," wrote Berdyaev, "to him Darwinism was not a biological theory subject to debate, but a dogma, and one who did not accept the dogma . . . awoke in him an attitude of moral suspicion."

Marxism was held by Russian Marxists in ways which astonished Marx himself. Thus N. I. Sazonov, landowner from the Russian steppe, who became one of the world's and not merely Russia's first Marxists in the 1840's, said to Marx: "I, a barbarian . . . love you more than any of your fellow countrymen do." Marx was astonished, even embarrassed, that his first disciple should be Russian and use the un-Marxian language of love.

As Russia came to reject Byzantium, yet made of Byzantine orthodoxy the orthodoxy of "the Third Rome," so Marxism was nationalized, the Marxism of the West rejected as heretical and revisionist, and Marxism made into a Russian Church. It became not merely a theory of economics and history and sociology, but the basis for a total rejection of all existing institutions (a rejection, incidentally, that formed a genuine constituent of Marx's own complex and ambiguous doctrines). It was held totally and exclusively, and totally applied like all the isms that preceded it. In power, it became a totalitarian system of thought and life, embracing absolutely everything, and employing total force and total control of the means of communication to prevent any other ism from succeeding it, as had been customary every half decade with the earlier isms. Lenin made of it a "profession" in both senses of the word, a profession by which and through which one lived and made one's living, and a profession of faith. It was Russian religiousness turned inside out and intended to end the long pursuit of a faith which had occupied Russia's intellectuals for a century. As a Dostoevsky could proclaim that the Russians knew and loved Christ more than the Christians of any other land, indeed, were the only ones truly to know and love Him, and therefore must teach the true faith to the world, so a Lenin could persuade himself that all Marxists were lukewarm or apostates, save only those who hearkened to him. Thus intellectual borrowing became not so much appropriation as expropriation even as the borrowing represented a terrible simplification and improverishment of what was borrowed.

THE BORROWING OF TECHNIQUES

Technological borrowing is simpler than the borrowing of institutions and ideas; it is more direct, more mechanical. Yet, even technological borrowing has its institutional prerequisites and possesses aspects involving the subtle world of the spirit.

The industrially less developed country cannot begin to implant the structures and techniques of modern industry until, by methods engendered in its own history, it has overcome certain obstacles in its own life. Thus Germany could not become a great industrial land until it had put an end to its fragmentation into petty principalities, while Russia could not begin its industrial advance until it had abolished serfdom.

With centralization achieved in Germany's case and emancipation in Russia's, there still remained the problem of the accumulation and concentration of investment capital. This problem had been solved in England over centuries. Germany and Russia would take but decades, for often they borrowed only end results without the profound spiritual and cultural development that had engendered them. And each would meet the problem differently, by inventing and mobilizing each its own characteristic institutional devices, and rallying the spiritual energies for the great sacrifices and expenditures of industrialization under its own distinct ideological banner.

To overcome its particularism and fragmentation, Germany required a series of wars. These made Germany not more like the England it was "imitating," but less like it than before. Out of Bismarck's *Blitzkriege* came the strengthening of Prussian militarism, Prussian *Junkertum*, and imperial power; the predominant emphasis on heavy industry, and the close tieup of militarism and industrialism—so characteristic of post-industrial Germany and so alien to the England of the Industrial Revolution.

Within a few decades, however, indeed before the turn of the century, German industry became big enough to outgrow the tutelage and control of the banks. Enterprises broke the monopoly of a single bank by working with several, or grew strong enough to switch banks, while the mightiest giants, like the electrical industry, established banks of their own. Though a close relationship continued between banking and industry, industry was liberated from tutelage and control, "the master-servant relation gave way to cooperation, and sometimes was even reversed." [12]

In Russia, after emancipation, the financial situation was so much worse, capital so scarce, standards of honesty and competence in business so low, that no banking system could attract the huge sums needed to finance industrialization. Hence, Russia reverted to the ancient institutional device so deeply ingrained in her history: compulsory exactions by government. Taxation; tariffs; loans; government-guaranteed orders, often paid for long in advance of manufacture; abnormally high prices to domestic production and rejection of lower foreign competitive bids; concessions; subsidies; direct government ownership, construction, control and investment—such were the devices employed. Thus did the Russia of Alexander III use the mighty machine of a "state stronger than society" (Miliukov) to undertake from above what the feeble, government-dominated society could not undertake from below.

Since the beginning of the seventeenth century, and especially since Peter I's day (1682-1725), moved by the needs of war and power, the Russian state had several times "modernized" the industries necessary for war with the technologically more advanced armies of the West. Now again in the last decade and a half of the nineteenth century—as so often in the past—"the State swelled up while the people shrank." (Kliuchevsky) And so it would be again under Lenin, Stalin, and Khrushchev.

As the alliance between industrialism and militarism and a close fusion of banking and industrial capital distinguished the industrialization of backward Germany from its English model, so the fusion of statism with industrialism distinguished the Russian model from the German and the English.

Modern socialist theory was grievously derailed by a misunderstanding of industrialization. It was Rudolf Hilferding's attempt to generalize the investment banking system as it developed in Germany into a "universal" institution proper to "modern capitalism" in general that constituted the fundamental error in this serious Marxist thinker's *Finanzkapital*, an error that led Marxist theoreticians to misunderstand the whole process of modern banking and "monopoly capitalism." Lenin, for his part, his grasp of economics being largely limited to the illustration of accepted dogma by the culling of suitable examples, compounded Hilferding's error when he turned it into the formulae of his *Imperialism: The Highest Stage of Capitalism.* From this error, too, he derived his simplistic, utopian schemata for the economics of the seizure of power in his fantastic recipes of the year 1917. For his October coup he pictured "a

12. Alexander Gerschenkron, *Economic Backwardness in Historical Perspective,* Cambridge, 1962, p. 20.

single bank—mightiest of the mighty—with branches in every district, every factory" as the simple institutional means for the seizure of economic power and the administration of the new economy. It was, he declared, "already nine-tenths of the socialist apparatus . . . something in the nature of the skeleton of socialist society. This 'state apparatus' . . . we can 'take over' and 'put in motion' with a single stroke, by a single decree. . . ."

Four years later he wrote ruefully: "On the State bank, a great many things were written by us at the end of 1917 . . . which turned out to be no more than mere words on paper." [13]

THE LINK BETWEEN MODERNIZATION AND BACKWARDNESS

In 1931, Joseph Stalin told a conference of Soviet managers:

The backward are beaten. . . . The history of old Russia . . . consisted of the fact that she was always being beaten because of her backwardness. She was beaten by the Mongol khans. She was beaten by the Turkish beys. She was beaten by the Swedish feudalists. She was beaten by the Polish-Lithuanian gentry. She was beaten by the Anglo-French capitalists. All of them beat her —because of her backwardness, because of her military backwardness, cultural backwardness, governmental backwardness, industrial backwardness, agricultural backwardness. They beat her because it was profitable and could be done with impunity.[14]

Stalin's test is a simple one—victory or defeat in war is the measure of the level of civilization. But his history is strangely one-sided, for it can as well be read in the opposite direction. Russia in time beat the Mongol khans, the Swedish feudalists, the Polish-Lithuanian gentry, the Turkish beys. For every "beating" Stalin cited—with the exception of the Crimean War ("the Anglo-French capitalists"), which ended without advantage to either side, there was a subsequent Russian comeback and ultimate triumph. It was these beatings and counter-beatings that form so much of the pattern of Russian history and have contributed so much to Russian institutions and the shaping of the Russian spirit.

When Peter I, still far from being "the Great," fled from Narva in 1700 and his armies melted away before those of Charles XII of Sweden, this "beating" became the spur to the first great modernization of Russia's army, her navy, and her war industries under the ruthless hand of the greatest of all industrializers of Russia prior to the days of Witte, Stalin, and Khrushchev. By 1721, Peter's refurbished armies had broken

13. *Lenin,* 4th Edition, XXVI, p. 82; XXXII, p. 68.
14. *Stalin,* XIII, p. 38.

the power of the "Swedish feudalists" and sent their king flying. And so after him, Russia would annex the Kingdom of Poland and Lithuania. And this same backward Russia, which Stalin pictured as forever beaten, would crush Frederick the Great of Prussia and disperse his armies, then defeat the still greater Napoleon and occupy Paris.

In his own day, Marx, too, regarded Russia as backward, but this did not prevent him from noting that backwardness had never precluded Russia's sudden stormy advances in military technique for the purposes of equipping mighty armies and turning defeat into victory and ultimate conquest. The once obscure Duchy of Muscovy had been expanding for the better part of the last three centuries, to North, South, East and West, becoming in the process the world's greatest land empire. "In the last sixty years," he wrote in the *New York Tribune* on June 14, 1853:

The Russian frontier has advanced:
Towards Berlin, Dresden and Vienna about .... 700 miles
Towards Constantinople .... 500 miles
Towards Stockholm .... 630 miles
Towards Teheran .... 1000 miles [15]

Marx's picture is, as he intended it to be, frightening. The expansion of Russia did not cease in his lifetime, nor after his death, nor did it cease in our time. At the beginning of the century in which Marx lived, one European in seven was under Russian rule; at its end, one in four. By the middle of our century, when Stalin died, one European in every two—either directly or through puppet regimes—was under Stalin's control.

Far from testifying to Russia's progress, this immense expansion of the Duchy of Muscovy into the greatest empire in the world was one of the causes of her backwardness. "It might be said," writes Berdyaev, "that the Russian people fell victim to the immensity of its territory." Almost continuous warfare over centuries, the maintenance of huge armies, the forced development of war industries and military service, strained to the utmost the poor country's human and material resources. She was forever spending beyond her strength to maintain and extend her illimitable bounds. The Eurasian plain was an armed camp, living under the harsh and autocratic laws of war. The social function of the Autocrat was an important one: to "gather in" the Russian (and not only Russian) lands; to raise, equip, and lead her armies; hold the Empire together; drive back the Mohammedan Mongol and Turk, the Roman Catholic Pole and Frank; to defend Russia's wide boundaries and freedom—the only free-

15. *New York Tribune*, June 14, 1853; Werke, IX, p. 116.

dom Autocracy and unending war could permit—freedom from the foreign invader, from foreign ways and foreign faiths.

Little wars were always being waged somewhere on the Empire's metes and bounds, and in nearly every generation there was a great war that strained Russia to the utmost, leaving her exhausted, in a mood for stagnation and reaction against the excessive strain and the forced military-technological disturbance of her traditional life.

Each such effort imposed an intolerable burden upon the generation whose life span coincided with the crisis. To extract from that generation the manpower, wealth, and energies for so great a struggle, an already over-powerful government had further to expand its powers and its exactions, subjecting the people to yet more severe measures of oppression and coercion, curtailing the right of each crisis generation to live for its own purposes or any purpose save service to the state and its monstrous growth.

Peter's industrialization may well serve as a paradigm of this process. What he sought in Europe, as Kliuchevsky said, was "Western technique, not Western civilization." To be able to fight the two-decade long Northern War, he wanted Russia to become a shipwright, building men-of-war; an iron-miner and smelterer, casting cannon and forging barrels and bayonets; a weaver of woolen cloth, to uniform regiments.

If he cut off his nobles' beards with his own shears, it was not merely to humble them but to make them look like officials of the West. Like Ivan the Terrible, but on an all-embracing scale, he created state service nobles who held their *pomestiye* at his will and as reward for service to him, not by virtue of absolute hereditary right. The long struggle between the Crown and the independent hereditary nobility, which began as the power of the prince grew in the fourteenth century and became a furious war on the boyars in the time of Ivan IV, was brought to an end when Peter reduced the free nobles to the status of state-service gentry. Thereafter the old nobility continued to exist only in a residual sense, as a memory of aristocratic descent, a feeling of personal dignity and *noblesse oblige*, an awareness that there were still some high callings like top diplomatic and administrative posts, which even a Peter hesitated to fill with *parvenu* "service people."

Peter completed the humiliation of the boyars so ruthlessly initiated by Ivan the Terrible. From now on, at least until 1762, the gentry, to use the apt words of Martin Malia, were bound to serve the state in the same way that the peasants were bound to serve their masters—as "serfs, although highly privileged serfs, of the Autocrat." By ukaz, or by direct command, Peter made nobles into industrialists, made technicians of their younger sons, humbled the nobility, made merchants into serf owner-manufacturers, and created a laboring class not of wage earners but of serfs from the crown lands adscripted to factories, to be bought and sold along with the plant. Thus, in Ivan's as in Peter's Russia, it was the State that created the classes, rather than—as Marxism asserted—classes that created the State. The State "belonged" to no class, but all classes belonged to and owed service to the State.

Peter's barbaric cruelties to his subjects, the thousands of his tortured and slain, was in part a product of the caprice and anger that only those whose power knows no limit can indulge. But as often as not he was punishing men for resistance to his innovations, offering them up as a sacrifice to the Moloch civilization of war and despotism. His secret police spied out their unfavorable opinions of his deeds and innovations and their "treason" in seeking to evade state service. His exactions rose annually from some million and a half rubles at his accession to eight and a half million at the end of his reign. He and his advisers showed positive genius for inventing new taxes on everything, from rents paid on "corners" of rooms, to private bathhouses in peasant huts; from marriage outside the Church, to the wearing of moustaches and beards.

But the heart of the reaction which was the reverse side of Petrine "progress" was the systematizing and universalizing of bondage. The mines and smelters he founded in the Urals, like the city he laid out on the marshes to be a "window on Europe," were constructed and manned by assigning bondsmen—and not only bondsmen—to these tasks. He ordered nobles to open and run factories, ordered wealthy merchants to reside and trade in his new city.

It would take two centuries for the town thus founded to become a potential locus of countervailing power comparable to the fortified and charter-possessing towns of the West. Instead of Russian cities being a refuge for those who fled in search of freedom, it was long the case that strict government measures were necessary to prevent flight *from* the Russian cities.

When the nobility did not suffice to create a manufacturing class, Peter gave merchants the privilege of purchasing and owning serfs, with the proviso that when they sold their factory the serfs were to go with it.

As there was no *soslovie* of manufacturers, the decree of January 18, 1721, authorized merchants to share the hitherto exclusively noble privilege of purchasing and owning serfs. Here the State created not a new "estate" but, out of some merchants and nobles, a new "class."

Peter's endless wars, his servile-labor factories, his systematic endowment of officers and bureaucrats with land and serfs as compensation for their service to him, his great constructions, and the very energy and sweep of the reforms thus enforced—all combined to universalize and systematize bondage. In the century when feudal serfdom was being uprooted in the West, Russia, though it had no feudalism, developed a harsh and universal serfdom, destined to retard development and inject its evils into the social life of the next century and a half.

Russia's bondage had neither the contractual mutuality, nor the comparative autonomy, nor the natural foundations, of Western feudalism. In the kingdoms of the West, nature and society imposed limits on the flight of the serf by the absence of unoccupied land. In the ever enlarging lands of the Russian giant there were forest, steppe, river bottom and shore, deserted or laid waste by war or newly conquered, to which the peasant reduced to serf might flee unless he were riveted to his place. The purpose of bondage was literally to establish fixity (*krepost'*) so that tax collector and recruiting sergeant would know where to find every man. It became the duty of each village to supply a new recruit for every soldier who dropped out, whether by reason of desertion, illness, injury, or death, so that the Russian soldier, as Florinsky has written, was "immortal."

The Petrine reforms were genuine, as his "Westernization" was genuine, but Autocracy was their driving force, war and the power of the state their objective, subjection of society and the binding of everyone from serf to serving noble, their method. "Peter did not hesitate," wrote Lenin admiringly, "to use barbarous methods in fighting barbarism."

What Lenin did not note was that technological progress and social reaction, the "civilization" of iron works and the "barbarization" of bondage, were two sides of the same coin. And so it would be again under Lenin and his successors. The decreeing of technological advance from on high for the purpose of war and power and the social retrogression implicit in absolute power, absolute servility, and universal bondage were two sides of one and the same process, by virtue of which Autocracy grew and Russia itself expanded. Paradoxically, as Russia became more "Western" in her war industries, she became more "Russian" in her despotism, her universal statism, her rural bondage, her servile factory labor, her subordination of society and all its members high and low to the omnipotent state.

The appearance of stagnation in nineteenth-century Russia, what was it but the persistence of serfdom until 1861, of absolutism until 1905, and of collective village responsibility until the Stolypin reforms loosened the bonds that tied the peasant to the *obshchina*? In the nineteenth century, the earlier autocratic industrialization in the fashion of Peter, with its all-pervading serfdom, was to prove the chief obstacle to the development of a "modern" industry and state.

IDEOLOGIES AND INDUSTRIALIZATION

A word should be said here about Professor Gerschenkron's illuminating analysis of the *ideological banners* under which industrialization has been undertaken, justified, and exalted, in various types of backward countries. To Saint Simon and his disciples in France he traces the glorification of the investment banker as a "missionary" ushering in a Golden Age of flourishing industry and "happiness for all." In Germany, which lacked France's political revolution and national unification, ardent nationalism was the ideological banner. But "in conditions of Russian 'absolute' backwardness, a much more powerful ideology was required to grease the intellectual and emotional wheels of industrialization."

Though the main impetus for industrialization came from the Russian government, which needed no more banner than that of military might and governmental power, there was a notable change in the attitude of the intelligentsia toward industry in the course of the eighties and nineties. Earlier they had opposed industry and its values, seeking their justification in the will of the peasant, agriculture, and the commune. The switch from regarding nonagricultural activity as unnatural and unworthy to exaltation of industry came under the banner of "orthodox Marxism."

It is this that explains the sudden rise of "legal Marxism," the government's toleration of it, and the fact that, for a moment, Marxism took possession of such liberals as Peter Struve and such profoundly religious spirits as Bulgakov, Berdyaev, and Frank. It seeped into the university chairs of history, economics, and law, affecting to some degree even men like Miliukov.

So too Professor Gerschenkron suggests some insights into present-day Soviet ideological banners. In Russia's long delayed industrialization and long perpetuated serfdom, he sees two of the causes "responsible for a political revolution in the course of which power fell into the hands of a dictatorial government to which in the long run the vast majority of the population was opposed." Since power cannot be retained exclusively by force regardless of the sweep of terror, the Soviet Government has sought "to make people believe that it performs an important social function which could not be discharged" without it or by using other than its methods. These methods involve "reversion to a pattern of economic development that should have remained confined to a bygone age, substituting collectivization for serfdom, and pushing up the rate of investment to the maximum point within the limits of endurance of the population." In doing these things, "the Soviet Government did what no government relying on the consent of the governed could have done." As a result, muted opposition and "day-to-day friction" are inevitable. The banner under which the Government seeks to make its harsh course less unacceptable bears two simultaneous devices: *Nationalism* and *Socialism*. To rally *nationalism* behind it the government has need of a military menace from abroad so that it may pose as the indispensable form in which the country-in-danger can be defended, the sole guarantee that Russia will not be "beaten." The *socialist* device on its banner is "the promise of happiness and abundance for future generations." This is the meaning of the endless scholastic exercises in analysis of the road "from socialism to complete communism." Thus, writes Gerschenkron, "economic backwardness, rapid industrialization, ruthless exercise of dictatorial power, and the danger of war, have become inextricably intertwined in Soviet Russia." [16]

The reforms forced upon the people by Peter, like the bondage imposed on them, met with sullen resistance. Thus a split between people and State, between the masses and the bureaucrats, between the State church and the Old Believers, and later between the masses and the intelligentsia—a split which would prove fatal in Russia's "Time of Troubles" in the twentieth century. The people were not better but worse prepared after such a "reform" for initiation of reforms themselves.

Moreover, until the twentieth century, all important reforms came from on high, from the Tsar and his advisers. Peter's military industrialization; Catherine's Rescript (which remained largely on paper); Speransky's administrative reform proposals (some of which Alexander I and Nicholas I introduced, others remaining in their desks, while the most important of them—a constitution and a reign of law binding on rulers as well as ruled—have not been realized to this day); Alexander II's emancipation of the serfs in 1861; finally, the great industrialization at the end of the nineteenth century under Alexander III and his son, Nicholas II, the last of the Tsars—all these assaults on backwardness, indeed, the very consciousness of backwardness, came largely from the throne and its chosen advisers.

The greatest of these reforms was the Emancipation of the serfs by Alexander II (1855-1881) in the year 1861, two years before Lincoln emancipated America's slaves. Once more, as with Peter, it was the ineffectiveness of Russia's serf armies in war, which brought home a sense that Russia must be "modernized" from above.

Unlike Peter's reforms, which have been overpraised, Alexander's have been overcriticized. Since the landowners still constituted the chief support of the throne, he had perforce to make some concessions to them, but he forced the liberation upon them by reminding them of two centuries of peasant mutinies. "It is better," he said, "to abolish serfdom

16. Gerschenkron, *Economic Backwardness*, pp. 22-29.

from above than to wait until it begins to abolish itself from below." The chief defect of this complex of measures was not that the serfs got less land than they had expected and had to pay for it and for their own redemption in a long series of annual installments. Nor was it the fact that the nobles had to give up privileges they were reluctant to part with, receiving payments that were not large enough to enable them to enter into industry or trade. The root defect was the ancient evil characteristic of Russia from before Peter's day: the tying of the peasant into his village community by constant communal repartition of the land, by village dictation of backward agricultural methods, and by collective responsibility for taxes and recruits. The peasant's tax ruble and the peasant soldier continued as before to be "immortal." At long last, in the brief period from 1907 to 1917, this burden of collective responsibility and bondage to the *obshchina* was removed, only to be restored in altered, more sweeping, and more exacting form in the Stalinist *kolkhoz*.

Whatever its defects, we need only remember that Alexander's Emancipation endowed the peasants with most of the land they had been tilling as serfs and compensated the landowners, while our Emancipation left the slaveowners ruined and the freedmen without farms. In the light of the history of agrarian reform in Western Europe and in our own South, there is much justice in Professor Karpovich's verdict that the Emancipation of 1861 was "the greatest single legislative act in the world's history."

Moreover, it made necessary four other great reforms from above: rural self-government by *zemstvos* (county councils), 1864; a reform of the law courts, 1864; municipal self-government (the municipal dumas), 1870; and a reform of the army, 1874. At the moment he was assassinated in 1881 by revolutionaries who found his reforms inadequate, Alexander II was working on the outline of a shadowy semiconstitution.

The cutting of the bonds of forty million peasants led to a general loosening of the bonds that constricted Russian society. The subject was in a fair way to becoming a citizen. The army ceased to exempt the nobility from conscription and made the obligation to service equal for all, at the same time shortening the term of service from twenty-five years to six (later reduced to four years), with strikingly shorter terms for students and with exemption for each family's breadwinner. The reform of the courts did away with class privilege before the law, made the courts independent of the bureaucracy, provided for qualified, irremovable judges, not subject to political dictate, set up trial by jury, and an autonomous bar. Though in time of stress the police sought to bypass them by administrative exile and court-martial, the Russian courts remained a shield against injustice, inferior to no other in the modern world—until the Bolsheviks returned to removable judges, subservient bar, political dictation of judicial decisions, and summary judgment by bureaucracy, party, and dictator.

It was the *zemstvos* that proved to be the greatest step forward in the awakening of an articulate "public" in rural, and not only in rural, Russia. However limited their budgets and their powers, they introduced into Russian life the principle of self-government, and of nongovernmental, nonbureaucratic, public initiative. They constituted the beginning of a multicentered society, a school of administration, a means of initiating and gaining social assent to social action. The *zemstvos* and the city dumas provided the foundations for a new representative system, foundations which seemed to the Russian intelligentsia to cry out for a national parliament and responsible cabinet "to crown the edifice."

Though the bureaucracy was jealous and suspicious (by 1914 only 43 of Russia's 70 provinces had as yet been permitted to set up rural self-governing institutions), yet by that date the *zemstvos*, led by the enlightened gentry, had in their employ some 5000 agronomists, had made significant strides on the road to universal education, had trained most of the men who were to be the leading liberal spokesmen of the Duma, and had built up a veritable army of new plebeian intellectuals: doctors, nurses, teachers, agronomists, veterinarians, engineers, statisticians, economists. It was these whom the peasants returned in overwhelming numbers to the Duma as their representatives. In the First World War, Nicholas's best generals and ministers, and Nicholas himself, turned to the *zemstvos* and the city dumas for help in mobilizing the country's agricultural resources, industry, and transport for war and for aid in caring for the refugees and the wounded. When, in 1917, the Russian people for the first and only time in their history were given the opportunity to choose their representatives freely by universal suffrage, it was the Socialist Revolutionary Party led by this rural plebeian intelligentsia and expressing above all the aspirations of the peasants, who received the overwhelming majority throughout the nation.

Thus to the consciousness of Russia's backwardness on the part of a Peter, a Catherine, or an Alexander, was at last added a consciousness of backwardness arising from below—in that new social formation of the nineteenth century, the intelligentsia, and what they themselves called "society," i.e., literate public opinion. Conditioned by all the past, they still turned to the sovereign for reforms. But to give their opinions and petitions force, they strove to inject their ideas, necessarily coarsened and simplified, into the masses of peasants and, later, into the masses of peasants and workingmen. Thus were born the revolutionary parties.

The peasants had been there from time immemorial, as peasants, then as serfs, then as freedmen. But before there could be workingmen, the peasants had to be free to go to the cities, and the cities themselves had to become centers of mighty industry. The last "reform" to come from the sovereign and his ministers without pressure from below was the great wave of industrialization in the last decade and a half of the nineteenth century and the first decade of the twentieth.

INDUSTRIALIZATION UNDER THE LAST TSARS

Emancipation had been a necessary condition, but by no means a sufficent one, to start this stormy upsurge. The merchants, small manufacturers, and nobles were too poor in capital and in spirit to undertake vast enterprises. An unstable ruble, a low state of credit, private and public, a corrupt officialdom, the lack of an adequate internal market were barriers to an influx of any significant foreign enterprise or capital. From the Emancipation to the middle of the eighties, the rate of industrial growth continued to be low. For the first few years after the Emancipation, industrial production even dropped because the serfs bound to factories were free to abandon them and many works simply shut down.

But from the middle of the eighties on, the State itself once more assumed the task of building up the industry it needed most. To be able to cope with the technologically changing and rapidly moving armies of the West; to be able to bring its vast reserves of manpower to bear on any point of its far-flung boundaries; to connect distant parts of the Empire for rapid transport of reports, officials, supplies, troops—the government undertook the construction of a railroad system of unprecedented proportions.

Railroads required iron and steel, rails and locomotives, coal and wood and ties, stations, telegraph lines, engineers and trainmen, miners and machinists and steelworkers, and enormous quantities of capital. To borrow capital abroad, the government had to strengthen its credit, firm up its ruble, purify in some measure the economic and bureaucratic life of the country. Railroad building became the lever of an industrial upsurge so great, and an inner market so much wider than before, that in the end industry and finance developed a momentum of their own—a self-propulsion quite new in Russia's long history. When the State under Nicholas II lost much of its interest in the great enterprise, industry and finance continued their growth from 1907 to 1914 without massive aid from the State. Thus there was every prospect—were it not for world war and revolution—that the "modernization" of Russia might have continued on its own, not from on high as under earlier Tsars and later Commissars but from below, not for the purposes of war and the power of the State but for the purposes of the market, the profit of the entrepreneur, and the satisfaction of the consumer.

If industrialization in and of itself is to be regarded as a "progressive" achievement, as Marxists tend to regard it,[17] then credit for Russia's industrial upswing at the turn of the century must go to Alexander III (1881-1894) and to his successive Finance Ministers, to whom he gave unstinting support. N. C. Bunge, a former university professor, was Minister of Finance from 1881 to 1886. I. A. Vyshnegradsky, also a university professor and a successful businessman, held the post from 1887 to 1892. Then S. J. Witte, a professional railroad man who worked himself up in sixteen years of railroading from the post of station master to Director of the South Western Railways, then to Minister of Transport, and then served as Finance Minister under both Alexander and Nicholas II, from 1892 until his opposition to Russian imperial adventures in the Far East caused him to lose favor with Nicholas in 1903.

Bunge introduced the first serious labor legislation as a paternal activity of the autocratic state. He abolished the hated poll tax; appointed tax inspectors to see what burdens the people could bear; encouraged the export of grain "even though Russia starve"; increased substantially the burden of indirect taxation upon the masses; curbed the ruble-printing presses; began the slow accumulation of financial reserves which would encourage foreign investment, increase the investment resources of the Russian state, and thus enabled Witte, at long last in 1897, to tie the ruble to the gold standard.

The nineties were the beginning of the golden age of Russian industrialization. Vyshnegradsky introduced a high tariff to encourage domestic industry; under him, Russia's tariff became, and after him remained, the highest in the world. He continued the struggle for a balanced budget, a stable currency, an inflow of foreign capital both for investment and government loans, and a great increase in indirect taxation, which, by 1892 accounted for seventy-two per cent of Russia's rapidly mounting public expenditures.

The chief stimulus to economic growth in the nineties was the intense activity of the government in railroad building. Under Bunge and Vyshnegradsky, a number of shorter lines were built by the state while others were purchased by it and operated under state management. By 1894 the government had taken over twenty-four lines with an aggregate length of eight thousand miles. But the grand enterprise of the period was the Trans-Siberian Railroad, begun under Vyshnegradsky in 1891 and pushed steadily to completion throughout Witte's term. It had just come

17. And not only Marxists. Today the idea that heavy industry is the measure of progress and the greatness of a state is widespread among new nations and among older nations faced with the possibility of total war. The idea of Denmark, that it can remain a prosperous, "modern, progressive," and happy land, on the basis of intensive agriculture and dairy farming for the markets of more heavily industrialized countries, is rare indeed.

into operation as a single track line when the Japanese War broke out in 1904.

The climax of Russian railroad building came in the five years from 1896-1900, when over ten thousand miles of road were built. No five-year period before or since, not under the Bolsheviks either, has equaled it. Here is a general picture of the rate of railroad construction:

1886-1890	1,898 miles
1891-1895	4,403 miles
1896-1900	10,035 miles

By the end of the nineties, the total investment in railroads was estimated at 4,700,000,000 gold rubles, a huge sum by any standard. The government's direct share was three and a half billions; private interests and foreign companies provided the rest. The State was the owner, the great builder and railroader. It willingly paid domestic iron and steel makers from 110 to 125 kopeks per pood (thirty-six pounds) of rails, while private buyers were paying only eighty-five to eighty-seven kopeks. When the construction of the great Trans-Siberian began, the British offered rails at seventy-five kopeks a pood delivered, but the government decided to stimulate domestic production by giving long term orders and huge cash advances at the rate of two rubles a pood. When the Bolsheviks decided to develop autarky by big subsidies to and big losses in heavy industry at the expense of the population, they were not introducing an altogether new principle into Russian life.

But autarky in the modern totalitarian fashion was not the aim of Alexander III and his finance ministers. They aimed at the development of domestic metallurgy, wisely welcoming foreign capital to share the heavy burdens of industrialization. Encouraged by the stabilization of the ruble and the enlargement of the domestic market, the inflow of foreign capital increased more than sixfold in the course of the nineties, most of it in the last five years of the period. Nearly half of it went into mining in the new Don metallurgy and mining area, but something like sixteen per cent went into machine building. By 1917 the total foreign investment in Russian banking, commerce, and industry was 2,243,000,000 rubles. Mining came first, metallurgy second, banking third, and textiles fourth.

FOREIGN CAPITAL AND INDUSTRIALIZATION

The respective national shares of this investment have been computed as: France, thirty-three per cent; England, twenty-three per cent; Germany, twenty per cent; Belgium, 14 per cent; the United States, five per cent; and the rest shared by Holland, Switzerland, Denmark, Austria, Italy, and Norway. But ownership by the Russian state and Russian investors exceeded all of these added together while the State or Crown was also the largest landowner in Russia.

In their absurd development of the "Leninist" notion that foreign investment enslaves the recipient and renders the latter "semi-colonial," Bolshevik writers have been hard put to specify which of these investing countries did the enslaving, or on whose behest this huge imperialistic "semicolony" got into the "imperialist war."

The notion, at least as applied to Russia, is "Leninist" rather than Lenin's, for he regarded Russia as an imperialist power, not a semicolony, and was convinced of Russia's responsibility for the outbreak of the war, which she entered for her own "imperialist aims."

Michael Pavlovich set Russia down as a semicolony of France, which dragged her as a vassal into the war for France's imperialist aims. Pokrovsky denounced Russia as chiefly responsible for the war, and even the assassination at Sarajevo, and pictured the French government as headed by politicians who had been *bought* by Russian landowners. Later he changed his picture and had Russia playing a dependent role, "a reflection of the interests of stronger imperialist powers." Stalin began in 1924 by describing Russia as "an immense reserve of Western imperialism" (in *Foundations of Leninism*) and ended by picturing her (in the *Short Course*) as being weighed down with the golden chains of Entente capital and government loans from Britain and France. These "chained Tsarism to British and French imperialism and converted Russia into a tributary, semicolony of these countries." This decline of "Tsarism's independent role in European foreign policy" he dated from Russia's having been "beaten" by the "Anglo-French capitalists" in the Crimean War!

Latterly, Soviet writers have come to acknowledge the absurdity of the whole notion . . . for Russia! This has solved for them the problem of picturing Tsarist Russia simultaneously as an imperialist and an enslaved power. *Voprosy Istorii* in 1956 published an article entitled: "Was Tsarist Russia a Semicolony?" which answered the question in the negative:

Capital from various imperialist groups was ensconced . . . in all kinds of industries . . . primarily [sic!] to obtain maximum profits and not always [sic!] with the direct aim of accomplishing general political state purposes. Exaggerating the political role of foreign capital in Russia, some research workers turned "the complex intertwining of finance-capital relationships" and purely commercial deals "into a dramatic episode of a conscious patriotic struggle of various groupings of foreign capital, allegedly acting as agents of the respective foreign governments." [18]

18. B. B. Gravye, "Was Tsarist Russia a Semicolony?," *Voprosy Istorii*, No. 6, June, 1956, p. 63-74; Michael N. Pavlovich, "Soviet Russia and Capitalist France," Moscow, 1921, p. 21 (he compares the Russian army to "the black-skinned troops who also had

Concerning Tsarist Russia's industrialization, also, Soviet writers have attempted to prove two inherently contradictory things. On the one hand, they have pictured Tsarist Russia as backward, stagnant, virtually devoid of industry and incapable of industrialization. On the other, they have sought to show that Russia had a great enough industry, a large enough working class, and an industrial tradition sufficient in 1917 to make the country "ripe" for a "socialist" revolution. Without our trying to decide what "ripe" for socialism means, we can recognize that neither side of this dilemma will stand up under examination.

From 1885 to 1916, Russia was industrially backward. Yet her industry, in terms of per cent of increase per annum, grew faster than that of any other great power.[19] Only in the stormy period from 1900 to 1906 (a world depression, the Russo-Japanese War, the Revolution of 1905), did the rate of increase falter. If we take the growth by five-year periods, as became fashionable with the five-year plans, Russia's annual percentage of industrial increase was higher than Germany's in every period but that of 1901-1906, higher than that of France, of England, and—except for the two periods 1885-1889 and 1901-1906—higher than that of the United States. For the whole three decades from 1885-1914, Russia's average increase in industry was 5.72 per cent per annum, America's 5.26 per cent, Germany's 4.49 per cent, the United Kingdom's 2.11 per cent.[20] From the Emancipation to 1900, Russian industrial productivity increased more than seven times, German almost five times, French two and one-half times, English a little over twice.

Thus did Russia begin her giant strides toward "catching up with and surpassing" (dognat' i peregnat'—the phrase is Lenin's) the industrial countries of Western Europe. The secret behind the big percentage increases is twofold. On the one hand, it is a matter of simple arithmetic: the lower the base from which you start, the easier it is to double, treble

---

to die for the glory . . . of the French Shylocks"); the Pokrovsky quotes and sources are in Gravye's article; Stalin, VI, p. 75; *Short Course,* p. 156; and J. V. Stalin "On Engels's Article, 'The Foreign Policy of Russian Tsarism'" is in *Bolshevik,* No. 9, 1941, p. 44. Stalin's article in *Bolshevik* was originally a letter sent by him to the editors of that journal in 1934, when he ordered them not to publish Engels' article in their issue commemorating the twentieth anniversary of the outbreak of the World War in 1914. His letter and his order to suppress Engels' article were kept secret until their publication during the Second World War.

19. It is frequently forgotten that Tsarist Russia also led the world in book publishing with 34,000 titles in 1914, many of them translations.

20. For these comparative figures as for much of the statistical material in the present article, I have drawn on Alexander Gerschenkron's ground-breaking study of "The Rate of Industrial Growth in Russia," *Journal of Economic History,* Vol. VII, Supplement 7, pp. 144-74. Gerschenkron's comparative tables include Sweden whose rate of growth during the same decades surpassed even Russia's, without either government subsidies or a lowering of living standards. Sweden, like the United States, suggests how widely methods of industrialization may differ, according to differing situations, traditions, outlooks, and institutions.

or quadruple it. On the other, there is a real advantage in backwardness, once industrialiaztion has begun, for the more backward an industrializing country, the greater the backlog of technological innovations that it can take over from the more advanced countries. The larger the imports of foreign machinery, foreign know-how, foreign capital, the faster industrialization can proceed. The industrializing country sets up only the latest type of plant; it is not burdened by a wide range of obsolescent and semi-obsolescent factories as is the older country from which the latest models only are borrowed. That is why "the German blast furnaces so soon became superior to the English ones, while in the early years of this century blast furnaces in still more backward Russia (South) were in the process of outstripping in equipment their German counterparts." [21] Indeed, we can lay it down as a general law that if a country is of the critical size and can summon up the institutional and economic resources to begin general industrialization, the later this begins in history and the more backward the country is, the faster its industrialization will proceed.

There was something in the lateness of her development, as there was something in Russia's statism and in her physical size and natural extremism of spirit, that combined to reinforce the tendency toward bigness of plant, which both Germany and Russia manifested, and the tendency of Russia's bureaucratic industrializers to concentrate on heavy industry to the detriment of the lighter consumer goods industries. The very shortage of skilled labor is an incentive to introduce the most modern, large-scale, labor-saving machinery.

In Germany the banks had been attracted to coal mining, iron and steel-making, electrical and general engineering, and industrial chemistry to the neglect of textiles, food-producing, shoe, and leather goods. In Russia the government of the nineties showed no interest in light industry either. Railroads, iron, steel, oil, coal—these were the industries that were government-constructed and operated or that received the subsidies, the long-term orders, the generous credits, and the guarantees.

From 1890 to 1899, during the greatest period of Witte's railroad construction, Russian industry as a whole increased annually at the formidable rate of 8.03 per cent. (Compare this with the rate of 5.44 per cent in Germany and 5.47 in the United States during the same decade!) Most of this increased national product was in the fields of heavy industry.

This upsurge was cut short by the world depression in 1900. (In Russia the depression was cushioned and a slow rate of increase kept up by railroad building.) Then came war with Japan, the massive unrest of 1905, and the peasant jacqueries of 1906. But in 1907 there began a transformation in the economic rhythm and structure of Russia and the

21. Gerschenkron, *Economic Backwardness*, p. 8.

pattern of thought and life of Russia's intelligentsia, which seemed destined to change the course of her history.

The State continued its railroad building, on a more modest scale: about 4,700 miles in the *nine* years from 1905 to 1913, as compared with the 10,000 miles in the last *five* years of the nineties. But this cutback did not cause industry to falter.

On the contrary, in place of stagnation, there was a new upsurge, primarily on the basis of autonomous, i.e. nongovernmental, financing for a nongovernmental or free market. This time the expansion included textiles. For the first time in her history the sphere of operations of the managerial state began visibly to contract and the sphere of operations of nongovernmental society to expand. To reverse Kliuchevsky: The State shrank, the people grew healthier. "Industry," Professor Gerschenkron writes, "had reached a stage where it could throw away the crutches of government support and begin to walk independently."

To be sure, it still needed the protecting wall of a high tariff. But this cannot be compared to the outright refusal of the government of the nineties to purchase English rails at less than half the price of Russian and still less to the absolute exclusion of cheaper and better competitive products by the autarkic Soviet economy. A protective tariff is a common feature of all newly industrializing lands though Russia, in this as in so many things, exceeded the common magnitude.

What was most strikingly new was large-scale financing by private banks. Just as Germany was beginning to outgrow the early stage of industrialization by investment banks and shake its industry free from control by bankers, Russia began to enter the stage in her development that Germany was leaving. Until then, since the Government had fulfilled the functions of investment banking, there had been room in Russia only for deposit banks, resembling the English commercial bank system.

But as the government withdrew, as business men became more trustworthy and enterprising, and as independent sums of capital accumulated, the Moscow deposit banks began to be overshadowed by the development of St. Petersburg banks conducted on principles already familiar in German rather than in British banking. To follow Professor Gerschenkron's phrasing, financing of industry by investment banking instead of the government represented "a new and higher stage in Russia's backwardness."

What of the workingmen and peasants during this quarter century of stormy growth of industry? During the first fifteen years from 1885 to 1900 it was from them that much of the "primitive accumulation" came to enable the government to finance industry. The high protective tariff, the rising prices, the great leap in indirect taxes, the higher tax on village

lands than on those of the large landowners, the export of grain, the
heavy taxes on such articles of common use as matches, alcohol, and tobacco, later the rising sale of spirits by the government alcohol monopoly
—all served to shift much of the cost of the great enterprise to the peasantry and the rapidly developing working class.[22] The wages of workers
in textile and other light industries did not rise at all during that period.
Wages in metal factories, though still very low, were about double those
in textiles, and rose another ten to fifteen per cent during the nineties.
Since prices also rose, the standard of living of the metal workers increased slightly while those of the textile workers deteriorated.

But here, too, the years between 1907 and 1914 showed a change for
the better and demonstrated that, under conditions of relative freedom
from state financing and state controls, industrialization—once it had
gotten over the first hurdles—could produce a more favorable market for
the peasant's product and begin to raise the workingman's wages and
living standards.

The worker now acquired some, albeit much harassed, freedom to
organize nongovernment unions, much more freedom for press and
political parties, complete freedom to form cooperatives and insurance
and benefit societies. Factory legislation was better enforced. Studies of
real income for the period are confusing since wages now rose rapidly
(in textiles, too, which tended to catch up with the wages of metal
workers), while agricultural prices rose forty-one per cent between 1900
and 1913, and general prices some 28.7 per cent. Such studies of real
income as have been made indicate that there was a genuine rise in the
standard of living of the working class as a whole, and a greater rise of the
poorer paid, between 1907 and 1913.

Improvement in the village was even more marked. After the catastrophic decline of the nineties, there was a rapid recovery until the village
was better off than it had been at any time since the Emancipation. Redemption payments and poll tax had been canceled. Collective responsibility for taxes was abolished in 1903. The umbilical cord which bound
the peasant to the village was cut by the Stolypin reform of 1906-1907
(confirmed by Duma legislation in 1910). The village captain's power
over passports and free movement to the towns was taken away. The
towns, free to invest in what the market required, began to turn to the
manufacture of things the peasant needed. The growing and more prosperous urban population created a better market for what the peasant

22. "Taxation by price" was what Preobrazhensky called it when in the twenties
he proposed the development of Soviet industry through "primary socialist accumulation."
And "taxation by price" has been the method of pressing out of the masses the
sums for Soviet industrialization. The turnover tax has been levied and is still levied
on articles of mass consumption on a scale that would have shocked Vyshnegradsky
and Witte as well as Marx and Engels.

produced. The terms of village trade with the expanding industrial centers improved by some twenty-five per cent between 1900 and 1913. The cities drained off some of the rural overpopulation while continuing to send devoted technicians and teachers to assist the countryside. By January 1915 (although it was less than a decade since the Stolypin Reform and he himself was assassinated in 1911), about thirty-three per cent of all peasant households had withdrawn from the hitherto obligatory commune and became independent farmers.

The freedoms granted by the Tsar's Manifesto of October 1905, although they were applied unevenly and grudgingly, presented no limitations to the burgeoning of peasant cooperatives. By 1914, nearly half of the peasant households of Russia had joined the cooperative movement. Their total capital rose from 37½ million gold rubles in 1905 to 682⅓ millions in 1916. Government banks, in disregard of sound financial principles, lent up to ninety per cent of the value of their land to the peasants who left the communes. The governmental Peasant Land Bank bought millions of acres of land from the gentry and resold them to the peasants. By 1914, over seventy-five per cent of all the arable land of European Russia was held by the peasants. No wonder Lenin thought that if the agrarian reform should continue to operate for another decade, the possibility of a revolution such as he envisaged would vanish and he would never live to see it.[23] Indeed, it would take a world war, and a widening whirlpool of folly at Court, to reverse the trend toward a more open and independent society that was at long last beginning to develop in Russia.

—June 1967

---

23. *Lenin*, XV, pp. 30-31.

III *DAS KAPITAL*
ONE HUNDRED YEARS
LATER*

On August 16, 1867, at two o'clock in the morning, Karl Marx wrote to his friend Engels, "Dear Fred, Have just finished correcting the last sheet of the book." The sheets were page proofs, the book *Das Kapital, Kritik der politischen Oekonomie*. It was Volume One of a projected six-volume work. Marx lived another sixteen years, writing and rewriting endlessly, but he never got out another. Though the author was the descendant of long lines of rabbis on both his father's and his mother's side, and his lifelong collaborator, Friedrich Engels, a manufacturer's son, first the manager then the half owner of the Ermen and Engels textile factory in Manchester, "the book" was to become, in Engels' words, "the Bible of the working class." Most workingmen did not and could not read their "Bible," yet it gave comfort to those with faith in it, for its real purpose was to provide "scientific insight into the inevitable disintegration of the dominant order of society."

Das Kapital, as a centenarian, still has astonishing vitality. Philosophers, economists, sociologists, political scientists, politicians expound upon it. Rulers of great lands quarrel with each other as to who is following it most faithfully, who "revising" or "betraying" it. Certainly, no other economic treatise, from Adam Smith's *Inquiry into the Nature and Causes of the Wealth of Nations*, published in 1776, to John Maynard Keynes's *General Theory of Employment, Interest, and Money*, published in 1936, is known to so many men in so many lands in name and comforting "insight" if not in content.

The century that has elapsed since its publication, and the two additional decades since the *Communist Manifesto* pronounced "the downfall of the bourgeoisie" and the victory of the "proletariat" equally imminent and "equally inevitable," have not dealt kindly with Marx's predictions. Yet, while other nineteenth-century social thinkers and social critics are today little more than names in textbooks, the name of Marx remains a banner and a household word for millions.

Today those who are free to study Marx's writings dispassionately—

* First published in the *Antioch Review*, Winter 1966-67.

as dispassionately as men can study writings so charged with passion—
are likely to see in him a social critic, a moralist, and a seminal thinker
of a bygone day, some of whose insights, and some of whose errors, have
been incorporated into the social disciplines (let us not fall into his mistake of calling them sciences): history, sociology, economics, and political
philosophy.

Many of the practitioners of these disciplines are embarrassed by their
awareness that man's values form a constitutive part of his examination
of his own activities. Were it not for this false shame, political philosophy
would not now be so nearly in eclipse, nor so reluctant to acknowledge a
debt to Marx and his fellow utopians for certain suggestive insights into
that branch of political philosophy which may properly be called social
criticism, a branch concerning itself with the imperfections of any society-
in-being as measured against its own potentialities and against man's
flickering yet undying vision of the good life. Such social criticism is, of
course, a branch of moral philosophy, becoming dangerous only when
the *hubris* of the social critic persuades him that it is a branch of exact
science.

There are many Marxes. Though he began as a humanist and a
utopian, borrowing freely from Rousseau and Condorcet, Saint-Simon
and Fourier, Hegel and the Young Hegelians, Proudhon and Weitling,
he was not content to remain in their debt, nor to be one utopian among
many, believing in an hypothetical "natural" or "generic" man who had
somehow been deformed by the movement of history and whose true
nobility could be suddenly and completely restored by following certain
utopian prescriptions. There was a prickly and arrogant side to Marx's
personality as is often the case with prophets; and a succession of quarrels
with his fellow utopians, a consciousness of his own great intellectual
powers, his desire to excel, and the disappointments arising from the
failure of the revolutions of 1848 caused him to repudiate his earlier self
as expressed in the *Economic and Philosophical Notebooks of 1844*, which
he chose to leave unpublished. Within a year after he jotted down those
notes, he abandoned the trade of philosopher and moralist for that of
"scientist." Then it was that he and his friend Engels discovered how
devastating the epithet "utopian" can be, not so much on the lips of the
opponents of socialism as in the struggle for predominance among socialists themselves. It was, as Martin Buber has written, "the earliest example of the Marxian device of annihilation by labels."

HOW MARX BECAME A "MARXIST"

When, late in October, 1843, Karl Marx took his newly wedded bride, Jenny von Westphalen, to Paris—a love match if there ever was one—he was still an anticommunist. He had been editing a "bourgeois democratic" journal, *Die Rheinische Zeitung*, in Cologne. When a rival paper accused him of being "communistic," he had answered haughtily, yet with prophetic foreboding:

We do not allow even *theoretical reality* to Communist ideas . . . still less do we wish to see their *practical realization*. . . . We intend to subject those ideas to a fundamental critique . . . but surely the *Augsburge Allgemeine Zeitung* must recognize that you cannot criticize such writings as those of Leroux, Considérant, and above all the penetrating work of Proudhon, off the top of your head with casual or superficial ideas, but only after long, persistent, and thorough study. . . .

We firmly believe that not the *practical attempt* but the theoretical exposition of Communist ideas constitutes the real danger. For practical attempts, even on a mass scale, can be answered with *cannon* as soon as they become dangerous, but *ideas*, which conquer our intelligence, which master the feelings that conscience has fused with our reason, these are chains that one cannot break away from without breaking one's own heart, they are demons which man can only conquer by submitting to them.

This was Karl Marx's only significant comment on communism before he reached Paris—significant for what it suggests of the passionate temper of his intellect; of his need to make a "long, persistent, and thorough" study of the socialist doctrine in order, as he thought to "criticize" it; significant, too, of his subconscious but vivid fear lest his conscience, his heart, and his intellect be caught in its toils; and his penchant for replacing "the weapons of criticism with criticism by weapons," a penchant which would thus seem to antedate his conversion to socialism.

The young Marx had a job waiting in Paris. An older and wealthier "young Hegelian," Arnold Ruge, to whom Marx had apprenticed himself, was founding a new journal, the *German-French Yearbooks*, and wanted Marx as co-editor. Marx's daily and Ruge's democratic-philosophical annual, the *Hallische Jahrbuecher*, had both been suppressed by their government for rather minor criticisms of the Prussian autocratic regime, so the two men moved to Paris with the modest intention of uniting "German philosophy" and the French radical-democratic tradition in a common effort at the further enlightenment of man. This was a bit presumptuous, for France had long been the hearth and beacon of revolutionary radicalism, democratic political theory, and socialist-utopian doctrines, while Germany was still stagnating in its medieval particularism and theological and political authoritarianism. It was Frenchmen who for over half a century had striven and suffered, fought, disputed and dreamed, and tried to turn the world upside down—to remake it *de novo* according to some one of a series of contending blueprints. Meanwhile, German thinkers had continued to watch meditatively, and German philosophers in cap and gown, or nightcap and slippers, had spun complicated theories transposed in cloudy fashion from French activities. Now two of these German philosophers had come to Paris to give the French a "philosophical" account of what the latter had been up to.

The ambitious venture never really got started. Eminent French thinkers ignored their invitations to contribute as did eminent thinkers inside Germany. Thrown into the proximity of exile and surrounding silence, Marx and his patron found that their temperaments and their households clashed, and their ideas as well. One double number of the *German-French Yearbooks* finally appeared in February, 1844, then publication ceased. It was at this moment that the young Marx, without a job, without a definite profession or material resources, exposed with his growing family to the hazards of uncertain fortune, discovered the proletariat. Along with the proletariat, in the same flash of lightning, he discovered socialism.

And, from the solitary number of the *French-German Yearbooks*, he discovered the German manufacturer's son, Friedrich Engels, who writing from his father's textile mill in Manchester had contributed an article (some twenty-five pages in the *Marx-Engels Werke*, Vol. I), entitled *Umrisse zu eine Kritik der Nationaloekonomie* (Outlines of a Critique of National Economy). Marx's admiring letter to the author began a friendship that was to last a lifetime.

In September, Engels crossed the Channel to visit Marx. The two friends spent ten days and nights in the cafés of Paris, eating good food, drinking good wine (Engels was a free spender and gourmet), sharing admirations and prejudices, talking good talk concerning German philosophy, French politics, and English economics, concerning Hegel who though dead some thirteen years, held sway over German thought, mocking at the various varieties of "Young Hegelianism" into which his school was splintering, and planning joint literary enterprises. They talked of Moses Hess, the humanistic socialist who had converted Engels to socialism, of the philanthropic manufacturer-utopian, Robert Owen, whom Engels, as a manufacturer's son, dreamed of emulating and for whose *Moral World* he was writing. They discussed with excitement the various dreams of socialism filling the Paris air (the very word, *socialisme*, was then only twelve years old).

The young Doctor of Philosophy, without a chair and without a journal to edit, and the young manufacturer's son, separated from felicity and his homeland by the cares of his father's English factory, found themselves in basic agreement on everything from their admiration for Wilhelm Weitling and Pierre-Joseph Proudhon, two declassed workingmen turned theoreticians, to their contempt for the Young Hegelians who only yesterday were their close comrades and to whose "critical" annihilation they were to devote the first two works they now planned to write together.

Engels was the younger by some two years. He unhesitatingly subordinated himself to the older, more titanic, and more highly charged mind of Marx; yet in this first encounter, he gave Marx incomparably more than he received. He had studied British political economic theory, British industry, and the British working class. He knew more about socialist thinkers and had already reported in Owen's journals on the many varieties of the socialist movement. Unlike Marx, he knew workingmen at first hand, through his overseership of textile workers in his father's factory, through a study of Parliamentary Blue Books and English statistical reports, and through a work-in-progress, *The Condition of the Working Class in England*, dedicated "To the Working Classes in Great Britain," in which dedication he told them that he had forsaken "the dinner parties, the port-wine and champaign [sic] of the middle-classes and devoted my leisure hours almost exclusively to the intercourse with plain Working Men! I am both glad and proud to have done so. . . ."

It was these fields of knowledge that were to become the foundation stones of Marx's future *magnum opus*. Engels generously ceded the title and subject of his *Umrisse zu einer Kritik der Nationaloekonomie* and the exclusive right for Marx to fill out those *Outlines* in a series of volumes all of which were destined to bear the title or subtitle *Critique of Political Economy*.

In any case, they hit it off instantly. Engels became a Huxley to Marx's Darwin, a junior partner in joint enterprises, a Ford Foundation for Marx's lifelong research-and-writing fellowship, a defender, popularizer, systematizer, vulgarizer, and after Marx's death the only authorized "revisionist" of the Master's thought and doctrine.

The words "critique" and "criticism," which have kept recurring in the pronouncements and plans of Marx and Engels, were as fashionable in Young Hegelian thought then as the words" existentialist," "alienation," and "absurd" are today. Moreover, "criticism" was one part of his fragmentary heritage from Hegel that Marx was to retain all his life, for it suited both his temperament and his writings and expressed his attitude toward the Germany of his day, toward prevailing economic theory and existing social and political institutions, and toward competing schools of socialist thought.

"Critical thought," a constituent part of Hegel's philosophy, proliferated in his more radical disciples when the old master was gone. David Strauss criticized theology; Ludwig Feuerbach, all transcendental religion; the three Bauer brothers, Bruno, Edgar, and Egbert, went on a critical spree in a philosophical journal they founded. Then Marx and Engels tore critically into all the Young Hegelians in their first two joint works.

To the Bauer brothers ("the Holy Trinity") Marx and Engels devoted what was planned during those ten days together as a "short satirical pamphlet." Engels duly dashed off his half in some sixteen manuscript pages before he left Paris. But Marx, a slower writer with a more prickly temper and a more ponderous style, took the rest of the year and over 300 pages to do his "half." The "little pamphlet" was entitled *Die Heilige Familie, oder Kritik der kritischen Kritik (The Holy Family, or Critique of the Critical Critique)*. By the time it appeared the very journal of the "Holy Family" had ceased publication and been forgotten; the polemic dropped noiselessly into oblivion.

Their second joint work, *The German Ideology,* was several times longer and more ambitious. It would settle accounts with all German thought and contemporary German thinkers. The authors sent two stout volumes in octavo to an interested publisher, who kept the manuscript but decided in the end not to publish. Those who in the course of duty have had to read it cannot blame him. Its original title suggests its tone and bulk: *The German Ideology, a Critique of Recent German Philosophy and Its Representatives, Feuerbach, Bruno Bauer, and Stirner, and a Critique of German Socialism and Its Various Prophets*. Engels remarked drily that its critique of Stirner was as long as Stirner's stout book. The devoted Marx biographer, Mehring, found it "arid, discursive," in many places "puerile." Marx himself wrote, "We abandoned our manuscript to the gnawing criticism of mice with little regret . . . because our main object had been achieved, an understanding with ourselves." Such were the unpromising first fruits of one of the most touching, devoted, and influential friendships in intellectual history.

THE MARVELOUS YEAR

But the year 1844, his first year of leisure in Paris, was for Marx a marvelous year, the most important in his life, for it was the year in which the ideas of socialism in the Paris air and the revolutionary impulses communicated from the City of Light to all Europe made Marx into a "Marxist."

From French "bourgeois historians" who had written the "class history" of the French Revolution while the habit of thinking in terms of
the medieval estates was still fresh, Marx learned that "all history is the
history of class struggles" and its nodal points those moments "when one
ruling class displaces another." Thus to his tendency to reduce individual
man in all his variety and uniqueness to "generic man" in his abstract and
timeless humanity was added yet another abstract construct: "class
man." But strangely enough, this man who made the term "class" into
an unexamined cliché never analyzed nor defined the term. When he
attempted to do so on paper, he left the manuscript—a single sheet of
paper—unfinished.

That year, too, he began a fascinated study of the French Revolution
until his mind was possessed by it as the prototype of events about to
occur in his own land and all Europe. He intensified his critique of the
world as it was until criticism became total rejection. He filled his head
with the critique of society by the great French utopians, accepting much
of their generous, crotchety, utopian vision of the world as it would be,
once their blueprints had been implemented. From Saint-Simon he
learned that "politics is the science of production," and that in utopia
"the political rule over men will be converted into the administration of
things, the direction of the process of production . . . the abolition of the
state . . . and of the present anarchy of production." From Fourier he
learned that "under civilization poverty is born of superabundance itself."

From Babeuf's *Conspiracy of the Equals* he derived the conviction
that "the French Revolution is the precursor of yet another, more magnifi-
cent revolution which will be the last." From Proudhon that "property
is robbery." From Bakunin, a demonic vocabulary: that socialism requires
revolution, "insofar as it has need of *destruction* and *dissolution*." From
Blanqui, perpetual conspirator perpetually in prison, he derived the idea
that revolutions can be made by a secret, conspirative organization which
seizes the symbolic points of power, using them to awaken that sleeping
titan, the proletariat, an idea that later Marx was to reject and Lenin
revive. From Engels, Bakunin, Saint-Simon, and Proudhon together,
Marx derived that incongruous touch of anarchism which made his
authoritarian spirit predict the proximate disappearance of the State, even
while he was laying down a program calculated to extend its powers, its
property and economic possessions, its sphere of action, and its unitary
centralism.

An awareness of the debt of Marx to the French Enlightenment, to
"bourgeois class historians" such as Guizot and Thierry, and to the French
utopians is important to the analysis of Marxian thought and the conflict
that within the year was to begin between French socialism and what
Marx himself called "the German theory." But this indebtedness should

not be taken to deny originality to his powerful mind and unique synthesis. Those writers who have piled up parallel passages in an attempt to reduce his imposing structure of thought, analysis, passion, and prophecy to a rubble heap of plagiarisms are like those who have thought to reduce Shakespeare to a mere plagiarist by matching passages from Holinshead and Plutarch.

Within that same marvelous year Marx's debt to French socialism was to be obscured by an outbreak of bitter quarrels, such as were to be a part of Marxian efforts and Marxian pronouncements thenceforward. There was a break with Proudhon, the excommunication of Weitling, then of Moses Hess for protesting Weitling's expulsion, and the beginning of what was to be a Hundred Years' War between French socialism and "the German theory."

The smell of powder of the coming uprisings of 1848 was already in the air. All his life a compulsive and passionate reader, day and night, often forgetting to sleep, Karl Marx read political and economic theory, social criticism, utopian visions, filling innumerable notebooks with long excerpts, appreciative or ironical comments, and original corollaries (how much more he might have written had Xerox been invented), all the while developing his own views and characteristic synthesis with incredible speed.

"We Germans have *thought* in politics what other *nations* have *done*," he wrote when his studies had run a mere six months. By a peculiar *non sequitur*, Germany would now "elevate its *praxis* to the level of its principles," and in revolutionizing itself would revolutionize Europe. *"The emancipation of the German will be the emancipation of man."* The "material force" is ready at hand to *"realize* German philosophy." "Theory itself can become a material force as soon as it has taken possession of the masses." The "theory" was the one he was even then elaborating, the material force was "the native representative of [German] society . . . the class bold enough to cry out the defiant challenge: *I am nought, I must become all."*

Though the "theory" was even then issuing fully grown out of the Jovian head of Karl Marx and could not possibly have "taken possession" of backward Germany's rudimentary proletariat, Marx wrote:

One must admit that the German proletariat is the *theoretician* of the European proletariat. . . . One must admit that Germany has just as much a *classical* vocation for a *social* revolution, as it has incapacity for a political one. . . . Only in socialism can a philosophical people find its corresponding practice. . . .

As the lawyers say, *What is admitted does not have to be proved.*

Thus, in two articles of 1844, written six months apart, was Marx's claim staked out, thus the time proclaimed at hand when "the weapon of criticism must be replaced by criticism by means of weapons." Out of this matrix was born in three years the best known and most widely read of Marx's works, the *Communist Manifesto*, signed by Marx and Engels—the latter's role being ancillary—and issued in the name of an insignificant league of German handicraftsmen in Paris, as the program the world required for the uprisings about to begin in most of the capitals of Europe in 1848.

TESTED IN THE LABORATORY OF HISTORY

The *Communist Manifesto* came out too late to influence the revolutions of 1848, but these upheavals tested its formulae as in a great social laboratory. The uprisings in Paris, Vienna, Budapest, Prague, and Berlin did not issue into "proletarian revolutions." The bourgeoisie, whose "scarce one hundred years of rule" the *Manifesto* celebrated as having "created more massive and more colossal productive forces than all preceding generations together," did not "prove that its existence was no longer compatible with society."

Moreover, whether that creation of productive forces should be credited to "the bourgeoisie's rule" or to scientists, workingmen, managers, investors, cumulative capital, cumulative technological change, rising living standards, growth of laboring and consuming population, expanding markets—or all of them—the century from 1850 to 1950 was once more to repeat and surpass the feat of the century from 1750 to 1850, creating again "more massive and colossal productive forces than all preceding generations together."

Far from marking the end of nationalism as the *Manifesto* anticipated, 1848 represented an upsurge of nationalism such as Europe had not known before. New nations were to be formed in Germany and Italy, where hitherto there had been mere congeries of local sovereignties plus fragments of foreign empire. National feeling was to prove a successful rival to international socialism, and fuse with socialism and communism into all sorts of startling and explosive mixtures. Then nationalism would spread to parts of Asia, Africa, and the Pacific Archipelago that hitherto had not known the nation. The name of Marx and Marxism were to be invoked in some of those new nations, though they possessed neither the modern industry nor the industrial proletariat that Marx had laid down as absolute preconditions for his anticipated "higher social order."

In Europe in Marx's day, there arose as many varieties of socialism as great nations, and even contending varieties within some of them. The

First International, dominated ideologically by Dr. Marx, who was brought in by the British trade unions to write its by-laws and program, was in the end torn to pieces by the great struggles and intrigues of French Socialism, the German Theory, Slavic and Latin anarcho-communism and anarcho-syndicalism. The English, the only real workingmen's movement in the International, left in disillusion when they heard their leaders attacked by Dr. Marx as "sold to the bourgeoisie and the government" and watched him pack a Congress to expel Bakunin. Moreover, they were winning electoral and labor reforms at home and felt no desire for all-out overthrow of their government. There was indeed no way in which German, French, British, Italian, and Russian ideologues, and English trade unionists and low-church Christian socialists, could be made to think and feel like each other.

The Second International founded in Engels' last years, was shattered on the same rock of nationalism. In the nineties, Engels and Bebel repeatedly declared their readiness to defend Germany rifle in hand, since it possessed "the strongest Social Democratic movement in Europe," against simultaneous attack by Russia and France. In the August days of 1914, French and German workingmen, armed and uniformed, many with Red Cards in their pockets, faced each other as "the enemy" in No Man's Land, though for more than a quarter of a century their leaders had been assuring them that their only enemy was within.

The Third or Communist International, founded by Lenin with what he deemed to be built-in safeguards against the defects of the Second, had the selfsame flaw built into its foundation by Lenin himself. His certitude that his seizure of power and his methods of totalist and centralist dictatorship in party and state were both the prelude and the archetypal model for revolution in all lands made it a Russian international from the outset, and made of his leadership the "General Staff of the World Revolution." He and his successors gradually turned the Communist Parties into instruments of Russian diplomacy and power politics. The Second World War gave Stalin his opportunity for the "liberation" of neighboring lands as his armies carried with them his designated rulers of states to each conquered country, but an interregnum after Stalin's death and devaluation revealed the persistence in those satellites of their own sense of history and tradition, their own national interests and national rivalries. With the Sino-Soviet rivalry, and the partly deceptive, partly necessary growth of autocephalic tendencies in Eastern Europe, it is obvious that, though international communism with its pattern of one-party dictatorships and totalitarian states is not dead, the Communist International is.

FROM REVOLUTIONARY VOLUNTARISM
TO SCIENTIFIC INEVITABILITY

When the storms of 1848 had died away, Marx and Engels found themselves stranded on England's quiet shore. With astonishment they contemplated the upsurge of prosperity and expansion in the Victorian Age and, with no less wonder and even admiration, the westward movement, the rise of industry and commercial agriculture, and the gold rush in the United States.

After some ineffectual attempts to bring back the storm by imitating the voice of thunder, in September, 1850, Marx broke with the Communist League and with the expectations of imminent revolution as outlined in the *Communist Manifesto*. Characteristically, the break took the form of a denunciation of those remaining faithful to his doctrine of yesterday. He charged them with:

replacing critical observation with dogmatism . . . regarding their own naked will as the driving force of revolution instead of the real facts of the situation . . . crudely flattering the German proletariat instead of calling the attention of the German workingmen to thair undeveloped character . . . and making *the proletariat* into a holy being.

With that the Marx of revolutionary voluntarism yielded to the Marx of scientific inevitability; the agitator gave way to the investigator. But still he remained a prophet. This vocation Marx would not relinquish.

Engels went back from German barricades to the textile factory in Manchester, and Marx buried himself—until the day of his death—in the British Museum in London. From criticism by weapons he was returning to the weapon of criticism. The name of the weapon was *Critique of Political Economy*. In 1858 he completed but did not publish *Grundrisse der Kritik der politischen Oekonomie* (it appeared for the first time in the present century). In 1859 he published *Zur Kritik der politischen Oekonomie* (Contribution to a Critique of Political Economy). In 1867 he published *Das Kapital, Kritik der politischen Oekonomie, Erster Band* (Volume I). His outline shows that this was volume one of an intended three-part study of capital, to be followed in turn by further volumes on landed property, wage labor, the state, international trade, and the world market, six studies in all, each to consist of one or more separate books.

Though Marx had many segments fully written, and many others in outline or in notebooks, and though he continued to labor endlessly on his mole's work of tunneling through the books, manuscripts, and reports in the British Museum, writing and rewriting endlessly as well, this great "torso," as Marxologists such as Rubel and Sternberg have reverently called it, was all he published to the day of his death.

Its avowed aim is in its subtitle. It was a critique both of prevailing economic theory and of existing society. Determined not to be thought a "utopian," Marx ceased writing about socialism. But a critique of capitalism is not a blueprint for a future society, as Lenin was to discover with dismay after he took power. More than once we find in his works such plaints as the following:

It did not even occur to Marx to write a word on this subject; he died without leaving a single precise quotation or irrefutable instruction on this. That is why we must get out of the difficulty entirely by our own efforts.

When Lenin did try to follow some utopian recipe or polemical obiter dictum of the earlier Marx, it invariably led to deep trouble so that he had to retreat from utopia lest his power perish. Hence, as the economist Abba Lerner has written, "Marxists must be described as people who concentrate on destroying what we have without considering what we will get in its place."

Yet this "science of capitalism" really does have socialism as its central concern. In it Marx was seeking "scientific" solace for the shipwreck of his dreams of the 1840's. His aim was to prove scientifically that the society he had hoped to overturn on the barricades contained the seeds of its own destruction, and that it must "inevitably" come to a cataclysmic end. The work would lay bare "the law of motion of capitalist society," to prove that the fastest changing economic order in human history was not destined merely to change and transform itself, as it obviously has done beyond the possibility of Marx's recognition, but was fated to grind to a fearful breakdown, and "burst asunder."

As a result of the battle between the conscience of a would-be scientist and the vision of a prophet, *Das Kapital* is possessed by a contradiction between its empirical investigation and its foreknown conclusion. Along with turgid and dull stretches, it contains many brilliant pages, great treasures of empirical material, critical appraisals and adaptations of all that had been said in economic theory up to Marx's day, suggestive historical sketches, sociological observations, passages of striking irony, wrath, poetry, and prophecy.

In 1850 Marx had told the Paris workingmen that it was "a senseless utopia" to expect even "the slightest improvement in its position *within* the bourgeois republic." But substantial sections of *Das Kapital* derive from the reports on industry and recommendations for legislation of the *Parliamentary Bluebooks*, thereby testifying to the awakening conscience of British society and showing that the dark picture Marx was painting was of an age that was ending or had ended as he was beginning his work.

He writes a paean of praise of the Ten-Hours Bill and other labor legislation:

Capital is under compulsion from society. . . . The factory magnates have resigned themselves to the inevitable . . . the victory of a principle in which the political economy of the bourgeoisie has capitulated to the political economy of the working class. . . . Most of the continental countries are accepting the English factory laws . . . in England itself their influence is widened by parliament from year to year.

The picture seems clear enough, even comforting. The empirical material has obtruded into Marx's consciousness an awareness of "the system's" capacity and will to reform and transform itself. But suddenly in the book's closing sections we run up against what is supposed to be the general conclusion of all this empirical and theoretical investigation, the *terminus ad quem* toward which the whole of industrial development has been tending, the "absolute general law of capitalist accumulation."

Capital, we learn in the language now of a Hebrew prophet, came into the world conceived in original sin, "a congenital bloodstain on its cheek, dripping blood and dirt from head to foot, from every pore." By the inexorable workings of "the immanent law of capitalist production itself," it is destined to leave the world as bloodily as it entered, in an inevitable apocalypse:

Along with the constantly diminishing number of magnates of capital . . . grows the misery, oppression, slavery, degradation, exploitation. With this grows too the revolt of the working class. . . . The monopoly of capitalism becomes a fetter upon the mode of production. Centralization of the means of production and socialization of labor at last reach a point where they become incompatible with their capitalist integument. This integument is burst asunder. The knell of capitalist private property sounds. The expropriators are expropriated.

What of those who will expropriate the expropriators or, in Lenin's slogan, "rob what has been robbed"? How will history prepare the new redeemers of society for their work of salvation?

In proportion as capital accumulates, the lot of the laborer must grow worse. The law [the general law of capitalist accumulation] establishes an accumulation of misery corresponding to the accumulation of capital. Accumulation of wealth at one pole is at the same time accumulation of misery, the agony of toil, slavery, brutality, ignorance, moral degradation, at the other.

This picture may excite our pity or indignation, but it is hardly conducive to inspire our confidence that we can trust the work of building a better world to those who are destined to be reduced to ever greater "brutality, ignorance, and moral degradation."

At the outset of Marx's career he had written: "It is not a matter of what this or that proletarian, or even the entire proletariat, *imagines* at one time or another to be its goal. It is a matter of *what it is*, and what in accordance with this *being* it will historically be forced to do."

But in Marx's day, and in the century that has elapsed since *Das Kapital* reaffirmed the mission of the proletariat, the workingman has simply refused to accept the task thus thrust upon him. He has not consented to become increasingly proletarianized or "pauperized." He has displayed stubbornness, tirelessness, courage, skill, incapacity to know when he is licked, ability to enlist political representatives and the sympathy of other "classes" in fighting against this prophetic assignment. Unlike the "alienated" intellectuals who offer the workingmen "Marxist" leadership, they themselves have had no stomach for being reduced to nought in order to prepare themselves to become all. It is precisely against this that their "class struggle" has been directed. They have fought to become something in the world in which they have their existential being, not everything in a world that exists—blurred at that—only in the fantasy of the utopians, of which Marx was perhaps the greatest. Marx's words were incorporated into the socialist anthem, "The International": "We have been nought, we shall be all." But once they have become something, the scheme loses its tidy outlines.

In the face of the evidence he himself has adduced in his "general law," Marx asserts that the proletariat cannot improve its lot without revolution:

The greater the social wealth . . . the growth of capital . . . the size of the proletariat, and the greater the productivity of its labor, the greater will be the industrial reserve army [i.e., the unemployed] . . . and the greater the official pauperism. *This is the absolute general law of capitalist accumulation.*

Near the turn of the century, Eduard Bernstein, literary executor of Engels, became uncomfortably aware that it was impossible to continue to assert Marx's "law of increasing misery." His attempts to re-examine reality were repulsed as "revisionism" by Kautsky, Plekhanov, Parvus, Luxemburg, Lenin, Boudin, and a host of other Marxist stalwarts. But fifty or sixty years later even devoted "orthodox Marxists" like Fritz Sternberg found it necessary to say: "One hundred years after *Das Kapital* we must acknowledge: It is the general tendency of capitalist production to raise the average real wage not lower it." Nikita Khrushchev, visiting

America in the sixties, declared in Iowa (not for home consumption): "I have seen the slaves of capital, and they live well."

Finally, in November, 1965, the ideological spokesman for Austrian Communism, addressing himself in *Weg und Ziel* (The Way and the Goal) to the Communist Parties of Western Europe, wrote: it is necessary to recognize "that the standard of living and real wages are visibly rising."

Curiously, there is evidence in *Das Kapital* itself that Marx may have been aware of the upward trend in real wages in his own day. Though his study of British statistics in health goes up to 1865, in factory inspection to 1866, and in general all statistical data are as late as he can make them, he has not one word to say on the movement of wages after 1850!

In 1873, he revised the statistical series for the second edition . . . except on the movement of wages! A third edition prepared in 1882-83 and published posthumously has the same silence, a silence much louder than words. Fritz Sternberg, in his last work, *Anmerkungen zu Marx-Heute* (Notes on Marx Today), published posthumously in 1965, suggests that Marx left the entire work "a torso" and failed to complete the further planned volumes because he became aware that a taking into account of the new upsurge of productive forces and the rising movement of wages would require "considerable alterations in his basic conception and a substantial reworking of the first volume."

THE PERVERSENESS OF HISTORY

In a sober moment Marx wrote, "No social order ever perishes before all the productive forces for which there is room in it have developed." On examination this proves no more explicit than any other of his sweeping generalizations. Nor any truer, as the Russian and Chinese Revolutions were to demonstrate. With singular perversity, history was to vouchsafe violent revolutions in lands on the eve of or just beginning industrialization and deny them in the advanced industrial societies whose law of motion Marx believed he had uncovered.

The industrial society Marx studied was scarcely at the beginning of its development. The industrial revolution he knew was a change from man, animal, wind, and water power to steam, and from cottage handicraft to machino-facture. Since then there have been many such "revolutions": from steam to electricity to electronics to atomic energy, the belt conveyor, the combustion engine, automation, lasers, and the end is not yet. Nor is there any evidence that an open society—or even a closed society—has to be blown up to accommodate them.

The polarization Marx foresaw has not occurred. The intermediate classes that were to be proletarianized and disappear have greatly changed in character and greatly multiplied. The industrial working class has gained in power through its unions but lost in numbers relative to the total population. The service trades which Marx treated with aristocratic contempt as a slave class, "parasitic servitors to parasites," have increased steadily in number and variety, outnumbering the industrial proletariat in prosperous societies, where the relative weight of these last is shrinking, and have become servitors to the working population as well.

The problem of whether we should sympathize with the "class most numerous and poor" and help it improve its lot has gotten completely separated from the problem of whether we should entrust to it our fate and expect the "brutalized, dehumanized, and degraded" to acquire through their dehumanization the ability to redeem the world. To the first question history has answered, yes; to the second, no.

Nor has the state proved amenable to Marx's prophecies. Instead of shrinking into a ruthless "executive committee" of a dwindling class, it has become democratized, its activities made subject to the labor vote, the farm vote, and the classless impulses and prejudices, fears and hopes of the "man on the street." When it comes to picking streets, every politician knows that Main Street has more votes than Wall.

THE CRISIS IN MARXIAN ECONOMICS

When the classical economists who were Marx's masters wrote their works, the early mercantilist regulation of industry by government was on its way out, and the age of political non-intervention or *laissez faire* seemed about to triumph. To Adam Smith and Ricardo, as to their disciple Marx, it seemed legitimate to abstract from the political factors and construct a theoretical model of the economy in which there was a "free play" of economic forces, "undisturbed" by political interference.

Marx went his teachers one better. Because of his dogma of the primacy of economics over politics (actually that is all he ever meant by his famous "materialism"), Marx not only abstracted from political forces in his model of the economy, but held them to be nugatory. "Legislation," he wrote, "civil law as well as political law, does no more than enunciate or verbalize the will of economic relations." From this it was but a tiny step to "scientific inevitability" and "automatic laws of capitalist development."

Yet precisely when Marx was writing his *Capital* and Engels publishing its rough-hewn sequels, a striking series of politico-economic novelties were being initiated that represented new and sweeping forms of intervention of the state into economic life. In the course of the century since Marx's *magnum opus* was published, state regulation has come to include (along with the factory acts Marx noted): protective tariffs; quotas on imports and exports and on the production of certain goods and crops; government marketing and withholding from the market; government ownership and government regulation of common carriers, means of communication, public utilities; mixed ownership of oil and power; government regulation, subsidy, takeover, or direct initiation of all sorts of enterprises of potential military importance, of national prestige importance, or of concern to industry as a whole; vast construction programs of roads, harbors, fleets, both merchant and air, hydroelectric developments, bridges, dams, railways, canals; government central banking and bank regulations, fixing of interest and discount rates, deposit insurance, stock exchange regulation; cost-plus contracts; costly innovations like atomic energy and satellite communication systems; insurance of profits in certain industries either in trouble or deemed useful and essential, or involving great numbers of the population and of the voters; price floors and price ceilings; state-fostered cartels and state-enforced competition; currency manipulation, regulation of inflow, outflow, or "flight" of capital; fixing of exchange rates; deficit spending conceived not as a temporary misfortune but as a deliberate policy; tax policy as a regulator of the business cycle; the over-all organization, mobilization, and planning of the entire economy in time of total war, including men, money, and materials; supranational economic structures such as the Common Market and Comecon; world-governmental banks and technical and financial aid-systems; and—in vast areas of the world—autarchy. Particularly the great states that invoke the name of Marx as guide are the ones that have declared war on their own peoples to remake them according to their blueprints; they try to regulate every aspect of life down to art, music, thoughts, and dreams, and the forms of the use of leisure, and to keep their people in a state of total psychological mobilization for the perpetual war to win the world, and for the expected invasion that is a paranoid projection of hostile intent.

Whether all these novelties are to be welcomed or feared, geared to the more or less of a mixed economy or made total, exalted as blessings to be served, promoted, and revered, or regarded as perils to the openness of society and the autonomy of the individual spirit, the fact remains that the *laissez faire* state and the "free market" economy have vanished insofar as they ever existed, or have been continued in a new mixed economy many aspects of which are politically regulated, planned, and determined.

Taken together, all these features have produced a world which makes the projections of Marx, as those of his classical predecessors and his contemporary opponents, irrelevant to the world of the twentieth century. The central problem of this new age which makes the very terms capitalism and socialism obsolete would seem to be whether the state should remain an instrument of society, or whether society should become but an instrument of the state, and all non-state organizations, parties, unions, churches, associations of artists, writers and the like become state instruments as well. The autonomous economic constructs of the first half of the nineteenth century from which Marx's picture of the "law of motion" derives are as useless for understanding contemporary society as Watt's steam engine for running a jet plane or a space capsule.

Unkindest cut of all, the state that was to wither away, having set out to wither by taking over everything, "planning" everything, and running everybody in every activity of life, now finds its total, centralized "planning" in profound crisis. In the Western world, despite the growth of state intervention, the market continues to perform many of the functions of determining the optimal allocation of scarce resources. But in the totally centralized, totally statized, command economy of Russia, where the "anarchy of the free market" was duly abolished as Marx bade, the central problem has become the mathematical determination of the marginal or differential yield in alternative uses and allocations of scarce resources—capital, skills, management, labor, materials—among competing ends. Every rational directive of the total planners is hampered by stringent political priorities and involves a theory and a mathematical computation in units that cannot be derived from Marx's labor theory of value, but only from the officially despised linear programs, input-output, allocative mathematical economic theory now prevailing in the West.

Planner Glushkov has warned his political bosses that with present methods the planning bureaucracy will grow thirty-six-fold between 1960 and 1980 and require the services of the entire adult population for its paperwork. *Ekonomicheskaia Gazeta* on November 10, 1962, noted that the project for the Novo-Lipetsk steel mill alone comprised ninety-one volumes totalling 70,000 pages and undertook to "blueprint the emplacement of each nail, lamp, washstand . . . everything except for one thing—its economic effectiveness."

Unless some of the proposals for "reform" of Professor Birman, Professor Liberman, mathematician Volkonskii, mathematical economist Kantorovich, and others are adopted, and even if they are, the *Economic Gazette* is filled with gloomy forebodings concerning the dangers involved in the "transition from charismatics to mathematics in Soviet economic planning."

The political bosses who determine priorities and have the last word on decisions are proving recalcitrant. In any case, the new theories, the technical experts, and the political bosses—not to mention the plant managers who must doggedly violate one directive to make a semblance of complying with another—are all making mincemeat of Marxian economic theory. After one hundred years, in place of a stimulus, poor Marx and his doctrine have become a fetter on the further growth of the productive forces in the land that invokes his name.

PART II

War as the Womb
of Revolution

Give us ten more years and we are safe.
——S. I. Shidlovsky [1]

We need peace: a war during the coming year, and especially in the name of a cause the people would not understand, would be fatal for Russia and for the dynasty.
—Stolypin to Izvolsky in 1911 [2]

. . . A general European war is mortally dangerous both for Russia and Germany, no matter who wins . . . There must inevitably break out in the defeated country a social revolution, which will spread to the victor.
—P. N. Durnovo to the Tsar after the Balkan alarms of 1913 [3]

Let Papa not plan war, for with war will come the end of Russia and of yourselves.
—Telegram of Rasputin to Vyrubova on learning of the mobilization [4]

1. S. I. Shidlovsky was a well-to-do liberal landowner, a Zemstvo leader, an ardent advocate of peasant reform, Chairman of the Land Commission of the Third Duma. Later he became Chairman of the Progressive Bloc. It was his theory, as it was Stolypin's and Lenin's, that the Stolypin land reform if carried out over a decade or two would solve Russia's agrarian problem and modernize and liberalize Russia. Lenin wrote that its success would make a "bourgeois revolution" impossible, "not only the present revolution but any possible democratic revolution in the future." *Lenin,* Vol. XIII, p. 419; Vol. XV, p. 30. See also, *Three Who Made a Revolution,* Chapter XXI, "Lenin and Stolypin," and Bernard Pares, *The Fall of the Russian Monarchy,* pp. 113-14 and 238.

2. Premier Stolypin wrote this to A. P. Izvolsky, Russian Ambassador in Paris, on July 28, 1911. Thoroughly at home in domestic matters, Stolypin was lost in foreign affairs and fearful lest Russia's alliance with France might get her into a war before agrarian reform, democratic parliamentarism, and an enlightened and patriotic public opinion had had time to develop. Izvolsky as Foreign Minister had favored the Franco-Russian Treaty. To win Stolypin's confidence, he had appointed Sazonov, Stolypin's brother-in-law, Deputy Minister. Then he resigned in Sazonov's favor in order to get the ambassadorship to Paris, where he could further cement the alliance. He was Ambassador to Paris from 1910 to 1917, and one of the leaders of the pro-French wing of the Russian bureaucracy. Other interesting sentences in Stolypin's letter read: "Every year of peace fortifies Russia not only from the military and naval point of view, but also from the economic and financial. *Besides, and this is the most important, Russia is growing from year to year; self-knowledge and public opinion are developing in our land. One must not scoff at our parliamentary institutions.*" The letter is in Kerensky, *The Crucifixion of Liberty,* New York, 1934, p. 188 n., who was permitted by Izvolsky's daughter to copy it. I do not know whether the italics were in the original or have been added by Kerensky.

3. P. N. Durnovo was Director of Police, then Minister of the Interior (under Witte). His secret report to the Tsar, dated February 1914, was inspired by the near outbreak of war between Russia and Austria-Hungary during the Balkan crisis of 1912 and 1913. If Marxism, as Stalin has written, really gives "the power to find the right orientation in any situation, to understand the inner connections of current events, and to perceive not only how and in what direction they are developing, but how and in what direction they are bound to develop in the future," then there was no better "Marxist" than this ex-Police Director and Minister of the Interior. The entire report is fascinating in the clarity of its analysis and pre-vision. It is in *Krasnaya Nov,* VI, Nov.-Dec., 1922; in English in Golder, *Documents of Russian History, 1914-1917,* New York, 1927, pp. 3-23.

4. Rasputin, wounded by Guseva, one of the victims of his lust, was recovering in a hospital when the war began. Anna Vyrubova was a lady-in-waiting to the Tsarina. The telegram is in Vyrubova's *Memoirs,* p. 49. A slightly different text is given by Lili Dehn's *The Real Tsaritsa.* She makes it read: "The war must be stopped—war must not be declared; it will be the end of all things." (p. 106.) Vyrubova's version seems closer to the style of Rasputin.

I WAR COMES TO RUSSIA *

Saint Petersburg, stormy capital which a decade earlier had looked on processions shouting, "Down with the Tsar," once more beheld workingmen marching from the workers' quarters to the Winter Palace. Ilyin-Genevsky, revolutionary student home from Switzerland, saw men in blue overalls marching with banners and roaring out a song. His heart filled with immense joy: "It must be the Revolution!" Disillusion was not long in coming, for now he could see portraits of the Tsar and hear the words of the song. The voices were chanting "Reign to confound our enemies."

Even that unflinchingly internationalist and prosaic Theodor Dan writes in more animated style than usual:

> The streets which but yesterday were filled with roving masses of strikers, today were dominated by "patriots." One demonstration followed the other to the Winter Palace and sank on its knees before the Tsar standing on the balcony. . . . Nor did the bacchanal leave the working class untouched: not a few of those who the day before had been on strike, today marched in the ranks of the patriotic demonstrators. Even in the ranks of Social Democracy itself, confusion reigned.

In the Winter Palace, the President of the Duma was telling the French Ambassador, "The Russian people has not experienced such a wave of patriotic emotion since 1812." Bernard Pares, looking out of the palace windows, saw "a vast multitude fall on their knees and sing 'God Save the Tsar' as it had never been sung before." Repeating word for word the oath which Alexander had taken before him in 1812, and which Stalin would take after him in 1941, Nicholas II swore to the populace that he would never cease from struggle until the last invader had been driven from Russia's holy soil. The British Ambassador wrote in his

* Written as a chapter for a work in progress and published separately in the *Russian Review*, April 1963.

memoirs: "Those wonderful early August days! Russia seemed to have been completely transformed." [5]

In the provincial capitals, too, strife was stilled. But foreign policy being more remote, the first reaction was bewilderment. General Mikhail Dmitrievich Bonch-Bruevich,[6] remembering in his old age how war came to his regiment in Chernigov in the Ukraine in 1914, will serve as a paradigm for all provincial notables who have written memoirs of those days:

Summer was at its peak. Tables somehow knocked together at the town fair were bursting under the weight of rosy apples, silver pears, flaming tomatoes, lilac-colored sweet onions, five-inch thick pieces of salt pork that would melt in your mouth, fat-dripping, home-made sausages, all the things in which the flourishing Ukraine is so rich. A cloudless, blinding blue sky hung over the dreaming town. Nothing, it seemed, could disturb the measured flow of peaceful provincial life. . . . The regimental ladies vied with each other in cooking up jams and jellies, putting up delicious salted cucumbers in casks; the gentlemen officers after unhurried accomplishment of their duties went to a meeting where on starched white cloths awaited sweating bottles of chilled vodka; the regiment was in camp, but the blinding whiteness of the placards, the shaped flowerbeds neatly trimmed by the soldiers, the carefully sanded paths, strengthened the feeling of undisturbedly peaceful life that dominated us all. Suddenly, at five in the afternoon on the 29th of July, the adjutant brought me a secret dispatch from Kiev . . . for the immediate putting of all units of the garrison on a *premobilization footing.* . . . Three days later came an order for general mobilization. . . . But *with whom* were we to fight? No one knew. Only on the 2nd of August did it become known that Germany had declared war on Russia. And only somewhat later did there at last arrive to Chernigov the news that along with Germany, Austria-Hungary had also declared war on Russia, and we were told that the XXIst Army corps . . . was to proceed into action against the Austro-Hungarian Army.[7]

To the villages war came in still more unintelligible guise. Here was no press, no oratory, no talk of world affairs, no knowledge of what

5. A. F. Ilyin-Genevsky, *Between Two Revolutions,* Moscow, 1931; Theodor Dan, *Die Sozialdemokratie Russlands nach dem Jahre 1908,* Berlin, 1926, p. 273; Maurice Paléologue, *An Ambassador's Memoirs,* New York, 1925, p. 56; Sir George Buchanan, *My Mission to Russia,* cited in Trotsky, *My Life,* p. 233; Sir Bernard Pares, *The Fall of the Russian Monarchy,* New York, 1939, p. 187; M. V. Rodzyanko, "Gosudarstvennaia Duma i Fevralskaia Revolutsia," in *Arkhiv Russkoi Revoliutsii,* Vol. VI, Berlin, 1922, pp. 16-17. Rodzyanko reports that "agrarian, and indeed all manner of disturbances in the villages, suddenly ceased."

6. Brother of the well-known Bolshevik, Vladimir Bonch-Bruevich. Tsarist justice did not persecute innocent members of a family for the political or common crimes of the guilty member. His brother's activities were no obstacle to his advancement in the Tsar's service, but of great help to him under the Bolsheviks. He served the latter just as faithfully as he did the Tsar but the passage quoted here suggests a deep nostalgia for the "good old days."

7. Memoirs of General M. D. Bonch-Bruevich, *Vsia Vlast Sovetam,* Moscow, 1957, pp. 11-13.

Austria-Hungary or Germany might be, nor of any world more distant than the nearest market town and the Tsar in the Kremlin far away. What was Serbia or Belgium to the Russian village? War came to him as a command from afar off, incontestable and incomprehensible, breaking the seasonal round of his days, summoning him to give up horses and carts, sons, himself, for unexplained service in unknown regions of the world against an unknown foe.

> *The capitals are rocked with thunder*
> *Of orators in wordy feuds.*
> *But in the depths of Russia, yonder,*
> *Ever the age-old silence broods . . .*

sang the poet Nekrasov. "At 100 versts from the big cities," Count Kokovtsev told a foreign correspondent, "all politics is stilled." Miliukov, seeking to sum up in his Memoirs the reaction of the peasants to the war, found it in the formula, "*My—kalutskie*, [We are men of Kaluga] that is, to our Kaluga Wilhelm will not get." He felt that the "*age-old silence* hid within itself its unspent forces and waited—for its 'Pugachev from the Russian university.'" [8]

Fyodor Stepun [9] was in the tiny hamlet of Ivanovka, two versts from the village of Znamenka, both remote from the world though they were in Moscow Province. One day the mail brought him a summons to appear in Znamenka "with his riding horse." How could he comprehend that this was the beginning of war?

He found Znamenka bursting with unwonted activity. In the village square in front of the Tavern sat "a commission"; a military officer, a clerk, a veterinarian, and, as equine experts, the two local horse dealers. The square was strewn with hay, overflowing with carts and horses, more carts coming from all directions, horses in front, horses on each side, horses tied to the rear, all trying to crowd into somnolent Znamenka. The commission was possessed by "bureaucratic exaltation." Without a word of explanation it was fixing prices, handing out receipts, requisitioning horses. Nobody spoke of Germany or Austria-Hungary or the defense of Russia, or of war.

The requisitioning turned the peaceful village into "a boiling kettle of human passion, gloom, and anger." Above the commands, quarreling and shouting, rose "strong Russian curses." Few had faith in the fairness of the commission. They looked with contempt at "his Excellency," with mockery and distrust at the local experts, the veterinarian, the two horse

---

8. The Miliukov statement, and that of Kokovtsev, are both from P. N. Miliukov, *Vospominaniia*, New York, 1955, Vol. II, pp. 183-84; cf. Kokovtsev, *Out of My Past*, Stanford, 1935, p. 388.

9. Sociologist and philosopher of the school of Soloviev.

traders. The poor were firmly convinced that the rich would not give up their horses: they would nail them up, rub tobacco into their eyes, buy their way out. "The Commission will take *yours* away at a fixed, low price, then that gypsy, Malanichev [the local horse dealer was a "gypsy," i.e. a horse-stealer], will bring you a new skinny nag at his own price, which he will take away again. You will feed him all summer with your own good oats, and in the Autumn he will see to it that he is paid again for a well-fed one." [10] Obviously, more widespread literacy and a government press and radio system—such as Stalin was able to count on in 1941 —would have been of enormous advantage to an old-fashioned despotism about to engage in mass mobilization.

To Siberia, Kaiser Wilhelm and the lands of Europe were even more remote. Wladimir Woytinsky, out on the Siberian *taiga*, did not know the war was on until a month or so after it had begun, when he got to Yakutsk: Here is his account:

A steamer arrived [at Nelkan on the Maya River] from the Lena, the last of the season. . . . The captain invited us to share his meals. . . . One day, he casually mentioned at the table that he had heard in Yakutsk that recruits were being conscripted, though he did not know why. . . . We did not learn about the beginning of war until we reached Yakutsk. Even now, after decades of research, historians have found it difficult to retrace the chain of events leading to the conflagration, but to people in the Siberian wilderness the events had a nightmarish quality. . . . In the middle of August, as our steamer passed villages along the way . . . landing places were crowded with men who had been called up. There was a spirit of sullen resignation among them and in the watching crowd. . . . The sudden shift from the solitude of the taiga to the turmoil of political events, rumors and passions was overwhelming.[11]

In this gulf between the garrulousness and enthusiasm of the capitals, the remote quiet of the provinces, and the age-old stillness of the village, between the literate "public" and the politically and alphabetically il-literate peasant mass, lay possibilities of misunderstanding, alienation, dis-cord—a breach through which any "Pugachev from the University," or any rumor-monger, might enter. The peasant was loyal enough to *his* Russia, obedient, enduring, strong and courageous to serve as a stubborn wall of flesh against the invader. Still, as long as *this Welhelm* did not get to Kaluga . . . or Yakutsk, the *Kalutskie* or *Yakutskie* would not know why they were fighting.

Thus the war began auspiciously for Russia. Deeply moved by the

10. Fedor Stepun, *Byvshee i Nesbyvsheesia*, New York, 1956, Vol. I, pp. 334-35.
11. W. S. Woytinsky, *Stormy Passage*, New York, 1961, p. 223.

ordeal that had come upon his land, Nicholas summoned the Duma, which had so often given him trouble, for a one-day session to vote the war budget, and to dramatize the unity of the "public" with the Tsar. In his Manifesto of August 2, Nicholas sounded this note of conciliation:

At this hour of threatening danger, let domestic strife be forgotten. Let the union between the Tsar and His people be stronger than ever, and let Russia, rising like one man, repel the insolent assault of the enemy.

Rodzianko answering on behalf of the Duma, told Russia's enemies:

You thought we were divided by strife and hatred, and yet all the nationalities dwelling in boundless Russia were welded into a single family when danger threatened our common fatherland.

Miliukov, for the Constitutional Democrats (Kadets), was equally reassuring:

In this struggle we are all as one; we present no conditions or demands; we simply throw into the scales of battle our firm determination to overcome the violator. . . . Whatever our attitude toward the internal policies of the Government may be, our first duty remains to preserve our country one and inseparable and to maintain for it that position in the ranks of world powers which is being contested by our foes.

The spokesmen of the various nationalities, Lithuanians, Jews, Moslems, Baltic Germans and Volga German colonists,[12] all spoke in defense of the common Fatherland. Deputy Friedman, speaking for his Jewish constituents, was typical:

We, the Jews, have lived and continue to live under exceptionally harsh legal conditions. Nevertheless, we have always felt ourselves to be citizens of Russia. . . . In this hour of trial we Russian Jews will stand as one man under the banners of Russia. . . . The Jewish people will do their duty to the last.

Yet faintly a note was sounded which was a harbinger of storms to come. Miliukov expressed the hope that "in passing through the sore trials which confront us, the country may come nearer to its cherished aim [of freedom]." Kerensky, who spoke for the Trudoviki (Labor Group, a legal, moderate offshoot of the Social Revolutionary Party) and who

---

12. It is worthy of note that Nicholas did not find it necessary to imprison or deport the Baltic or Volga Germans as Stalin did in World War II. It took the brutalities of dictatorship, Cheka, forced collectivization, and purges to shake their loyalty.

had spoken against the last military budget as pregnant with possible war, sounded a somewhat stronger note of discord:

> We are unshakably convinced that the great, irresistible power of the Russian democracy . . . will defend the native land and culture created in the sweat and blood of generations! We believe that on the fields of battle . . . there will be born a single will to free the country from its internal shackles.

He hailed the efforts of the socialists of France, England, Belgium, and Germany to avert war, protesting that "only we, the Russian democracy, were prevented" from openly joining that effort. "Citizens of Russia," he cried:

> Remember that you have no enemies among the laboring classes of the belligerent countries . . . remember that this frightful war would not have come had the great ideals of democracy, liberty, equality, and fraternity inspired the activity of Russia's rulers and the Governments of all other countries.
> Unfortunately, our Government, even at this dreadful hour, has no desire to forget internal strife. It denies amnesty to those who are fighting for the freedom and the happiness of our country . . . it does not seek reconciliation with the non-Russian nationalities, who have forgiven everything and are . . . fighting enthusiastically for our common fatherland. . . . Instead of ameliorating the condition of the laboring classes . . . it imposes upon these the main weight of war expenditures. . . .
> You peasants and workers . . . gather all your forces, and then, having defended our country, set it free. . . .[13]

The stand taken by the Social Democratic Deputies was not very dissimilar from that of Kerensky and the Trudoviki. Among the Social Democrats, as among the masses who had elected them, there was a yearning for socialist unity. The Bolshevik Duma Deputy, Roman Malinovsky, agent of the police and spokesman for Lenin, on the instructions of both his masters had succeeded in splitting the reluctant Fraction in two. But three months before war broke out, he had suddenly resigned his seat to avoid exposure as a police agent.[14] This left five Bolsheviks, all smallish men accustomed to have Lenin or Kamenev write speeches for them, and seven Mensheviks, of whom the most articulate was Chkheidze. With Lenin far off in Austrian Galicia (Cracow) and his mouthpiece

13. For the Tsar's Manifesto, Rodzyanko's, Miliukov's, Friedman's and Kerensky's declarations, see Golder, *Documents*, pp. 29-37.

14. General Dzhunkovsky, humane and honorable, had just been put in charge of the police. He withdrew the police spies from the army and the schools and, when he discovered that there was a police agent in the Duma, he informed the Duma Chairman of that fact. For his own account of these matters see his testimony in *Padenie Tsarskogo Rezhima*, Moscow, 1926, pp. 68 ff.

Malinovsky gone, instinctively the twelve Social Democratic Deputies moved toward each other again. Since the two fractions felt that they had no differences in their internationalist feelings—after all Martov and Lenin had both supported Rosa Luxemburg in her amendments to the Stuttgart Resolution—Bolsheviks and Mensheviks agreed on a joint declaration on the war.

According to the account written by the Bolshevik Duma Deputy Badaiev, a first draft for this common statement was made by the Petersburg lawyer, N. D. Sokolov, a nonparty attorney who defended clients from both groups and who, over the years, inclined now more to the Mensheviks now more to the Bolsheviks. According to the Menshevik leader, Boris Ivanovich Nicolaevsky, who had been arrested in the prewar raids of the last days of July, 1914, but was still in detention in Petrograd where he could follow the events closely, the declaration was of purely Menshevik origin. It was drawn up by the Menshevik leader, Peter Abramovich Garvy, who was not a Duma Deputy but was one of the ablest socialists in Petrograd at liberty at the moment. After he had drafted it, he went over it with Genrikh (Heinrich) Ehrlich, a leader both of the Bundists and of the Menshevik organization in Russia, and with Cherevanin-Lipkin. When the Declaration was already finished, the Menshevik Deputy Khaustov was approached by the Bolsheviks with a proposal to draft a joint declaration. Khaustov replied: "Our statement is ready; if you would like to see it and make it a common declaration, we will be delighted." The Bolsheviks had no draft of their own. They read Garvy's statement, and subscribed to it. In any case the Declaration is Menshevik—Lenin would have said *Kautskyan*—in thought and tone. At the Duma Session of August 8, the Menshevik Deputy, Khaustov, read it as the stand of "the Social Democratic Fraction of the Duma."

Like Kerensky's statement, the Socialist Declaration began with an attack on the horrors of war; praised the international socialist movement "with the German proletariat at its head" for attempts to prevent it; protested that the Russian government by its last minute closing of journals and prohibition of meetings had stopped the Russian proletariat from joining in the effort to avert war. Like Kerensky, too, the Declaration rejected responsibility for the war, blaming it on "the greed" of the ruling classes of all belligerent countries. Where Kerensky spoke of the readiness of "the Russian democracy . . . to defend the native land and culture created in the sweat and blood of generations," the Socialist declaration read:

The proletariat, constant defender of the freedom and interests of the people, at every moment will fulfill its duty and will defend the cultural treasures of the people from all attacks, from whatever they may come— whether from abroad or from within the country.

In this defense of Russia's "cultural treasures," however, the Socialists repudiated "the hypocritical call for unity" with a government which does not "carry out the conscious will of the people" and under which the people are without rights though they bear the heaviest burdens of war. In its outlook for the war's end, the Socialist Declaration departed somewhat from Kerensky's statement, in the direction of a greater degree of pacifism and internationalism.

We are deeply convinced that in the international solidarity of the proletariat of the entire world, humanity will find the means to the speediest possible ending of the war. And may the peace terms be dictated not by the diplomats of the predatory powers, but by the people themselves taking their fate into their own hands.
. . . We express the deep conviction that this war will finally open the eyes of the popular masses of Europe as to the real source of violence and oppression from which they suffer, and that the present frightful conflagration will be the last such conflagration.[15]

When the vote was taken, the five Bolsheviks, the seven Mensheviks, and Kerensky, and the Trudoviks, neither wishing to vote for nor against the credits, nor publicly record themselves as abstaining, simply walked out of the Chamber together. Their failure to participate in the voting enabled the newspapers to report that the Duma had voted unanimously "to stand up in defense of their country." [16] And in fact both the Trudoviks and the Social Democrats had pledged themselves "to defend the cultural treasures" [Kerensky said "the native land and culture"] from "all attacks from abroad." A year later, the Bolshevik Deputies then being in prison, the Mensheviks repeated their walkout. This time the Trudoviks

15. For the Bolshevik version of the drafting on the joint Declaration, see Badaiev, *The Bolsheviks in the Tsarist Duma*, New York, n. d., pp. 199-200. Written in 1929 when it was regarded as shameful to have agreed with the Mensheviks on the war, Badaiev's account contains a number of evasions. Thus on page 199 he acknowledges that there was a joint declaration but on page 200 he has resort to the passive voice ("was read") to avoid stating that the Menshevik Deputy, Khaustov, read the Declaration, and he has the Bolsheviks march out of the Chamber alone, with no mention of the Mensheviks and Trudoviks who marched out with them. A Menshevik account of the matter is in Dan, *op. cit.*, p. 282. Boris Nicolaevsky gave me the information concerning the role of Garvy, Ehrlich and Cherevanin in the preparation of the document and showed me unpublished materials confirming his version. The text of the Declaration is in Kalinychev, *Gosudarstvennaia Duma v Rossii v Dokumentakh i Materialakh*, Moscow, 1957, pp. 595-96. The fact that it was a common declaration of Bolsheviks and Mensheviks is concealed here, as it has been in all party histories from Zinoviev's in 1923 to Stalin's "Short Course." The new *Istoriia Kommunisticheskoi partii Sovetskogo Soiuza* (Moscow, 1959) suggests that the Mensheviks made a show of not being for the war as a "maneuver caused by the fear of losing all influence whatsoever in the working class," but it says nothing about the joint Declaration of Bolsheviks and Mensheviks.

16. In Germany, too, one Reichstag Deputy, Kühnert, walked out to avoid voting. Since it was only a single Deputy, his absence was not even noticed until he himself reported it a few months later.

were not with them, and one of the Menshevik Deputies, Mankov, decided to remain and vote for the credits. He was promptly expelled from
the Menshevik Fraction.

All that Lenin detested most was in that manifesto to which his
followers had subscribed. As soon as he got out of his Austrian prison
and was safely in neutral Switzerland, he would excoriate the Declaration
without referring to his party's share in making it. Every idea in it was
"Kautskyanism, the most dangerous position of all and that most calculated to deceive the masses." In it were all the main targets of his
wrath: (1) the "priestly humanitarianism" which dwelt on the horrors
of war in disregard of the fact that the Socialists themselves needed war
for their own aims; (2) the "priestly pacifism" which speculated on the
hope of an early peace, instead of foreseeing a prolonged war that could
only be ended by its proper continuation, i.e., its transformation into a
universal civil war; (3) the "treacherous and deceitful" idea that this
war might be "the last conflagration," without any reference to the fact
that more wars were certain as long as capitalism endured; (4) a "shameful" expression of a hope for "international solidarity," without any mention of the necessity of smashing the Second International and building a
Third; (5) social-chauvinism, i.e., defensism covered with socialist phrases,
in the pledge to defend Russia's cultural heritage from the inner and outer
foe; (6) the propagation of the dangerous illusion that the peoples might
dictate a just peace by their pressure without a prior world revolution. In
short, the Declaration his followers had endorsed was pure Menshevism,
pure Kautskyism, and Kautsky, as Lenin was to write to the first follower
to whom he could send a letter after the war broke out, "is now *the most
harmful of them all.*"

But here it was, and Lenin had to make the best of it until he should
be able to whip his followers into line, or, as he had so often done before,
get rid of those whom he could not convince and make a fresh selection.
In the meanwhile, part of his stock in trade was to claim that all parties
everywhere had committed treason to international socialism and the
Stuttgart Resolution *except* the Russian Bolsheviks in the Duma.

At this juncture came a lucky break. As often before, the police solved
one of Lenin's internal problems for him. He sent the Bolshevik Duma
Deputies a copy of his own views on the war with a demand that they
adopt his views as theirs. The core of his document was a call for the defeat of Russia "as the lesser evil" (Thesis 6) and a call for the "transformation of the imperialist war to civil war" (Thesis 7). The Deputies were
shocked, as was Kamenev, Lenin's Central Committee representative in
Russia. To them it seemed obvious that Lenin had no idea what it was
like to live in a country at war and feel the pulse of its people. Dutifully,
however, they called a conference of their five Duma Deputies and five

representatives from the local organizations, plus Kamenev for the Central Committee, to consider Lenin's views. Small though the conference was, at least two police agents in the party were privy to it. As if to make matters easier for the police, Deputy Muranov, in charge of the secret arrangements, was stupid enough to convene it at Ozerki, near Petrograd, in the northern war zone already under martial law. The police raided the meeting on the night of November 16-17 (November 3-4 Old Style), capturing not only all the participants and Lenin's *Theses*, but on the person of the not overly bright Muranov a complete list, uncoded, of the names and addresses of all the local Bolshevik leaders with whom as Duma Deputy he was in touch.

Because it was a zone of martial law, it was easy for the police to override the parliamentary privilege of the Deputies, and avoid a public trial. They were tried on February 10-13, 1915. Kerensky, the noted labor lawyer and future rival of Lenin, took up their defense in court and intervened elsewhere on their behalf, even appealing to Foreign Minister Sazonov. He urged the adverse effect upon Russia's democratic allies of news that Duma Deputies who had made an essentially patriotic declaration should be jailed for possessing a document drafted by Lenin. It was Lenin, he said, who should be tried *in absentia* to make his defeatist views more widely known. At their secret trial, the Deputies expressly repudiated both the defeatist and civil war points in Lenin's *theses*. They pointed out that his document was in contradiction, as indeed it was, to "that declaration which in the name of both Social Democratic Fractions was read out in the Duma on August 8." Kamenev for his part declared that Lenin's views were rejected "both by the Social Democratic Deputies and by the Central Instances," i.e. the Central Committee whose spokesman he was. But the police charged all participants in the Conference with the "dissemination" of Lenin's defeatist views and shipped them all off to Siberia.

Lenin was beside himself with fury at Kamenev. He wrote cautiously on March 29, 1915, that "they did not show sufficient firmness at the trial." But he pretended to believe that they had concealed their true convictions merely to trick the police. It was right to trick the police "but to attempt to show solidarity with the social patriot, Mr. Yordansky,[17] as did Comrade Rosenfeld [Kamenev's real name], or to indicate disagreement with the Central Committee . . . this is impermissible from the standpoint of revolutionary Social Democracy." Yet, in the same article, Lenin praised his Duma Deputies as having given an example of the use of parliamentarism for revolutionary purposes such as was unequaled in the entire history of socialism. In any case, Kamenev and the Bolshevik

---

17. A socialist journalist who testified in court that Kamenev had provided for an article of his the title: "Let There Be Victory."

Duma Deputies were silenced for the duration. Their joint statement with the Mensheviks on the day the Duma voted the war credits could henceforth be ignored while Lenin could distinguish in his propaganda between the Bolshevik Deputies, who had been arrested and sent to Siberia, and the Menshevik Duma Deputies, whom the police left "untouched." For the rest of the war, the great wastes of Siberia would stand between the two fractions in the Duma and their yearning for unity,[18] while the real conduct and convictions of his Duma Deputies and Russian Center could not trouble Lenin's defeatist propaganda.

18. For Lenin's discussion of the conduct of the Duma Deputies see Vol. XXI, pp. 149-54 and pp. 290-93. In the latter account (in his pamphlet, "Socialism and War"), Lenin wrote of the two attitudes toward parliamentary activity, that of the "opportunists" of Germany, France, and Italy and of "Chkheidze and Plekhanov" and the Menshevik fraction, on the one hand, and that of the Bolshevik fraction on the other. "The parliamentary activity of the former leads to ministerial chairs, the parliamentary activity of the latter leads them to prison, to exile, to penal hard labor. The one is socialist-imperialist. The other is revolutionary Marxist." The distinction is something less than candid.

For the discussion of Kerensky's intervention on behalf of the Bolshevik Duma Deputies, see Pares, *The Fall of the Russian Monarchy,* New York, 1939, pp. 333 and 347, and Kerensky, *The Crucifixion of Liberty,* New York, 1934, pp. 250-52. That Kerensky was concerned with the fate of the Bolshevik Duma Deputies is proved by the fact that in 1916 when an upright man, A. A. Khvostov, became Minister of the Interior, he petitioned Khvostov to do justice to the exiled deputies by granting a free pardon. The minister offered to forward Kerensky's appeal with its legal documentation to the Tsar, but as Khvostov lasted only two months, nothing came of it. On this see Khvostov's testimony in *Padenie Tsarskogo Rezhima,* Vol. V, p. 454.

—April 1963

II WAR COMES TO
RUSSIA-IN-EXILE *

It is hard for those who have never been uprooted to understand the misery of the political émigré's estate. "If a tooth could feel after being knocked out," Gorky wrote from lovely Capri, "it would probably feel as lonely as I . . . " In defeat or isolated flight, with no prospect but the continuing night of exile, there is only the dubious sustenance of the closed-in colony of lonely, high-minded, self-righteous, warring handfuls. Lenin's personal letters are full of expressions of distaste for the controversy, recrimination, intrigue, and schism of which he was perhaps the greatest master. "Emigrant life is now a hundred times more difficult than it was before the Revolution of 1905," he wrote to Gorky after his flight from Russia in 1907. His letters to his mother are full of inquiries about the snows, the festive holidays, and the coming of the Spring on his native Volga.

The émigré colony, most numerous in Paris before the War as again after 1917, were, we must remember, the irreconcilables, voluntary and involuntary revolutionary exiles from their native land because of principle. Not for that was the deprivation any less deep: separation from family, friends, country, from immersion in native language, intercourse, feelings, culture, scenes, from all the familiar round of activities that go with belonging to some land's daily life. The very principles which raise the refugee in his own eyes above the ordinary citizen serve also to deprive him of organic relation either to the land of his longing or the land of his refuge, contracting his life to something less than the ordinary citizen's estate.

To a writer who has been forced to flee abroad, every Russian word is sacred, for his roots may wither for lack of feeding from the springs and elements of his native soil. The political émigrés were most of them in some measure intellectuals, too, coming from that intelligentsia which tried to live by ideas alone. Whether declassed intellectuals or declassed workers, their means of making a living in their new home that was not

* A chapter from a work in progress published separately in the *Russian Review*, April 1963.

home were mean and marginal, which made their unsatisfied longing for their native land the more intense. Now war came, catching up everybody around them, giving every man a place for weal or woe in the community of his nation. What were these irreconcilables to do in this hour? They had declared war to the death on tsar and regime. Many had escaped from hard labor, from Siberian outposts or administrative exile in the frozen north. Some had broken out of jail, fled from prison terms, or from death sentences. Among the Anarchists and Socialist Revolutionaries, some had been involved in attempts on the lives of tsarist officials. Yet their war to the death was now submerged in universal war.

"The worker has no country," they had repeated, but nostalgia for their native land took possession of them all the same. They became aware of love of their own people as never before and of solidarity with their nation in its hour of danger, a feeling to which they had believed themselves immune. Those who had been abroad longer had had time to mingle with love for their lost home a love for their second home, France, where they had learned to know freedom as something more than a sacred word.

Yesterday their war had been with each other. They did not intend it that way, for they had a common enemy, the Government in St. Petersburg. But that enemy was out of reach; so they had turned on each other, accusing each other of "objectively" strengthening the enemy by advocating the "wrong" methods of fighting him. So it had been yesterday. But today a wholly new division cut across hitherto warring groups, a new division and a new solidarity that broke up all the old factions, reducing them to a shambles overnight.

"A SMASHED ANT HEAP"

A. A. Argunov, Social Revolutionary leader writes:

The Paris Center of the Socialist Revolutionary Party was turned by the outbreak of war into a smashed ant heap, with the ants running off in all directions biting at each other as they ran.[1]

The biting was between those who wished to defend Russia, or France, and those who held to the old "internationalist" formula. The rift cut across all tendencies and shadings, yet it did not bring solidarity to the "internationalists." These continued their faction wars and tactical controversies as before, adding new ones on the proper tactics toward the

---

1. A. A. Argunov, *Pravoe i levoe*, an unpublished manuscript quoted by Oliver S. Radkey in his *The Agrarian Foes of Bolshevism*, New York, 1958, p. 88.

war. But it brought the "defensists" of all socialist groups into close comradeship.

Lydia Krestovskaia, who has written the best account of the movement of the Russian émigrés to volunteer for the French Army, tells of the torment these dedicated Russians went through as they tried to reconcile lifelong antiwar positions with the moods welling up within them:

... the drama of people who had no land of their own when the land which has given them shelter finds itself in danger . . . How react to the events? What to do? Each felt that silence was a crime, that life demanded an immediate answer.[2]

Many signed up to dig trenches, strengthen the fortifications of Paris with fresh masonry and earth, produce shells in ammunition factories. Women, too, entered into the munition works. "But the basic question remained: *volunteering*." For more than two weeks a debate raged in all party centers, in cafés until closing time, then in lodgings, or, where landlords protested about the noise, in the streets.

People fought furiously with each other, with hatred, and from the first day there arose two hostile currents, cutting short at one stroke relationships that had been created over years . . . Some plunged into an activity of silent thought and reexamination of all the commandments that had been until now the basis of their entire view of life. . . . N. V. Sapozhkov [the top Bolshevik Paris leader] for two whole days and nights lay alone in bed, refusing to get up, to answer questions, to say a word, while he appraised and weighed *pro* and *contra*. Then he arose and said simply to his intimates: "I am going to volunteer!" Neither questions nor appeals could draw from him a word of explanation or of argument.[3]

Sent to the front at once, Sapozhkov fought recklessly and gallantly, volunteering for all dangerous reconnaissance missions. That same autumn, going out on a detail of six and sensing danger ahead, he bade the others stay back while he crawled forward . . . to his death. The prowar socialists did not last as long as the antis as in time death greatly reduced their earlier numerical superiority.

After two furious weeks of debate around the clock, more than nine

2. Lydia Krestovskaia, *Iz istorii russkogo volunterskogo dvizheniia vo Frantsii*, Paris, N. D., p. 10. This 145-page pamphlet is a compendium of documents, excerpts from the author's diary, bearing dates in 1914, letters with dates in 1915 and 1916, actual political documents with their dates, and again letters, reflections and diary excerpts dated in 1917, 1919, and one in 1920, after which the pamphlet unaccountably returns to matters of 1914. This chaotic organization gives all the items the strong flavor of contemporaneity in which there has been no retouching. Other matter pertaining to the present study is to be found on pages 11-12, 43-45, and 121-122.

3. *Ibid*. p. 11.

thousand Russian émigrés (not counting those who had gone into labor battalions and munitions factories), singing Russian and French revolutionary songs, marched to the Recruiting Bureau in the Maison des Invalides. Next day, about four thousand of these were found fit for active service—the test of fitness being not too exacting—and, after a week or two of training in camps, were dispatched to the front. They were a motley army, consisting, Krestovskaya writes, of "journalists, writers, artists, craftsmen, clowns, and antique dealers," and, she forgets to add, professors, doctors, lawyers, hereditary nobles, and members of all the variegated nationalities that made up the Russian land. "Naturally, at their head had to be that vanguard of the Russian volunteer movement from which now their remains but a handful . . . scattered over the world." [4]

The "vanguard" to which she refers, a strange parody of Lenin's vanguard yet the same breed of men, the "most conscious revolutionary elements," were not content merely to enlist. They formed a "Russian Republican Detachment." Thus they could demonstrate that they were serving Russia but not the autocracy and defending in France the idea of the republic and of the French Revolution. Was not Germany, like Russia, an empire headed by a semi-absolutist monarchy? So the first four thousand found in the Republican Detachment its conscience and its leadership, "the spiritual and ideological vanguard of the Russian volunteer movement in Paris."

The Republican Detachment was indeed composed of men accustomed to lead the émigré colony, some seventy-five to eighty party activists drawn from the Bolsheviks, Mensheviks, and Socialist Revolutionaries. At the head of this little band marched S. N. Sletov, one of the founders and top leaders of the Socialist Revolutionary Party and N. V. Saposhkov (Kuznetsov), who since 1910 had been secretary of the official Bolshevik Committee supposed to direct not only the Paris Bolsheviks but all Bolshevik organizations abroad.[5]

---

4. *Ibid.* p. 11.

5. A note in Vol. XVIII of the Third Edition of Lenin's works, p. 426, gives the number making up the Republican Detachment as eighty. Krestovskaya's account, written earlier, records the names of seventy-four but is incomplete. Of these she lists twenty-one as already having been killed in action, thirteen wounded, four deserters, and twelve as *ref.*, an abbreviation which is most likely a transcription into Russian of the French word for being returned to the ranks after having been wounded. On the fate of twenty-two she could get no information, and she records that one is in Russia and two are prisoners of war. The Socialist Revolutionary leader, Argunov, in an unpublished manuscript cited by Radkey (*The Agrarian Foes of Bolshevism*, p. 119 n.) gives a list of sixty-eight of these Republican volunteers. He numbers thirty-five as Social Democrats, without distinction between Bolsheviks and Mensheviks, seventeen as Socialist Revolutionaries, nine as Anarchists, and seven as undetermined. Krestovskaya's breakdown according to national origin gives twenty-six Russians, thirty-eight Jews, four Georgians, two Poles, the rest scattered or unknown. Argunov's figures are thirty-three Jews, twenty-nine Russians, and six of other communities.

POPULISM LOSES ITS TOLERANCE

Until August 1914, the humane temper of Russian Populism as contrasted with Russian Marxism had expressed itself inside the SR Party in the friendly spirit, so rare among Russian intellectuals, with which they differed with each other and the tolerance which their various groupings and tendencies showed toward each other within the same organization. Left and right, terrorists and peaceful enlighteners, had followed a voluntary division of labor, disagreeing without rancor, conducting their debates without the endless splits, personal attacks, and bitter feuds which characterized the Social Democratic or "Marxist" faction wars.

Now war engendered a more exacerbated rift than the SR's had ever known before. The émigré leaders, out of old habit, were still able to hold a unified conference at Beaugy-sur-Clarens, Switzerland, on August 22, 1914. But the debate there became sharp and bitter between "defensists" and "internationalists." For the first time the idea of "betrayal," so readily used by Lenin, was hesitantly voiced in an SR conference. The sword drew a line between them: they began to think of each other as "betrayers of the International" or "betrayers of Russia." The word *traitor*, once it rises to the lips, no longer permits of comradeship. Tolerance was stretched beyond the breaking point, with consequences that would become apparent in 1917.

At the Conference, the prowar or "defensist" elements were in a majority. Three founders of the party were present. One, Victor Chernov, declared himself an internationalist. A second, Chernov's brother-in-law, S. N. Sletov,[6] proclaimed that he was enlisting for the defense of French democracy. The third founder, A. A. Argunov, declared for the defense both of France and Russia. To the defensists rallied such outstanding spokesmen as N. D. Avksentiev, Ilya I. Bunakov (Fondaminsky), V. V. Rudnev, who in 1917 would become Mayor of Moscow, Boris Savinkov, a leader and ideologist of the terror, I. A. Rubanovich, the party's representative in the International Socialist Bureau. On the other side with Chernov stood Mark Natanson (Bobrov), venerable link with nineteenth-century Populism, and three lesser figures, B. D. Kamkov (Katz), Dalin (M. A. Levenson) and Peter Alexandrovich (Dmitrievsky), later to serve in the Soviet Cheka. In 1917, this little band would split again, Natanson, Kamkov and Alexandrovich breaking with Chernov in favor of a line which would for a while resemble Lenin's. Down in the ranks of the

---

6. When Sletov was killed in action, Chernov stirred up great bitterness at his funeral by a speech in which he lamented that his brother-in-law had died under the tricolor instead of the red flag.

SR party in 1914, the prowar sentiment was even stronger than in the leadership.[7]

Perhaps the Populist sensitivity to the uniqueness of their native land, its history and its institutions, and their devotion to the *narod* (which in Russian means both "the people" and "the nation") made their love of country especially strong. But the other groups of "irreconcilable" émigrés seem to have been no less vulnerable to the unacknowledged feeling of love of country.

Of the four founders of Russian Marxism, Plekhanov, Axelrod, Deutsch, and Zasulich, only Axelrod took an "internationalist" stand. Plekhanov became the chief spokesman for the idea of volunteering. Only his age and poor health prevented him from doing so himself. He made the farewell speech in honor of the Republican Detachment of socialist volunteers who were enlisting in the French Army. To Deputy Burianov, his closest follower in the Duma, he wrote:

It would be most distressing if our fellow-thinkers should hinder the cause of the self-defense of the Russian people by any thoughtless step. A vote against the credits would be a betrayal of the people, abstention would be cowardice. Vote *for!*

Among the Menshevik leadership, as among the SR leaders, the proportion of "internationalists" was somewhat higher than among the rank and file. Martov and Axelrod led the internationalist remnant abroad, while in Russia six of the seven Menshevik Duma Deputies kept the banner of "internationalism" flying. But Dan, himself an "internationalist," wrote in his history of those years:

Among the Russian socialist émigrés in foreign lands, especially in the lands of the *Entente*, the great majority stood under the influence of the ideology of the "Defense of the Fatherland." [8]

Lenin would have loved to gloat at this "treason" of SR's and Menshevik Social Democrats. However, the news of his own faction, slowly coming to him from Paris, gave him pause.

---

7. Radkey, *op. cit.,* Chap. IV.

8. Plekhanov's letter to Burianov is cited in Yaroslavsky, *Ocherki po istorii V. K. P. (b),* Moscow, 1937, p. 248. The Dan quotation is from his *Geschichte der Russischen Sozialdemokratie* (continuation of a work carried by Martov up to 1908), Berlin, 1926, p. 275.

THE BOLSHEVIK VOLUNTEERS

Though in practice Lenin held all the threads of command in his hands and picked the members of the various committees, the official center supposed to direct the Bolshevik émigrés was located not in Cracow but in Paris. Its Secretary was N. V. Sapozhkov, whose reactions Krestovskaya has already described for us. He was an old Bolshevik who so much enjoyed Lenin's confidence that he had been a delegate to the London Congress of 1907, and had been named Secretary of the Paris Center in 1910, while Lenin still lived in Paris. In the last days of July he tried frantically to get in touch with Lenin, but the telegraph office refused to accept a wire addressed to Cracow, in Austrian Poland, for Austria-Hungary was already at war. Sapozhkov then sent telegrams to Bolsheviks in neutral Switzerland, begging them to get in touch with Lenin or Krupskaya and communicate Lenin's instructions to Paris. These messages, too, remained unanswered. Once France was invaded, Sapozhkov, as we know, refused to meet with his Committee, say a word to any of his comrades, or even explain the process by which he had arrived at his decision to volunteer.

As unemployment hit all but the war industries, everyone was for the moment free from morning until night to discuss the war. Here is a description of the discussion among the Bolsheviks by one who took part in it:

On August 1 a poster was put up announcing mobilization. The café overflowed with emotion. *To accept or not to accept the war?* Acceptance found more supporters. Immediately and fatally arose the question of volunteering. . . .

In the little restaurant on the rue des Cordelières, almost all the members of the group were present. On the order of business, only one question: *volunteering.* The meeting is disorderly, the discussion anarchic, passions high. The meeting breaks up in general tumult. . . . Partisans and adversaries of volunteering exchange brutal words. At last the group of "defensists" marches demonstratively out of the meeting. Some one cries after them: *Renegades!* But the cry finds no echo, nor much sympathy either. . . .

. . . On the Place des Invalides, where volunteers were being accepted, the first groups of Russians applied. They were, for the moment, separate individuals. But in a few days the movement took on a more organized character. In the rue de la Reine-Blanche, near the Avenue des Gobelins, in the poor meeting hall of the Workers' Club of which Antonov-Ovseenko was the Secretary, there begins, under his direction, the enrollment of émigré volunteers. Bolsheviks, Mensheviks, SR's, Anarchists enroll there. In a few days the first Russian Republican regiment was constituted, into which entered the following members of the Bolshevik group: Sapozhkov, Antonov-Popov, Mikhail Davidov, Ilya Japaridze (Moiseev), and others. On their initiative there was drawn up the declaration that, now that war was here, it was necessary to face it and decide, as Marx and Engels had, the question of the victory of which side would be of most advantage to democracy and socialism.[9] The war was caused by the aggressive imperialism of Austria and Germany. These two lands had always been the bulwark of the Russian autocracy. The victory of feudal Austro-German militarism over the democratic powers of Western Europe would fatally strengthen international militarism and reaction . . . arrest social evolution in Europe . . . strengthen autocracy and backwardness in Russia. But the defeat of the German and Austrian ruling classes would bring not only a republic and socialism to Germany and Austria, but, by removing the last supports of tsarist reaction, in Russia as well. . . . The signers of the Manifesto are profoundly convinced that we serve faithfully the interests of the international proletariat. They are entering the armies of Republican France under the slogans: Long live democracy! Long live the German Republic! Down with Tsarism! Long live German socialism! [10]

Thus Bolshevik activists supplied not only the recruiting agent, Antonov-Ovseenko, and the recruiting center, their workers' hall, but the Manifesto by which SR's, Anarchists, and Mensheviks as well as Bolsheviks justified their volunteering. From other sources we learn that the author of the document was the Bolshevik Mukhin, who used the *nom de guerre*, Ekk.[11] Alexinsky, who had been Lenin's chief spokesman in the Second Duma but had later gotten into conflict with him on tactical matters and joined the Left or Vperyodist Bolsheviks, became the editor of a prowar Russian social-democratic paper, *Rossia i svoboda (Russia and Freedom)*, to which Plekhanov became the most distinguished contributor. In September this group of Bolsheviks and former "Party Mensheviks" (as Plekhanov had called his group) came to an agreement with Avksentiev, Bunakov, Voronov, and Argunov of the prowar SR's to merge their paper into a joint organ of all defensist socialists to be called

9. Cf. Lenin's favoring of the victory of Japan in the Russo-Japanese War of 1904-05. *Collected Works,* 4th Russian Edition, Vol. VII, p. 183; VIII, pp. 31-39, 239, 448-51. The key quotation reads: "The proletariat . . . does not forget, however, not for a moment . . . that while class rule remains it is not possible to evaluate wars from only a democratic sentimental point of view, but in every war between exploiting nations it is necessary to distinguish the role of the progressive and reactionary bourgeoisies of one or another nation." In a number of the other passages indicated he makes clear that in this war the Japanese bourgeoisie is the progressive side and its victory desirable both from a Russian proletarian and an international proletarian point of view.

10. Aline (Alin). *Lénine a Paris,* cited in Rosmer, *Le mouvement ouvrier pendant la guerre,* Paris, 1956, pp. 466-68. The text of the Manifesto of the Republican Volunteers is given in French in Rosmer, pp. 468-69, and in Russian in Krestovskaya, pp. 123-24. It is characteristic of Bolshevik activism that Lenin's group provided both the recruiting agent, Antonov-Ovseenko, and the ideologist, Mukhin, who drafted the Manifesto for signature by Bolsheviks, Mensheviks and SR's. And it was Plekhanov, waverer between Bolshevism and Menshevism from 1903 to 1914 and teacher of all of them, who delivered the solemn farewell address.

11. The Manifesto, dated August 21, 1914, was issued over the signatures of a committee of two Bolsheviks, two Mensheviks, and one SR.

Prizyv (a Russian word that can mean either a call or a call-up for military service). Thus, at long last, did Plekhanov begin to reverse the split between Marxists and Populists which he himself had initiated back in 1883.[12]

The Bolshevik Leading Committee of Organizations Abroad fell to pieces. Two of its five members volunteered for the French Army (Antonov-Britman and Sapozhkov), a third resigned both from the Committee and the Party, leaving two badly confused and demoralized members to wait for some word from Lenin. How many Bolsheviks volunteered is uncertain. Aline, who was there at the time, says that a majority were in favor of volunteering. Krupskaya in her memoirs writes a little gingerly:

> In our groups abroad . . . there was not such firmness. . . . The problem was unclear for many. . . . In Paris in the end [*v kontse kontsov, i.e.,* in the long run] a majority of the group came out against the war and volunteering, but a part of the comrades—Sapozhkov [Kuznetsov] Kazakov [Britman, Sviiagin], Misha Edisherov [Davydov], Moiseev [Illya, Zefir] and others— entered as volunteers into the French army.[13]

Since some of the prowar Bolsheviks like Antonov-Ovseenko, after acting as recruiting agent for the Republican Volunteers, later became antiwar under the influence of Trotsky, and since some of those who "did not declare themselves" in favor of volunteering were by age, sex, or condition of health prevented, it is not unlikely that Krupskaya's "minority" and Aline's "majority" represent substantially the same picture.

Among the Bolsheviks who did enlist immediately, we know that Japaridze was wounded, Kazakov, Sapozhkov, and Davydov killed in action, and only the fate of Mukhinov (Ekk) among the leading Bolsheviks was unknown when Krestovskaya compiled her list of the "Russian Republicans." Krupskaya continues even more circumspectly: "In other groups also (*i.e.,* other émigré centers) the question was not clarified to the end."

---

12. For *Rossiya i svoboda* and *Prizyv,* see Dan, *op. cit.,* p. 275. Radkey reproduces many SR writings from *Prizyv.*

13. For the disintegration of the Bolshevik Center in Paris, see Lenin, 3rd Edition, p. 426; Krupskaya, *Vospominaniia o Lenine,* Moscow, 1957, pp. 230-31. For a Bolshevik account written nine years after the events, which gives the number of Bolsheviks who volunteered for the French Army as 11 out of a membership of 94, see I. P. Khoniavko, "V podpolie i v emigratsii," in *Proletarskaia Revoliutsiia,* No. 4, 1923, p. 168. The picture of what happened to the Bolshevik movement inside Russia is less clear, except for the equivocal stand of the Duma Deputies and their overseer, Kamenev. But we know that a number of outstanding Bolsheviks were prowar (see below, note 14), and that even such an old Bolshevik as Voroshilov, with seven years of prison and exile behind him, volunteered for the Tsar's army. (Erich Wollenberg, *Ostprobleme,* July 21, 1951, p. 895.)

THE ELITE OF THE LENINIST PATRIOTS

"Not clarified to the end" is a rather remarkable understatement, for the number of outstanding Bolshevik intellectuals both in exile and inside Russia who rallied to the defense of their country was truly astonishing. Among them were the two translators of *Das Kapital* into Russian, I. I. Skvortsev-Stepanov and V. A. Bazarov (Rudnev); the Bolshevik leader in the Second Duma, Alexinsky, who founded his prowar journal in Paris; the Bolshevik writer and editor, A. A. Troyanovsky; the Central Committee Member I. P. Meshkovsky (Goldenberg); Lenin's earliest comrade in arms and intimate, Krzhizhanovsky; the bomb-maker, fundraiser, and troika member of 1905, Krassin, and lesser journalists and propagandists like Finn-Yenotaevsky, chronicler of the revolutions of 1917. To be sure, Lenin had already written off Bazarov and Alexinsky when he quarreled with the former on philosophy and the latter on tactics, and both of them had joined in the formation of the "left" Bolshevik *Vpered* Group that Lenin read out of the Party in 1912. But Skvortsev-Stepanov was an esteemed contemporary, born like Vladimir Ilyich in 1870, a veteran of the revolutionary movement, which he joined in 1891, a historian and economist of some reputation, the translator of a number of Marx's works, the author of studies on the Paris Commune and the French Revolution, a four-volume textbook on political economy and a volume on "Historical Materialism and Natural Science." Lenin had regarded him as so dependable that he had chosen him to represent the Bolsheviks at the Stockholm "United" Party Congress, and as a Duma candidate for Moscow. Moreover, he had spent eight years in jail which proved him a "rockhard." Meshkovsky-Goldenberg, too, had been a man to rely on: a Bolshevik member of the "united" Central Committee from 1907-09, representative of the Committee to the Third Duma Fraction, a delegate with Lenin to the Stuttgart Congress of the Socialist International.

During the war they were "traitors," but when Skvortsev-Stepanov returned to the fold in 1917, Lenin named him Commissar of Finance in the first Soviet Government, assigned him to make two provocative addresses to the Constituent Assembly just before it was dispersed, and entrusted him with many other important tasks. In 1922, Skvortsev wrote on the project closest to Lenin's heart, "The Electrification of the RFSFR," and Lenin wrote an introduction. Leonid Krassin would become Lenin's Commissar of Trade and chief negotiator of economic accords.

So, too, did Meshkovsky-Goldenberg rejoin the Bolsheviks after 1917, and receive assignments involving confidence in his ability and probity.

The case of Troyanovsky was more complicated. A Bolshevik from 1904 on, he had been one of Bolshevisms's important journalists, writing for and serving on the staff of *Zvezda*, *Prosveshchenie* and *Pravda*. To Gorky Lenin wrote in 1913, "Troyanovsky and his wife are good people. . . . Everything we know of them till now speaks in their favor. And they have means. They might be able to return [to Russia] and do a lot for the journal." Troyanovsky was close enough to Lenin then to prepare the materials on which Malinovsky and Lenin based their argument to justify the split of the socialist Duma Delegation. But Troyanovsky became an ardent defensist, eloquently appealing to Russian socialists to defend their country. His return to Bolshevism was difficult and circuitous: a Menshevik in Russia from 1917 to 1921; then a Bolshevik once more in 1923, after which he was entrusted with the ambassadorships to England and the United States.[14]

This is not the place to discuss the reaction to the war of Bolshevik leaders inside Russia, but one interesting case worth considering in this context is that of Leonid Borisovich Krassin. Krassin had been one of Lenin's big three in the stormiest and most critical years: the year 1905 with its efforts at armed uprising, and the years 1906 and 1907 when the secret *troika*, Lenin, Bogdanov, Krassin, directed the revolutionary hold-ups or "expropriations." During those days, Krassin was Lenin's chief source of funds. He it was who lined up his employer, the wealthy Morozov, Maxim Gorky, and others to contribute. As an engineer with considerable technical ability and a conspirator whose skill in that difficult art aroused Lenin's admiration, Krassin managed to retain respectability as a manager and director of electrical enterprises while he manufactured bombs for both Bolshevik and Maximalist holdup attempts. The year 1914 found him in Russia as the Manager-Director of the Petersburg Branch of the Siemens-Schueckert Elektrische Gesellschaft. His wife in her biography of her husband tells how he was filled with gloomy fears for the future of Russia when Germany attacked. He felt restless and disturbed because he could not figure out how he could be useful in Russia's defense.

In time, however, he found scope for his energies in organizing a number of war hospitals out of funds provided by the concerns of which he was managing director. . . . Under his able direction, our little relief organization made great strides. An opportunity came in 1915 for Krassin to do some work of real national importance. . . . An effort had to be made to mobilize the trading resources of the country. . . . Krassin was chiefly instrumental in

14. The biographical details of the lives of Skvortsev, Meshkovsky and Troyanovsky are taken mainly from the biographical notes to the Third Edition of Lenin's works. The letter to Gorky is in *Lenin i Gorkii, Pisma etc.*, Moscow, 1958, p. 93.

establishing this organization on a working basis under the title of the War Industries Committee.[15]

Once an activist, always an activist. For Russia now as once for Lenin, he raised funds, recruited industrialists and workingmen for the war effort, worked day and night without rest to bring into being the War Industries Committee, which committee Lenin attacked most bitterly as representing a betrayal of the cause of revolution, class struggle, and socialism. But this "treason" did not hinder Lenin from enlisting Krassin's energies and commercial and technological skills to negotiate peace and trade agreements, to run the Commissariat of Foreign Trade, to represent the Soviet government at Genoa, Rapallo, the Hague, and London. Could it be that Lenin did not really mean the word *traitor* as other men do? Or that treason no longer mattered in those who could be useful again and who, in the latest separation between sheep and goats, had returned to the side of the sheep in the fold?

Thus the internationalist socialist and the internationalist working-man, like the cosmopolitan man of the eighteenth century, and like Marx's "international bourgeoisie," had shown after all that he was really the Englishman, the German, the Frenchman, and the Russian.

Lenin might charge, as he found it politic to do, that all parties had wavered and betrayed "*except* the Bolsheviks." Yet he could not help but know that his "rockhard Bolsheviks," gathered painfully one by one over the years, selected for their energy, their firmness, their orthodoxy, their hardness, their agreement with "the correct line," had wavered and "betrayed" like the others. And that the masses had been caught up by the enthusiasm and fevers of war as much as—nay, more unreservedly than—the leaders.

In the last month of his political life, a few days before a stroke stilled his tongue and pen forever, he wearily acknowledged what in his heart he had known all along:

It must be explained to the people how great is the secrecy with which war arises, and how helpless are the ordinary organizations of the workers, even those calling themselves revolutionary, in the face of a really oncoming war.

It is necessary to explain to people with all concreteness again and again how matters stood at the time of the last war and why it cannot be otherwise.

It is necessary to explain, especially, the significance of those circumstances which make it inevitable that the question of "the defense of the fatherland" will be decided inevitably by the overwhelming majority of the workers in favor of their own bourgeoisie.[16]

15. Lubov Krassin, *Leonid Krassin: His Life and Work,* London, 1929, pp. 21-22. The author was Krassin's wife.

16. "Notes on the Question of the Tasks of Our Delegation to the Hague," written Dec. 4, 1922, Lenin, Vol. **XXXIII**, pp. 409-10.

But in 1914, in an Austrian prison, then on the road to neutral Switzerland, Lenin was able to force this awareness out of his consciousness. He turned the matter over and over as he elaborated his own *sui generis* position on the war. Had the war come "with great secrecy" or had it been cynically and openly plotted for years? Why, cynically and openly plotted for years, of course, for this made the guilt of ruling classes and socialist leaders the graver. Had the masses reacted as patriots, sometimes carrying with them, sometimes silencing, their leaders? No, the leaders had betrayed the masses, and now the leaders and organizations which had committed treason had to be destroyed and the masses redeemed from their Judas-leaders. Had there been a strong strain of patriot and *defender of the Fatherland-in-danger* in Marx and Engels? But this war was not the one they had foreseen but a different one. Their choice of *"victory for which side will be more advantageous for progress"* was applicable only to their time, not to this different age. (For the first time Lenin permitted himself to be a "revisionist" ready to declare that some basic approach of Marx and Engels was outdated.) Had the German Social Democracy, which he had admired above all others for its organization methods, its power, and its orthodoxy shocked him into disbelief,[17] grieved and outraged him as nothing else had ever grieved and outraged him? Then he would declare that he had seen it degenerating for years, that its treason was the worst, and the pacifist apostasy of its theoretical spokesman, Kautsky, the "most dangerous of all."

STARTING ONCE MORE FROM SCRATCH

Some of these thoughts a close disciple might conceivably have anticipated, yet as he turned things over and over in his mind, while in prison and in flight, he would devise a position which not even those closest to him would be prepared for. The stand he proclaimed in his *Seven Theses on the War*,[18] would be foreseen by no one and, for a long time, be shared by almost no one. It would draw a line not only between him and the prowar elements inside his group and outside of it: it would draw a line betwen him and the *antiwar* elements. It would divide, as with a sword, Lenin from all other antiwar and internationalist tendencies. It would separate him from the internationalists, Martov and Axelrod and

17. At first, according to Zinoviev and other memorialists, Lenin thought that the issue of *Vorwaerts* announcing the voting of war credits by the Social Democratic Deputies was a forgery of the German General Staff.

18. See *Three Who Made a Revolution,* Chap. XXXVI, "Seven Theses Against War."

Chernov. It would draw a line between him and Rosa Luxemburg and between him and Trotsky.

Thus in August and September 1914, Lenin alone knew what "the Bolshevik" stand was to be. Fleeing with Zinoviev and Krupskaya from Austria to Switzerland, Lenin "carried with him about all that was left of the Bolshevik organization abroad," [19] together with the ideological basis on which it was to be reconstituted. In his head were the shibboleths which were to divide yesterday's Bolsheviks from today's, divide Bolsheviks from non-Bolsheviks, Leninists from would-be Leninists, Left Zimmerwaldists from Zimmerwaldists, and even one little group of Left Zimmerwaldists from another.

Had Austria kept him in jail, where they at first put him, and held him incommunicado as an "enemy alien" until the war's end in November 1918, how different would everything have been, at Zimmerwald and Kienthal, in the International, in Russia in 1917. History is full of such *ifs* and *almosts*, for what is *ex post facto* proclaimed to have been "inevitable" is only what has happened. Having irrevocably happened, it acquires its appearance of having been inevitable all along.

From Switzerland Lenin began anew, as he had done so many times before, to pick "Leninists" one by one, gathering them around his new platform. *His* new platform, from which he would not deviate, nor add one thought of another, nor compromise a single expression. "Never, it seems, was Vladimir Ilyich in such an irreconcilable mood. . . . There were differences with Rosa Luxemburg, Radek, the Dutch [left], with Bukharin, Pyatakov, in part with Kollontai." [20] As so many times before, he would pick out one by one the individuals who accepted his line from the first word to the last and followed him unconditionally. He was too selfless, or too unconscious of self, to say "Leninist," but now as in the past, wherever Lenin and two or three were gathered together, there was Bolshevism. "Bolshevism" was not what that handful might vote it to be, but what Lenin laid down, for he would select them, not they him, working out his position first, then selecting them one by one by the infallible test that they approved "the only correct position" as he had formulated it.

Who could believe then that this man, starting once more from scratch to pick adherents, would in three years be ruler of a great land? Certainly, Lenin could not believe it, for as late as January 22, 1917, he told an audience at the Zurich People's House: "We old ones perhaps will not live to see the decisive struggles of this coming revolution." [21]

19. Gankin and Fisher, *The Bolsheviks and the World War,* Stanford, Calif., 1940.
20. Krupskaya, pp. 264 and 271.
21. *Ibid.,* p. 271.

If in 1914, Lenin stood all alone, Nicholas II seemed more secure than any Tsar since Alexander I had defied Napoleon in 1812, for in this hour of Russia's danger, the workers ceased their strikes and marched to the Winter Palace to sing "God Save the Tsar," while the irreconcilable battalions of the enemies in foreign lands disintegrated or rallied to the defense of the Fatherland or of its ally, Republican France.

—April 1963

III TITANS LOCKED

IN COMBAT *

> In its scale, in its slaughter, in the exertions of the combatants, in its military kaleidoscope, the struggle on the Eastern Front far surpasses by magnitude and intensity all similar human episodes. . . . Hard and somber war; war of winter; bleak and barren regions; long marches forward and back again under heavy burdens; horses dying in the traces; wounded frozen in their own blood; the dead uncounted, unburied; the living pressed again into the mill. . . . Here all Central Europe tore itself to pieces and expired in agony, to rise again, unrecognizable. . . .
>
> —Winston Churchill in *The Unknown War*

The giant nation girded for war. The air cleared as if a storm had blown itself out. For years the thoughtful and informed had feared this moment, for they knew that Russia was playing the great-power game "on credit only." [1] Yet, now that war had come, fear vanished. Men breathed easily, hearts were uplifted, old wounds seemed to heal over. From Grand Dukes lacking employment worthy of their rank and generals looking for

* A chapter from a work in progress, published separately in the *Russian Review*, October 1964 and January 1965.

1. The "thoughtful and well-informed" seemed limited to the successive Finance Ministers, who alone showed awareness of the fact that Russia was deperately poor and could not really afford to play the great-power game. From Reutern (1862-78) to Kokovtsev (1904-14), all the Finance Ministers were opposed to war. Reutern, Witte, and Kokovtsev each lost his post for reminding his Sovereign of this too insistently. Virtually the entire rest of the bureaucracy, the Court itself, and the articulate public, preferred to believe that Russia was in every sense a great power. If a few staunch conservatives counseled against war with a country like Germany, it was not out of financial consideration but because of the social costs. N. K. Giers, Foreign Minister from 1882-95, warned that defeat would unleash a revolution "which would make the Paris Commune look like a mere children's game." In February 1914, old Durnovo, former Police Chief and Minister of the Interior, then nearing seventy, prepared an unsolicited memorandum to his Sovereign which brilliantly predicted the line-up of nations large and small, if war should break out over the Balkans and involve both Germany and England. Such a war, he said, could only end in a revolution in both Germany and Russia, no matter which of the two was victorious. Thus a true vision of the future, denied to such Marxist adepts as Lenin and Plekhanov and to such historians as Miliukov, was vouchsafed to an aging, conservative former police official.

For the text of Durnovo's Memorandum, see *Documents of Russian History, 1914-17*, edited by Frank Golder, New York, 1927, pp. 3-23. For a discussion of Russia as a great power on credit only, see Theodore H. Von Laue, "Problems of Modernization," in *Russian Foreign Policy*, Ivo J. Lederer, Ed., New Haven, 1962, pp. 69-106.

laurels on the field of battle to the "public" who felt that their exclusion from public life by the bureaucracy would now end, from the students who uncovered the Tsar's picture to march with it in the street to the workingman who knelt before the Winter Palace to sing "God Save the Tsar," and even the diehard opposition in foreign exile whose organizations were torn apart by a fever of volunteering—the arc of unity was more inclusive than it had been since Napoleon stirred Russia by taking Moscow over one hundred years before. Though he had faced the prospect of general war with a heavy heart, Nicholas was as uplifted in spirit as his subjects. "Now Rodzyanko," he said to the Chairman of the Duma, embracing that hitherto disagreeable symbol of a check on his autocratic rule, "I am your friend until death. I will do anything for the Duma. Tell me what you want." [2]

But the Duma did not know what it might want beyond the chance to serve. Its main concern had not been foreign affairs but domestic reform. Loyal to the monarchy in principle, it had wanted nothing so much as the unity of Monarch and Duma that this moment seemed to establish. To be sure, the very existence of the Duma had been extorted from the Tsar in the aftermath of an unpopular war. But this war seemed different. The conflict with Japan in 1904 had been brought on by a cabal of rascally adventurers at Court and had linked Russia's destinies with Asia, hence with all that was backward, despotic, and humiliating in Russian life. This new war, it seemed, had been forced upon Russia against the Tsar's desire, and it linked her destinies once more with Europe—still better with Western against Central Europe, with constitutional England and republican France against semi-absolutist Germany and Austria-Hungary, both in the past supports of all that was reactionary in Russia.

MISPLACED CHIVALRY

Swept off his feet by the same wave of enthusiasm that caught up students, workingmen, and articulate opposition, "the simple impressionable Tsar," in the words of the historian doubling as wartime liaison officer, Sir Bernard Pares, "was himself conspicuous in his chivalry to his country's allies." Instead of waiting until mobilization was completed, or keeping his armies on the defensive and poised for withdrawal into the depths of the Russian land—a tactic that had worked so well against Darius of Persia, Charles XII of Sweden, and Napoleon, as it would work once more against Hitler—the Emperor rushed hastily improvised armies into East Prussia and Galicia so that the "Russian steamroller" might

2. M. V. Rodzyanko, *The Reign of Rasputin*, London, 1927, p. 111.

come to the rescue of invaded France and as yet unmobilized England. How could the liberal, democratic "Westerners" of the Duma doubt that out of this fervent national union of parliament and Tsar and this fraternal alliance with the democracies of the West the reforms they longed for must come?

Even the Russian peasant responded to the call to the colors as never before. The mobilization of the largest army in all history took place without a hitch. Despite sparse and deficient railways, nonexistent roads, and slow river highways, despite the vastness of the land and the three months required to complete the call-up (Germany's mobilization took only nine days), ninety-six per cent of those called for duty reported within the time prescribed. By September 30, 4,215,000 men had been mobilized.[3]

After a few hours of patriotic addresses, the Duma voted the huge budget (which like all the war budgets of all the participants was to prove so pitifully inadequate) and adjourned until the Emperor might call them, for the members were eager to take up the new public duties that the war had opened up to them. Within a week, every outstanding leader of rural zemstvo, city duma, and Imperial Duma, had found some public work.[4] The well-known liberal zemstvo leader, Prince Georgy N. Lvov, assumed the Chairmanship of the Civilian Red Cross. By the end of a month, his organization had prepared a million hospital beds.[5] Various bodies made up of those public-minded men hitherto excluded from public life by the bureaucracy, set up a whole network of organizations to care for sick and wounded, for refugees and invalids, for the needy families that the war was bound to produce. At the same time the Empress and many noble ladies became patrons and nurses in hospitals under religious and Imperial patronage. Moving passages in Alexandra Federovna's letters to her husband testify to the emotional depth and devotion of her work as patroness and as actual working nurse. In this field, too, the arc of unity seemed all-embracing.

As the war continued to swallow everything in its insatiable maw, the routinary bureaucracy proved unequal to the task of keeping up a steadily increasing flow of munitions, supplies and transport. Thereupon the same leaders of the "public," augmented now by patriotic industrialists and patriotic workingmen in the war industries, set up a chain of War Industry Committees to keep the vast machinery moving at an even greater speed. Only the case-hardened bureaucracy and police regarded the sud-

3. Kohn and Meyendorff, *The Cost of the War to Russia,* New Haven, 1932, p. 14; N. N. Golovin, *The Russian Army in the World War,* New Haven, 1931, p. 202.
4. They had found what the founders of the American Republic called "public happiness."
5. Bernard Pares, *The Fall of the Russian Monarchy,* New York, 1939, p. 189 and note.

den upsurge of national unity with misgivings. In language strangely like Lenin's they reported sourly on the "noisy wave of chauvinistic excitement." [6]

Later many liberals and socialists would wish to believe that they had not been swept off their feet by that first tidal wave of unity and enthusiasm. But those who were honest with themselves, consulting their diaries or their memories, could not doubt that it had been so. Writing nearly a half century later, I. B. Ilyin would still recall in all its poignant confidence his exultant mood in the first weeks of the war and his simple conviction that the Russian people "were the same people as in the time of Suvurov or Kutuzov . . . marching to defend their country!" [7]

Of that "people of Suvurov or Kutuzov," the keenest of French political thinkers of the nineteenth century, Alexis de Tocqueville, once wrote in his notebook:

There are people who live under despotism, but yet have a strong feeling of nationality . . . making immense sacrifices to save a fatherland in which they live without share and without rights. But then, one must note, it is always religion that takes the place of patriotism. . . . In defending the country they defend that holy city in which they all are citizens. . . .

The Russian, who has not even a share in the land on which he is born, is one of the bravest soldiers in Europe, and he burns his crops to ruin the enemy. . . .

Despotic governments [are] formidable . . . when the people whom they rule are moved by religious enthusiasm. Then the unity of power instead of damaging social cohesion simply directs it. Nations in such condition have the strength of free people without the disadvantages of liberty. . . .

The more harsh and oppressive the government is, the greater the efforts [the people] makes to protect a soil it does not possess, the less men are attached to life, the better they defend it. . . . And they die the more easily, the more wretched they are. . . . [8]

This was the servile people who had defeated Napoleon, and who, serfs once more under Stalin in a system of forced "collectivization" supplemented by concentration camps, would defeat Hitler, "an inexhaustible supply of men . . . hardy, fatalistically brave."

On the same page of his notebook, Tocqueville reminded himself that when the faith of a servile people weakens, its fighting power weakens, too. The people of Turkey, he wrote, had never taken any part in the

6. S. Melgunov, *Na putiakh k dvortsovomu perevorotu* (hereafter referred to as Melgunov, *Na putiakh*), Paris, 1921, p. 11; Reports of the Ministry of the Interior at the beginning of the war in *Krasnyi Arkhiv*, No. IV.

7. I. S. Ilyin, "The Revolution,' *Novyi Zhurnal*, No. 56, March 1959, p. 210.

8. De Tocqueville, "Unpublished Fragments," edited by J. P. Mayer, *Encounter*, April 1959, pp. 17-22.

direction of their affairs either. But as long as they saw in the conquests of their Sultans the triumph of the religion of Mohammed, they had been invincible. "Now that their religion is going and they have only despotism left," Turkey is facing its downfall.[9]

AN AUTOCRACY WITHOUT AN AUTOCRAT

How was it with the people of Holy Russia? Were they really still the people of Suvorov and Kutuzov? Or had their faith weakened, leaving only the hollow shell of despotism? How long could they hold up under the anomaly of an autocracy without an autocrat? How long respect a government whose Ministers were designated and dismissed at an ever faster tempo according to the coarse-grained impulses of a cunning holy peasant and the touchy fantasies of a sickly woman surrounded by venal flatterers? How could the articulate public have confidence in a government from which the most able were one by one unceremoniously ousted for giving upright opinions or showing initiative in carrying on their work? How could a government increasingly made up of accidental nonentities lead a great nation in war when its members were treated like personal servants in the servants' hall of a touchy private household?

True, the war had started with an unexpected show of unity, but would the unity stand the strains of inevitable defeats and inevitable deficiencies?[10] How long would the unprecedented unity stand up against the noisy quarrels between routinary bureaucracy and inexperienced public? the rumors concerning Rasputin and his disreputable train and concerning "that German woman"? the intransigeant attacks upon the ministers from the public forum of Duma and the daily press? the reckless slogans of obscure circles of the revolutionary opposition? the longing for peace which would grow in all lands as the years of war stretched out endlessly? the rumors set afoot by German psychological warfare?[11] Not since 1812 had Russia been put to such a test. But this time, such are the ironies of history, the very progress Russia had made—the emancipation of the peasant, the germs of a constitution, the growth of the press, Duma and articulate public, the development of an economy independent of the state, the emergence of political parties and unions—all made the test infinitely harder. Firmly established democracy can stand the hardships and reverses of war without weakening as can firmly established autocracy. It is the land in which autocracy has weakened and democracy

9. *Ibid.*

10. These problems were not peculiar to Russia. Each of the belligerents suffered its share of reverses and sought scapegoats for its deficiencies.

11. With modern total war this method of warfare took on a scope and a significance unknown in earlier centuries.

not yet become complete and customary that is most likely to crack under strain.[12]

At the outset, men expected a short war. All the nations nourished the same illusion. "You will be home before the leaves have fallen," the Kaiser told the first departing troops. "Ten weeks," calculated Count Hochberg. "I shall have breakfast in the Café de la Paix on the anniversary of Sedan," one officer said to another. (The anniversary of the Battle of Sedan was September 2.) The General Staff had an exact timetable for the outflanking of the French frontier forts by driving through Luxembourg, Belgium and Holland,[13] the seizure of Paris, the chopping up of the surrounded French armies, then the swift destruction of the armies of Russia.

In Saint Petersburg the optimism was no less. The Vice President of the Duma, S. I. Shidlovsky, has written that "everyone" was agreed that "more than 3-4 months it cannot last." When England declared war on Germany on August 4, Jurisprudence Professor K. S. Stankevich was so sure of Germany's defeat "in a couple of weeks" that he bade himself maintain a "pacifism on principle and preserve neutrality of spirit." (Later he was to volunteer, become one of the most ardent and deeply concerned of patriot officers, and, after the fall of the Tsar, serve as Commissar for the Provisional Government on the Northern Front.) Serious journals wrote of dictating peace terms in Berlin before the end of the year.[14]

In France they were so sure of early victory that they did not try to defend the iron ore of Lorraine, as they would "soon get it back at the peace table," an error which cut off eighty per cent of French iron and steel for four long years. England, thinking an expeditionary force of volunteers would suffice for quick victory, gave no thought to calling up the Empire or introducing conscription.

Everywhere was the same fatalistic lightheartedness arising from a century of short wars, each followed by swift recovery for both victor and

12. Writes Crane Brinton of four revolutions, the English, American, French and Russian: "Our revolutions clearly were not born in societies economically retrograde; on the contrary, they took place in societies economically progressive." (*The Anatomy of Revolution*, Revised Edition, New York, 1937, pp. 30 and 33.) What Brinton said about economic progress may also be said about political progress. Indeed, Tocqueville had already made the same observation. To cite Brinton once more: "The men who made the French Revolution were getting higher and higher real income—so much that they wanted a great deal more. And above all . . . they wanted much that cannot be measured by the economist." (*Ibid.*, p. 32.)

13. At the last moment Holland was omitted from the Schlieffen Plan, a change which narrowed the invasion gap and retarded the outflanking movement.

14. Melgunov, *Na putiakh*, pp. 22-23. Virtually all memoirs of this period testify to the same. The expectation of a short war in Germany, France, and England is documented in the memoirs of the respective countries and in such secondary works as Barbara Tuchman, *The Guns of August*, New York, 1962, where most of the relevant passages are quoted.

vanquished. No one dreamed that this war would become total, its battle lines freeze in bloody stalemate, the fighting drag on endlessly despite unimaginable cost in lives and treasure, without visible prospect of decision.

With incontestible columns of figures, economists had proved that the countries would all be bankrupt within a few weeks or at most a month or two. And so indeed they were. But the fact was papered over by the new wizardry of mortgaging the future, piling up astronomical debts, rationing necessities except those intended for war, on which there was no limit, and printing money with accelerating speed. Like a sorcerer's apprentice governments knew how to start the presses but not how to stop them again as they peeled off endless sheets of bonds and banknotes with less and less behind them, less and less that they could buy, and less and less meaning to each added scrap of paper and string of zeroes.

"GERMANY HAS LOST THE WAR"

Before we look at the fortunes of war and changing moods in Russian society, we might do well to take a look at the best military machine in Europe, the German. On September 2—that anniversary of the Battle of Sedan which was to see German officers breakfasting on the Rue de la Paix—one of them wrote in his diary: "Our men are done up. They stagger forward, their faces coated with dust, their uniforms in rags. They look like living scarecrows." When Moltke became aware of the fact that the beaten French were retreating in good order, preserving their armies intact, free from panic and, half dead with fatigue, yet at the sound of a bugle able to take up their rifles and renew the attack; when he found himself stopped at the Marne and faced with the need of dispatching troops to the west to stop the Russians in East Prussia and in Austria—he wired his Emperor: "Your Majesty, we have lost the war!" [15]

The judgment cost Moltke his post, though in the end, his verdict would be verified. The consequences of the failure of the Schlieffen Plan, however, would be concealed by Hindenburg's victory in East Prussia. It would take four more years to turn Moltke's words into actuality—four years of stalemate and unstinted bloodshed, of the spread of the war from seven countries to thirty, and the growth of the numbers in arms from six millions to sixty-five. The third year would see the exit of Russia and the entrance of America. In the fourth year, with the German lines still

15. Hanson Baldwin, *World War I*, New York, 1962, p. 26. The best short military history of the war is Baldwin's. Russia's part in it is treated at great length in Pares, *op. cit.*, in General Sir Alfred Knox, *With the Russian Army, 1914-17*, 2 Vols., London, 1921; General N. N. Golovin, *The Russian Army and the World War*, New Haven, 1931; the Memoirs of Generals Danilov, Brusilov, Gurko, and Polivanov.

holding in France, Belgium, and Poland, and with German soil nowhere occupied, it would take the appearance of multitudes of perfectly fresh, young American troops, and an endless flow of American supplies, to make it manifest to Hindenburg and Ludendorff that they had indeed lost the war.

If in the West the land was too narrow for the clashing armies so that movement soon ground to a halt in a war of position, on the Eastern Front the land was too wide. Even Russia's millions were thinly dispersed over its many fronts. The armies of Russia and Germany clashed in East Prussia; those of Russia and Austria-Hungary rolled back and forth over Poland and down to the Carpathians; the armies of Russia and Turkey grappled in the Caucasus; and when in 1916 Rumania joined the Allies, the Russian front had to be unhealthily extended deep into the Balkans to save Rumania from extinction.

Only one of these three or four interlocking wars was lost by the Russian armies; the others they won. But because both Western Allies and "Westerner" public in Petersburg had their attention centered on Germany, the defeat in East Prussia outweighed morally the victories over Austria-Hungary and Turkey.

I am not afraid of military reverses [F. V. Rostopchin wrote to Emperor Alexander I when Napoleon attacked in 1812]. Your empire has two powerful defenders in its vastness and it climate. The Emperor of Russia will always be formidable in Moscow, terrible in Kazan, and invincible in Tobolsk.[16]

THE RUSSIAN ARMIES INVADE THE TWENTIETH CENTURY

Nicholas, too, could have been invincible in Tobolsk, had he chosen to wage a defensive war. But the French pressed, with an understandable if not an intelligent selfishness, for the Russian armies to give battle far beyond their frontiers where the peasants in gray uniform were no longer on home ground nor able to feel that they were fighting to defend their native fields. Before his armies were so much as one-third mobilized, the "chivalrous and impressionable Tsar" sent three of them into Germany where the network of German railways was excellent, the railwaymen long trained for troop movements, German military telephone and telegraph apparatus in splendid array, German generals fighting on well-known and drilled-over terrain. East Prussia had been a favorite training

16. M. Florinsky, *Russia, A History and an Interpretation.* New York, 1959, Vol. II, p. 675 n.

ground for summer war games against Russia. Years before, General von Schlieffen had anticipated and prepared for just such an attack.

Without adequate maps, without decent intelligence, without a lateral railway network behind them to concentrate troops where needed, without any transport but the horses of the cossacks and the slogging feet of the infantry, without a network of telephone and telegraph lines or adequate signal equipment or codes, without a proper food or munitions supply system, armed only with the chivalry of the officers, the tenacity of the men, and the superiority of numbers, the Russian armies pressed forward into the chain of Masurian lakes and unfamiliar pine forests of East Prussia.

General Paul Rennenkampf commanded the First Army, north of the Lakes; General Alexander Samsonov the Second, south of them. Another army, the Tenth, moved slowly up with the intention of connecting the first two.

Though they possessed superiority in numbers, they were pitifully inferior in heavy artillery, light artillery, machine guns, supplies, and intelligence. Their officers, less trained for modern warfare than the Germans, had not learned the unchivalrous art of taking cover. Every intended "surprise" blow was telegraphed to the enemy by the inevitable slowness of the buildup and concentration of troops. Either they did not have a proper code or did not have the habits and instruments for employing it; at key moments, when they were planning to spring a trap which might have annihilated the armies opposing them, they revealed their plans by communicating by wireless in clear!

Nevertheless, panic seized the German Eighth Army Commander, General Prittwitz. He called GHQ on the Western Front to report to Moltke that he was abandoning East Prussia to save his army. The harassed Moltke removed Prittwitz, called from his retirement the aging "wooden Titan," Hindenburg, giving him Ludendorff as Chief of Staff. From France, with the lightning speed of the splendid German railways, two additional army corps were shipped to East Prussia, thereby further disrupting the timetable of the Schlieffen Plan.

Military historians do not credit Hindenburg with the moves that reversed the Russian trap, for these were conceived and started by the Chief of Operations, Colonel Hoffmann, before the new Commander arrived. But popular beliefs are another matter. The legend which grew up about the victory of Hindenburg and Ludendorff at this second great battle of Tannenberg [17] was to be fateful for the subsequent history of

17. Tannenberg had left a scar in the German memory, for it was here that in 1410, Polish, Lithuanian, and Russian troops stopped the advance of the Teutonic Knights into Slavic lands, a defeat that the new victory avenged.

Germany, and for the world. In any case, it is not hard to be a superior general when heavy guns (in the fire power ratio of better than four to one), telephones, rail lines,[18] and familiar terrain, are all on your side.

Yet, for a whole week, the battle was in doubt. The Russians outnumbered the German defenders. In hand to hand fighting and night offensives, the Russian soldier was definitely superior. But Zhilinsky, supposed to connect Samsonov and Rennenkampf, was unequal to his task. The Tenth Army, which was to close the gap between the two, was still in the process of formation, and what there was of it could not get past the Masurian Lakes. Tempted by the Fortress of Königsberg (now Kaliningrad), Rennenkampf moved northward, farther and farther away from Samsonov, instead of maintaining contact with him, a move which Zhilinsky encouraged as Chief of Operations. "He need only have closed with us," writes Ludendorff, "and we should have been beaten."

By August 30, part of the Russian force having been fighting for four days without bread, with the gap between the First and Second Armies widening and communication between them non-existent, the audacious plans of Colonel Hoffman bore fruit. Using an excellent lateral railway, most of the Eighth Army was transported with great speed a distance of 130 miles, to pour into the gap, surround Samsonov, and cut his army to pieces. Samsonov shot himself, his last words reportedly being, "The Tsar trusted me." Then, with the same speed, the Eighth Army was shipped back again, 130 miles to the North, where Rennenkampf was still plodding foward toward the Fortress of Königsberg. So poor was Zhilinsky's staff work that Rennenkampf had no inkling of disaster until he perceived that his forces were being encircled and that he was alone. Then he retreated, with delaying counter-offensives, managing to extricate a good part of his army, and, once back in Russia, his lines held. But the "irresistible Russian steamroller" was smashed, the disaster obscuring both the German defeat at the Marne and the simultaneous tremendous Russian victories over Austria. The confident mood of St. Petersburg gave way to alarm, mistrust, division, a search for scapegoats.

"MISCHIEVOUS IMPORTUNITIES" OF THE ALLIES

Even as the grim news reached the capital, French Ambassador Paléologue was making another of his importunate and unceasing calls on Sazonov to send yet more invading troops into Germany. Hitherto the

18. The German railway density per inhabitant was more than twelve times greater than that of European Russia. Everything in Russia had to be transported on an average five times farther. Against Germany's motorized transport and fine roads, the Russians had only cavalry and tracks of dirt and mud.

Foreign Minister had answered each importuning with fresh assurances. Now he grieved, "Samsonov's army is destroyed; that is all I know." Paléologue withdrew in silence. This did not prevent him, as Pares has written, from "renewing his mischievous importunities" within a few days, and, in mid-September, calling on Sazonov for "a new direct offensive against Germany." [19]

The blow was enough to put a less durable nation out of the war. Russia's losses in East Prussia were estimated as 300,000 men, 650 guns, an enormous amount of equipment, including rifles flung away in flight. The shock was the greater because the hope of victory had been high and because not Austria-Hungary, which had started the war, but Germany was the real object of popular hatred.

Tannenberg aroused in the army, both in the general staff and the rank and file, an almost superstitious belief that the German military machine was so superior in equipment and maneuverability as to be unbeatable. What else could men think who were pounded from a distance by big guns and had no adequate artillery to reply and were cut to pieces by sheer weight of metal before the Germans came within fighting distance? The Russians had to oppose rifles to machine guns, until ammunition ran out, then try to take machine-gun nests by bayonet charges. And what were the commanding generals to think when they saw how much swifter and more secretively the Germans could move their armies to block a slowly gathering offensive or take advantage of an opening? After a few such experiences, General Russky told a session of the Council of Ministers in August 1915: "The demands of contemporary military technique are beyond our powers; in any case, we cannot keep up with the Germans." [20]

If to many it seemed that Ivan Ivanovich was always replaceable by another Ivan and the Russian soldier therefore "immortal," it was soon clear that the loss of experienced officers was a serious matter. Major-General Knox, who was with the Russian Army as a British adviser from 1914-17, did not think very highly of its officers above the rank of company commander, but at the war's beginning he found "many excellent officers" up to that rank.[21] These officers of the line, however, out of archaic notions of chivalry, ordered their men to crawl forward while they themselves fought standing. They led with drawn swords in bayonet charges. This inspired confidence, even devotion, in the men, but such

19. Maurice Paléologue, *La Russie des Tsars pendant la Guerre*, Paris, 1922, Vol. I, pp. 104 and 128. Pares, *op. cit.*, p. 205.

20. All accounts of what went on in the Council of Ministers (except where otherwise indicated) are from the notes taken by the Assistant Secretary of the Council, A.N. Yakhontov, published under the title, "Tiazhelye dni," in *Arkhiv Russkoi Revoliutsii*, Vol. XVIII, Berlin, 1926.

21. Knox, *With the Russian Army*, p. 264.

officers did not last long. Even on fronts where Russian arms were victorious, the mortality among the officers was terrifyingly high. Before the war was a year old, virtually the entire middle officers' corps, those close to the soldiers, knowing how to lead them and respected by them, had disappeared.[22] The posts from junior lieutenant to company commander had to be fleshed out again and again with hastily promoted non-coms, green students fresh from school, lawyers, professors, and other recruits from the often devoted but distrusted, distrustful, and latently extremist, intelligentsia. Moreover, the needs of a swiftly expanding army of ten millions could not be met because of the relatively small percentage of the educated classes in Russia. The ignorance and panic shown by young officers when the troops in Petrograd refused to obey orders in late February 1917, the readiness with which some trigger-happy soldiers shot and killed passing officers often unknown to them, the going over to the Duma and the Revolution of a number of officers who personally led their men to the Tauride Palace, are all attributable in great measure to the fact that only uniforms, emblems, and rifles were the same, but the officers' corps had been "renewed" several times over.

Nor was Ivan as immortal as the constant refilling of the ranks by new callups suggested. The trained, experienced soldiers who numbered 1,400,000 before the war began, disciplined, knowing their commanders and their duties, habituated to obey orders, bear hardships, and fight on, soon disappeared, too. "In a year," General Brusilov wrote, "the regular army vanished." New recruits were "disgustingly untrained . . . our army [was] . . . like an ill-trained militia." By the time the war had been going ten months, Russia's armies, the defeated and victorious together, had lost 3,800,000 men.[23]

The Tsar was not unaware of this state of affairs. In his visits to the Stavka he received reports from Grand Duke Nicolai Nikolaevich, the Supreme Commander and spoke of them in his letters to the Empress. As early as November 19, 1914, he wrote:

> . . . again an insufficiency of munitions. In consequence, . . . the brunt of the fighing falls upon the infantry [and] losses at once become colossal. Some of the Corps of the line have become divisions; . . . brigades have shrunk into regiments . . . half [of the reinforcements] have no rifles. . . .[24]

22. The evidence on the disappearance of the officers of the line, derived from Generals Danilov and Knox, is in Pares, *The Fall of the Russian Monarchy*, pp. 210-11.

23. Figures from a personal report of Sir Bernard Pares to the British Government as given to him by the Russian War Ministry. Sir Bernard writes, "I have reason to think that it was an understatement." (*Ibid.*, p. 237.)

24. All quotations from the letters of the Emperor and Empress are respectively from *Letters of the Tsar to the Tsaritsa*, New York, 1929, and *Letters of the Tsaritsa to the Tsar*, London, 1923. In the present work quotations are identified by the date of the letter rather than the page of any given edition.

On June 12, 1915, he wrote that the "Second Category" would have to be called up. This Reserve Militia (*opolchenie*) was made up of men between the ages of 21 and 43, with absolutely no training, all of whom had been previously rejected or exempted. Only twice before, in 1812 and 1854 (the Napoleonic and the Crimean Wars), had the situation been deemed grave enough for this. Companies, regiments, divisions, were now fleshed out with these raw men, with only skeleton forces of experienced soldiers to give some staying power.

On June 23, 1915, Nicholas wrote:

. . . the army at present is only just a trifle stronger than in peace time. It should be, and at the beginning of the war [after the first callup] it was, three times as strong. . . . Of course, I am giving this information only to you. Please do not speak of it, darling.

That Nicholas should feel it necessary to ask his wife not to speak of such confidential things, is a matter we shall have to return to . . .

One thing Nicholas did not seem to sense is that the crack guards regiments, too, on whom his personal defense was supposed to depend, had been hollowed by losses and replacements like all other forces. When he reviewed one or another of the élite guard regiments with boyish enthusiasm, it was always resting far in the rear, spruced up, in holiday mood. As late as October 1916, he was still able to write that Grand Duke Paul "was in high spirits" after seeing "the whole of the Guards." But Sir Alfred Knox, only two days earlier, had written in his diary:

I hear whispers that the Russian infantry has lost heart and that anti-war propaganda is rife in the ranks . . . little wonder that they are downhearted after being driven to the slaughter over the same ground seven times in about a month, and every time taking trenches where their guns could not keep them.[25]

The famous guards had been in those seven assaults to give them backbone and by now were hollowed out and packed with raw men just like the less élite parts of the army. In February 1917 this would give Nicholas one of the most bitter of his surprises.

RUSSIA WINS HER WARS WITH THE NINETEENTH CENTURY

While Germany was being held at the Marne and Russia beaten in East Prussia, on August 23 the Austro-Hungarian Armies, already fully mobilized, flung a million troops into the invasion of Russian Poland. In

25. General Knox, Diary entry for October 28, 1918, *op. cit.*, p. 488.

East Prussia a nineteenth-century army had invaded the twentieth century and been repulsed and cut to pieces. But in Poland two nineteenth-century armies faced each other. If the Austrian army was earlier mobilized and well led by General Conrad, the Russians had good generals too, Plehve, Sievers (both, like Rennenkampf, with German names), Brusilov, Alexeev, Lechitsky, and the Grand Duke Nikolai Nikolaevich, who personally directed overall operations at the later stages of the colossal battle.[26] The Austro-Hungarian Armies were sent reeling back. The Austrians saved their shattered lines by withdrawing from Serbia. The Russians destroyed the renowned Hungarian cavalry, inflicted a quarter of a million casualties, took over 100,000 prisoners including countless officers, vast quantities of materiel. Conrad's offensive ended with his armies resting on the Carpathians, 135 and 150 miles away from their starting points. They had been driven out of Russian and then out of Austrian Poland. Austria had lost most of its officers of the line, something even more serious for Austria than for Russia, since the Austrian officers were seventy-five per cent German-speaking while their troops were multi-lingual and included a majority of Slavs, the officers providing the cement which held the army together. Austria was so badly hurt that she considered suing for a separate peace. Only the hasty dispatch of reinforcements and materiel by Hindenburg stabilized the beaten army. From this time dates the constant need of German support of the Austrian lines, which was to reach extravagant proportions before the war ended with German command of the combined forces.

Galicia, much of whose population was Ukrainian, greeted the Russian armies with torches and flowers. But a regime of crude Russification and persecution of the Ukrainian autonomists or independence adherents and of the Roman Catholic Eastern Rite Uniate Church by emissaries of the Orthodox Church of Russia soon dissipated this enthusiasm.[27]

26. There were no Napoleons in any army in World War I. At the beginning of the war, some generals held their posts in the Russian Army by virtue of birth or because of seniority or because they were favorites of the Tsar. But as the war continued, only those who could win battles or retreat without losing their armies continued at the head of important bodies of men on key fronts. Some of these were of plebeian origin; most had risen to commanding posts by virtue of their achievements. Grand Duke Nikolai Nikolaevich felt so ill-prepared for the post of Supreme Commander that when he was appointed by his cousin, the Tsar, he wept in consternation. Yet he proved a good enough soldier to win the respect and affection of generals and soldiers and to earn high tribute from such of the enemy leaders as Hindenburg and Ludendorff. Physically a giant, he towered head and shoulders above the slight Tsar; morally he was of more decisive character and with a higher regard for public opinion; in a military sense he was irreplaceable. When the Tsar decided to take the post himself in August 1915, the army was de facto without a Supreme Commander.

27. Among those banished from their native Ukrainian Galicia to close police supervision in Russia were the well-known historian Michael Hrushevsky and the Uniate Metropolitan, Count Andrew Szepticki. Nikolai Nikolaevich and the Duma favored a more liberal autonomy policy toward the Ukrainians and a proclamation of an autonomous

By late autumn the Russian offensive came to a stop. But there were now German divisions mingled with the Austrian (poison gas would be used for the first time by the Germans on this front on January 2, 1915). The road transport of the War Department had proved so inefficient that more and more of it had to be taken over as a function of the civilian Red Cross. The lack of officers was already alarming. Only the civilian Red Cross took adequate care of the wounded. More died from disease than from wounds until the Red Cross set up field bakeries. Munition reserves, which had been built up with the idea that the war could not last till Christmas, were already exhausted; batteries that had normally fired some 45,000 rounds a day were now categorically limited to three rounds a day under threat of court martial. New recruits were coming up, but at least a third of them were without rifles now. In many sectors, without training and without arms, they were sent into the second line of offensives with the hope that the men in front of them, when killed or wounded, might provide them with rifles. The officers were officially informed that they could expect no real remedy of the munitions and rifle muddle until March 1915.

General Knox, who pays tribute to the gaiety and bravery of the picturesque Russian troops with their variety of uniforms and nationalities, paints "a picture of mingled muddles and heroism; no patrols, dreadfully futile cross movements, wading through sand or mud, late orders, no telephone, no cipher, no notes of their units taken from the prisoners, enemy officers not questioned, no roads assigned for transport, petrol short; and on the other hand, triumphant good temper as a substitute for order." [28] To add to the confusion, each Russian Army commander was following his own strategy. Ivanov and Alexeev wanted to pursue the beaten Austrians to Vienna, Kornilov was descending into the Hungarian plain, Danilov was in favor of a fresh attack on East Prussia. France absurdly clamored for the almost munitionless horde to march on Berlin, and the War Minister, Sukhomlinov, whether out of lightmindedness or false pride, was telling Joffre that munitions were adequate and that sufficient rifles were expected any day from America.

If we cast up the balance of these first two gigantic engagements on the Eastern Front, we can see that, as so many times in the past, the sorely battered and beaten army that had invaded Germany was able to reform, stand its ground, and face the enemy when on Russian soil while

---

united Poland under a Russian protectorate, but the Court, and particularly the Empress, the conservatives, the Pan Slavists, and the "Union of the Russian People," were against these moves so that Russian attempts to recruit Poles and Ukrainians to active participation on their side were largely paralyzed throughout the war. Stalin repeated the same "Great Russian chauvinist" policies toward Poland and the Austrian Ukraine and general Ukrainian autonomy during and after World War II.

28. Pares, *op. cit.,* p. 210.

the victorious army that had been attacked by the Austrians in Poland had driven the attacker back almost 150 miles and conquered more ground in the East than Germany on the Western Front. The premature offensive in East Prussia, entered into on France's desperate urging, like the counter-offensive in Austrian Poland, had together served the big objective of weakening Germany's Blitzkrieg in France and compelling Hindenburg to begin the conversion of the Austro-Hungarian into a German army by the dispatch of more and more of his own troops.

1916: THE LAST VICTORIOUS OFFENSIVE

The same costly arithmetic whereby Russia began ill-equipped and not yet quite ready offensives in the East whenever her Allies were most sorely pressed in the West was to continue all through the years 1914, 1915, and 1916. In March 1916, when Russia had once more filled up her decimated ranks and the munitions problem was at last largely solved,[29] enough infantry weapons having been produced and imported to arm every soldier and enough shells to supply every gun, a great coordinated offensive was prepared to occur simultaneously on the Eastern and Western Fronts. But the Austrian invasion of Italy, which had entered the war late and ill-prepared, plus the German attack on Verdun, compelled fresh frantic appeals to the Tsar, who once more "chivalrously" ordered a premature and one-sided offensive. In June and July, Brusilov with his green armies[30] and imperfect, if greatly improved, transport, ploughed through the Austrian defenses once more until he again reached the passes of the Carpathians. This time, countless Austrian Slavs, including whole regiments of Czechoslovaks, marched under fire with banners flying

29. As early as February 20, 1916, General Knox wrote, "The rifle situation is definitely improved." By the middle of May he was able to say, "All units at the front possessed their full complement. The number of machine guns had increased to an average of 10 to 12 per 4-battalion regiment. Most of the infantry divisions had now 36 field guns, and there was a reserve of some 8 million of 3 in. shell. Most of the corps had a division of eight 4.8 in. howitzers. A considerable number of trench mortars and hand grenades had been provided." (Pares *op. cit.*, p. 355.) For a detailed study of the munitions problems and the gradual overcoming of the shortage in rifles, bullets, big guns and shells, see General Gurko, *War and Revolution in Russia, 1914-17*, New York, 1919, pp. 118-28. He writes: ". . . it was only in the Spring of 1917, while preparing for the coming [offensive] operations, that the different armies were made happy by being able to reckon on having several tens of thousands of shells for the 6-inch guns, and about 100,000 4.8 inch mortar bombs. . . . By the end of November 1914 the Germans were using a 12-inch gun in field battles, whilst we had nothing heavier than a 6-inch gun till the spring of 1916." (Pp. 127-28.)

30. They came wretchedly trained to the front but the problem of making good soldiers of them was now being solved by giving them thorough training after they arrived.

and drums beating to surrender or to join Russia. By late June, for all the German stiffening, Austria was once more on the edge of catastrophe. Hindenburg and Ludendorff scooped up every division they could spare from in front of Verdun, and the Austrians abandoned their attack on Italy while German artillery on the Eastern Front now became comparable in density of fire power to that on the Western Front. Though Rasputin, who was close to the feelings of the peasants, urged that the attempt to storm over the Carpathians be abandoned, Brusilov attacked again and again, all through August and September, until at last the Tsar, persuaded by Rasputin and the Empress, ordered the slaughter to stop.

The Brusilov offensive in 1916 was the greatest Russian victory of the war. Only the Tsar's refusal to consider a separate peace and the overwhelming presence of German troops prevented Austria from leaving the war officially. In that offensive, the ancient Habsburg Empire died, and in November, grief-stricken, Franz Joseph I died, too. The offensive caused 600,000 casualties, including some 400,000 prisoners, many of them ready to join the Allies. But the Russian armies had lost a million men, dead, wounded, missing, and deserting. Verdun had been relieved and Italy saved, but at what a cost! [31]

Now Rumania, which like Italy had been bargaining ignominiously with both sides for preposterous "imperialist" territorial gains (the small countries and late comers were the great imperialists of the war!) picked what it took to be the winner, compelling Germany to add 250 miles of front to her thin and dwindling lines and sacrifice 60,000 casualties to knock Rumania out of the war while one quarter of all the armies of Russia then in being were drawn into the defense of what was left of the latest ally, whose entry had proved to be not a help but a trap.

THE FRONT HOLDS UNTIL THE TSAR FALLS

Each winter, when other armies could scarcely bear the rigors of the climate, Russia, at the petition of the Allies, had started a fresh offensive. Each offensive, at least until 1916 when the munitions and supply problems and to some extent the military transport problems had been con-

31. In March 1919, Marshal Foch told a *Times* correspondent, "If France was not wiped off the map of Europe, we owe it first of all to Russia." As late as May 30, 1916, the Tsar wrote to the Tsaritsa: "New regiments are being formed now in order to be sent to France and Salonika." On April 8, other Russian troops had arrived "safely and just for Easter," the Tsaritsa wrote in one of her letters on April 9. These Russian troops serving in two brigades of the French Army were given exposed sectors and "badly handled." After the Tsar's fall they mutinied and "artillery fire had to be turned against them." (Baldwin, *World War I,* p. 101.)

quered, involved the cruel arithmetic of substituting overwhelming numbers for materiel.[32] Yet the Front was preparing still another offensive for the late winter and early spring of 1917—at the moment when the Tsar fell. Along with the Tsar discipline fell, too. It was only after the fall of the Tsar that the Russian armies were to prove no longer capable of mounting an offensive as Kerensky and Kornilov were to learn to their sorrow.

True, the army and, still worse, its officers of the line were now almost wholly green, raw men. Desertion was growing, and grumbling along with it. But there were no mutinies on the Front until after the Tsar fell and the Kerensky July offensive was ordered. In the spring of 1917, the first really great mutinies at the Front occurred, not in Russia but in France, mutinies so grave that General Pershing called Woodrow Wilson in code to send over American recruits untrained to hearten the French army, overawe the mutineers, and restore morale. In his military history of World War I, Hanson Baldwin writes:

The French Army mutinied—probably the largest mutinies in a great army in modern history. . . . Camps were placarded with notices declaring the intention of the soldiers to refuse to go back to the trenches. . . . A battalion ordered to the front dispersed in a wood. Soldiers coming home on leave sang the Internationale in the trains and demanded peace. Mutinies occurred in sixteen different Army Corps. . . . A number of young infantrymen marched . . . baa-ing like sheep to indicate that they were being driven like lambs to the slaughter. . . . Pétain . . . told the British that they must shoulder the main burden on the Western Front while the Allies waited for American manpower to help turn the tide.[33]

32. On war losses we can accept the estimates of the military writer, Nikolai Galay, based on all the available documentation. In the *Bulletin of the Institute for the Study of the USSR,* Feb. 1958, p. 23, he writes:

"During the First World War the Russian Army lost 1,650,000 killed, 3,850,000 wounded, 2,410,000 taken prisoner, out of a total of 15.5 million men, to which should be added more than a million deserters and refugees after the February Revolution." Similar figures are to be found in General N. N. Golovin, *Voennye usilya Rossii v mirovoi voine,* Paris, 1939, Vol. I, pp. 125-53. This would mean that the losses in killed, wounded, missing, and prisoners, not counting deserters, was over half of the total number called up.

In World War II, Galay estimates, 28 to 30 million were drafted, and there were 5 million dead and 11.5 million wounded, or well over half, this time not counting either prisoners or deserters. Thus in both wars the proportion of losses was about the same.

The political-military differences between the two wars lay chiefly in the fact that in the First World War the two antagonists were semiautocracies and in the second totalitarian regimes; that in the Second World War the Allies were able to give effective material help in the form of food, ammunition, weapons, tanks and trucks and planes; and the difference between the slack and crumbling autocracy of Nicholas II and the tight and total dictatorship of Stalin and his party machine.

Finally, it should be noted that the Kaiser and his Generals had no scruples against fomenting revolution in Russia but Hitler had ideological obstacles to playing the same game (witness his negative attitude toward Vlasov).

33. Baldwin, *op. cit.,* pp. 100-01. The citation includes some sentences which Baldwin has taken from the *War Memoirs* of Lloyd George.

This was quite different from the act of the raw recruits in Petrograd, refusing to fire on strikers and on women demonstrating against a temporary shortage of bread.

It is well to remember, since it has been so speedily and generally forgotten, that despite shortages and bungling, despite desertions and grumbling, the Russian Fronts held until after the Tsar's government collapsed through actions taking place in the rear. Russia's was the only Allied army that fought on German soil. Though its invasion of Germany was beaten back, its lines held. In two and one-half years it took over 2,700,-000 prisoners and 3,850 big guns. The cruel arithmetic of substituting human waves for materiel did not break the Russian Army then as it did not later under Stalin. Had the Gallipoli campaign been successful (the Turks were within a day of surrender when the English abandoned the siege) or had the Murmansk railway been completed in 1914 instead of the end of 1916, the Allies might have made up for the Russian shortage in materiel as they did in the case of Stalin in the Second World War. But the sickness at the heart of Russia was deeper than the shortage of materiel.

Russia proper was not successfully invaded until after the government collapsed. Alexander I yielded to Napoleon the sacred city of Moscow and scorched the earth in between. Stalin lost all the great industrial regions of European Russia except the two capitals, his armies retreating all the way to the Volga before the German forces lost their punch. But the Germans were not even able to take Riga on the Baltic Coast in World War I until after the fall of the Tsar. It was not a collapse of the front that brought on the fall of Tsarism, but the fall of the Tsar that carried in its train a collapse of the fronts. We must turn to the capital to find the secret of the Tsar's fall.

—January 1965

IV THE TRIPLE POWER: THE ROLE OF THE BARRACKS AND THE STREET *

Historians and political leaders are accustomed to speak of "the dual power" that prevailed in Petrograd during the spring of 1917. On the one hand there was the Provisional Government, generally recognized as the lawful government of Russia until Lenin overthrew it; on the other, the Petrograd Soviet of Workers' and Soldiers' Deputies. The Provisional Government issued out of a provisional committee of the Duma; the Petrograd Soviet was convoked by a self-appointed "Executive Committee," made up of socialist journalists and leaders of socialist parties and factions. Both committees were organized on the same day, February 27 Old Style (March 12 on the Western calendar), and both met in the same building, the Tauride Palace, home of the Duma. The Soviet had no intention of setting up a rival power, merely of protecting and voicing the interests of the popular masses in an uncertain situation. But two days later, the principal actors in the drama became aware of the duality of power when the Soviet issued its "Order No. 1" to the soldiers and sailors of the Petrograd District, bidding them keep control of their arms, elect committees, send deputies to the Soviet, and "execute orders of the military commission of the State Duma only in such cases as do not conflict with the orders and resolutions of the Soviet Workers' and Soldiers' Deputies." [1]

The order was drafted by a semi-Bolshevik lawyer, N. D. Sokolov, aided by soldiers who milled around him as they made suggestions. Then it was ratified by the Executive, published in the Soviet organ *Izvestia*, and reprinted as a leaflet and spread far and wide by the Bolsheviks who

---

* This chapter is based on a talk I delivered in April 1967 at the Harvard Conference on "Fifty Years of Revolutionary Russia." The organizers of the conference, following the usual concept of "dual power," had asked Leonard Schapiro to discuss "The Ideology of the Provisional Government" and Oskar Anweiler to present "The Ideology of the Petrograd Soviet." I was asked to comment on their two papers but instead chose to present a third ideology, that of the Barracks and the Street.

1. For the text in English of Order Number 1, see *Documents of Russian History, 1914-17*, edited by Frank Alfred Golder, New York, 1927, pp. 386-87. For the best account in English of the genesis of Order Number 1, see John P. Boyd, "The Origins of Order No. 1," in *Slavic Studies*, Glasgow, Jan. 1968, pp. 359-72.

saw in it a means of demoralizing the Front, for which it was not intended, as well as the Petrograd Garrison. When officers complained of its effect, new "orders" and proclamations were issued to soften its impact, but the mischief was done. Moreover, it was clear now that there existed a division of power; immediately, both sides began negotiations to insure full support of the Soviet for the Provisional Government.

When Lenin arrived at the Finland Station shortly after midnight on April 3, his first act was a declaration of war on what he himself called in that self-same declaration "the freest government in the world." "We must," he wrote in his notes for the defense of his *April Theses,* "skillfully, carefully, by clearing their minds, lead the proletariat and the poorest peasantry *forward* from the 'dual power' toward the *full power* of the Soviets." And on April 9, his own mind having become clearer, he wrote in *Pravda:*

The most highly remarkable distinguishing feature of our revolution is that it has created a *dyarchy.* . . . Of such a dual power *no one* thought before, nor could any one think of it. In what does this dual power consist? In this, that alongside of the Provisional Government, a government of the *bourgeoisie,* has been built a still weak and embryonic but all the same undoubtedly existing and growing *second government:* the Soviet of workers' and soldiers' deputies. What is the class composition of this second government? The proletariat and the peasantry (dressed in soldiers' uniforms). What is the political character of this government? It is a revolutionary dictatorship, that is a power resting directly on revolutionary seizure, from below, on the direct initiative of the popular masses, *not on a law* passed by a central state power. . . . Inasmuch as these Soviets exist, *inasmuch* as they are a power, we have in Russia a state of the *type* of the Paris Commune. I have emphasized the words, "inasmuch as," for it is only an embryonic power. By direct agreement with the bourgeois Provisional Government and by a series of actual concessions, it has itself *surrendered and is surrendering* its positions to the bourgeoisie.[2]

Lenin called his article "O dvoevlastie" (On the Dual Power), thus maintaining, as did others who followed his lead, that there were two powers in Russia, each with a distinct ideology, each—or so he claimed—representing a different class, each possessing a share of governmental power which the leaders both of the Duma and the Soviet were striving to merge into a single and unitary power vested in the Provisional Government. The Soviet, with its soldier and workingman delegates, enjoyed the greater confidence of the populace of the capital. But the Provisional Government had more of the air and purpose of a government though its mass support depended in large measure upon its reinforcement by the

2. *Lenin,* XXIV, p. 13 and pp. 19-22; in English translation, XXIV, pp. 32-33 and 38-41.

Soviet. This is the generally accepted picture of the dyarchy or dual power.

But actually there existed at that moment in Petrograd a third power, to which, without formulating it clearly in their minds, both the Provisional Government and the Petrograd Soviet appealed and Lenin as well. For brevity we may call that third power the *stikhiia*, the elemental, uncontrollable, perpetually fluctuating force of the barracks and the street.

Here indeed was a real "class" difference. Both the Provisional Government and the Petrograd Soviet were led by intellectuals, men with political and social theories. All the political parties were led by intellectuals. But down in the lower depths, inarticulate, normally sullen and passive but aroused now to sudden acts of impulse and fury, was that *stikhiia* that Lenin had fought since 1902 as the direct opposite of socialist political consciousness.[3]

Nowhere in Europe was there greater hostility toward the educated classes, from which the leadership of both government and soviet were drawn, than there was in the villages of Russia. When the peasants came from the villages to the city to work in the factories, or to loaf in the barracks of Petrograd, they brought this suspicion and hostility with them.

The two leading bodies, the Duma Committee and the Soviet Executive, negotiated with each other and came to agreements on a number of matters. But we must note that the ministers of the Provisional Government continued to act pretty much as their own judgment dictated or as they were moved to act by pressures coming from the street. On the other hand, Soviet decisions, majorities, and attitudes remained fluid, too, changing from day to day in response to the changing moods and day-to-day accidental makeup of that vast mass meeting called the Soviet and the scarcely less fluid and unwieldy Executive Committee. They too felt the pressure and influence of that underlying third power, the *stikhiia*. Now they made attempts to enlist its support, again to placate it, and yet again to restrain and direct its reactions. But always the *stikhiia* made iself felt.

The downfall of Foreign Minister Miliukov is a typical example of how the street asserted itself. To be sure, Lenin and his partisans did their best to stir up and utilize this reaction of the street, but the street acted on impulses of its own, particularly the soldiers from the barracks acted out an obscure feeling that the repudiation of the Foreign Minister and his pledge to carry out prior agreements with Russia's allies

---

3. Lenin began this attack in his first full-length "Leninist" work, *Chto delat?* (What's to be Done?) published in Stuttgart in 1902. Chapter II of that book is called "Stikhinost mass i soznatelnost sotsial-demokpartii" (The Elementalness of the Masses and the Consciousness of the Social Democracy). *Lenin*, Vol. V, pp. 345-367.

would somehow make the continuation of the war by Russia impossible. Most of the major actions of the barracks and the street in 1917 flowed from this same deeply rooted desire to get out of the war now that the apparatus of compulsion and consent, of command, obedience, and discipline had broken down.

THE PROBLEM OF LEGITIMACY

This brings us to the problem of the unexpected and sudden rupture of legitimacy in the midst of total war. Total war is a stern and jealous god that demands of a people automatic, traditional, unquestioning, total obedience. Total war demands, too, an unparalleled effort on the part of society to find or create charismatic leaders and to organize with unprecedented strain and imagination the total mobilization of men, money, materials, and emotions. The last tsar was no charismatic leader, nor was he capable of finding anyone equal to the tasks of total war or willing to entrust power to such a leader had one offered himself. After Nicholas fell, neither a Guchkov nor a Kerensky nor a Tseretelli nor a Martov nor any other of the individuals who made up the complex of the Provisional Government and Soviet, was comparable to a Lloyd George in England or a Clemenceau in France. Thus the continuation of total effort in the war was complicated alike by the rupture of legitimacy, by the lack of charismatic or even adequately dynamic leaders, and by the lack of the will of the people to continue the all-out effort, the strain, the sacrifices, the unquestioning loyalty and obedience that total war requires.

Even in time of peace, it is hard enough to organize a new order after the legitimacy of the old has been ruptured. But during a time of grant of more than ordinary trust and credit by masses of men who were task required superhuman wisdom, a large measure of consensus, and a grant of more than ordinary trust and credit by masses of men who were bewildered and confused by the breakdown of their traditional institutions, traditional leadership, and traditional habits of obedience.

ECLIPSE OF OFFICERS AND INTELLECTUALS

The tsar fell because some soldiers, impulsively and unexpectedly to themselves, disobeyed the command of their officers to fire on a demonstrating crowd. It was fear of punishment for their violation of discipline that frightened the demoralized soldiery, causing them to appeal to other regiments, give up their rifles and seek to lose themselves in the crowds.

And the same fear caused the mutineers to look eagerly for larger justifications and meanings for their first impulsive act.

If order were restored they would be doomed. One of the reasons for the well-aimed, "accidental, stray bullets" that killed young officers and even the high officer on an inspection tour in an automobile with War Minister Guchkov was that the soldiers were frightened but with weapons in their hands. They had violated discipline unexpectedly even to themselves. Fearing punishment, they asked the Duma committee, the Soviet, and the unknown spokesmen of unfamiliar parties to give their mutinous action sanction, legitimation, and guarantees that punishment would not follow. All these things they got in full measure.

After a moment of hesitation and fear, society gave them celebration and glorification. Men who had disobeyed orders learned that they were conquering heroes who had freed the nation from unbearable chains. With adulation came self-confidence, whereupon the problem arose of discipline and control by their frightened and inexperienced officers (most of the officers in these inactive reserves were, like the men, scratched together from the bottom of the barrel). Discipline became an insoluble problem from that moment. Moreover, their desire to avoid transfer to the front was now proclaimed a revolutionary duty, for they were the guardians of the glorious revolution they had wrought.

Their deeds were welcomed by the men who had been conspiring at Court and in the Duma circles, and in the *zemgor* or War Industries councils, to replace Nicholas II by a more active and able tsar with advisers—themselves—deemed better fitted to the demands of total war.

As was the habit of the Russian "public," they thought in terms of analogy with French revolutionary history. Since the French Revolution had begotten victorious armies that swept over Europe and great military leaders such as Carnot and Napoleon, they persuaded themselves that this revolution too would beget invincible armies, victorious generals, and glorious victories. They forgot that France was at peace and prospering when its revolution occurred and that its revolutionary wars did not begin until the third year of revolution, while Russia was in its third year of an exhausting and indecisive struggle that had worn out its human and material resources. The French peasant, as Lewis Namier has reminded us, went to the front to retain the land he had seized, while the Russian peasant in uniform deserted the front to go home and seize his share of the land.[1]

In order to illuminate the moment of anarchy when disobedient soldiers from the demoralized Petrograd reserves brought on the downfall of the tsar, I turn to a close and highly articulate observer, Vladimir Stankevich. His memoirs are particularly revealing on the relationship

1. L. B. Namier, *Avenues of History,* London, 1952, pp. 6-7.

between the Provisional Government, the Soviet, and the *stikhiia*. He writes: [2]

Officially they celebrated, glorified the revolution, cried hurrah to the fighters for freedom, adorned themselves with red ribbons and marched under red banners. . . . Everyone said *we, our* revolution, *our* victory, and *our* freedom. But in their hearts, in solitary talks—they were terrified, trembled, felt themselves prisoners of a hostile elemental force [*stikhiia*] that was moving in some unknown direction. Bourgeois circles of the Duma who essentially had created the atmosphere that called forth the explosion were completely unprepared for such an explosion.

There follows a picture of Rodzianko, "that ponderous nobleman," striving to walk with dignity through the disorderly mob of soldiers filling all the corridors of the Tauride Palace, his face marked with suffering and despair as he went out to address fresh detachments of arriving soldiers as "heroes." "Officially this was supposed to mean that 'the soldiers have come to support the Duma . . . ,' but in fact the Duma was eliminated from the outset."

This is particularly interesting since Stankevich himself was the first officer to lead his own regiment in good order, drums beating and flags flying, to the Duma to offer it support, an event which so moved Chkheidze that he fell on his knees and kissed the banner that Stankevich presented on behalf of the regiment. Clearly, the Chairman of the Soviet (Chkheidze was a leading socialist in both bodies) feared the disorderly soldiery too and devoutly hoped that this first orderly act of an army detachment might be a portent of things to come.

Stankevich looked at the soldiers filling the corridors of the Tauride Palace, and into the dining hall where

all day and all night the soldiers were welcome to eat by turns without paying anything. . . . The soldiers sat concentratedly chewing, not letting their rifles out of their hands, not even speaking to one another, not sharing their impressions, yet herdlike seeming to possess some common feeling, thinking in their own individual fashion each in his own special way, incomprehensible, inaccessible to the understanding.

The officers themselves were demoralized by the sudden turn of events that had broken all rules of order and discipline appropriate to a modern army.

It was not a matter of Orders No. 1 and 2 or any other formal measures. . . . It was the fact that the soldiers, breaking discipline, left the barracks not merely without their officers but even despite their officers, and in many

2. V. B. Stankevich, *Vospominaniia 1914-1919 g.*, Berlin, 1920, pp. 70-71. What follows is from pp. 71-77.

cases against their officers, even killing some of them who tried to fulfill their duty. And now by universal, popular, official acclaim, obligatory for the officers themselves, the soldiers were supposed to have realized by this a great deed of emancipation. If this was indeed a heroic exploit, and if the officers themselves now proclaimed it, then why had they not themselves led the soldiers out onto the streets—for you see that would have been easier and less dangerous for them than for the soldiers. Now after the victory is won, they adhere to the heroic feat. But is that sincere and for how long? You see, during the first moments they were upset, they hid themselves, they changed into civilian clothes. . . . Even though next day all the officers returned. Even though some of the officers came running back and joined us five minutes after the going out of the soldiers, all the same it was the soldiers who led the officers in this, and not the officers the soldiers. And those five minutes opened an impassable abyss cutting off the troops from all the profoundest and most fundamental presuppositions of the old army.

(Actually Stankevich is talking of himself in particular when he speaks of officers who hid themselves for only five minutes. When he heard that his soldiers had left their barracks he began to run toward the barracks, but a junior officer stopped him with the words, "Don't go there; dead officers are lying in the doorway, and soldiers shoot at other officers as they appear." He hid then for a few minutes, but overcame his fear and went to his regimental mess hall. He found only a few soldiers drinking tea, the rest being out in the streets. He began by rallying those he found, and they formed the nucleus for the first march of a disciplined regiment to the Tauride Palace. But his regiment, too, had been out, and he had been away and had hidden himself for some five minutes so that between his reconstituted regiment and the old army there was the same impassable abyss.)

Under what slogans had the soldiers gone out? They had gone out obeying some obscure mysterious voice, then with visible indifference and coldness they afterward permitted to be hung upon them all possible slogans. Who led them when they conquered Petrograd? When they burned the district court? Not a political thought, not a revolutionary slogan, not a conspiracy, and not a mutiny. But an elemental movement that suddenly reduced the whole old regime to ashes with nothing left over: both in the cities and in the provinces, and the police power, the military power, and the power of self-government. Unknown, mysterious, irrational, welling up out of the deepest layer of popular feeling, suddenly the street overflowed with a gray mass, bayonets sparkled, shots rang out, and bullets whistled. It was this mysterious unknown human force that was approached [by the leaders of the government, the Soviet, and the parties] to take control of it. And not being able to formulate objections nor knowing how to resist, the mass began to repeat slogans alien to it and words not its own and permit itself to be inscribed into parties and organizations. Naturally, the least organized and the least demanding of organizations proved the most acceptable to the spirit of this mass. The Soviet, that meeting of half illiterate soldiers, appeared as their leader because it demanded nothing of them, serving only as a façade to cover up a complete anarchy.

LENIN'S SPECULATION WITH THE STIKHIIA

Over against these three forces and vague ideologies, we can from the outset see yet a fourth, that of Lenin's planned speculation with the *stikhiia*, its unrest, uncertainty, inexperience, and vulnerability to plausible, attractive, demagogic slogans. It was precisely the *stikhiia* that he had always deeply detested, as he made clear from 1902 on, and that, after he was in power, he would declare "more terrible than all the Denikins, Kolchaks, and Yudeniches put together." But Lenin, this sworn enemy of the *stikhiia*, saw in it in 1917 the dynamite that might be used to blow up the Provisional Government. His ideology in 1917 was a peculiar admixture of utopian beliefs, ad hoc demagogic slogans to stir up the *stikhiia* against the Provisional Government, and the old Leninist centralist organizational predilections. He planned to use the *stikhiia* as the battering ram to smash his way to power, but in the back of his mind was clearly the determination to use that power according to the formula of 1918 in which he said, "We must organize everything, take everything into our hands."

In the Provisional Government and the Soviet we must note a symmetrical opposite of Lenin's attitude, a planlessness toward the *stikhiia* and toward Lenin and his use of it. This planlessness is dramatized by the naming of the incompetent Tolstoyan, Prince Lvov, to be not only premier (a designation at least justified by the notion that his leadership of the *zemgor*[4] and voluntary war organizations fitted him to run a country at war) but simultaneously Minister of the Interior. To name him Minister of the Interior meant that there would be no administration, and no Department of the Interior. As a matter of fact, he never lifted a finger to set up a new administration and control after the old administration broke down, tore off its uniforms, and went into hiding. But this meant that the *stikhiia*, and Lenin's speculation with it as an explosive force, would go unchecked. Except for an occasional speech to a particular mob or mutinous regiment by some trouble shooter from the Government or the Soviet, there was no administration in Russia and no Ministry of the Interior.

4 *Zemgor,* a contraction from *zemstvo* and *gorod,* standing for the rural and city organizations set up to aid the war effort.

Once in a radio interview I asked Kerensky, "Why did you not suppress the Bolsheviks after they openly declared their determination to wage war on what Lenin himself called 'the freest Government in the world,' and he avowed his determination to overthrow it?" He answered, "What force did I have to suppress them with?" And, indeed, what did he have? But we must ask the further questions: from what ideology did it spring that there was no serious attempt to build up an administrative machine and that a Lvov was appointed to the Ministry of the Interior and then never once asked to report on what he was doing to set up a machinery or order an administration? Moreover, did not Lenin have the benefit of a self-paralyzing belief of other Social Democrats that he was just another slightly more impatient type of Social Democrat? And did Lenin not have powerful protection within the Menshevik camp?

Martov, and not Tseretelli, has always been glorified as the outstanding leader of Menshevism by the Mensheviks in defeat and exile. But it was the Martov "Internationalists" in 1917 that advanced the notion of the overriding solidarity of all socialists, the idea that socialists cannot disarm or suppress any organization calling itself socialist, nor any paramilitary formation calling itself an armed workers' Red Guard. From Martov to Kerensky there ran through the scarcely formulated ideology of both Provisional Government and Soviet the feeling that the only real danger was that of a counterrevolution from the right or a monarchist restoration. This was accompanied by the dangerous, indeed, fatal ideological delusion summed up in the formula *"pas de'ennemi à gauche."*

To be sure, Tseretelli and some of his friends urged the disarming of Lenin's workers' guard. But when they proposed this in the Soviet, Martov in his hoarse voice (he already had cancer of the throat) cried out, V*ersalets!* (Versaillan!) Since his voice was hoarse, the assemblage thought they heard him cry *Merzavets!* (Scoundrel). At this breach of the niceties of debate everybody was more shocked than by his real intention, which was to compare Tseretelli and his associates to the men of Versailles who had disarmed the Commune of Paris in 1871.

The proposal to disarm Lenin's paramilitary formations was voted down, or rather shouted down. No *enemy on the left!* And yet on the left stood anarchists and Bolsheviks and Lenin's impudent gamble on stirring up the *stikhiia* to undermine and destroy the nascent democracy embodied in the Provisional Government, the Soviet, and the forthcoming Constituent Assembly.

The Duma Committee sought to legitimate itself as best it could, but it was self-appointed and lacked true legitimacy. It did not spring from the Duma, nor was it chosen by the Duma, nor did it report to the Duma, but it sought its legitimation precisely where there was none to be found, in the street and the barracks. But by so doing it gave a sort of legitimacy, not to its own existence but to the mutiny and the *stikhiia*. Thereafter, it could urge, plead, admonish, but not govern the turbulence nor build an administration.

Yet there was one sense in which it did lay the foundations for its own temporary legitimacy. This was not through its loyalty to the old government's promises to its allies, nor its attempts to continue the war with a no longer manageable army. These loyalties failed to take into account the new situation and served but to hasten the government's downfall.

The glory of the Provisional Government, as I see it, is the fact that it had the grace to call itself *Provisional*. Thereby it said what few governments arising out of revolution have said: "We do not regard ourselves as a permanent successor government to the one that has fallen. We do not set up our dictatorship. We regard ourselves as the temporary guardians of the power that has been entrusted to us (Alas, it could be asked, *by whom?*). We look upon ourselves as prelegitimate, a prelegitimate government whose chief task is to convoke an assembly representative of the entire people that will write a new constitution for Russia and thereby replace the monarchical hereditary legitimacy that has been ruptured with a new democratic legitimacy that will represent the will of the people of Russia, or the peoples of Russia." Whatever its errors, whatever its sins of omission and commission, this was the Provisional Government's grace and glory. I know that "grace" and "glory" are words bearing a moral connotation, and I use them because in my judgment this is the acid test of a government that arises amid the discontinuities and chaos of revolution, namely that it recognize its provisional and prelegitimate character and acknowledge as its first duty that of bringing into being a new legitimacy based on the consent of the governed, who have made the revolution.

It was the setting of a date for elections to a Constituent Assembly that led Lenin to set a precise date for his coup. The date he chose makes clear his keen sense of the realities of power in the midst of revolution. "Verily, verily," he said twice in his brief letter to the Central Committee on the date for an uprising, "Verily, verily, delay is like unto death." His preciseness in the setting of a date lay in the fact that the coup (it was not really an uprising) had as its function to forestall the consolidation of two potential loci of more legitimate power, to present two institutions with the *fait accompli* that power was already in the hands of his dictatorship and his party. The first institution was the Soviet itself in which he expected to have a pro-Bolshevik majority, but he knew that that majority was only nominal and was assured only by the fact that many of the "deputies" did not really know what he stood for. Had they realized that what he sought was a dictatorship by his party, which meant ultimately by Lenin himself, his majority would have melted away.

The second institution was the Constituent Assembly, which he knew would destroy his chance of taking power if it ever completed its work.

His quarrel with his Central Committee, even with his closest collaborator in the seizure of power, Leon Trotsky, turned on what seemed a hair-splitting difference between the seizure of power on October 24 and the sanctioning of "its own" power by the Soviet scheduled to meet on October 25. Lenin prevailed, so that the symbolic strongpoints were seized by his shock troops on the night of October 24, the night before the new Soviet was to assemble. From the actions of *Vikzhel*, the railwayman's organization, of the other parties, and even of the majority of his first body of People's Commissars, we can deduce that without the *fait accompli*, the new Soviet Congress might have voted for a government of all socialist parties or all Soviet parties but not for the single dictatorship of his party. From the actions of the one-day meeting of the Constituent Assembly before he dispersed it by force of arms, we can deduce that, meeting in freedom, they would indeed have adopted a new Constitution and created a new democratic legitimacy. Thus Lenin's sense of timing was proved right.

And thus was ushered in a period of dictatorship and chronic illegitimacy, a period that has now lasted fifty years. As we examine that revolution and the half century now coming to a close, we must recognize that in fifty years the regime thus founded has shown no signs of engendering a legitimacy. Indeed, it has not even worked out a legitimate mode of determining the succession. The Soviet Government has the trappings of legitimacy: soviets that do not govern; elections in which the people do not choose or elect; parties (that is, parts of society) of which there is only one, and that one moribund and emptied of internal life; a constitution that might well choose as its epigraph: "Paper will put up with anything that is written on it."

Now at the end of a half century, we must recognize that this regime has no intention of creating such a legitimacy. At any rate, at this moment I cannot foresee any organized faction that might arise in the ruling party or oligarchy or in the discontented but unorganized yet overorganized body of the Russian people that might publicly declare its intention of submitting to the judgment of the people of Russia the government's present actions, or its actions of the last fifty years.

Consequently, for me the great ideological divide of 1917 lies between those who accepted, as did both the Provisional Government and the first Soviet, the idea that the government was provisional and prelegitimate and must aim to establish a new democratic legitimacy and those who were determined, following Lenin, to establish a dictatorship.

If this be so, and if this be the crucial nature of the ideological divide, then despite all the fashionable "convergence" theories and "models of an advanced industrial society," we stand about where we might expect: with a dictatorship that does not seek nor possess legitimacy in the sense in which I have defined it, but is ruled by a series of "diminishing dictators," over the ultimate outcome of whose diminution we must puzzle at the present moment.

—November 1967

PART III

Permanent Dictatorship
and the
Problem of Legitimacy

I SOCIETY AND
THE STATE*

The power of the state, measured both by the fields it embraces and the amount it can take for taxes and for war, has increased steadily during the last eight or nine centuries. If we go back to the beginning of that period, we find armies diminutive, unstable, mustered for only forty days, paid out of the private resources of a king who was but the first among his peers. War lacked scope then, since power lacked scope; it could neither impose taxes nor conscript men. Slowly, in the course of centuries, monarchs centralized their domains with plebeian support against aristocratic privilege and aristocratic liberties. Indeed, liberty itself is aristocratic in its origins. When the monarch had so far centralized his realm that he could impose taxes, he could also set up a standing army. Yet "so long as the monarchy lasted," writes Bertrand de Jouvenel in his book, *On Power*, "it never dared attempt the conscription of men." Jouvenel is correct so far as French history is concerned, but in Germany conscription came under a semiautocracy after unification of the German Empire under the King of Prussia, while in Russia the tsars established universal conscription with obligation to serve for twenty-five years without benefit of democracy or a republic. But in his native land from which Jouvenel derives his generalization, it took the great French Revolution that overthrew the monarchy, to complete the latter's task of centralizing France, sweeping away private interests, local jurisdictions and loyalties, nonstate organizations, social authorities, barriers of jealously guarded charter, status or privilege, the whole pluriverse of painfully cultivated medieval forms in favor of the unitary, centralized, modern bureaucratic state.[1] And it took the French revolution with its cry "The Repub-

* This chapter is based on two articles first published in the *American Mercury* in March 1948 and January 1949, entitled respectively "The Individual versus the State" and "The Problem of Power." They represent early attempts on my part to analyze totalitarianism.

1. In retrospect I find this "clean sweep" effect of the French Revolution an exaggeration. Thus, only in the second half of the present decade did France finally abolish the requirement that vegetables must be transported from all regions of France to *les Halles* before they could be reshipped for sale in all the regions of France.

lic is in danger!" to introduce conscription of the manpower and resources of France for the armies of Carnot and Napoleon.

Nor did the monster then cease to grow. At the end of the Napoleonic wars, all the nations of Europe together had a total of three million men under arms. A century later, in World War I, more than five times that many were killed and wounded! World War II involved the total conscription of labor and manpower in most of the nations engaged, and these aimed the total annihilation of all the centers of industry and population of the enemy that could be effectively reached with bombs. The power of the state increases steadily, while, by a coincidence that is more than mere coincidence, the power of men to do mischief to their species continues to increase along with the power to marshal all man's forces for total, all-embracing war.

THE STATE FOR THE PEOPLE
OR THE PEOPLE FOR THE STATE?

When the historian of the next century looks back upon our own, I fancy that it will be with amusement at our excitement over the question of "socialism versus capitalism." All states, he is likely to record, and all societies were moving simultaneously, each according to its own tempo, history and tradition, in the general direction of greater "socialization," greater state intervention in various fields of social life. One state moved ahead with foresight and caution, seeking to carry along what was best in its past and slough off what had been outgrown. Another rushed headlong, arbitrarily, drastically throwing overboard the accumulated heritage of freedoms and restraints imposed by custom and tradition upon power. The past took its own peculiar revenge by reasserting what was worst in it instead of what was best. A third walked backward toward the future, shouting "free enterprise" even as it insured deposits, regulated securities, put floors under farm prices, set up social security systems, TVA's and what-not. (The reader may recognize in these three "types" England, Russia and the United States.)

The chief problem of the twentieth century, the historian of the twenty-first is likely to say, was not "socialism versus capitalism" at all, but whether the state could enter into so many fields and so many aspects of social life become "socialized" or statized without the state's becoming total in the process and without liberty vanishing and democracy perishing. To put it in political terms, the real problem of the twentieth century was limited state or total state, democracy or totalitarianism or, to adapt a familiar theological metaphor, whether the state should exist for the people or the people exist for the state.

For totalitarianism is not a mere epithet as many who use it imagine, but a serious philosophy of government, with a corresponding governmental structure. And democracy is not a mere breeding ground for totalitarianism, as some of its conservative critics assert, but a rival twentieth-century philosophy of government, with a corresponding structure of government.

THE FATE OF VOLUNTARY ASSOCIATIONS

The essence of the total state is not tyranny nor terror but the fact that the state aspires to be "total." Totalitarianism asserts that the state is identical with society and coextensive with it, that all the purposes of the state are identical with the purposes of society and that society can have no purposes that are not state purposes.[2] Therefore it denies autonomy to the individual, his private purposes, his judgment, his conscience, his moral responsibility. By the same token, it denies autonomy, *a fortiori*, to nonstate organizations as against the state: to unions, to clubs, to churches, to parties, to lodges, to foreign policy associations, to chambers of commerce, to Boy Scouts, to Masons. "Under the dictatorship," wrote William Z. Foster in *Towards Soviet America*, "all the capitalist parties—Republican, Democratic, Progessive, Socialist, etc.— will be liquidated, the Communist Party functioning alone as the Party of the toiling masses. Likewise will be dissolved chambers of commerce, employers associations, Rotary Clubs, American Legion, YMCA, Masons, Oddfellows, Elks, Knights of Columbus, etc." And Mr. Foster really meant that "et cetera." Whatever nonstate organizations exist when the total-state dictatorship is formed must either be coordinated into the state apparatus or be charged with being antistate and treasonable, and liquidated. That is what is happening today to the unions, the parties, the churches and associations of every sort in the countries behind the iron curtain.

Having thus secured control of every social organization, the totalitarian party and state seek to penetrate every aspect of life, assume control of every interest, undertake systematic organization of every activity, convert every individual interest and activity and every social interest and activity into a state activity. "The duty of Russian women," the inimitable Vyshinsky told those Canadians who wanted to get their Russian wives out of Russia and into Canada, "is to produce Soviet children, not children *for the Canadian Government*." It is this attempt to penetrate all

2. This is not diminished but reinforced when the state itself is not autonomous but controlled by the single infallible party which penetrates and directs every organization including the state.

organizations and direct all activities, not excluding love and art and music and leisure and dreams, that forces the totalitarian state to become a universal police state.

The essence of democracy is that it regards the state as a servant of society and not its master, that however many functions the state assumes, society still remains enormously more extensive than the state, and the state, however expanded, still remains but one of the organizations and one of the instruments of society. The party struggle, which so repels many of democracy's critics, is a symptomatic test of democracy. As long as there is freedom to organize parties, to propose rival men and rival measures, as long as there is a conflict of interests, organizations, lobbies, pressure groups, each seeking to influence the state and enforce its will in one or another particular, so long there is no total state. As long as there is free trade in ideas, clash of opinions, freedom of opposition, freedom of criticism, freedom of press, so long can we know that the expanding state has not coordinated and reduced to transmission belts the various organizations meant to lead a life independent of it, and even to influence and to make pressure on it. As long as there are occupations and activities that are autonomous and independent of party and state dictation, the state is not all-embracing. This is so simple that it might seem a tautology. Yet this simple formulation is the heart of the matter.

What constitutes democracy in the Anglo-American sense of the word (the French Roussellian conception is quite different) is: (1) the existence of a society that is wider than the sphere of action of the state; (2) the setting of definite limitations upon the powers of the state (our Bill of Rights characteristically begins: "Congress shall make no law respecting . . ."); (3) the existence of recourse within the state itself against arbitrary acts of officials (*habeas corpus*, rules on search and seizure, on due process of law, on punishment for false arrest);[3] (4) the presence

---

3. These safeguards and freedoms have even been extended to Communists and Nazi Bundists, who seek to use them in order to abolish those very freedoms once they have won power. A wise democracy that believes in its own freedoms will not grant absolute freedom to those who conspire to abolish freedom. Yet it is necessary to safeguard democracy by ways worthy of democracy, by ways that will not themselves be destructive of it. Hence, we have properly granted to Communist and Nazi fifth columnists, as we have to racketeers and waterfront killers, the protection of the Fifth Amendment; a stubborn judge has rightly compelled the FBI to produce its secret papers on Judith Coplon and subject its informers to cross-examination or give up the case against her; "due process" has been applied to the administrative power of the State Department over the issuance of passports and the right of our citizens to travel abroad. The problem here, as with all complex conflicts of interests, of rights and of laws, is to find the sometimes razor-thin line where democracy is better safeguarded by curbs on those who would destroy it or better safeguarded by extending even to those who would destroy its safeguards which are essential to its own health. One of these difficult meeting places, as Justice Holmes has pointed out, depends upon the magnitude of the threat ("clear and present danger"). Another, as Sidney Hook has aptly put it, is the dividing line between heresy

of opposition as a right, and even as a fundamental and constructive element of government, with the consequent presence of the spirit of discussion and compromise, of give and take and of accountability to the electorate, which is the essence of parliamentarism; (5) the right of the people to turn out the government of which they disapprove.

That is not all, but will suffice to make clear the differences between the total-state dictatorship and the limited democratic state, even under the difficult conditions of modern war and expanding statehood.

DANGERS FOR DEMOCRACY IN OUR TIME OF TROUBLES

If the reader had picked himself a century to get born into, he could hardly have picked a more exciting one. If you have reached the "middle years," it has been your fate to live through two world wars and to be in fear of a third, to have witnessed a startling revolution and counterrevolution in Russia and others no less startling in Germany, Italy, Spain, China, and many other lands. You have been through three, perhaps four, world-wide depressions, you have watched the richest country in the world go into the most dizzying of all economic tailspins, and you are holding your breath at this moment while you wonder whether the "cold war" presages a new global hurricane.

The private individual (an extremely recent and precarious invention) is quite dwarfed and overwhelmed by the all-embracing character of total wars and totalitarian governments, by the elephantiasis of the machine, the megalopolitan swelling of urban life, the nine to twelve zeros at the end of the statistics of gain and loss, taxation and expenditure, life and death.

Is the individual, then, a mere momentary caprice of history, soon to be dissolved in the new flood of gigantism and corporatism? Can freedom and democracy (two other late and precariously rooted sprouts) survive for long in a jungle world of further total wars? Will private possession, free enterprise, freedom of movement and occupation, and freedom of organization, continue to flourish under the twin spreading shadows of giant monopoly and state enterprise? How shall that anonymous hero of

---

and conspiracy ("heresy, yes; conspiracy, no"). Democracy in health and in peril involves a moving equilibrium of conflicting forces in which complacency gives way to alerted sense of danger, sense of danger begets exaggerated administrative or legislative action, the courts curb the excesses, and so on. Latterly, it seems to me, our courts have been so zealous concerning the rights of criminals that they have somewhat neglected the rights of society to be protected from crime. Underlying these fluctuations are the ebb and flow of public opinion which, in a healthy democracy, can be trusted in the long run to keep an even course.

democracy, the sovereign voter, decide on the wisdom of the various items in a multi-billion-dollar budget? [4]

In the nineteenth century things were lively enough, but at least they happened with some regularity of pattern; the century had some time to come to terms with events and formulate their meaning into systems of theoretical generalization. But things in the twentieth century are happening so fast and are so unprecedented in magnitude and nature that the explanations limp behind the speeding events and soon lose sight of them. Since our century has no theories adequate to cope with this historical novelty, we turn to the clashing creeds of the eighteenth and nineteenth centuries, anxiously re-examining them for new combinations of their elements and guides to a new orientation for a new time. In England, for example, the Labour party is trying to match pieces out of John Locke and John Stuart Mill with pieces out of Karl Marx, William Morris, and "Jesus the Carpenter," with results that are still uncertain but are bound to prove surprising and instructive. In Russia they are compounding bits of Marx and Lenin with generous portions of Nicholas I and Genghis Khan, with results that have already proved terrifying. In all lands there is a frantic taking of stock in the midst of a five-alarm fire, a reconsideration of the basic elements in the combinations: individual-society-state; liberty-equality; planning-security-freedom; private initiative-public enterprise; tradition-change or, if you prefer, evolution-revolution.

In our stocktaking, in the comparative evaluation of individual institutions, we dare not lose sight of the ultimate danger, the danger of a total state totally identified with society rather than the state as an element of society. In totalitarianism, all the possible aims and purposes of society, or any part of it, are identified with the aims and purposes of the state and taken entirely, without a residual remainder, under state control, regulation, and direction. Actually it is an organization of a new type still calling itself, out of old habit, a party or the party, that claims to regulate and control and determine everything. It works through the totalitarian state as its principal "transmission belt" and through it denies autonomous existence, autonomous aims, and autonomous activities to all nonstate organizations, and autonomy of action, feeling, thought, or conscience to the individual. Where unions, parties, churches, clubs, lodges, discussion groups, and schools exist, they must either be absorbed

---

4. The first draft of the Budget for 1969 calls for one hundred and eighty-six billion dollars (actually $186,100,000,000) but there is a general expectation that the actual expenditure will be higher. When I published a draft of this article in *The American Mercury* in January 1948, the budget was $39 billion. I have lived long enough to remember the front-page headline in the New York *Journal:* "America Has Its First Billion-Dollar Budget." I saw that headline only a little over a half century ago, America was still at peace, but defense spending was shooting up. The year was 1914.

("coordinated") [5] or crushed by the one-party state. When they have been coordinated, they cease to be organs of their members and become so many additional organs of the state and party. Hence the thing called a "party" is no longer a party, and the thing called a "union" is no longer a union. Indeed, contrary to the general impression, the total state is not really a one-party state; it is a no-party or nonparty state. For "party" implies part, or faction: an autonomous organization of autonomous individuals formed to influence the state or gain temporary control of its activities, not an organization of the state to control social life. Where there is only one "party," all party life ceases, just as, if there were only one "sex," all sex life would cease.

On the other hand, even where there are two or more genuine parties they must in a democracy share a large degree of consensus and basic views in common, or the party struggle may take on exacerbated forms which can threaten the foundations of democracy: riots in the chamber of deputies, street fighting, disruption by force of rival campaign meetings, smashing of presses, burning of party headquarters, paramilitary partisan auxiliary formations, gross misuse of power by the party in power to perpetuate its rule, and so on. Democracy requires for its healthy functioning the presence of democratic habits and traditions, a live will to freedom on the part of the majority, a public opinion which sets "civilized" and "honorable" limits on party strife, a readiness of those in power to recognize the right of the opposition and a readiness on the part of the opposition to cooperate with as well as criticize the party in power and to recognize the latter's right to rule until it is properly turned out. Without this general consensus and healthy tradition, without these limitations imposed by society both on the state and on party contests, party strife itself may but prove the prelude to civil war and the demise of the substance and even the forms of democracy. Such things cannot be safeguarded merely by a written constitution but lie in the "spirit of the laws," in the tradition or "constitution" of a people. They are historically evolved over a period of time but can perish or weaken in a single moment of crisis. It is in this deep sense that "eternal vigilance is the price of liberty" and love of country above love of party. The real problem of the young republics of Asia and the unstable republics of Latin America is that they have installed the institutions of democracy without yet having developed the underlying tradition, the climate of opinion, the sense of the need of limitations on one's self, one's party,

---

5. "Coordinated" is a feeble and inadequately expressive translation of Hitler's *gleichgeschaltet*. In Part V, below, dealing with the absorption of their various fields of culture by the party-state machine, I have used the expression, "the *conditioning* of culture." Actually, the rulers of the new Russia employ Lenin's word, *partiinost*, also untranslatable since the very concept does not exist in our language. It is sometimes inadequately translated as "partyness" or "party spirit."

and the state. To a lesser extent this, too, is the problem posed by a demagogue or by a moment of popular hysteria or irresponsible opposition in the older democracies—or by the new storm-troopers on campuses.

THE EXPROPRIATION OF THE HUMAN SPIRIT

The would-be totalitarian party-state is the overshadowing phenomenon of the mid-twentieth century. Fascism, nazism, communism—Mussolini, Hitler, Stalin—these are the new isms and the new men of power who hold or have held in their hands the fate of millions. With Hitler and Mussolini gone it is estimated that at this moment there are 200 million people in the Soviet Union and a total of perhaps 800 million [6] in the vast Soviet empire under the power of a totalitarian and absolute state, under a totalitarian and absolute ruler.

Frequently, the front page of *Pravda* has carried this slogan: *Interesy gosudarstva vyshe vsego:* "The interests of the state are above all else." Here is the essence of totalitarianism described by an official organ of the world's most powerful totalist state, the Union of Socialist Soviet Republics. Literally, this means not only that every citizen owes his country a natural loyalty, but that in all things, at all times, and in all ways he must make the interests of the state, as dictated by an omnipotent party and leader, his own.

In a deeper sense it means that totalitarianism is actually attempting to reshape the very nature of man and society. Its doctrine claims that men have no end in life but to serve the party and the state. As such it must aim at destroying all philosophies and doctrines that would limit the rights of the state. There can be *nothing* beyond its control. There can be no institutions with the right to remain independent, to have an autonomy and a validity of their own. There can be no room, no scope for the individual, his judgment, his conscience, his private purposes, hopes and dreams, his love for those who are close to him, his personal dignity. The party-state is determined to own everything, not only material things but men themselves—to own them body and soul.

This means that the party and its state must wage constant and unending war upon the entire population because the spirit of man is more complicated than any institution he has contrived and it is *not* in man's nature to submit himself without a residue to any man-made institution.

In the one-party state's war against its own people, these are the weapons: mass propaganda, terror, isolation, indoctrination, total or-

6. This estimate was made before either Tito or Mao had broken with the Kremlin or Czechoslovakia been invaded by Big Brother and four "brother countries."

ganization, and total regulation. These means are something new in history. In fact they could only exist in an era of advanced technology where the state can reach with loudspeaker, newspaper, telephone, police wagon, tank and plane all the far corners and most secret places of its domain. It is that monster which Herzen prophetically foretold when he wrote:

If all our progress should continue [as it has in the past] to be accomplished only through the government, we should be giving the world a hitherto unheard of example of autocratic rule armed with everything that freedom has discovered; servility and force supported by everything that science has invented. This would be something in the nature of Genghis Khan with the telegraph, the steamship, the railroad, with Carnot and Monge in the general staff, with Minié weapons and Congreve rockets, under the domination of Batu Khan.

Genghis Khan with the telegraph—today the telephone, the wireless, the loudspeaker on every square and in every public place. *With the steamship and railroad*—today the airplane and the sputnik. *With the Minié ball and the Congreve rocket*—today the atom bomb, hydrogen bomb, the rocket, and the missile that will reach not only the target over the hill or in the stratosphere, but orbit the earth or reach Venus and the moon. *Servility and force armed with everything that has been engendered in the matrix of intellectual freedom and supported by everything that science has invented.* Is this not the nineteenth-century prophet's foreboding of the nature of totalitarianism?

As we have already noted, whenever the total state takes over, one of its first objectives is to infiltrate, gain control of, or destroy all nonstate organizations: political parties, trade unions, churches, clubs—the whole network of independent organizations that men form for themselves in free societies. In the totalitarian state the political party must be reduced to a state party. The churches must either be changed into state churches or crushed. The trade unions, formerly precious instruments of the workingmen, owned and controlled by them and used by them to defend themselves against the employer, must be changed into instruments of the state, itself the employer, and used by the state to speed them up and chain them down. In short every nonstate organization is either converted into an instrumentality of the state or else destroyed.

Hitler's word for this process was *Gleichschaltung* (coordination). Stalin's phrase—the term originated with Lenin—was "transmission belt." He more than once declared that, in the Soviet Union, party, trade unions, clubs, and organizations of all kinds were transmission belts, instruments of command and control, by means of which the leaders *transmitted* their will to the masses. Where organizations did not lend themselves to use as transmission belts, they were immediately charged with high treason and liquidated. This explains the plague of purges that afflicted each satellite as it was subjugated. And it explains, too, why the accusations were so wild and false. The state first decides to destroy an organization, then arrests and sentences its leaders and loyal followers, then finds a crime to fit the punishment.

Thus, in a full-blown totalitarian state, the mass organs calling themselves clubs, parties, unions, etc., are agencies of the party, the police, and the state. As such they serve a double or a triple purpose. They are not only propaganda agencies constantly reminding their members of the omnipotence and omniscience of the leader, constantly marshaling them into all the current campaigns and interpreting the currently accepted Communist dogmas, but also instruments of command, control levers, regulating the citizens' activities in such a way that the immediate aims of the party and the state may be carried out. They leave the individual atomized yet herded into organizations, with neither privacy nor the right to form organizations of his own.

The totalitarian state has been ably described in a single sentence by Benito Mussolini. His motto was: "All through the state, all for the state, nothing against the state, and nothing outside the state." But Mussolini would be the first to admit that Joseph Stalin did a more able and thorough job in realizing this dream.[7]

The Soviet state has existed longer, is more total, the power of Stalin and his successors more absolute, the purges bloodier and more sweeping and more continuous, the concentration camps larger and more "useful" than anything Mussolini dreamed of or Hitler introduced. Only in his

---

7. On the third anniversary of his seizure of power, October 28, 1925, Mussolini said: "La nostra formula è questa: Tutto nello Stato, niente al di fuori dello Stato, nulla contro lo Stato." (Address in the Teatro della Scala.) In the fourteenth volume of the *Enciclopedia Italiana* (1932) Mussolini himself summed up "La Dotrina del Fascismo." Though some of its formulations and then the article itself disappeared from later editions, this authoritative statement has been reprinted many times and translated into many languages. It is here that Mussolini first introduced the term, "totalitarianism." A few quotes are worth remembering in the history of political thought: "The fascist system stresses the importance of the State and recognizes the individual only insofar as his interests coincide with those of the State. . . . The Fascist conception of the State is all-embracing; outside of it no human or spiritual values may exist, much less have any value. . . . No individuals or groups, political parties, associations, economic unions, social classes are to exist apart from the State. . . . A party wielding totalitarian rule over a nation is a new departure in history. . . . For Fascism the State is absolute, individuals and groups are admissible insofar as they act in accordance with the State. . . . The State is not only the present, it is also the past and above all the future. . . . The Fascist State lays claim to rule in the economic field no less than in others; it makes its action felt throughout the length and breadth of the country by means of its corporate, social, and educational institutions." I have used the English translation by E. Cope from the Third Edition of *Benito Mussolini: The Doctrine of Fascism*, published in Florence, Italy. Its official character is attested by the fact that on April 24, 1940, a copy of this edition was donated to the Hoover Library by the Italian Ministry of Popular Culture.

crematoria built during World War II did Hitler's imagination exceed the deeds of Stalin.

Indeed, as Hannah Arendt has pointed out (in her *Origins of Totalitarianism*), only a truly great and populous country can afford the expenditure of human lives necessary to terrorize and atomize on the scale proper to totalitarianism. Mussolini's regime counted its assassinations. Hitler tormented the Jews but did not dream of murdering Jews or Slavs until he thought he had all the population of Europe at his feet to draw on for manpower. The would-be fascists of certain prewar Balkan or Baltic countries, of Spain or Latin America, had to content themselves with old-fashioned military and personal dictatorships, with mere trimmings of police and paramilitary terror when they came to power, because they did not have Stalin's hundreds of millions to work with and millions of lives to spend in order to atomize and terrorize all the rest. Communist China, on the other hand, taking power in a land that has so longed watched millions die in famine, and having at its disposal one-quarter of the human race, has already officially reported purging and putting into concentration camps more millions in a few years than the bolsheviks did in their entire first decade.

—March 1948—January 1949

II LENIN,
THE ARCHITECT OF
TWENTIETH-CENTURY
TOTALITARIANISM*

There is one thing on which virtually all who have written on Lenin, whether historians, biographers, disciples or opponents, are agreed: had he failed to get back to Russia from Switzerland during the fateful year 1917, there would have been no Bolshevik seizure of power, no October Revolution, no one-party dictatorship, no world Communist movement. And today we would be living in a vastly different world.

Lenin had to make his bid for power during that brief interval when there was no universally recognized legitimate government, and power, so to speak, lay in the streets. "It was as easy," Lenin would say later, "as lifting up a feather." On March 15, 1917, the Tsar abdicated, rupturing the old monarchist hereditary legitimacy. On January 18, 1918, the Constituent Assembly was to convene to write a new constitution for Russia. If Lenin had not been in a position to disperse that assembly by force of arms, it could have created a new democratic legitimacy. Between the fall of the Tsar in the spring and Lenin's *coup d'état* in the fall, power was held by a government of uncertain legitimacy, named partly by the old Duma, partly by the new Soviets. Unlike Lenin's permanent dictatorship, it had the grace to call itself "provisional," that is, to regard itself as a prelegitimate government whose chief task was to carry on until a Constituent Assembly could create a new democratic legitimacy.

Between those two dates, Lenin had somehow to get to Russia through the lines of his country's wartime enemy, had to conquer his party, infuse into it his will to power, his sense of timing, his awareness of those time limits, had to get arms for his little band of followers, had to sow sufficient confusion by skillful demagogic slogans to paralyze the armed forces of the capital which might be used against his *coup d' état*. Of the actual armed seizure of power the chief organizer was Leon Trotsky as Chairman of the Petrograd Soviet and the Military Revolutionary Committee. But the party that seized power was Lenin's party, the sense of timing and

* This chapter is condensed from four articles published between 1965 and 1968 (see note at the end of this essay).

awareness of the precarious time limits were Lenin's, the will to seize power his will, the demagogic slogans, the day-by-day tactics, the confidence that it could be done, access to the funds needed to flood the country with leaflets, newspapers for soldiers and for peasants, and journals of every description, were all Lenin's.

Leon Trotsky in his three-volume *History of the Russian Revolution* sought to prove that the October Revolution was "inevitable" and both the weakness of Nicholas II and the strength of Lenin "inevitable links" in that chain of historical inevitability. But in his Diary for the year 1935, published after his death, Trotsky wrote:

Had I not been in Petersburg in 1917, the October Revolution would still have taken place—on the condition that Lenin was present. . . . If neither Lenin nor I had been present in Petersburg, there would have been no October Revolution. . . . If Lenin had not been in Petersburg, I doubt if I could have managed to overcome the resistance of the Bolshevik leaders . . . but granted the presence of Lenin, the October Revolution would have been victorious.[1]

The possibility that Lenin might not have gotten to the Russian capital in time was a real one. In 1907, for example, fleeing from Finland where the Russian police, or so Lenin thought, were looking for him, he hired two guides to conduct him at night over the ice to an island port of call of a steamer for Stockholm. The guides were drunk, the ice thin; somewhere in the darkness it began to crack and shift under his feet. "What a silly way to die," he thought.

Again in 1914, the World War caught him vacationing in an enemy country, in the Carpathian Mountains of Austrian Poland. Normally, he would have been interned as an alien enemy for the duration of the war and could not have reached Russia until a full year after the date on which the bid for power had to be made. The local peasants had watched with suspicion this bald-headed foreigner climbing the mountain tops, "surveying the terrain," making notes in a little notebook. The local constable who arrested the "spy" found mysterious cryptograms (agricultural statistics) in its pages. His wife heard peasant women in front of his jail debating whether Lenin should be lynched or merely have his eyes put out if the authorities released him. In this wild corner of the Carpathians, who would know of his fate? his internment? his lynching? And what would happen if this self-proclaimed defeatist should fall into the hands of the Russian armies advancing on Przemysl, Cracow, Nowy Targ, and Poronino, where he was vacationing?

But Austrian and Austro-Polish Social-Democratic Deputies, Victor Adler, the party's leader, Diamant, Daszinski, Marek, Dr. Dlyssky, class

1. Leon Trotsky, *Diary in Exile,* 1935, Cambridge, 1958, p. 146.

enemies all by Lenin's simple schema, men whom he would denounce more ferociously on the morrow than he had the day before, intervened on his behalf with the Austrian government. It did not occur to them not to help out a fellow socialist in trouble. Besides, they were moved by another consideration. "Ulyanov was an enemy of Russian Tsarism," Dr. Adler told the Minister of the Interior, "when Your Excellency was its friend. He is its enemy now. He will be Tsarism's enemy when Your Excellency may again have become its friend . . ."

"In the opinion of Dr. Adler," the Minister of the Interior reported to the Austrian Chancellor, "under present circumstances, Ulyanov may render great services." Hence Lenin, his wife, his chief lieutenant, Zinoviev, and the latter's wife were given safe-conducts to cross through the enemies' lines into neutral Switzerland. From Switzerland Lenin was able to continue his war on the Tsar and his own government.

"This is one of two occasions," [2] Lenin's follower Karpinsky wrote in his *Memories of Lenin*, "in which our enemies helped Lenin. Just try to imagine what turn the fate of the Russian Revolution would have taken if Lenin had been interned and had gotten back to Russia, not on April 3, 1917 but only in the autumn of 1918." Try to imagine, indeed, for April 3, 1917, when Lenin arrived at the Finland Station in Petrograd and forced through his reluctant party his famous April Theses was one of those fateful days that marked a turning point in history. Without the help of the Austrian government and the German General Staff, there would have been no November 7th, or, as the old Russian calendar has it, no October Revolution.

THE SELFLESS EGOIST

What kind of man, then, was this great man of the first quarter of our century, or, as Sidney Hook writes in his *Hero in History*, this "event-making man"?

When I first wrote of Lenin as a "selfless egoist" editors and proof-readers wanted me to choose between the two contradictory terms. But his selflessness has been stressed by virtually all who have written of him. We never catch him glancing in the mirror of history. His work contains almost no autobiographical touches or expressions of personal feeling. He lived simply and austerely. He sought neither the perquisites and privileges nor the cult of admiration that so often go with the absolute power he achieved.

---

2. The other case was that of the "sealed train" through "enemy" Germany in which the German General Staff arranged for Lenin to cross their country to arrive in Petrograd in April 1917.

This selflessness, however, was only the outer shell. At the core of his spirit was an unquestioning belief in himself and the least of his views or prescriptions, an absolute certitude that he was the best, indeed the only true master of an infallible science called Marxism. For his own eyes he wrote, "Out of every hundred Bolsheviks, seventy are fools, twenty-nine rogues, and only one a real socialist." And again, "After a half century, not a single Marxist has understood Marx." Obviously, the one who could write such a judgment in his *Philosophical Notebooks* recognized one exception: himself.

He was certain of his rightness in every controversy, large and small. Indeed, given his temperament, there were no "small" controversies. He tended to make the rejection of his viewpoint on any theoretical, tactical, or organizational matter a pundonor, a splitting point. To the secretary of his faction he wrote in 1904: "For God's sake, don't trust the Mensheviks nor the Central Committee but unconditionally carry out everywhere and most resolutely, splits, splits, and splits." The Mensheviks who were not to be trusted were supposedly his comrades while the Central Committee was his own handpicked Central Committee, but since it had set itself against his splitting mania, it too was to be split. The Russian word he used, *raskol*, means both a split and a heretical sect. Both meanings are applicable, for Lenin was an inveterate splitter and a fanatical sectarian who saw heresy in every difference of opinion. Whatever the difference of the moment, he was sure that just that difference divided the saved from the damned.

From his quarrelsome belief in himself followed the conviction that he must have absolute authority and power in whatever sphere he happened to be working: power in the *troika*, or three-man team, with which he was accustomed to give a collective appearance to his decisions, power in any Editorial Board of which he formed part, power in the Central Committee, the faction, the party, power in Russia, and in the international Communist movement. Any organization he could not control he was ready to split. Again and again he withdrew with a mere handful, but always he gave his split-off fragment some large-sounding name like "The Party" or the Bolsheviks (Majorityites), for wherever two or three were gathered together with Lenin, there was Bolshevism, there the majority of true revolutionaries, there the Party.

At a Party Court of Honor where he was put on trial for slandering his own comrades during the electoral campaign of 1906, Lenin coolly admitted that he had chosen "obnoxious terms calculated to evoke hatred, aversion, contempt . . . calculated not to convince but to break up the ranks of the opponent, not to correct the opponent's mistake but to destroy him, to wipe this organization off the face of the earth." His excuse? He had taken it for granted that a difference on how to nominate candidates for Duma Deputy would become a "splitting point." Since he expected a split, that meant war, and in war one acted as if one were at war. "And I shall always act in that way whenever a split occurs . . . in the event of the development of a split, I shall always conduct a war of extermination." When Lenin said extermination he meant it. When the occasion arose, it must be said that he was faithful to his pledge.

Lenin was thus the organizer of his own faction and party. He was its self-chosen leader, he personally selected his own lieutenants in high places and low, he was its commander-in-chief exacting from his followers the discipline of an army. He defined and redefined its doctrines and its tactics. He instilled into it his own total rejection of all existing institutions. He was its will and its intellect. I would be tempted to say its heart as well, were he not by grave and serious conviction opposed to all sentimental considerations, all emotions save the emotion of class hatred, all general moral rules applying to the treatment of one's fellow man merely because he is human. To the Young Communist League he would say in 1920:

Our morality is completely subordinated to the interests of the class struggle. . . . For Communists, morality consists entirely of compact united discipline and conscious mass struggle against the exploiters. We do not believe in a timeless morality and we expose all fairy tales about such a morality.[3]

This ruthlessness and cynicism were partly natural to Lenin, partly the result of a blueprint he had devised for himself in accord with what he thought a revolutionist should be like. It was this amorality that made it possible for him to arrange the counterfeiting of Russian rubles and direct holdups by his followers to obtain funds for his action, though public opinion was shocked and a congress of his party had expressly forbidden such acts. This it was that made it possible for him to use such unscrupulous lieutenants as Victor Taratuta, Joseph Stalin, and Roman Malinovsky and defend them against exposure. This it was that made it possible for him to use the funds and physical aid made available to him by the German General Staff from 1915 to 1918, so long as the source was properly disguised.[4]

---

3. Address to the Young Communist League, October 2, 1920.

4. The scope of the present analysis prevents the documentation of these matters. On aid from the German government and General Staff, see George Katkov, "German Foreign Office Documents on Financial Support to the Bolsheviks in 1917," *International Affairs,* London, April 1956, pp. 181-89; Werner Hahlweg, *Lenins Rückkehr nach Russland,* 1917, Leiden, 1957; Z. A. B. Zeman, *Germany and the Revolution in Russia, 1915-1918,* Oxford, 1958. On the revolutionary holdups, see the chapter "Arms and the Man," in the writer's *Three Who Made a Revolution.* On Lenin's blueprint for his own spirit, see my "Leninism," in *Marxism in the Modern World,* edited by Milorad M. Drachkovitch, Stanford, California, 1965, pp. 51-54.

PARTY, STATE, AND PROLETARIAT

Though Lenin sincerely regarded himself as an orthodox Marxist, his Marxism was authoritarian quotational Marxism. For every controversy, wrote Krupskaya, "Ilyich consulted Marx." He ran through the vast, ambiguous, orphic many-sided writings of Marx, looking for a quotation to use as a club. When he found one made to his order, he used it again and again as if every *ipse dixit* of the founder were proof positive and sufficient. But when he saw a quotation that contradicted him, he over-looked it or forced it out of his consciousness.

Moreover, in his Marxism, as he himself proudly noted, there was a strong admixture of Jacobinism and of the extreme terrorist, centralist, conspiratorial tradition of Tkachev, Bakunin, Zaichnevsky, and Nechayev.

When the average socialist leader spoke of class struggle, he thought of the organization and education of the entire working class, of a struggle for universal suffrage, labor legislation, social security, the formation and legalization of unions and a party of labor, of the attempt to win general social support for labor's needs and demands, or of a simple nationalization of all major industries. Social revolution was either a figurative term for an accumulation of such changes and reforms until "quantity was trans-formed into quality," or a fundamental transformation of the political, economic, and social structure of society by a ruling socialist or labor party through a series of democratically adopted legislative acts after it had won power by democratic means. Force, if it were to be used at all in democratic societies, Marx and Engels held in their last years, was to be kept in reserve against the possibility that a ruling minority might enforce its dictatorship or attempt to hold onto power by force against the generally expressed will of the majority.

But when Lenin said class war, he meant war. It would, of course, be a war for the good of humanity, but for the good of humanity, a good part of humanity would have to be dealt with according to the rules of war. Even on fellow socialists, when they differed with him, he waged "a war of extermination."

When we get power [Lenin wrote in 1916] we will establish a dictatorship of the proletariat, although all evolution moves toward the elimination of rule by force of one part of society over another. Dictatorship is the rule of a part of society over the whole of society, and, moreover, a rule basing itself directly on force.

This he wrote in 1916 when he was but dreaming of his possible dic-tatorship. But on December 5, 1919, after he had been dictator in fact for two years, he wrote: "Dictatorship is a harsh, heavy, and even bloody word." And on October 10, 1920, near the end of the third year of his rule, he bade advocates of democracy remember:

The scientific concept of dictatorship means neither more nor less than unlimited power, resting directly on force, not limited by anything, not restricted by any laws, nor any absolute rules. Nothing else but that.

This formulation is beautiful in its pedantic clarity, for the first giant step in the establishment of a totalitarian power is the destruction of all the restraints that limit power, the restraints of religion, morality, tradition, institutions, constitutions, and laws, that may place any restrictions upon the atomization of a people. The history of all totalitarian regimes has proved the rightness of Lenin's "scientific definition." If one adds to that Lenin's total rejection of the existing world and his conviction that he was the infallible interpreter of an infallible doctrine that told him what mankind should be like, to what blueprint it must be made to conform, and what "History" wants man to do; and further the ambition expressed by Lenin in the summer of 1918, "We must organize everything, take everything into our hands," we have a fair definition of totalitarianism.

This ambition to organize everything tidily, accurately, and totally was actually inherent in Lenin's doctrine from the start. We have only to read attentively his outburst against the first and chief of the cardinal sins in his Decalogue: *stikhiinost* (elementalness, spontaneity, initiative from below). To him it was the opposite of *soznatelnost* (consciousness, the instruction or direction that comes from above from the "vanguard" or "center"). In his first characteristic credo of 1902, he declared war on *stikhiinost*. In early 1918, when he was already in power, he pronounced the elemental, uncontrollable spontaneity of the "million-tentacled hydra" of the "petty bourgeois" peasantry and the workers affected by them to be "the main enemy." And in 1922 and 1923, after he had been four years in power and was discovering that the great "machine refuses to obey the driver's hand," he reiterated the denunciation, adding the grim corollary: 'Petty bourgeois spontaneity is more terrible than all the Denikins, Kolchaks, and Yudeniches put together."

The same dictatorial regime applied inside his party. Before the party had ever been formed, at the "unification" Congress called by the six editors of *Iskra* in 1903, Lenin split away from the other five (from the fifth after a few months of temporizing) because they disagreed with him on the definition of a party member. The definition he offered for article one of the bylaws was intended to be more restrictive and give more control of the party center over each member. When it was voted down, he flew into one of the uncontrollable rages for which he was known, then posted guards to exclude the other heretical *Iskra* editors from the "*Iskra* caucus" he called to decide what to do next. This was the real point of departure for the ultimate formation of two Social-Democratic Parties, Bolshevik and Menshevik, instead of one.

In his notes for the debate, he wrote: "*There are no rights* in party membership—RESPONSIBILITY." When one of the delegates spoke in liturgical language of the projected Central Committee that it would be a "Spirit omnipresent and one," Lenin wrote in his notes and cried out from his seat, "*Ne dukh, a kulak!*" ("Not spirit, but fist!") Even before there was such a thing as a Central Committee, Lenin had written (in 1902):

The committee should lead all aspects of the local movement and direct all local institutions, forces and resources. . . . Discussion of all party questions, of course, will also take place in the local circles, but the deciding of all general questions of the local movement should be done only by the committee. The independence of local groups would be permitted only in questions of the technique of transmitting and distributing. The composition of the local groups should be determined by the committee which designates delegates to such and such a district and entrusts these delegates with setting up the district group, all the members of which must in turn be confirmed in their positions by the committee. The district group is a local branch of the committee that receives its powers only from the latter.

Other socialist intellectuals might dream of the day when Russia would be free enough for workingmen to organize freely, select their officials and determine their program. Not so Lenin. To him this was not Marxism but treason to Marxism:

The task of the bourgeois politician [he wrote] is to "assist the economic struggle of the proletariat." The task of the Socialist movement is to make the economic struggle assist the Socialist movement. . . .

Thus, at the outset, Lenin found his answer to the question whether the workers exist for the party or the party for the workers. And thus did he lay the theoretical foundation for the dictatorship of the leader over the Center, of the Center over the local branches, and of the party machine of the "vanguard of the proletariat" over the working class itself. The machine was a general staff issuing commands, not a representative delegate body selected by and receiving instructions from the proletariat.

Marx might insist that in the long run the working class in the course of its struggles would found its own party, elaborate its own consciousness, develop its own wide, inclusive organization ("Every step of a real movement is more important than a dozen programs."), but Lenin invented for this view a completely new language of reprobation, derision, and condemnation: "opportunism in the organization question"; "*khvostism*" ("tailism," dragging at the tail of the proletariat instead of dragging it forward); "cringing before spontaneity"; "slavish kowtowing to the backwardness of the masses"; "demagogic flattery of the working class"; "bourgeois trade unionism," and many related deviations or heresies.

Thus, to his distrust of the court and the gentry natural in a revolutionist, his distrust of the "bourgeoisie" and the liberals understandable perhaps in a socialist, and his distrust of the peasantry as property-minded because they wanted to possess the land on which they toiled, Lenin alone among socialists added an openly expressed distrust of the working class and even of the lower ranks and local organs of his own party.

There had not been, there was not, [he wrote] nor could there be Social-Democratic consciousness in the workingmen. This can be brought to them only from the outside. . . . Left to their own resources, the working class is capable of working out only a trade union consciousness [i.e., a mere concern with better wages and working conditions, a "petty bourgeois" concern with the market price of their labor under capitalism]. . . . The *spontaneous* development of the workers movement leads precisely to its subordination to bourgeois ideology. . . . Trade unionism means precisely the ideological enslavement of the workers to the bourgeoisie. . . . Therefore, the question: What is to be done to bring to the workers political knowledge? cannot be answered by "go to the workers." . . . The Social Democrats must *go into all classes of the population* . . . send in *all directions* the detachments of its army . . . direct all manifestations of this all-sided struggle to be able "to dictate a positive program of action" alike to rebellious students, to dissatisfied *zemstvo* figures [i.e., liberal gentry], discontented members of the dissenting religious sects, indignant schoolteachers, and so on.[5]

Thus, what Lenin was aiming at in 1917 was a dictatorship, not only of his self-constituted and self-appointed "vanguard of the proletariat" over the working class but a dictatorship over the entire population "dictating a positive program to every class of society."

That "dictate" was never with him a mere figure of speech Lenin made clear when he was still one of the six editors of *Iskra*. To the other five he sent a memorandum explaining that "we should show every kindness to the peasantry" but "not yield an inch" in "our maximum program." "If the peasants do not accept socialism when the dictatorship comes, we shall say to them: 'It's no use wasting words when you have got to use force.' " On the margin of this memorandum Vera Zasulich wrote, "Upon millions of people? Just you try!" When he came to power, that is just what he tried.

5. For sources, context and analysis of these formulae, see the writer's "A Party of a New Type," in *The Comintern: Historical Highlights*, edited by Milorad M. Drachkovitch and Branko Lazich, New York, 1966.

LENIN'S IDEA OF THE CLASS WAR

As we have seen, the operative word in what Lenin called the class war was not class but war. This involved not merely an acceptance of terror and a loving concern with the idea of its application but also a pedantic elaboration of terroristic methods that distinguished him from other socialist leaders.

In 1901, he wrote in the Marxist theoretical journal, *Zarya*, an apostrophe to lynch law: "Trial by the street breathes a living spirit into the bureaucratic formalism that pervades our government institutions."

In 1905, he did not hurry back to Russia while Tsarism was reeling, as did Martov, Leon Trotsky, and Rosa Luxemburg, but he showered his followers with detailed and bloody instructions from afar. In January 1905, he wrote his "Plan of the Battle of Saint Petersburg": "Revolution is war. . . . The workers will arm themselves. . . . Each will strain with all his might to get himself a gun, or at least a revolver."

Subtly he recalled the cry of Zaichnevsky:

"To the Axe!"
No, with axes you won't be able to do anything against sabres. With an axe you can't get to him; perhaps with a knife, but that is even less. No, what we need is revolvers . . . still better, guns.

In a call for a Congress of his party, he suggested as the order of business:

Organization, relation to the periphery, uprising, arming of the workers—setting up workshops for making dynamite.

Workshops for making dynamite on the order of business of a socialist Congress—who but Lenin could write that? and his draft "Resolution on Armed Uprising" said:

The Congress resolves . . . that by preparation of the uprising it understands not only the preparation of weapons and creation of groups, etc., but also the accumulation of experience by means of . . . individual armed attacks on the police and the army . . . on prisons, government institutions, etc.

For these armed groups he exceeded himself in the ardor of his incitements and the detailed pedantry of his instructions:

The bomb is a necessary part of the equipment for arming the people. . . . Bombs can be prepared everywhere and in all places. . . . In this, frenzied energy is needed, and yet more energy. With consternation, by God, with consternation, I see that there has been talk of bombs for more than a half year, and not a single bomb has been made. . . .

In his "Tasks of the Detachments of the Revolutionary Army," written at the moment when the Tsar was promising a constitution and large sections of the opposition were calling off their activities to see what the promise meant, Lenin instructed his revolutionary detachments to "engage in actions on their own and assume leadership over mobs." They must:

arm themselves as best they can (guns, revolvers, bombs, knives, brass knuckles, cudgels, rags soaked in kerosene to start fires, rope or rope ladders, spades for erecting barricades, barbed wire, tacks against cavalry, etc., and so forth). . . . Select leaders or officers, work out signals . . . cries, whistles, passwords, signs to know each other in darkness or in tumult. . . . Attack a policeman or cossack who has gotten separated and take away his weapons. . . . Climb on roofs or upper floors to shower stones on troops, boiling water, etc. [Always there was that etc. for fear that they would do nothing without his instructions, and perhaps he had forgotten something.]

He gave directions for securing the help of friendly officers, for procuring explosives, learning the layout of prisons, police stations, ministries, arms deposits, banks, instructions for employment of the aged, the weak, women, and children.

These directives, and the train of thought they bespoke, are unique in the history of modern socialism. The ruthlessness of Nechayev, the romantic exaltation of criminals and barricades by Bakunin, the call of Zaichnevsky to the axe, are mere violent posturing in comparison.

Up to August 1914, the overwhelming majority in every socialist party and of Russian workingmen and revolutionary intellectuals rejected both Lenin's view of dictatorship over the working class and other classes, his methods of organization, and his prescriptions for waging the class war. They were outraged by his quarrelsome splitting, his bank holdups, his money counterfeiting. Had they understood more fully what he was saying and believed he meant it literally, they would have been still more outraged. These methods isolated him and reduced his following to a little band of "rockhards"—a word he loved to echo—of men who admired him for his ruthlessness and cynicism, plus men in key posts, who, as it turned out when the police files were opened, were agents of the police. These agents included the man in charge of procuring bank note paper and explosives for holdups and planning the passing of counterfeit bills, Zhitomirsky; the man who led his Duma faction and his union activities and attended his most secret conferences, Roman Malinovsky; two editors of *Pravda* privy to the names of all workingmen who sent in money or articles or acted as distributors; the founder of a Bolshevik paper in Moscow; and other key "men of confidence." Small wonder that Lenin's underground organizations were constantly being broken up, and that every lieutenant who was sent by Lenin from Austrian Poland to reorganize his shattered forces was arrested shortly after crossing the frontier.

WAR WAS LENIN'S OPPORTUNITY

But in August 1914 began the terrible years—four long years of a frozen war of position, brutalizing years in which statesmen and generals treated their male citizens as so much human materiel to be expended without stint or calculation in the pursuit of undefinable and unattainable objectives. Men learned to accept as commonplace the mud and blood of the trenches and the ruthless logic of mutual extermination. They learned to master their fear of death and their revulsion against inflicting it. They developed a monstrous indifference to suffering, their own as well as that of others. Universal military discipline made Lenin's vision of military discipline in his party and public life seem less alien. Total war, which saw in entire nations a total enemy, made Lenin's idea of exterminating entire "hostile classes" less shocking. Universal war so brutalized European man that, as Reinhold Niebuhr wrote, "It became possible to beguile men into fresh brutalities by the fury of their resentment against brutality." Now that all things were being subjected to the arbitrament of bullet and bayonet, why not war and peace and the "system" that was declared to have made the sterile carnage possible and, according to Lenin, "inevitable." (It would take Lenin's disciples fifty years and an awareness of the atomic stalemate before they would grudgingly admit that universal war might not be inevitable).

"Since it was a time of horrors," Raymond Aron would write in retrospect, "at least violence might have peace as it objective." If Lenin still rejected peace in favor of prolonging war until it could be transformed into a universal civil war,[6] this fine point of distinction was now less noticeable, for was he not "rejecting" the imperialist war and declaring war on "the system that begot it"?

6. Actually, when Lenin got back to what he pronounced "the freest country in the world in wartime" and sought to overthrow its new freedoms, for the first time in his life he found himself face to face with mass meetings of real peasants and workingmen in uniform. Then he found it convenient to urge peace and not prolongation of the war, and limited his slogans to suggestions of fraternizing in the trenches, grounding arms, turning arms on your own officers, desertion of the imperialist war to seize land in one's native village. The transforming of the imperialist war into universal civil war proved so impractical for the seizure and holding of power that within two months of his *coup d'état* he was threatening to "appeal to the sailors of Kronstadt" against his own Central Committee if they continued to vote for "revolutionary war" in place of a separate peace with Germany.

Thus, war was Lenin's opportunity, since it made his fantastic prescriptions on military discipline and class war seem less unnatural. For, before there could come the reign of what Churchill would one day call "the bloody-minded professors of the Kremlin," there had first to be the bloody mess of Flanders Field, in which, as England's wartime leader, Lloyd George, himself would write, "Nothing could stop Haig's compulsion to send thousands and thousands to their death against the enemy's guns in the bovine and brutal game of attrition."

THE BEGINNINGS OF TOTAL POWER

The completeness of Lenin's belief in himself was matched by the completeness of his distrust of everybody else, from the proletariat to his own lieutenants, local bodies, and rank and file. Once in power he tried to define and prescribe everything, give detailed orders and write detailed decrees and instructions on everything, check upon everything's execution. His correspondence is filled with such detailed prescriptions and reports.

Uncomfortable as always in the presence of spontaneity, complexity, ambiguity, partial truths, shadings, pluralism, openness, the not-yet-known, the imperfectly known, or the unknowable, Lenin treated all questions of government and human conduct as if they had only one right answer, one simple, definite solution. The striking exception was his retreat in 1921 from the complete nationalization of everything down to the last bit of wool out of which a housewife might otherwise have knitted a sock or sweater, the last typewriter, scrap of paper, and inkwell, and the last exchange of rural grain for city-made hammers or nails, an impossible procedure partly brought on by the exigencies of civil war and partly by the primitive and credulous nature of Lenin's original "Marxist" dogmas. The retreat gave Russia Lenin's "New Economic Policy," or NEP, from which Stalin was to return to all-out nationalization.

Apart from this, Lenin's answer to whatever failures and irrationalities arose from his fantastic blueprint and his excessive centralization and control was yet more control and yet more administrative machinery.

A "terrible simplifier" in his remedies, he tended to cut through any complexity or muddle with the simplest of remedies: *arrest!* Set up another overseer committee to oversee the remiss or defective one, and "arrest a few scoundrels as an example."

A perpetual conspirator himself, before he came to power one of his weapons of confusion and demagogy was to bombard the Provisional Government with demands for the arrest of the "wealthy conspirators," the "ten capitalist ministers," and a stipulated number of bankers, manufacturers, and millionaires.

When the Provisional Government, simultaneously attacked by Lenin from the "left" and Kornilov from the "right," guiding itself by the false maxim *pas d'ennemi à gauche*, armed the Bolsheviks along with the other socialists and democrats against Kornilov, Lenin privately told his followers, "We will support Kerensky as the rope does the hanged man." But publicly he "supported" Kerensky with the demand, "Arrest Miliukov, arrest Rodzianko." In the "Threatening Catastrophe and How to Combat It," written a little over a month before he seized power, Lenin demanded "the abolition of commercial secrets [Is there any country with more secrets today than the totalitarian regime he founded?] and the firing squad for hiding anything."

But it was after he took power in the state that was "to begin at once to wither away" that his imagination ran riot. On November 18, 1917, he called upon the people of Petrograd and Moscow to show initiative by "arresting and handing over to revolutionary tribunals" all those guilty of "damage, slowing up, undermining production . . . concealment of supplies . . . any sort of resistance to the great cause of peace," to the policies of "land to the peasants" and "workers" control of production and distribution." Every man his own judge!

Then he proposed that every man be his own executioner, too, provided only that he was one of the mob and not one of the "scoundrels, loafers, rich." The instruction came in a draft article entitled, with unconscious irony, "How To Organize Competition." Each commune, each village, each town, should show "initiative and inventiveness" in devising ways of "cleansing the Russian land of all noxious insects, scoundrel fleas, bedbug rich, and so forth and so forth.

"In one place they will put into prison a dozen rich men, a dozen scoundrels, a half-dozen workers who shirk on the job. . . . In another place they will set them to cleaning outside toilets. In a third they will give them yellow tickets [as identity cards] after a term in prison . . . so that the entire people . . . will act as the overseers of them as harmful people (wreckers). In a fourth they will shoot on the spot one out of every ten guilty of sloth . . . the more varied, the better . . . for only practice can work out the best measures and means of struggle."

Clearly, Lenin was being unjust to himself when he wrote: "We will suppress the resistance of the possessing classes by the methods they used," since "other means have not been invented." In the speech in which he thus belittled his own inventiveness, he invented the term "enemies of the people" for an entire political party, the Kadets, and outlawed them and their elected Deputies to the Constituent Assembly.

In three weeks he had invented the Extraordinary Commission (*Cheka*) along with the experimental "shooting of one in ten."

On January 27, 1918, he demanded that the entire working class join the terror. Workers who did not want to join in the hunt against "speculators" must be "forced to . . . under threat of the deprivation of their bread cards." Every factory and every regiment must pitch in to set up "several thousand raiding parties of ten to fifteen people each." "Regiments and workshops that do not accurately set up the required number of detachments [the word accurately is typical of this pedant of terror] will be deprived of bread cards and subject to revolutionary measures of persuasion and punishment. . . . Speculators caught with the goods . . . will be shot on the spot by the detachments. The same punishment for the members of the detachments convicted of bad faith."

As a socialist, Lenin had voted for the resolution of the parties of the Second International in favor of abolishing the death penalty for any crime. No one dreamed then that in the twentieth century the death penalty would be restored for theft, crimes against property, or "speculation."

But Lenin was furious with his lieutenants for abolishing the death penalty in October 1917. Even before the Civil War began—a war provoked largely by such arbitrary acts as are here described, by Lenin's insistence on one-party rule and the outlawing of other parties, and by his dispersal by force of the Constituent Assembly when he found that the Russian people in their first (and last) free election had not given him a majority—he had restored the death penalty and was calling for "shooting on the spot." "As long as we do not apply terror—shooting on the spot—" Lenin told the representatives of organizations for procuring food on January 14, 1918, "we won't get anywhere." When the Civil War ended, the death penalty was abolished (on January 17, 1920) but restored in May of the same year. The first Criminal Code of the RSFSR provided the death penalty for seventy crimes. With ebbs and flows, the regime Lenin set up, returning now to "Leninist norms," has once more restored the death penalty for the various types of "aggravated speculation," theft, forgery, and crimes against the one real property, state-owned property.

Ce n'est que le provisoire qui dure. Lenin did not intend this "accurate" application of terror to chaos to be more than temporary. But there is an embarrassment of riches in Lenin's subsequent writings and speeches in the same vein. Let us skip to the Eleventh Congress, held during the gentler age of the NEP, in April 1922, the fourth and last year of his rule, when Lenin was talking of the problem of "purchasing canned goods in a cultured manner." Then he said: "One must think of this elementary culture, one must approach a subject thoughtfully. If the business is not settled in the course of a few minutes on the telephone, collect the documents and say: 'If you start any of your red tape, I shall put you in prison.'"

To take power, Lenin had flattered the proletariat and promised them "workers' control." But in power, he told them: "Just because the revolution has begun, that does not mean that the people have turned into saints." Far from it. Workers' control and ownership became "counter-revolutionary syndicalism." One of the primary duties of the "proletarian power" was "to resist the inevitable petty-bourgeois waverings of the proletarian masses," to combat the "demoralization" that war, and the party's own war against the Provisional Government, had introduced into the masses. "Only by an extraordinary, difficult, prolonged, stubborn road can we overcome this demoralization and conquer those elements who are augmenting it by regarding revolution as a means of getting rid of their own shackles by getting out of it as much as they can."

This is not the place to decide whether and to what extent Marx is responsible for his unique disciple. Here it is enough to say that Lenin's idea of the relation of class to party and Marx's can only be reconciled to each other intellectually—or rather, verbally—by four acts of Leninist *legerdemain*, four feats of semantic juggling, four fundamental deceptions achieved by four arbitrary acts of redefinition.

The first is the confounding of the proletariat with the people. The second is the confounding of the party with the proletariat. The third is the confounding of the party machine (Central Committee, Politburo, Presidium, Orgburo, Secretariat, Apparat) with the party. The fourth is the confounding of the *Vozhd* or Leader, with the Central Committee and the Apparat. Though Stalin and Khrushchev are entitled to credit for their further "creative development" of these four inventions, all four are creations of Lenin.

This man, who regarded himself as the most orthodox of orthodox Marxists, the only one to have understood Marx in fifty years, could rightly claim that he was building a "party of a new type"—a party Marx and Engels would have been astonished to contemplate. It was not only new in type; it was unique and exclusive. For while there might be other parties claiming to be socialist, there was room in society for only one party which claimed to be the vanguard of the working class and of all other discontented classes and which, once in power, would appoint itself the vanguard of the "ruling class," in whose name it would rule over all classes, not excluding the proletariat. For then, with the aid of exclusive and dictatorial power, at long last it could compel the working class to accept its revolutionary leadership, its doctrine and its consciousness.

Lenin is indeed unique in his conceiving and begetting his machine, in systematizing and developing his doctrine, and then—and this alone gives him his great historical importance—when power lay fragmented and in the streets, in suddenly perceiving that this was his opportunity, casting all doctrine and scruple behind him, seizing power and atomizing Russian society under his ruthless and completely self-confident dictatorship. "The point of the uprising is the seizure of power: after that we will see what we can do with it." And after that, the main point was to hold power, to make whatever changes in doctrine, to undertake whatever acts of concession, persuasion and terror seemed necessary, to hold on to power and to "organize everything." This was the heart of his mystery. And this made what might otherwise have been one more page in the book on which are inscribed the names of Blanqui, Bakunin, Nechayev, and Tkachev, into the story of a truly great man in history, a man who changed the world into which he was born beyond all recognition.

—October 1967

III THE DURABILITY OF DESPOTISM IN THE SOVIET SYSTEM*

At every turn the historian encounters the unpredictable, contingency, historical accident, biological accident intruding itself into history, as when the death of a history-making person brings a change of direction, changes of mood, emergence of new situations, sudden leaps that seem to turn an accretion of little events into a big one, complicated interaction of multiple determinants on the production of every event, the unintended consequences of intended actions.

Still, history is not so open that any event is conjecturally just as likely as any other. As in the flux of things we note continuing structures, as in biology we note heredity as well as variation and mutation, so in history there is an interrelation between continuity and change.

Though all lands go through a history, and all orders and institutions are subject to continuous modification and ultimate transformation, there are some social orders or systems that are more markedly dynamic, more open, more mutable, even self-transforming, while others exhibit marked staying powers, their main outlines continuing to be discernibly the same through the most varied vicissitudes.

Though it may be difficult to determine except in retrospect just when a system can be said to change in ways so fundamental as to signify a transformation of the system, still it is possible and necessary to distinguish between self-conserving and self-transforming systems, between relatively open and relatively closed societies, between changes so clearly of a secondary order that they may be designated *within-system changes*

---

* In June 1957 a conference was held at St. Antony's College, Oxford, under the joint sponsorship of the University and the Congress for Cultural Freedom on "Changes in Russia since Stalin's Death." I was invited to participate, but when I informed the sponsors that I was more concerned with the continuities than with the changes, I was invited to present a paper on the opening day and provocatively entitled it "The Durability of Despotism in the Soviet System." I was the blank of target practice for a week, but three days after the conference adjourned, Khrushchev expelled Malenkov, Molotov, and Kaganovich. Most of the other papers were then withdrawn, and Oxford decided against publishing, returning to me the copyright. It was then published in *Commentary, Encounter,* in various symposia on the Soviet Union during the course of the year 1957, as well as in two issues of *The Russian Review.* It is probably the most frequently anthologized of my essays. It forms the basis of the present chapter.

and those so clearly fundamental that they involve *changes in the system* or basic societal structure. That this distinction may be hard to make in practice, that there may be gradations and borderline cases and sudden surprises, does not relieve us of this obligation. Merely to reiterate endlessly that all things change, without attempting to make such distinctions, is to stand helpless before history-in-the-making, helpless to evaluate and helpless to react.

If we look at the Roman Empire, let us say from the time of Julius Caesar to the time of Julian the Apostate, or from Augustus to Romulus Augustulus, through its many vicissitudes and changes, we can nevertheless perceive that for three or four centuries the Roman Empire continued in a meaningful and determinable sense to be the Roman Empire. In similar fashion we can easily select a good half millennium of continuity in the Byzantine Empire. Or, if we take one of the most dynamic regions, Western Europe, in one of its more dynamic periods, we can note that monarchical absolutism had a continuity of several centuries. This is the more interesting because monarchical absolutism, though it was one of the more stable and monopolistically exclusive power systems of the modern Western World, was a *multicentered system* in which the monarch was checked and limited by his need of support from groups, corporations, and interests that were organized separately and independently of the power center; the castled, armed, and propertied nobility; the church with its spiritual authority; the burghers of the wealthy, fortified towns.

It is the presence of these independent centers of corporate organization that makes Western monarchical absolutism an exception among the centralized, long-lasting power systems. It was these limiting forces, organized independently of the central power, that managed to exact the charters and constitutions, the right to determine size and length of service of armed levies, size and purpose of monetary contributions, thus ultimately transforming the absolute monarchy into the limited, constitutional monarchy of modern times. And it is from our experience in the milieu of this exceptional evolution that we derive many of our unconscious preconceptions as to the inevitability, sweep and comparative ease of change. To correct our one-sided view it is necessary to compare the characteristics of multicentered Western absolutism with other more "complete" and "perfected" forms of single-centered power and despotism.[1]

1. This comparison is a central part of Karl A. Wittfogel's *Oriental Despotism: A Comparative Study of Total Power*, Yale, 1957. His attention is centered on the countries in which "the state became stronger than society" because of the need to undertake vast irrigation and flood control works by corvée organization of tht entire population, with the consequent assumption of enormous managerial functions. But his study is full of insights into modern, industry-based totalitarianism highly suggestive for the purposes of our inquiry and the theme of the present chapter.

THE MUSCOVITE AUTOCRACY

In the *samoderzhavie* of Muscovy we find a more truly single-centered power structure, stronger, more completely centralized, more monopolistic, more despotic, more unyielding in its rigid institutional framework than was the absolutism of Western Europe. The tsar early managed to subvert the independent boyars and substituted for them a state-service nobility. The crown possessed enormous crown lands and state serfs. Bondage, both to the state and to the state-service nobility, was a state-ordained and state-instituted bondage, adjusted to the purposes of the recruiting sergeant and the tax-gatherer. When in the nineteenth century the emancipation came, it came as a state decreed "revolution from above" (Alexander's own words for it) and carried with it state supervision and the decreeing of collective responsibility to the state of the village *mir*.

To this universal state service and state bondage, we must add the features of Caesaro-papism, signifying a tsar- and state-dominated church in place of an independent one. In addition there was the administrative-military nature of the Russian towns, which checked the rise of an independent burgher class with independent corporate organization. Industrialization, too, came with state initiative and an enormous preponderance of state ownership and management. From Peter I to Nicholas II there were two centuries of state-ordained and fostered industrialization, with continuing powerful state-owned and state-managed basic industry, mining, metallurgy, munitions, railroad construction, and ownership, and some state commercial monopolies, all crowned with a huge and predominant state banking and credit system.

The rudiments of a more multicentered life were just beginning to develop in this powerful single-center organized society when World War I caused the managerial state to add to its concerns the total mobilization of men, money, materials, transport, industry, for history's first total war. The "model" country in this new form of state enterprise was wartime Germany. The system of total management by the state for total war has been variously, but not very intelligibly, termed "state capitalism" and "state socialism." In any case, Lenin was quick to welcome this development as the "final transition form." In it, as in the heritage from the tsarist managerial autocratic state itself, he found much to build on in making his own transition to the new totalitarianism.

A "SOCIALIST" RESTORATION OF AUTOCRACY

From Ivan the Terrible on, for a period of four centuries, "the state had been stronger than society" and had been ruled from a single power center as a military, bureaucratic, managerial state. Amidst the most varied vicissitudes, including a time of troubles, wars, conquests, invasions, peasant insurrections, palace revolutions, and revolutions from above, the powerful framework endured. Weakenings, even power vacuums, were followed by swift "restoration" of its basic outlines. When the strains of total war, of a magnitude beyond its inflexible powers to organize, finally caused its collapse, there came a brief interlude of the loosening of the bonds. Then Lenin, even as he revolutionized, likewise "restored" much of the four-century-old heritage. Indeed, it was this "socialist restoration of autocracy" which Plekhanov had warned against as early as the 1880s as a danger inherent in, or at least potential to Russia, whenever the longed-for revolution should come. He warned the impatient Populists that unless all the bonds were first loosened and a free 'Western" or "bourgeois-democratic" order were allowed to develop and mature, the seizure of power by would-be socialists could only lead to a "restoration" of Oriental, autocratic despotism on a pseudosocialist foundation with a pseudosocialist "ruling caste." Things would be even worse, he warned Lenin in 1907, if this new "Inca ruling caste of Sons of the Sun" should make the fatal mistake of nationalizing the land, thus tightening more than ever the bonds that bound the peasant to the autocratic state.

The term "Oriental despotism," applied to Russia in the course of this controversy among Russian socialists, reminds us that there are yet more durable social formations with yet greater built-in staying powers than those we have so far noted. These reckon their continuity not in centuries alone but even in millennia.

As a Chinese historian once observed to me: "Your Renaissance was a fascinating period. We had seven of them." If we substitute Restoration for Renaissance, both in the sense of restoration of vigor and restoration of basic structures, he was right.

For though China knew changes, suffered upheavals, invasions, conquests, falls of dynasties, rebellions, interregna, and times of troubles, a Chinese villager or a Chinese official of the nineteenth century, if transported to the China of two thousand or more years ago, would have found himself at home in a familiar institutional and ideological environment.

With the exception of Western monarchical absolutism, what all these enduring social structures had in common was a single power center, a managerial state, a lack of independent social orders and forms of property, an absence of checks on the flow of power to the center and the top, a powerful, self-perpetuating institutional framework.

TOTALITARIANISM—A CLOSED SOCIETY

Modern totalitarianism is one of these comparatively closed and conservative societies with a powerful and self-perpetuating institutional framework, calculated to assimilate the changes which it intends and those which are forced upon it, in such fashion that—barring explosion from within or battering down from without—the changes tend to be either inhibited or shaped and assimilated as within-system changes in a persistent system with built-in staying powers.

At first glance the word conservative may seem out of place in speaking of a society that is organized revolution. And indeed there is a striking difference between Communist totalitarianism and all previous systems of absolute, despotic, undivided (and in that sense, total) power. For whereas despotism, autocracy and absolutism were bent on preserving the status quo, Communist totalitarianism is dedicated to "the future." This powerful institutional structure which tolerates no rival centers of organization has a vested interest in keeping things in flux. It maintains the omnipotence of its state and ideology by carrying on, within and by means of its power system, a permanent revolution. Like Alexander's, it is a revolution from above. Indeed, much more truly than Alexander's and much more sweepingly and exclusively is it a revolution from above. Its aim is nothing less than to keep society atomized and to create, as rapidly and as completely as the recalcitrant human material and the refractory surrounding world will permit, a new man, a new society, and a new world.

Like the earlier systems referred to, and much more than they, it possesses a state that is stronger than society. Like them it represents a system of total, in the sense of undivided, power. Like them it lacks any organized and institutionalized checks on the flow of power to the top. Like them it possesses a state-centered, state-dominated, state-managed and for the first time, a completely state-owned economy.

If the other societies are distinguished by the high specific gravity of state ownership, state control and state managerial function within the total activity of the society in question, under Communist totalitarianism, state ownership and state managerialism aspire to be total in a new sense. In the other cases, we have been contemplating total power in the sense of undivided power: power without significant rival centers of independent organization. But now we must add to the concept of *undivided power*, the concept of *all-embracing power*.

No longer does the state limit itself to being "stronger than society." It now strives to be *coextensive* with society. Whereas the earlier power systems recognize certain limitations in their capacity to run everything, leaving room, for example, for pocket-handkerchief-sized farms and the self-feeding of the corvée population, for private arts and crafts unconnected with the managerial concerns of the state, for certain types of private trade and even finding room for village communal democracy under the watchful eye of the state overseer (what Wittfogel has aptly called "beggars' democracy")—the new totalitarianism strives completely to fragment and atomize society, to coordinate the system of dispersed villages completely into its centralized power system, to eliminate even the small private parcel of the *kolkhoznik* already reduced from a "pocket-handkerchief" to a mere swatch.

For the first time a total-power system in the earlier sense of undivided and unchallenged power aspires to be totalist or *totalitarian* in the further sense of all-embracing power and aspires to convert the state-stronger-than-society into the state-coextensive-with-society.

ILLUSIONS ON THE TRANSITORINESS OF TOTAL POWER

We cannot deduce much from a comparison with other modern totalitarianisms. For historical and physical reasons Italian fascism was more totalist in aspiration than in realization. And, though nazism and Stalinist communism suggestively moved toward each other, nazism did not last long enough to complete its evolution. But it did live long enough to dispose of certain illusions concerning the supposed incompatibility of totalitarianism with certain aspects of modern life.

Thus it is widely held that the monopoly of total power and the attempt to embrace the totality of social life and activity are incompatible with modern industry and advanced technology. But Germany adopted totalitarianism when it was the foremost country of Europe in industry and technology. This should also dispose of the idea that totalitarianism is the appropriate form for industrializing.

Indeed, it is precisely modern technology, with its all-embracing means of communication, its high speed transmission of commands and reports and armed force to and from any point in a country, its mass communication conditioning techniques and the like, which for the first time makes it possible for total (undivided) power to aspire to be totalist (all-embracing) power. If total power tends to arise wherever the state is stronger than society, totalitarian power can rule over a great area and in great depth only where the state is both stronger than society and in possession of all the resources of modern technology.

Closely akin to the illusion of incompatibility of totalitarianism with modern technology is the view that totalitarianism is "in the long run" (a run not generally conceived of as very long despite the slow geologic time implied in the popular metaphor of "erosion") incompatible with universal literacy, with advanced technological training and with widespread "higher" or secondary school education. Once more it is Germany that serves to remind us that one of the most highly literate and technologically trained peoples in the history of man adopted nazism when that people was both universally literate and possessed a high proportion of scientists, scholars and persons with secondary school training.

Whereas in preliterate societies it took long periods of conflict followed by ages of the development of tradition to indoctrinate a people into customary acceptance of centralized total power and customary acceptance of their lot as obedient servitors to a managerial-priestly bureaucracy, Nazi ideology spread like wildfire among a people who already knew how to read. For modern totalitarianism requires that everybody be able to read so that all can be made to read the same thing at the same moment. Not the mere ability to read but the possibility of choosing between alternative types of reading is a potential—and only a potential —liberating influence.

LENIN, STALIN, AND KHRUSHCHEV

When Stalin died in 1953, bolshevism was fifty years old. Its distinctive views on the significance of organization, of centralization and of the guardianship or dictatorship of a vanguard or elite date from Lenin's programmatic writings of 1902 (*Where to Begin; What is to Be Done?*). His separate machine and his authoritarian control of it dates from the split of 1903.

During these fifty years bolshevism had had only two authoritative leaders, each of whom in turn set the stamp of his personality upon it. Lenin, as we have suggested, inherited much from tsarist autocracy, yet, his totalitarianism is different in principle from the old Muscovite despotism. He regarded himself as a devout orthodox Marxist, building upon and enlarging some aspects of Marx's conceptions while ignoring, altering or misrepresenting others. His Marxism was so different from Marx's that a not unfriendly commentator, Charles Rappoport, called it *marxisme à la tartare*. Stalin's Leninism, in turn, differed enough from Lenin's that we might term it *marxisme à la mode caucasienne*. Yet there is discernibly more continuity between Stalin and Lenin than Lenin and Marx. The changes Stalin introduced involved the continuation and enlargement of certain elements in Lenin's methods and conceptions, along with the alteration of others. He inherited and used, now in Leninist, now in his own "Stalinist" fashion, a powerful institutional framework involving a party machine, a state machine, a doctrine of infallibility, an ideology, and the determination to extend the totalization of power to transform the Russian into the "new Communist man" and win the world for communism.

With Stalin's death, once more there are new leaders or a new leader. It is impossible to believe that this new personal imprint will not make alterations in Stalinism as Stalin did in Leninism. But it seems to me useful that we should remind ourselves at the outset, that the "new men" are not so new, that they have inherited a going concern with a durable institutional framework, a dynamics, and a momentum already powerful and powerfully established, and that actually we are examining changes in—or rather I think we should say *within*—a single-centered, closed, highly centralized society run by a power that is both total in the sense of undivided and totalist in its aspirations. Such societies, as I have indicated, have tended to exhibit built-in staying powers and a perdurability despite changes like the death of a despot, an oligarchical interregnum or a struggle for succession.

As for these "new men," they are, of course, Stalin's men. They would not now have any claim to rule over a great nation were it not that they managed to be Stalin's surviving close lieutenants at the moment of his death.

It is my impression that they are smallish men. There is a principle of selection in personal despotisms that surrounds the despot with courtiers, sycophants, executants, yes-men, and rules out original and challenging minds. This almost guarantees a crisis of succession, where there is no system of legitimacy, until a new dictator emerges. Moreover, the heirs are no longer young so that a fresh crisis of succession may well supervene before the present muted and restricted crisis is over.

I would not consider these "smallish men" too small, however, for when you have a sixth of the earth, 200 million population, a total state economy, and a great empire to practice on, you learn other trades besides that of courtier or faction lieutenant. Even so, not one of them at present exhibits the originality and the high charge of energy and intellect that characterized Lenin. Nor the grosser but no less original demonic force of Stalin.

Whenever a despot dies, there is a universal expectation of change. The new men have had to take account of it, and have taken advantage of it to introduce changes which the old tyrant made seem desirable even to his lieutenants: to rationalize elements of a system which has no organized, independent force, to change it from above, and to make limited concessions while they are consolidating their power. But the institutional framework they have inherited is one they intend to maintain. It is a solid and durable political system dominating a society that has been totally fragmented or atomized, and the state, or rather the party that is its core is the controlling core of all extant organizations.[2]

THE STRUCTURE OF THE APPARATUS

Some of the parts of this power machine are now more than a half-century old, others date from 1917, others from the consolidation of the Stalinist regime in industry, agriculture, politics and culture in the thirties. But even these last have been established for more than two decades.

In short, what the epigoni have inherited is no small heritage: an atomized society; a centralized, monolithic, monopolistic party; a single-party state; a regime of absolute force supplemented by persuasion or by continuous psychological warfare upon its people; a managerial bureaucracy accustomed to take orders and execute them (with a little elbow-room for regularized evasion); a centrally managed, totally state-owned and state-regulated economy including farms, factories, banks, transport, and communications and all trade, domestic and foreign; an established dogmatic priority for the branches of industry which underlie the power of the state; a bare subsistence economy for the bulk of the producers; a completely statized and "collectivized" agriculture which though it has never solved the problem of productivity, continues to reach out after greater gigantism and statification and threatens to reduce even the small parcel to a mere "garden adornment"; a powerful, if one-sided, forced-tempo industry centralized even beyond the point of rationality from the standpoint of totalitarianism itself; the techniques and momentums of a succession of Five Year Plans; a completely managed and controlled culture (except for the most secret recesses of the spirit which even modern technology cannot reach); a monopoly of all the means of expression and communication; a state owned system of "criticism"; an infallible doctrine stemming from infallible authorities, interpreted and applied by an infallible party led by an infallible leader or clique of infallible leaders, in any case by an infallible "summit"; a method of advance by zigzags toward basically unchanging goals; a system of promotion, demotion, correction of error, modification of strategy and tactics, and elimination of

2. This does not apply to the empire but only to the Soviet Union. In general in this chapter I have omitted any consideration of the empire.

differences, by fiat from the summit, implemented by purges of varying scope and intensity; a commitment to continuing revolution from above until the Soviet subject has been remade according to the blueprint of the men in the Kremlin and until communism has won the world.

It is in this heritage that these men were formed. In this they believe. It is the weight and power and internal dynamics of this heritage that in part inhibits, in part shapes, such changes as these men undertake and enters as a powerful shaping force into the changes which they make involuntarily.

It would require a separate study to attempt an inquiry into what is fundamental to totalitarianism so that a change in it would represent a "change in the system" and what is of a more superficial order so that a change in it may readily be recognized as a "within-system" change. Here we shall have to limit ourselves to a glance at a few post-Stalin political developments for purposes of exemplification. The first change that obtrudes itself is collective leadership.

The party statutes do not provide for an authoritative leader, a dictator or a *vozhd.* Just as this, the most centralized great power, still professes to be federal, a mere union of autonomous republics, so the party statutes have always proclaimed party democracy and collective leadership.

WHY COLLECTIVE LEADERSHIP IS TRANSITORY

It was not hard to predict that Stalin's orphaned heirs would proclaim a collective leadership at the moment of his death, even as they began the maneuvers for the emergence of a still narrower ruling group (triumvirate, duumvirate) and a muted struggle for the succession. Stalin, too, found it necessary to proclaim a collective leadership and pose as its faithful wheel horse for more than half a decade, and he took a full decade before he killed the first of his "rivals."

Stalin heirs had the same reasons as he for proclaiming the collective leadership of the Presidium, and some additional ones. The harrowing and demoralizing experiences of the thirties, the signs of the beginnings of a new mass purge just a few months before Stalin died, the state of terror in which even his closest collaborators lived and the justified fear of each of the others, all combined to make necessary the proclamation of a collective leadership.

To be sure, there is nothing inherently incompatible with total (undivided) nor with totalitarian (all-embracing) power in the rule of an oligarchy, or in a shorter or longer interregnum between despots or dictators. What is harder to understand is the seriousness with which experts discussed and are still discussing collective leadership as if it were a permanently institutionalized feature, or even the beginning of the dispersal of power. What is noteworthy in the case of this collective is the swiftness with which the first triumvirate—Malenkov, Molotov, Beria—were demoted and disgraced. It took Stalin ten years to shed the blood of potential rivals; Beria disappeared in a few months. In less than two years, the skeptical were obliged to recognize that Khrushchev was "more equal than the others," was demonstrating in a score of fields that "power is knowledge" and making all the important programmatic declarations with his hand on the lever of the party machine.[3]

The important point to remember is that triumvirates, duumvirates, directories, are notoriously transitional in the succession to a despot where there is no legitimacy to provide a successor, and where there are no *socially organized* checks, below and outside the central power, to restrain the flow of power to the top.

The whole dynamics of dictatorship calls for a personal dictator; authoritarianism for an authority; infallible doctrine for an infallible applier and interpreter; totally militarized life for a supreme commander; centralized, undivided, all-embracing, and "messianic" power for a "charismatic" symbol and tenant of authority.

As long as collective leadership does not swiftly and determinedly broaden itself instead of narrowing; as long as it does not openly recognize itself as "prelegitimate" in the sense of aiming to replace itself by a broader, nondictatorial organization of power; as long as power does not flood down into the basic units of the party (where it did not inhere even in Lenin's day) and then overflow the party dikes and spill out into self-organizing corporate bodies independent of the state and party, thus restoring some initiative to society as against party and state, as long as there do not develop rival organized or corporate bodies, freely functioning factions, and ultimately parties; as long, in other words, as there develop no organized checks upon the reflux of power to the top, not merely a slowing but actually a reversing of the whole trend of totalitarianism—there is reason to regard any directory or collective leadership or bureaucratic oligarchy as a mere interregnum between dictators.

Both purge and terror were instituted by Lenin and "perfected" and "over-perfected" by Stalin. Leaving on one side the purely personal element (paranoia and relish for vengeance), both purge in the party and terror in society as a whole serve many of the "rational" purposes of the totalitarian regime: the establishment of the infallibility of the party, its summit, and its doctrine; the maintenance of the party in a "state of grace" (zeal, doctrinal purity, fanatical devotion, discipline, subordination, total mobilization); the atomization of society as a whole; the break-

3. This was written *before* Khrushchev ousted Malenkov, Molotov, Kaganovich, Zhukov, and Bulganin.

ing up of all nonstate conformations and centers of solidarity; the turn-over in the elite, demotion of deadwood and promotion of new forces; the supplying of scapegoats for every error and dramatization of every needed change of line; the maintenance of the priority of heavy industry, of forced savings for capital investment, of unquestioned command and relative efficiency in production, of collectivization in agriculture, of con-trol in culture and a number of similar objectives of the totalist state.

All of these institutions have been so well established that to a large degree they are now taken for granted and have become to that extent "second nature." Stalin himself promised in 1939 that there would never again be a mass purge. Except in the army and among Jewish writers, the purge became physically more moderate, until, with increasing signs of paranoia, Stalin gave every sign of opening another era of mass purge a few months before his death. The first thing the heirs did around the corpse was to call off this purge, both because it had no "rational" pur-pose and because it had threatened to involve most of them.

THE ERA OF KHRUSHCHEV

But it would be a mistake to believe that the "moderate" purge has been dispensed with or is dispensable. In the preparation of the Twentieth Congress the heirs showed how well they had mastered the "Leninist norms" which had prepared every congress since the Tenth by a prior purge of the organization. All the regional Secretaries and leading com-mittees were "renewed," thirty-seven per cent of those who attended the Nineteenth Congress disappeared from public view, forty-four per cent of the Central Committee failed to be elected as delegates or to be re-elected to the new Committee. All we can say is that the purge resembled those of Stalin's "benign" periods or of Lenin's day. Yet the liquidation of Beria and at least twenty-five of his friends shows that the techniques of the blood purge had not been forgotten, only held in reserve in case of need. That the party ranks breathe easier and are glad of the self-denying ordinance of the leaders in their struggle for position we do not doubt. But there is no evidence that the party ranks ordered this change or could do so, or would venture to try.

The terror in society as a whole has also diminished. No longer are there such bloody tasks as forced collectivization to carry through. Habitual obedience, the amnesties and concessions of an interregnum, the shortage of manpower for industry, agriculture, and the army due to continued expansion and the deficit of wartime births that should now have been reaching the labor age—these and many other things account for the fact that artists and writers, workmen and peasants and managers do not at this moment feel that public reproof (which they are quick to hearken to) must necessarily be followed by arrest and concentration camp. With manpower shortages the concentration camp is the most wasteful and least productive way of using up a man. The camps are gentler and fewer in number now, yet the camps are there.

LAW UNDER DESPOTISM

The police has been downgraded and, in a regime so in need of naked force, the army has been upgraded, i.e., given more internal political functions. The public prosecutors have been given more control of trials and pretrial inquisitions—like making the fox the guardian of the chicken coop. There are some other minor law reforms. Above all there has been much fuss about a promise of a codification and regularization of the laws.

This new code was begun in Stalin's last months. It was promised "within sixty days" by Lavrenti Beria when his star seemed in the ascendent. Sight unseen, we can predict that the new code will not touch the foundations of the totalist state, i.e., not alter the subservience of courts and laws and prosecutors and judges and police to the will and purposes of the oligarchy or the single leader. It is necessary to remember that any total power, and *a fortiori*, any totalist power, may obey its own laws whenever it suits it to do so without giving those laws power over it or making them into limits upon its powers. A power center that is both legislator and administrator and judge and enforcer and even self-pronounced infallible "critic" of its own acts, may declare any activity a crime which it pleases. In the Soviet Union even loyalty to the underlying principles on which the state itself was founded has been declared a degrading crime and punished with incredible cruelty. How easily this totalist state may set aside its laws and negate its most solemn and "binding" promises is evidenced anew—after the repeated proclamation of "socialist legality"—by the sudden repudiation by the "workers' state" of the state debt to the workers themselves, without so much as the possibility of a murmur. The owners of the repudiated bonds and investors of their now wiped out compulsory savings were even obliged to hold meetings and pass resolutions in which they expressed their delight at being expropriated.

The longer such a regime endures the more it has need of regularization of the duties and expectations of its subjects, even as it keeps undiminished its powers of sudden reversal and unpredictable and unlimited intervention. The only guarantee against a totally powerful state is the existence of nonstate organizations capable of effective control of, or effective, organized pressure on, the governmental power. Otherwise, to attempt to check, or limit, or even question is to invite the fury of exemplary punishment for the purposes of preserving atomization.

"Betwixt subject and subject," Locke wrote of despotism, "they will grant, there must be measures, laws and judgments for their mutual peace and security. But as for the ruler, he ought to be absolute, and is above all such circumstances; because he has the power to do more hurt and wrong, it is right when he does it. To ask how you may be guarded from harm or injury on that side . . . is the voice of faction and rebellion . . . The very question can scarcely be borne. They are ready to tell you it deserves death only to ask after safety. . . ." [4]

It is well for us to remember that the most despotic rulers have on occasion handed down elaborate law codes. The famous and in many ways justly admired Roman Code was compiled and proclaimed only after the emperor himself had become a god, no longer subject to question or limitation, only to worship. Though laws must multiply and be regularized so that the subjects may know what is expected of them, and even what they can count on in their relations with each other where the central power is unaffected, the lack of independent courts, of independent power groups or corporate bodies, of an independent press and public opinion, deprives these laws of any binding force upon the rulers. In Communist totalitarianism, the place of imperial divinity is taken by the infallibility of doctrine, the dogmatic untouchability of the dictatorship, the infallibility of the masters of the infallible doctrine and by such spiritual demiurges as "revolutionary consciousness," "historical necessity," and "the interests of the revolution and of the people." Those who *know* where history is going, surely have the right and duty to see to it that she goes there.

"The scientific concept, dictatorship," Lenin reminds us with beautiful simplicity, "means neither more nor less than unlimited power, resting directly on force, not limited by anything, not restricted by any laws or any absolute rules. Nothing else but that." [5]

And to Commissar of Justice Kursky, when he was elaborating the first law code, Lenin wrote:

[My] draft is rough . . . but the basic thought, I hope, is clear: openly to set forth the proposition straightforward in principle and politically (and not merely in the narrow-juridical sense), which motivates the essence and *justification* of terror, its necessity, its limits.

The court should not eliminate the terror: to promise that would be either self-deception or [simple] deception, but should give it a foundation and a legalization in principle, clearly, without falsification and without em-

4. *Second Treatise on Government,* Chapter VII, 593.
5. *Collected Works,* 4th Edition, Vol. 31, p. 326.

bellishment. It is necessary to formulate it as widely as possible, for only a revolutionary consciousness of justice and a revolutionary conscience will put conditions upon its application in practice, on a more or a less wide scale. [Emphasis in the original] [6]

In these regards the new men do not have to "return to Leninist norms," for they have never been abandoned for a moment.

ORGANIZATION—THE CORE OF LENINIST IDEOLOGY

If we can hope for, perhaps count on, the diminution of the apocalyptic element in the ideology of a going and long-lasting society, we must remind ourselves that Leninism was peculiar in that its central "ideas" were always ideas about organization.

Bolshevism was born in an organization feud: what the statutes should say about the definition of a party member, and who should control the majority on a paper (*Iskra*), which should act both as guardian of the doctrine and core of organization of the party. "Give me an organization," Lenin wrote at the outset of his career as a Leninist, "and I will turn Russia upside down." The organization he wanted, he explained, must be one in which "bureaucratism" prevailed against "democratism," "centralism" against "autonomy," which "strives to go from the top downward, and defends the enlargement of the rights and plenary powers of the central body against the parts." The idea of the rule of the elite, the idea of a vanguard party, the idea of the repulsiveness of all other classes and the untrustworthiness of the working class, the idea that the working class also required a dictator or overseer to compel it to its mission—these "ideas" about organization form the very core of Leninism as a special ideology. Far from "eroding" or growing "weak" and merely "decorative," it is just precisely these structural ideas that have grown and expanded, become implemented and systematized.

It is these concepts of organizational structure and the dictatorship of an infallible elite that set their limits on the possibility of *organized* public opinion. Resentments, pressures, discontent, longing for a less oppressive regime and an easier lot, exist under despotisms, autocracies, total-power states and totalist states, even as in other social orders. Indeed, whenever hope or expectation stirs they are apt to become endemic and intense. The problem of "statecraft" in a despotism is that of preventing the discontent and longing from assuming *independent* and *organized* form. Since the totalist state penetrates all social organizations as their leading core and uses them as transmission belts (framing up and destroying whatever organization it cannot coordinate into its structure) it is particularly adapted to keeping discontent thus fragmented and unorganized. The earlier despotisms spied on their people not merely to weed out troublemakers but often to find out what changes it should introduce to lessen such discontents, where the changes did not affect its fundamental powers and aims. Here too, the totalist state is better adapted by virtue of its universal police and espionage penetration than was the primitive "espionage" of an incognito Haroun al-Raschid or Peter the Great.

By 1936, Lenin's central idea of an elite, single-centered dictatorship had gotten into the "most democratic Constitution in the world" as Article 126 which proclaimed the party to be "the vanguard of the working people and the leading core of all organizations both social and state." And in the summer of 1956, when Khrushchev and company were summing up the Stalin discussion, they declared in *Pravda*:

"As for our country, the Communist Party has been and will be the *only master* of the *minds*, the *thoughts*, the *only spokesman, leader, and organizer* of the people." (Emphasis added.)

It is foolhardy to believe that they did not mean it, self-deluding to convince ourselves that the forces pressing for concessions within the country are likely to find the road open to separate and effective corporate organization, which is the condition precedent to the development of a limited, multicentered state and society.

THE SECRET PLACES OF THE HEART

Even before Stalin died, we got evidence that the spirit of man is wayward and not as easily subjected as his body—the mass desertions at the war's end; the escape of millions who "voted with their feet" against totalitarianism, the two out of three "Chinese volunteers" in the Korean prison camps who, for the first time after any war, preferred exile under precarious and shameful "displaced person" conditions to return to their native scenes and homes.

Since Stalin's death there have been East Berlin and Pilsen, Poznan and Vorkuta, Warsaw and Budapest, to prove that men will sometimes stand up unarmed to tanks and cannon and machine guns. They have proved too that the armies of the conquered lands have never been the pliant instruments of the Kremlin that the faint-hearted thought them to be.

We have seen that forty years of *Gleichschaltung*, corruption and terror have not rooted out of the artist the ineradicable notion that sincerity to his creative vision is more to be desired than *partiinost* and *ideinost.* We have seen that the youth, though the faint-hearted thought they would be turned off the conveyor-belt as "little monsters," are still born young, and therefore plastic, receptive, doubting, capable of illusion and disillusion, capable of "youthful idealism" and youthful questioning of the elders and of the established and of youthful rebellion. Now the expulsions among the university youth are for the first time providing a pariah elite as a possible leadership to future undergrounds that may form under even this most terribly efficient atomizer of society.

Both Zamiatin in *We* and Orwell in *1984* with appropriate symbolism made the love of a man and a woman the crime of treason against the totalist state because love represents a solidarity outside the purview and control of the state, an antidote to total atomization. Even Ivan Petrovich Pavlov, he of the "conditioned reflexes" by which those who believe man to be infinitely manipulable chart their course, found among the primary reflexes in the inborn nature of men and animals: "the reflex of freedom." [7]

I would not have it thought, in presenting these remarks on the power and durability of the institutional framework of despotism in general and the totalist state in particular, that I do not take account of the "freedom reflex" and of the fact that the nature of man, too, is tough and durable so that when the screws are relaxed ever so little, it tends to spring back toward a more human shape.

Nor do I underestimate the power of illusion. Because of the ideology which they inherited, and because of the very nature of man and their contest to win man's allegiance on a world scale, the men in the Kremlin are compelled to engage in semantic subterfuge. While this is actually one of their devices for dominion over and atomization of those over whom they rule, it bears within it the possibility of vast and fateful misunderstandings. If in general it is dangerous to relax the screws ever so slightly or to measure out homeopathic doses of freedom, there is an additional specific danger that big announcements and big promises may seem to mean more than they intend. Illusion, to paraphrase Marx, once it takes possession of great masses of men, becomes itself a material force.

Nor, finally, have I ever for a moment ceased to cast about for grounds of hope: that weaker heirs might make less efficient use of the terrible engines of total power; that a struggle, or succession of struggles, for the succession might compel a contender to go outside the inner circles and summon social forces in the lower ranks of the party or outside of it into some sort of independent existence; that the army, disgraced as no other in all history by the charge that it gave birth to traitors by the thousands in its general staff, might develop the independ-

7. "The Reflex of Freedom," is the title of Chapter 28 in Ivan Petrovich Pavlov's *Lectures on Conditioned Reflexes*, New York, 1928, pp. 282-286.

ence from the party sufficient to make it a rival power center or an organized pressure body; that intellectuals, that technicians, that students, that writers and artists, might somehow break through the barriers that hinder the conversion of discontent into an organized independent force.

THE DANGER OF ILLUSIONS

If then, this analysis puts the emphasis on the nature of the institutional framework and its built-in staying powers, it is by way of bending the stick in the direction I thought it had to be bent in order to straighten it out. For, or so it has seemed to me, the western world has found it hard to gaze straight and steadily at the head of Medusa, even if only in the reflecting shield of theoretical analysis. Brought up in a world of flux and openness, we find it hard to believe in the durability of despotic systems. Our hopes and longings are apt to betray us again and again into readiness to be deceived or to deceive ourselves. And the "journalistic" nature of our culture has made us too ready to inflate the new because that alone is "news" while we neglect to put it into its tiresomely "repetitious" historical and institutional setting.

From the NEP to socialism in one country; from the popular front and collective security to the Grand Alliance and one world; from "peaceful coexistence" to the "Geneva spirit"—the occupational hazard of the western intellectual has been not to read too little but to read too much into planned changes, involuntary changes, and even into mere tactical maneuvers and verbal asseverations.

Each has been hailed in turn as the softening of the war of the totalist state on its own people and the war upon the world; as the long awaited "inevitable change" or "fundamental transformation"; "the sobering that comes from the responsibilities of power"; "the response to the pressure of the recognition of reality"; "the transition from terrorist to normal modes of societal regimentation"; the growing modification of totalist power by "a rationalist technocracy"; "the sobering effect of privilege upon a new privileged class"; the "rise of a limited and traditionalist despotism"; a "feeling of responsibility to Russia as against world revolution"; the "quiet digestion period of a sated beast of prey" no longer on the prowl; the "diffusion of authority which could lead to a constitutional despotism"; the "mellowing process that sooner or later overtakes all militant movements"; the second thoughts on the struggle for the world which have come at long last "from the recognition of the universal and mutual destructiveness of nuclear war"; the "preordained downward curve in the parabola of revolution"; the "inevitable work of erosion upon the totalitarian edifice." (Each of these expressions is quoted from some highly respected authority on Soviet affairs in the Anglo-Saxon world.)

Because of the nature of our mental climate and our longings, because, too, of the injection of "revolutionary methods" into diplomacy in a polarized and antagonistic world, we are not nearly so likely to overlook change and to test perhaps without sufficient scepticism the meaning of each verbal declaration. No, "the main danger," as the Communists would say, has not lain in insensitivity to hope, but in too-ready self-deception.

When Hitler's attack on Russia threw Stalin into our camp during World War II, I wrote an article, entitled "Stalin at the Peace Table," which contended that there would be no peace table or general settlement as after other wars, and that the peace would be settled piecemeal by the strategic acts of the war so that, if the war were not planned accordingly, there would be no decent peace. The illusions of the Grand Alliance were such that this view could not get a hearing.

This is not surprising in the case of a "Cassandra" who is merely a free-lance writer on totalitarianism and Soviet affairs. But Winston Churchill, participating in the directing councils of the Grand Alliance, tried in vain to get an agreement on a strategy for the joint occupation and liberation of the Balkans and eastern Europe, and even he could not prevail against the overpowering Grand Alliance illusions of both Anglo-Saxon lands. As a result, where the Soviet army was in sole occupation, there are conquered countries. Where there was joint occupation, there is a divided Germany and a divided Korea. Where the Soviet army was not admitted, there is a Japan free to criticize its occupier and determine its own destiny. Thus an awareness of the nature of Soviet totalitarianism and its aim would have made a difference in the freedom of hundreds of millions of human beings.

The case is, to be sure, exceptional in that the war created an exceptionally fluid world. But what we are trying to understand and estimate is at no time a mere exercise in sociological abstraction or historical generalization. For literally every judgment in the estimation of the nature of totalitarianism and the scope of the changes in it is fraught with fateful significance for the fate of millions of men.

IV THE STRUGGLE FOR
THE SUCCESSION *

Joseph Stalin had been dead for six hours and ten minutes before the Kremlin flag was lowered and the radio announced that the dictator was no more. In an age of split-second announcements of death, there was something strange in this delay. No less strange were the official communiqués on his last illness. "The best medical personnel has been called in to treat Comrade Stalin. . . . The treatment is under the direction of the Minister of Health. . . . The treatment is under the continuous supervision of the Central Committee and the Soviet government. . . ." Nine doctors watching one another; the Minister of Health watching the doctors; the Central Committee and the government watching the Minister. And all of this, by an inner compulsion, announced to the world. Who can fail to sense that the laws of life and death are somehow different behind the Kremlin walls?

Early on the morning of March 6, 1953, with all the morning papers missing from the streets, the radio announced that the Vozhd [1] had died at 9:50 the night before. The communiqué included a call to maintain "the steel-like unity and monolithic unity of the ranks of the [Communist] party . . . to guard the unity of the party as the apple of the eye . . . to educate all Communists and working people in high political vigilance, intolerance, and firmness in the struggle against the inner and outer foe." This call was repeated hourly all through the day.

Shortly before midnight the party chiefs, in continuous meeting since their leader's death, announced that a joint session of the Central Committee, the Council of Ministers, and the Presidium of the Supreme Soviet had come to the conclusion that "the most important task of the party and the government is to ensure uninterrupted and correct leadership of

* This chapter is based on the declassified portion of a top secret government document prepared by the writer and entitled *On Death in the Family*, this section having been declassified upon Stalin's death.

1. *Vozhd* is a title regularly applied to Stalin and, retroactively, to Lenin. Ushakov's Russian dictionary defines it as "leader of an army (*literary, obsolescent and rhetorical*); leader of a social movement, of a party; ideological leader." *Vozhd* has the same flavor and intention in Russian as *Führer* in German and *Duce* in Italian. All three are military-political terms.

the entire life of the country, which demands the greatest unity of leadership and the prevention of any kind of disorder and panic." "In view of the above," the communiqué continued, it was necessary to make at once a sweeping series of changes in the personnel and organizational structure of the leading party and government bodies. The changes completely undid all the personnel and structural arrangements made less than five months earlier by the Nineteenth Congress (October 1952) under the personal direction of the man who was not yet dead twenty-four hours.

The "call to steel-like unity and monolithic unity" and to increased "vigilance" and "intolerance . . . in the struggle against the inner and outer foe" continued to reappear in editorials and articles. It was repeated textually in Malenkov's funeral oration three days later. The warning against "disorder and panic" was paraphrased by Beria in his funeral oration and repeated verbatim in the leading *Pravda* editorial of March 11.

"DISORDER AND PANIC"

Disorder and panic! When United States President Franklin Roosevelt died during his fourth term in office, could it occur to the Vice-President who automatically succeeded him, or to the leaders of either political party, or to "the government," to warn against disorder and panic? When George VI of England or Gustav V of Sweden died while still in royal office, could such words creep into the communiqués or the funeral addresses of those who knew and loved them?

Not even in young states just being born in turmoil and conflict—not in Israel, when its first president, Chaim Weizmann, died, not in Turkey when Kemal Pasha died, not in Pakistan when Liaquat Ali Khan died, not in India when her unique political-religious leader Mahatma Gandhi was assassinated, not in China when Sun Yat-sen breathed his last—could anyone think of pronouncing the ominous words "disorder and panic." Those strange words bring us close to the heart of the mystery of the nature of this state, of the nature of the men who rule over it, of their relationship with each other, with the people they rule, and with the rest of the world.

One searches history in vain for a case of a peaceful and bloodless succession to a dictator who has climbed to power by force and based his rule upon force without troubling to restore the ruptured fabric of legitimacy. When Caesar was assassinated, the triumvirate that followed tore the Roman Empire apart. The *Directoire* that succeeded the terror of Robespierre was dislodged by Napoleon, who wrestled all his life with the problem of restoring legitimacy, only to end on St. Helena. Hitler's *Tausendjähriges Reich* perished in a flaming bunker in Berlin, and

Mussolini's *Imperium Romanum* did not outlast his hanging. There had been "disorder and panic" when Hitler and Mussolini died, for the lack of a procedure for the succession to a dictator was reinforced by the armies closing in on the rubble of their cities. But the "disorder and panic" which Stalin's comrades mentioned spring not from such external events but from their hearts and the essence of their system. A system that is based on an unending war upon its own people, and upon all other peoples, cannot develop a legitimacy. The word "panic" escaping the lips of the rulers of the world's most powerful government betrays a fear that is ineradicable in their hearts: they fear the prostrate people over whom they rule, they fear the outside world which they plan to conquer, and they fear each other.

The Soviet government is not a government by Soviets. The people have long ceased to elect or recall "deputies." The Soviets have long ceased to elect their leaders or decide anything. Nor is the Soviet government a party government. Parties are parts. They need each other, and party life ceases as soon as there is only one party and no opposition.

As the Soviets have long ceased to decide anything or select their leaders and officials, so the party has long ceased to decide anything or select its leaders. What was once a party has become a "transmission belt" (the phrase is Stalin's) to convey and enforce the will of the leaders upon the masses. Both decision and personnel selection are from the top downward: a military-ideological-organizational apparatus, a pyramidal power structure culminating in what Max Weber has called a charismatic leader.[2]

On the surface everything seems designed to last forever and to ensure a simple, quiet, peaceful succession. Was ever such monopoly of power wielded by so perfectly organized a mechanism? Thirty-six years of continuity in government (is it not still called "Soviet"?). Thirty years of continuity of personal leadership in the person of the all-wise, all-powerful *Vozhd*. Over a third of a century of uninterrupted happiness of the people, of nonexistence of opposition. More than two decades of unanimous decisions on everything. Not the unity of human beings, but the unity of a monolith. Where is there a crevice in which might sprout the seedcorn of doubt, much less of disorder and panic? The leader controlled the Politburo so long that at the Nineteenth Congress he could abolish it altogether in favor of a diffuse body so large and scattered that it could not be called upon to make day-to-day decisions. The Central Committee had long before become such a body.

The chain of command was so clear: the leader controlling the Politburo, the Politburo controlling the Central Committee, the Central Committee controlling the party. And the party, in turn, controls an

2. Or an *Ersatz*-Charismatic Leader, as in the case of an Ulbricht or a Brezhnev.

imposing apparatus of police, army, bureaucracy, press, radio, meeting halls, streets, schools, buildings, churches, factories, farms, unions, arts, sciences, everything. All the power levers seem to function so smoothly. What it had cost Lenin and his associates so much travail and struggle to build, and Stalin so much struggle and bloodshed to perfect into the all-embracing power apparatus of the total state, seems now so perfected, so smoothly functioning: a ready-made machine, the greatest power machine in all history. Yet the first words of the orphaned heirs on the death of the dictator are not human words of sorrow but ominous words about "disorder and panic," intolerance, vigilance, and uncompromising struggle "against the inner and outer foe."

DICTATORSHIP AS THE RUPTURE OF LEGITIMACY

In all this mighty machine there is oppressive quiet, but no peace to ensure a peaceful succession. There is a multitude of laws, but no legality to provide a legal and legitimate succession. The democratic revolution of March 1917 ruptured the legitimacy of tsarism, but it set to work at once to develop a new, democratic legitimacy out of the State Duma or parliament, out of the City Dumas, the rural Zemstvos and the Soviets. It looked forward to convening a Constituent Assembly that would adopt a new democratic constitution and provide a fresh fabric of consensus, consent, acceptance, collective and democratic determination of policy, a multiparty system, a parliament, to secure the habits of willing consent which are the tissues of all normal governments and which make the death of a particular head of state a cause for grief but not an occasion of fear of disorder and panic. To use the terminology of the Italian historian Ferrero, the Provisional Government set up by the first revolution of 1917 was a "prelegitimate government," moving as quickly as the troubled times permitted from the ruptured legitimacy of the monarchy to democratic legitimacy. That is what it meant when it called itself "provisional."

But the Bolshevik party, in November 1917, overthrew this "prelegitimate" Provisional Government by a violent *coup d'état*, and then dispersed the Constituent Assembly which alone could have laid a foundation of democratic legitimacy. When they outlawed all other parties, including the working-class and peasant parties, they thereby drained the Soviets of all power as a "workers' parliament" or "workers' and peasants' parliament," and the party began to rule in the name of the Soviets. Next Lenin outlawed all factions within the party, thereby draining it, too, of all political life. Always excessively centralist and hierarchical, it now became a transmission belt for the will of the Central Committee. When the "servant" of the Central Committee, its General Secretary, executed the majority of the members of the Central Committee which he was supposed to serve, that too ceased to be a decisive organ.

Even as Stalin purged all dissenters and all he had reason to suspect because they were injured or aggrieved or because they found it hard to sing the praise of his perfections, the whole machine of power and force and propaganda got into high gear to make of this unpopular, colorless, and unloved man a synthetic charismatic leader. The leader who possesses charisma ("divine" grace) acquires one by one the attributes of divinity: omniscience, omnicompetence, omnipotence. In him all power is concentrated. Whom he touches with his spirit partakes of his grace. Whom he denounces shrivels into nothingness. He decides everything: linguistics, genetics, the transformation of nature, the disposition of artillery on every front the quota and technique of every factory. Others get power only by emanation and delegation, and even then must be prepared to give him the credit for all success and take upon themselves the blame and punishment for all failures.

So, at the death of the dictator, there are no parties to establish a legal succession by electoral contest. There is no Soviet constitutional provision for a successor to the post of self-appointed genius. There is no party which any longer decides anything, debates anything, selects anybody. There is not even a provision for a dictator, much less for a successor, in the constitution or in a party statute.

There is no moral code, either, to restrain the aspirants to the succession from framing each other and killing each other. In so far as they follow the precedents bequeathed to them, and in so far as they follow the real inner laws of the total state, that is precisely what they will have to do. It is to themselves that they are speaking when they call to an awed populace for "steel-like unity and monolithic unity" of party and of leadership. It is from their own hearts that the words escaped concerning "disorder and panic."

Why not, asks the reasonable man trying to project himself into the irrational atmosphere of totalitarian dynamics, why not then a collective leadership? A triumvirate? A heptarchy? A decemvirate? The Presidium, maybe? The Central Committee? The Council of Ministers? The Secretariat?

Even in Lenin's day, before the Central Committee and Politburo had been drained of all political life and power, it proved impossible to arrange a succession by purely peaceful means or by means which, at least within the party purview, might be regarded as lawful and legitimate. Lenin got three solemn warnings from the "angel of death" in the form of three cerebral hemorrhages. Only after the second did this man, bursting with vitality and a will to power over the entire world, begin to believe in his heart that death was approaching. Then at last he tried to prepare a "legal" and "peaceful" succession. Recognizing that he had acquired enormous personal authority, that perhaps without willing it consciously he had dwarfed the party, and its leading bodies and become a personal dictator, Lenin began to fear that his lieutenants would tear each other to pieces if any one of them tried to become a Vladimir Ilyich the Second. With no clear understanding of the dynamics of the totalitarian process he had set in motion, he sought to re-establish the moribund authority of at least one "collegial" body, the Politburo. His testament proposed a collective leadership in which all his close lieutenants, working together, would replace him and together rule. For this purpose the testament was carefully constructed, with a warning of the "danger of a split in the party," with an adverse judgment on each of his associates to keep him from thinking that he was big enough to rule alone and a word of praise for each of them to indicate that none should be eliminated.

Collective leadership is difficult at best, but without democracy it is impossible. Where there are no constitutional rules for collective procedure, where in all fields there is dictatorship, where force settles all things, where opposition is not an accepted part of the game of politics but something to be eliminated and crushed, the whole momentum of the state and the system drives relentlessly toward personal dictatorship. So it was with Lenin; so it was with Mussolini; so it was with Hitler; and so it was with Stalin.

Even before Lenin was dead, Stalin began "disloyally" to gather into his hands the reins of power. The dying dictator, speechless now from his third stroke, yet managed to add a codicil to his testament: "Stalin is too rude, and this fault becomes insupportable in the office of General Secretary. Therefore, I propose to the comrades to find a way to remove Stalin from that position. . . ." But Lenin's will could not prevail against Stalin's determination and the innate dynamics of the machine which Lenin himself had set in motion. Stalin did not even permit it to be published in the Soviet Union.

Precisely because Stalin did not possess Lenin's moral authority over his associates, he found it necessary to use more physical power. The cult of Lenin's person among his disciples was spontaneous and personally distasteful to him. Lenin had frequently used his authority and prestige to get his own way in disputed matters, but he opposed the development of a cult of his person. The cult grew up only around his embalmed corpse, fostered above all by the very man who was undoing his last will. For Stalin could claim infallibility only by first developing the cult of infallibility around Lenin and then making himself into the "best disciple" and apostolic successor. Thus the last repositories of some kind of legality and legitimacy, the Party Congress, the Central Committee, and the Politburo, were deprived of their right to say yes or no to anything. Unanimity, monolithic conformity, and synthetic infallibility prevailed.

Lenin had defeated his opponents inside the party by debate, not infrequently fortified by organizational maneuver and frame-up; but once they were worsted, he was careful to salvage the person and the dignity of the defeated opponent. But Stalin could not win by debate. His method was to enlarge the organizational maneuvers and frame-ups that were already a part of Lenin's techniques, to compel his opponents to be-smirch themselves and to liquidate themselves morally by repeated "con-fessions." Then he killed them.

There is a fearful dynamic to totalitarianism that drives it to rupture the entire fabric of consent and consensus. From thence springs its fear that men will not believe and not obey. But once fear is present, it drives to the use of further terror. And terror exercised against one's people or associates begets greater fear. Fear and terror alike aim at atomization.

The free political process needs opposition; once opposition is out-lawed, there are no limits to terror and fear. The thermometer measuring opposition having been broken, the quicksilver of opposition is instinc-tively felt to be everywhere. Everywhere there is fear; therefore every-where there must be terror. Terror cannot be used against other parties and public bodies without invading one's own party and its leading bodies—until even one's own cronies, one's palace guards, and one's doctors are suspect. The more inert the body politic, the more suspect it is, and the more cause there is to fear it.

Stalin exacted a cult of his person that was the more extravagant because all who knew him knew his personal limitations. He was keenly sensitive to his inferiority as a theoretician and as a popular leader. He knew that the men around him were his equals, in some way his superiors. This drove him to kill off all of Lenin's associates, to kill off his "suc-cessors," and to surround himself only by lesser men, courtiers, sycophants, faction lieutenants, executants of his will. He exacted a cult of his person even from those he was about to destroy, and from the entire nation even as he tormented it. If Lenin's prestige was unable to bind his closest associates, who loved and revered him, to carry out the terms of his will after he was dead, how much less likely is the enforced, repugnant, humiliating Stalin cult to bring his associates or his party to execute his will?

Besides, this time there seems to be no will. "In his unconscious," Freud has written, "no man believes in his own death." It is this which enables the soldier to hold on the shell-swept field, where a third or two-thirds must die, yet cling to the conviction that "my number isn't up." In the case of a dictator who aspires to absolute rule over all things and all men, there is an exceptionally strong will to disbelieve in ordinary mortal limitations, so far as he is concerned. Lenin got three warnings from the "angel of death," but Stalin, though aging, was rugged. Foreigners who interviewed him a few months before his death wrote that he was in good health. After minor strokes, a massive one came suddenly, and in three days he was dead.[3]

Moreover, Joseph Jugashvili Stalin, as all who knew him can testify, was jealous, resentful, envious, capricious and suspicious by nature. No one dared bid him prepare for death; none dared to try on the crown in his presence. As American presidents realize, it is unwise even in a democracy to announce too early in your term of office that you do not intend to run again. The very men of your own party begin to abandon you for the bandwagon of your anticipated successor, and power and leadership slip from your hands. But in a dictatorship, which tolerates only a single power center, it would be fatal to let anyone else openly try on the crown. A rival power center would begin to polarize, and the whole totalitarian regime would be called in question. His very beneficiary and heir would become a danger to the dictator if he began this unnatural abdication or renunciation of part of his total power.

As soon as anyone around him began to shine, however faintly, by the light of his own deeds, Stalin was swift to remove him from the stage. Sometimes the removal by the law of fear-and-terror led to purge. At other times it led to mere rustication, a shift to a minor provincial post, as in the cases of Marshals Timoshenko and Zhukov. Sometimes rumors grew that some one man was the "heir apparent"; then, mysteriously, an assassin's bullet or a sudden illness or—if we are to believe Stalin's last frame-up—"poison-doctors" brought the heir to his end. When shall we really know how Kirov died and how Zhdanov died?

Thus the nature of the total state and the personal psychology of the particular leader combined in Stalin's case to make it ever harder for anyone to grow big enough or acquire the prestige to fill his shoes, or don the mantle of the apostolic succession. The cult of his person grew until it filled the horizon and overarched the sky. Those around him, many of them very capable in their own right, were systematically reduced to dwarfs around a giant. Each fresh extravagance exacted from them in this cult of the master-of-everything, each blasphemous phrase in the litany

3. Franz Borkenau predicted that he was near death seven weeks ·before he died, deducing it from a January 1953 resolution of the East German Communist Party in which Malenkov was cited at length by Ulbricht while the erstwhile "greatest genius of all lands and times" got only a half sentence quote dating from an utterance of 1910. For this master stroke of "Kremlinology" see Borkenau's article in *Commentary*, April 1954, p. 400, or the convenient summary of this point in Walter Laqueur, *The Fate of the Revolution*, New York, 1967, p. 181.

of worship of a living god, diminished further the stature of the men around him and made harder the process of building up a new charismatic leader after his death.

CANDIDATES FOR THE SUCCESSION

The only men who have a chance to try for the leadership are those who are in possession of the power levers which constitute the actual organs of government of the Soviet state. Molotov and Voroshilov, and to a lesser degree Kaganovich and Mikoyan, represent "old bolshevism." In so far as any new *Vozhd* may want to preserve an air of continuity with Lenin and the "men of October," such old bolsheviks are useful as symbols. But they do not represent a real power lever. Stalin killed off virtually all the men of October during the blood purges of 1934 to 1938. In 1947, on the thirtieth anniversary of the *coup d'état* of November 7, 1917, only 438 old bolsheviks who had joined the party prior to the seizure of power were still alive and in good standing to sign a letter of thanks to Comrade Stalin for what he had done to the party. The most important of these is now Molotov. Lenin pronounced him an "incurable dumbbell" and "the best file clerk in all Russia." He is obstinate as a mule. *Kamenii zad*, "Stone Behind," his own associates call him, and every diplomat who has tried to negotiate with him will agree. Unless he backs the wrong horse, he undoubtedly will be included in any entourage as a symbol of continuity, and someone like him or Voroshilov is likely to be vested with the title of Chairman of the Presidium of the Supreme Soviet or some other such honorary badge. But Stalin was boss before he had any state titles, and Molotov and Voroshilov could not be boss if a score of titles were showered upon them. For the men of October, of whom they are the enfeebled, diminishing shadow, are no more.

The new men, from whom the new *Vozhd* will emerge if the process is not interrupted before its completion, are the *epigoni*, the "sons," or perhaps the "grandsons." Stalin, killing off the men of October, became the spokesman of the "sons"; his Leninism became different from Lenin's as Lenin's Marxism was from Marx's. The Malenkovs and Berias, and men still younger, who aspire to power, are men who never knew the great dreams and humane ideals of the nineteenth-century Russian intelligentsia, never knew the excitement, the fervor and the misery of the tsarist underground and exile, scarcely know except by hearsay the "heroic days" of the storming of the Winter Palace and the Kremlin. The world will watch with interest what these men, wholly formed and brought up not as underground revolutionaries but under the new regime of bureaucratic and totalitarian absolutism, will make of the heritage of Marxism and Leninism and Stalinism in the course of their struggle with each other.

POTENTIAL POWER LEVERS

The real power levers in this struggle are three: the party machine, the secret police, the armed forces. Potentially, other power groupings may be in process of formation: an *esprit de corps* among the state bureaucracy, for example, or among the industrialists and technicians. But these are only embryonic forces and not real power levers at present.

Who is in control of the party machine? While Stalin was alive, he controlled it. Whether he was General Secretary, or Premier or simply *Vozhd*, all power and all decision emanated downward from him and in his name. Because he had designated Malenkov in recent years as Secretary of the party, or as first of a battery of three or five or ten secretaries (the number has fluctuated), it was assumed by the outside world, and by some in the Soviet Union—perhaps even by Malenkov himself—that he had his hand on the lever that moves the mighty machine. But often there is some central mechanism that is the key to the functioning of a machine, and, when that is removed, the levers no longer work. Stalin was such a central mechanism. All power concentrated in him, all cohesion. When he died, it soon became clear that no one was any longer in complete possession of the party machine.

For a few days, Malenkov acted as if he were, and the party seemed to act as if he were. On the day of Stalin's death, *Pravda* quoted some lifeless utterance of Malenkov in bold type in the lead editorial, as formerly it had quoted Stalin. It did the same on March 7, 8, and 9. On the 9th, *Izvestia* printed a photo of Stalin with Malenkov and a little girl. On the 10th *Pravda* published a photograph showing Stalin, Mao Tsetung, and Malenkov as a "big three," standing alone at the signing of the Sino-Soviety Treaty. Examination of the original photograph shows that Beria and Molotov had been cut off, as well as Vyshinsky, who actually was signing the treaty, and many others. Sovfoto released a photograph of Malenkov with two of his three chins missing. Operation Retouch had begun.

Greetings began to come from provincial congresses and gatherings to "the Chairman of the Council of Ministers of the USSR and Secretary of the Central Committee of the C.P.S.U., G. M. Malenkov." Then suddenly, the number of quotations diminished. The "fat type" gave way to ordinary print. Quotes from Molotov and Beria began to appear along with quotes from Malenkov. On March 13-15, *Pravda* ceased to use a dual title for Malenkov. From then on, in place of stress on his person, there was stress on "the Central Committee, consisting of people taught by Comrade Stalin, into whose hands Stalin gave the great Lenin banner."

THE PARTY MACHINE: MALENKOV AND KHRUSHCHEV

The Supreme Soviet, called to meet on March 14 to "ratify" the changes made on the day of Stalin's death, was postponed for a day without explanation. When it met, the list of cabinet ministers presented to it differed from the list that had been broadcast on March 6. Again no explanation. Secretly the "Central Committee of the Party" had met on March 14 and had come to significant decisions which were kept secret for a full week. The Soviet met for only one hour, one of the shortest sessions on record. It applauded the reports of the changes made on the day of Stalin's death, as mysteriously changed again by the secret meeting of March 14, but it did not go through the formality of voting its approval on anything. Malenkov told the deputies: "The strength of the Government will consist in its collective nature." Only on March 21, a full week later, was it announced that on March 14, Malenkov, "at his own request," had been removed as Secretary of the party and thereby deprived of the dual leading posts that seemed to mark him for the succession.

Neither the editors of the regional and provincial press nor the Supreme Soviet had been informed of the decisions of the secret top party meeting on March 14. It is inconceivable that it was a full Central Committee meeting as stated, for that is so large (216 persons) that the news would have reached the editors and secretaries of the Constituent Republics. As late as March 21 and 22, provincial papers continued to carry greetings to Malenkov in place of the column headed "News of the Day," and references to his dual titles and his position as "head of the party" or "the government" or both. Then suddenly this ceased. Most papers skipped one full day, without publication—in many cases not the usual off day—and a surprising number of them reappeared next day with the name of a new editor at the masthead.

When Malenkov first reported to the Supreme Soviet on the changes being made in the "Stalinist" party and government, he presented them as having been "contemplated and approved" by Stalin. Actually, they reversed in significant ways things that Stalin had done at the Nineteenth Congress. The Congress had abolished the Politburo in favor of a large and formless Presidium of twenty-five. Now the Presidium was reduced to ten, in most cases the old Politburo members. Never before has a deliberative body in the Soviet Union thus contained an even number of persons because of the danger of a tie vote. This suggests a state of dead-lock and of bargaining over a precarious equilibrium.

The Secretariat, increased by the Nineteenth Congress to ten Secre-taries, was now reduced to five, with Malenkov as First Secretary. On March 14, when Malenkov lost his secretarial post, he was replaced by Khrushchev. A few weeks later, Ignatiev, who had been elevated to the place of a party Secretary only on the death of Stalin, was peremptorily dismissed in connection with the "doctors' frame-up." Thus the Secretariat would now appear to be reduced from ten to four.

No less startling were the changes in Stalin's governmental arrange-ments. The inner cabinet of fourteen Deputy Premiers was reduced to five or six. Malenkov was made Premier, but he was surrounded by, and put under the obvious control of, members of the "old guard." To emphasize their importance, the party performed the miracle of appointing four "First Deputy Premiers" to work with him. Though all four are called "First" their names had to be mentioned in some order; Beria was named as first "First," Molotov second, Bulganin third, and Kaganovich fourth First Deputy Premier. In addition, one more member of Stalin's old guard, Mikoyan, was named a Deputy Premier, the only one with no "First" before his title.

THE SECRET POLICE: BERIA

The Ministry of the Interior and the Ministry of State Security were combined into one single body, and Lavrenti Beria, whom Stalin had "kicked upstairs," was restored to his old post as head of the com-bined secret police forces. The Ministry of War and the Ministry of the Navy were combined into one, and Bulganin was made Minister, with two "First" deputies, Generals Zhukov and Vasilevsky. Thus the army was brought back into the structure of carefully counterbalanced forces, and General Zhukov, whom Stalin had jealously exiled to a remote secondary post, reappeared as a kind of "representative" of the General Staff. Voroshilov, now aged seventy-two, was made Chairman of the Presidium of the Supreme Soviet. This might seem to be merely an honorary office, but in the delicate balance of forces it too proved to have power implica-tions, for on March 28, when Malenkov's recession had begun, it was Voroshilov, Chairman of the Presidium, rather than Malenkov, Premier and Chairman of the Council of Ministers, whose name was signed to the popularity-seeking decree on amnesty. If Stalin had chosen to issue an amnesty, he would never have let the chairman of a purely honorary body sign in place of him.

Lavrenti Beria seemed to be on his way out at the moment of Stalin's death. For more than a decade a favorite of Stalin's, he had first run Georgia as head of the Georgian police, and then risen to All-Union Security Chief. In 1946, after the post had been divided into two, a Minister of State Security and a Minister of the Interior, Beria was relieved of direct responsibility for either, and elevated to Deputy Premier "to devote full time to his main work." People assumed that the main work was either atomic energy and atomic espionage, or overall supervision of both security forces. Beria's men were put in charge of both, as earlier his men had been put in charge of Georgia when he left for Moscow.

The first visible sign of Beria's decline was a large-scale purge of his appointees in his native Georgia during 1952. Mgeladze, an anti-Beria man, became First Secretary of the Georgian Party, and with the assistance of Rukhadze, head of the secret police, "crushed in a Stalinist manner" many lesser leaders. Stalin, as was his fashion, forced Beria to discredit himself with his own followers by sanctioning these purges. At the Nineteenth Congress in October 1952, Stalin eliminated Beria's man, Abakumov, Minister of State Security of the USSR, from his party and government posts. And on January 13, 1953, the lightning struck again. After patient preparation by Stalin and Malenkov, it was announced that the top Kremlin doctors were "poisoners," and that the deaths of Scherbakov and Zhdanov, which had occurred while Beria was still a power in the secret police, were brought on by the doctor-poisoners. All this had happened because the security forces were guilty of "lack of vigilance." Things began to look ominous for Beria.

As a cerebral hemorrhage saved Stalin when Lenin was about to remove him as General Secretary in 1923, so death intervened to save Beria on March 5, 1953. The very next day, the ministries of State Security and the Interior were recombined into one, and Lavrenti Beria's hand closed firmly on the mighty power lever. Beria was one of the three speakers at Stalin's funeral. It was he who made the nomination of Malenkov as Premier. On March 21, Malenkov resigned the post of Secretary through which Stalin had paved his way to power. But Beria had two serious handicaps to overcome. First of these was the unpopularity that always has clung to the head of the secret police. Beria's speeches began to include vows to protect the civil rights of the Soviet citizen and uphold the constitution. On March 28, a sweeping amnesty of petty offenders was proclaimed, and the penal code was ordered revised "within 60 days."

On April 3, the "doctors' plot" was declared a frame-up, the anti-Beria police leaders held responsible and placed under arrest. In the name of undoing an injustice, a counterpurge thus got under way. On April 6, Semyon D. Ignatiev, whom Stalin and Malenkov had put into the post of

Minister of State Security when Beria was losing his grip, and whom Malenkov had just made a party Secretary, was accused of "political blindness and gullibility." On April 7, his ousting was announced.

Exactly one week later, on April 14, Beria struck back in Georgia. Secretary Mgeladze, Security Minister Rukhadze and "their accomplices" were charged with having framed up innocent Georgian leaders, "trampled down the rights of Soviet citizens," extracted "false confessions by impermissible means" (torture), "cooked up charges of nonexistent nationalism," and shown themselves to be "enemies of the people." The accused were rehabilitated and restored to their posts. That same day, new police chiefs were appointed in virtually all the republics of the Soviet Union. All published names seemed to be Russian, regardless of the nationality involved, and many of them were known Beria men.

THE ARMY AS A POTENTIAL POWER LEVER

The secret police has its tentacles everywhere, in every factory, in every *kolkhoz*, in every party organization. But the party, too, has its cells everywhere, even in the secret police. The army is riddled with party agents and secret police agents and has been the most jealously watched power instrument of all. It was built by Trotsky, who died in exile with a blow from an Alpine pick in the back of his head. It was mechanized by Tukhachevsky, who fell in the blood purges along with virtually the entire General Staff. Thereafter it bore a deep grudge against the secret police, which Stalin apparently was trying to mollify with his talk of "lack of vigilance of the security organs" in the "doctors' plot against leading military figures." Generals Zhukov, Timoshenko, Vasilevsky, Konev, Sokolovsky were moved about by Stalin as in musical chairs to prevent their popularity from growing too great, and watched over by a political "General, Marshal and War Minister," Bulganin. Yet the army has a strong *esprit de corps*, and if it can unite on a candidate it may well in a long struggle become the most powerful contender.

Moreover, in this totalitarian land the army is the only potentially "democratic" power instrument. The Russian and Soviet peoples cannot possibly identify themselves with the party machine which has enslaved and driven them and waged upon them an unending war of nerves. Still less with the secret police which has tortured, enslaved, purged. But the army did serve them in defending their frontiers and homes against the invader. And the army is a part of them and they of it, since all able-bodied males serve in it, and in it are better fed, clothed, and housed than at any other time in their lives. Finally, the army is thought of as for defense rather than for a deeply feared aggressive war. The people trust the army more than they do the party or the police, and around it they could most readily be rallied.

MAKEWEIGHTS OR MASS ORGANIZATIONS?

The three power levers, moreover, are not mechanical things, but living organisms with hundreds of thousands, even millions, of members. Such power levers can be used symbolically in maneuvering for position in a muted struggle. But they cannot be brought into actual play surreptitiously and behind the scenes. If the contenders do not manage to finish each other off, by some combination of subordination and purge, behind the scenes, then three great power machines, each embracing their millions of members and their families, may be brought into action in one or another combination.

Then whoever appeals to the party must appeal to some traditions, some program, something in the past and present and something proposed for the future. Whoever appeals to the army likewise. And to the secret police the same. If the struggle is prolonged and enlarged, there are other reserves of power to be tapped: the moribund trade unions, the regions and nationalities, the local party members, the nascent *esprit de corps* of officials and technicians, the *kolkhozes*, the factories. In any case the struggle to replace the charismatic leader with another of the same type is inseparable from the total state. And, overt or covert, the struggle is bound to smoulder for a long time.

If ever these power levers are to be not merely used as makeweights but brought into play as actual levers of power, then anything might happen. Then the empire,[4] which cannot take orders from an upstart as easily as it could from Stalin, may regain its independent life. The Soviet peoples, so long in chains, may then recover their freedom, while the outside world, safe only when Russia is democratic once more, may regain its lost hope of a genuine, just, and enduring peace.

But the current "peace talk" must not be confused with such genuine peace. The men in the Kremlin are moving from weakness and the uncertainties of their internal struggle. Just as during the famine of the early 1920s they made their strategic retreats of the NEP (Lenin's 1921 New Economic Policy) and offered "concessions" to foreigners, as during the anti-Comintern axis they talked "Stalinist constitution" plus "popu-

---

4. By *the empire,* I meant the satellite states of Eastern Europe. The muted struggle for independence that began with Khrushchev's destalinization speech has assumed new and diverse forms in the closing years of the nineteen sixties. Less overtly and under less favorable conditions there has been unrest among national minorities of the "inner empire."

lar front," as during the first onslaught of Hitler's invasion they "abolished" the Comintern—so once more they are moving from weakness and talking "peace." But during the NEP Lenin completed the political foundations of the total state. The Stalinist constitution was translated into life by the blood purges. The abolition of the Comintern was accompanied by the dispatch of its agents into the "liberated" countries to turn them into "People's Democracies." And once more the very decrees of amnesty and of justice to the doctors contain menacing phrases about renewed "vigilance" and are accompanied by fresh purges.

Still totalitarianism's difficulty, whether writ large or small, is freedom's opportunity. The world, in this writer's judgment, except for the dangers which may spring from its own failures to understand what it is watching, is safer for the moment while a regime based on total force and total dictatorship goes through its convulsive struggles to solve the insoluble problem of a "legal" and "peaceful" succession in a system that knows neither law nor peace.

—July 1953

V THE AGE OF THE DIMINISHING DICTATORS*

The men who have been ruling the Soviet Union since Stalin's death are *epigoni*, "sons," aftercomers. They owe their power to an apostolic succession and they style themselves disciples of Lenin and comrades-in-arms of Stalin.[1] The structure and dynamics of their rule are dictated by the same philosophy, incorporated in the same single-party police state; the rule continues to be totalitarian in scope and aim and is engaged in the same unending war on its own people, the same drive to reshape and control the globe. Still, they are new men, younger men, men with different formative backgrounds, and their regime has a new look.

The Khrushchevs and Malenkovs, and men younger still, who now form the post-Stalinist "collective leadership," are the men Stalin gathered around him in his rise to personal dictatorship. They were wholly formed in the Stalinist fight for a monopoly of power and in the iron age of forced industrialization, forced collectivization, and blood purge. They were brought up not as underground revolutionaries but under the new regime of bureaucratic totalitarianism.[2]

They do not even look like the men who were Lenin's close associates. As one contemplates the pictures of them lined up on Lenin's (then also Stalin's) tomb, one cannot but be struck by the fact that they are all fleshy, solid, square, and squat—"fat boys," to borrow an old "wobbly" term against labor bureaucrats. Harrison Salisbury has called our attention to a curious detail that none of them is over 5 feet 4 inches (Stalin's police record gives his height as 5 feet 3¾ inches)—as if they had been chosen not merely with regard to faction loyalty and party infighting and administrative capacity, but also that their height, spiritual and physical, should not dwarf the none-too-tall leader who had perforce to

---

* Reprinted from *Foreign Affairs*, January, 1955, copyright by The Council on Foreign Relations, Inc. Its original title was "A New Look at That New Look."

1. This was written before "destalinization."

2. Lenin was born in 1870, Stalin and Trotsky in 1879, Zinoviev in 1883, Bukharin in 1888. Khrushchev was born in 1894, but did not join the Communist party until 1918, after it had taken power. Malenkov was born in 1902 and joined the Communist party only in 1920. Brezhnev was born in 1906 and joined the party in 1931 (from the Young Communist League which he entered in 1923).

216

excel in all things.[3] Actually Stalin managed to look taller than they on Lenin's tomb by having a little raised platform built under him.

There is, to be sure, a remnant of old bolsheviks among the new "collective leadership." But these older men, Molotov, Voroshilov, Kaganovich, and Mikoyan, owe their places, indeed their very survival, to the fact that they were cronies of Joseph Stalin. Second-string figures in Lenin's day, from the outset faction adherents of Stalin rather than Lenin, they came out of the crucible of the purges refashioned, so to speak, as "new men."

What is collective about this collective leadership, and will it continue to be a collective? What can the world expect that will be new in the work and ways and aims of these new men who have taken over Stalin's power? And what of continuity? It is these questions that constitute the real problem of the "new look."

In theory it is conceivable that a committee government, a *Directoire*, a duumvirate, triumvirate or decemvirate, could wield autocratic, dictatorial, and total power. But the whole course of Soviet history and the whole dynamic of autocracy, dictatorship, and totalitarianism work against it.

DICTATORSHIP REQUIRES A DICTATOR

Lenin began by creating a party in which the Center selected the local committees, which in turn sent delegates to the conventions that confirmed the Center. He seized power by a minority conspiracy, drained democracy of authority by dispersing the Constituent Assembly, drained the Soviets of authority by outlawing all other parties and deciding all things in the Communist Central Committee and its fractions, drained the party of authority by forbidding factional controversy, drained the Central Committee of authority by setting up the Politburo, and the Politburo by settling matters by telephone, telegram, letter, and personal conversation. Inside the Politburo he never altogether sloughed off the appearance of "collegial" power; in his will he sought in vain to preserve that one last redoubt of collectivity.

It took close to a decade before the "collective leadership," of which Stalin appeared but to be the faithful *apparat* wheel horse, was openly dissolved in favor of his personal power. With his death his lieutenants are faced with the problem that in a dictatorship there is no legitimacy and no legal succession. These men have been taught in a hard school to make many moves in their head before they touch one piece on the

3. The one exception is the tall, gaunt, ailing Suslov, who as long as Stalin was alive always stood in back where his comparative height would not be noticed.

chessboard of power. The bloody list of their dead gives them every reason to combine forces against any man who moves too fast or too bloodily. That they would begin their orphaned rule with the proclamation of a "collective leadership" could have been predicted.

That first holding company included Beria, who was nominated by Malenkov, and Malenkov, who was nominated by Beria. Within a few weeks after Stalin's death, a newspaper build-up which seemed to portend Malenkov's rise to dominant power was put a stop to by some decision of his associates, and he was "relieved" of the post of party Secretary "at his own request." That brought Khrushchev into a top-ranking position as party Secretary. Beria's undoing came from his too rapid moves to make the secret police independent of the party and through it to strengthen his control of certain "republican governments" and the party machine. This aroused the fears of so many of his associates that, suddenly, they combined against him and there was one "collective leader" less.

As long as the power question is not settled and the pyramid of power is without an apex, these men will jealously watch each other and makes promises of reforms to their subjects. They will continue Stalin's policy of avoiding either all-out war or all-out peace. They cannot tolerate all-out peace, since the very excuse for the existence of their perpetual state-of-emergency regime is "capitalist encirclement." Like Stalin, they have two reasons for avoiding all-out war. The first is doctrinal; their central belief teaches them that they are the wave of the future, that the capitalist order is in decay, that time is on their side. The other is a readiness to risk war at the periphery with limited engagements and "calculated risks," without jeopardizing their power center, the loss of which in all-out war might change the course of history.[4]

To Stalin's hesitancies they add one more: as long as the power question is not settled, they dare not put live ammunition and overwhelming force in the hands of the army, lest "Bonapartism" settle the problem of power in its own fashion. Thus we could do well to remember that their present minuscule concessions in foreign relations come not only from their calculation that they may divide the free world, isolate America and cut off her support from some sector of Europe or Asia, but no less from recognition of their own internal weakness. "Collective leadership . . . the party and the government . . . the wise Central Committee"—so far they have cast about in vain for an overwhelming power symbol that can paralyze dissent, command obedience and worship in union and empire, such as was commanded by the Stalin cult and Stalin's word and name. The struggle may be muted and concealed, it

---

4. Since this was written a third, even more compelling reason has been added: the atomic stalemate.

may be long or short, it may be compromised and blunted again and again, but the whole dynamics of dictatorship cries out for a dictator, autocracy for an autocrat, militarized command and militarized life for a supreme commander, infallible government for an infallible leader, an authoritarian setup for an authority, a totalitarian state for a *Duce, Führer, Vozhd*.

EBB AND REFLUX OF THE STALIN CULT

The Stalin cult, whose high priests these men were, has made the problem of the succession more difficult. By attributing to Stalin all successes and to themselves and their subordinates all failures, shortcomings, or unpleasant consequences, they enlarged his person until it filled the horizon, diminishing their own to the point of nullity.

In this swollen form, the Stalin myth was dead as soon as his body was cold. For what right did such dwarfed men have to be individual or collective dictators? Moreover, in the end they were irked by his arrogation to himself of credit for all they did, thought up, ghost-wrote for him, by the precariousness of their positions dependent entirely on the caprice of one man, by the need each day to kindle greater clouds of incense to his name. Their cold funeral addresses, concerned with programs and power, testified to the fact that he had exacted so much "posthumous tribute" while alive that there was no reserve to call on after his death. These historians of the purge, who had rewritten recent history so often and continuously in order to enlarge and glorify Stalin's works and name, began immediately a fresh rewriting of history to cut him down to size—not to actual size, but to their own size, so that there could be some sense in their claim to individual or collective succession. Henceforth, Lenin is the author of the great theories and the initiator of the great works, and Stalin is reduced to continuator, developer, and disciple. They, for their part, are co-disciples of Lenin and comrade-in-arms of Stalin and, by virtue of membership in the same leading body, coauthors of all the theories, policies, and plans hitherto called Stalinist.

Many wrongly concluded that the process would not stop until Stalin's name had been extinguished and his policies abandoned. But his orphaned disciples had no intentions of doing one or the other. They cannot extinguish his name, for what other claim do they have to rule the Soviet land except association with Stalin and discipleship to Lenin in an unbroken apostolic succession? Nor do they wish to abandon his policies, for these are in fact their policies no less than his.

In Russia, the death of a despot has always awakened a lively expectation of change. The most unlikely princelings have been endowed with gentle attributes until their acts as tsars dispelled illusion. The greater the despotism, the greater the expectation of change. But only when the death of a despot coincided with some defeat to his system has the expectation in part been realized.

When Stalin died, the first picture of a nation all contracted in one brow of woe was soon replaced by more authentic reports of this general expectation of change. We now know that there was ill-concealed rejoicing, that men got drunk, that whole regiments celebrated in Germany, that in a far-off Vorkuta concentration camp inmates turned their hopes into a strike for better conditions and were given concessions even as force was being used and ringleaders executed. Sweeping promises had to be made to the satellites; workingmen struck in East Germany and Czechoslovakia and stood up, unarmed, against Russian tanks. All this exerted powerful pressures upon men whose power position was unsettled and whose succession is based upon neither constitutional nor hereditary legitimacy.

Nor was the free world exempt from illusion. One of Britain's leading authorities on Soviet history rushed out a book to prove that Stalin by barbarous methods had so civilized and transformed Russia that further Stalinist barbarism was impossible. Another stoutly declared that since all thinking was colored by emotion he preferred "wishful rather than despairing thinking." The same writers who had once assured us that the "realist and nationalist" Stalin had put an end to Trotsky's dream of world revolution and that "the wise old realist" was curbing the hotheads of the Politburo now declared that Stalin had been more than a little mad and that soberer and more realistic heads were taking over power.

Even the wise and wary Churchill, two months after Stalin's death, spoke of a "new regime" and what he hoped was "a change of attitude." He who had alerted America to the iron curtain and the need of united defense against aggression now permitted himself to dream that the last great act of his declining years might be a fresh four-power conference like those with Stalin and Roosevelt to settle unsettled things. On October 10, 1954, he put it quite soberly: "A year and a half ago, Stalin died, and ever since then I have nourished the hope that there is a new outlook in Russia, a new hope of peaceful coexistence with the Russian nation, and that it is our duty patiently and daringly to make sure whether there is such a chance or not."

In a land where secrecy and power are alike total, every smallest flutter of a leaf is likely to be magnified into the fall of forests. No longer badgered by his patron, Molotov proves a little gayer, makes fresh démarches, and tries altering his formulae without stopping to call up the Kremlin—but without yielding an iota of his essential, stubbornly held position; this is magnified into "concessions," a "new flexibility," evidence that there is real "departmentalization" and "separation of powers." General Zhukov echoes Ambassador Bohlen's toast "to justice"; on the stubborn iteration is built an entire structure of fantasy: army independence, army paramountcy, open conflict between army and party. Khrushchev hangs back for a last word when his comrades are departing from a state banquet; this is reported as evidence that the party Secretary is "an amiable chatterbox . . . hail-fellow well met." Malenkov picks flowers for an English lady, clinks a lady's glass and toasts "the ladies," and the new Premier becomes a bashful fat boy, "full of old-fashioned grace and courtesy . . . a Little Lord Fauntleroy." Hence it becomes important to inquire how new these new men really are.

THE "NEW" MEN

Khrushchev, the "amiable chatterbox" who then led the party machine, began the really important part of his biography in 1929 with the great forced collectivization drive in the Ukraine and the mass liquidation of all who held back. Then in Moscow he took part in the *Yezhovshchina*, without garrulousness contributing his share to the organization of the great blood purge. During the war he directed partisan warfare behind the German occupier's lines, visiting punishment on waverers and collaborators. He is credited with having strengthened Russia's support among the masses by acts calculated to increase the cruelty of the Germans and with giving orders to assassinate the gentler puppet mayors and spare the crueler ones as the best way of inflaming opposition to the occupiers.[5] After the war Khrushchev returned to the Ukraine as liquidator of small private land holdings, collectivizer, industrializer, Russifier, and avenger. This "chatterbox" worked quietly for a year and a half, then reported that "in the past eighteen months more than fifty per cent of all officials" had been removed from their posts. In 1950 he opened the war on the collective farm in favor of the development of *agrogorods* (agricultural cities). There was resistance, local criticisms by Arutiunian in Armenia and Bagirov in Azerbaijan, partial retreat. But the number of collective farms was reduced from 250,000 in 1950 to 94,000 in 1953. And when Beria fell, Arutiunian and Bagirov, Khrushchev's critics of 1950, died too. At the Nineteenth Congress, Khrushchev delivered the report on the revision of the party statutes that represented a further tightening of

5. For many of the biographical details in this article I am indebted to the researches and reports of Lazar Pistrak, of the United States Information Library and to Boris Nicolaevsky. Others come from wartime and postwar Russian refugees, and from Soviet documents.

totalitarian controls. After Stalin's death, he became First Secretary of the party, and led the new drives in agriculture.

As for Malenkov, he began his career as Secretary of the Communist cell of the Moscow Higher Technical School, where he gathered around him the Saburovs, Pervukhins and Malyshevs who switched like him from engineering to politics, becoming engineer-chekists, party commissars in technology and industry. It is on the entrance of these engineer-chekist associates of Malenkov into the ruling circle that so many commentators have based the contention that party rule is now giving ground to the claims of the new technocracy. But these men are instruments of party penetration into and control of technology, just as Bulganin is not a military general who has gotten into the Politburo but an agent of the party and the police-made Marshal and Minister of Defense to control the army.

In 1934, Malenkov became Chief of the Department of Leading Party Organs, which had charge of placements, removals, dossiers. In the bloody years of the *Yezhovshchina*, he was the chief organizer of the purges in so far as they had a planned, centralized, and systematic party character. As Yezhov advanced, Malenkov was made his deputy in this department, supplying the dossiers and the indications as to chain reactions when any leading official fell. In December 1937, *Partiinoe Stroitelstvo*, which Malenkov edited, carried the following lead editorial:

Under the leadership of the Stalinist People's Commisar, Comrade Yezhov, the Soviet Intelligence Service has inflicted merciless and devastating blows on the Fascist bandits. The Soviet people love their intelligence service . . . it is their flesh and blood. . . . The faithful guardians of Socialism, the men of the NKVD under the leadership of their Stalinist People's Commissar, Comrade Yezhov, will continue in the future to root out the enemies of the people, the vile Trotskyite-Bukharinite, bourgeois-nationalist, and other agents of Fascism. Let the spies and traitors tremble! The punitive hand of the Soviet people, and NKVD, will annihilate them! Our ardent Bolshevik greetings to the Stalinist Commissar of Internal Affairs, Nikolai Ivanovich Yezhov!

The *troika* that planned the purges under Joseph Stalin's personal direction was made up of Malenkov, keeper of the dossiers and supplier of leads, Vyshinsky, prosecutor and impresario of staged trials, and Yezhov, apprehender, inquisitor and executioner. When the fury had run its course, Yezhov was made the expiatory goat; Malenkov and Vyshinsky were promoted. The year Yezhov disappeared, Malenkov was made head of the new Administration of Party Cadres, which "keeps a strict personal register of every party member and candidate" in some 2.5 million dossiers on standing, public and private life, friends, talents, vulnerabilities, along with dossiers on perhaps 500,000 specialists in industry and agriculture.[6] It is this key index which Malenkov has now surrendered—reluctantly, I would imagine—to party Secretary Khrushchev. In any case, Malenkov's connection with the *Yezhovshchina* should help us to keep our perspective on this "Little Lord Fauntleroy."

COLLECTIVE CONSULTATION UNDER STALIN

Thanks to our penchant for personalizing and the impact even on us of the Stalin cult, we are prone to forget that Stalin did not work out his policies alone. When the informed think of the Stalinist agricultural policy, they think of Khrushchev. When they think of the Stalinist line in literature and intellectual life, they think of Zhdanov, and, after his death, of Khrushchev. In short, the Stalinist leadership was also a "collective leadership," with the difference that there was one top man who must always be credited, could never be blamed, and who had the sometimes arbitrary and capricious and always decisive last word.

Finding all about them the general expectation of change, faced with uncertainty as to their own authority and structure of succession, anxious to prevent "disorder and panic" (as the funeral ceremonies declared), the henchmen of the dead dictator were glad to take advantage of the credit opened to them on the theory that they were "new" men from whom a "change" could be expected. Yet one of their prime motives in cutting Stalin down to their size was to emphasize that all of them ("the party and the Central Committee"), not Stalin alone, were the authors of the "great" policies and doctrines. They even denied, and we know that they did so rightly, that Stalin was the author of the *History of the Communist Party: Short Course*, first published as the work of a collective and then arrogated to Stalin as Volume XV of his *Collected Works*.[7] And we must admit that the liquidation of Beria and his close associates was in the best "Stalinist" tradition.

The releasing of a few Soviet-born wives; gracious toasts at banquets; less surliness in conversation; repetition, as a rule in the self-same language, of the calculated utterances of Lenin and Stalin on "peaceful co-existence"—only against the background of Soviet truculence could this be taken as something significant. And then only if we permit ourselves to forget how many times this ebb and flow in the realization of an unchanging long-range aim has occurred before, either when internal weak-

6. This was in 1939; the number of dossiers has since increased several fold.

7. Actually "destalinization" prevented the publication in Russia of the closing volumes, XIV, XV, and XVI which were edited by Robert H. McNeal and published by the Hoover Institution in 1967.

ness or too quick a build-up of resistance abroad or the desire to cover an offensive with an umbrella of peace talk, has prompted Stalin to roar gentle as any sucking dove.

PEACEFUL COEXISTENCE

This is not the place to go through the long history of "peaceful coexistence." We can trace various facets back to Lenin's declaration in October 1915 that if he got power he would propose an unacceptable peace and "prepare a revolutionary war"; to Trotsky's pronouncement two weeks after they took power ("We desire the speediest peace on the principles of honorable coexistence and cooperation of peoples; we desire the speediest overthrow of the rule of capital"); to Lenin's 1920 coexistence statement to a Hearst reporter followed the same year by a warning to the Moscow party cell leaders (kept secret till after his death) that "as long as capitalism and socialism exist side by side we cannot live in peace"; to Litvinov's 1922 proposal of a "proportional reduction in arms" at a time when the Soviet Union was secretively arming with the aid of the German Wehrmacht. The whole sequence of these utterances, from the first down to Malenkov's amiable chat with Ambassador Bohlen and Congressman Wickersham while MIG's were shooting down one of our planes that had lost its way, boils down to this: divide and disarm your opponents while you work unceasingly for their destruction.

Nor is there anything these "new" men have so far done that would not accord with the last programmatic utterance on foreign policy by Joseph Stalin (in *Economic Problems of Socialism in the USSR*, 1952) in which he urged that through the "peace fight" they could undermine "bellicose governments," perhaps develop the peace movement into "a movement for the overthrow of capitalism," make more likely war between capitalist countries than between the non-Soviet and the Soviet worlds and isolate the United States. ("To think that Germany, Britain, France, Italy, and Japan . . . will not try to smash U.S. domination and force their way to independent development is to believe in miracles.")

The main foreign policy proposals were summed up by Marshal Bulganin in a speech delivered on November 7, 1954:

(1) "A collective security system in Europe, *i.e.*, Europe with Russia but without the United States.

(2) German unification by "peaceful means," *i.e.*, the continued disarming of Germany and the holding of "elections" such as have been proposed in Korea, and practiced so resourcefully in the "peaceful unification" of all postwar satellite coalition governments.

(3) Proportionate reduction of armaments, which would leave over-

whelming superiority to the heavily armed Soviet bloc; and "prohibition of weapons of mass extermination," which would eliminate the one weapon in which the free world has superiority, without the guarantees of a foolproof control and inspection.

The only thing one can find that is new in this third of a century of juggling with "peaceful coexistence" is that leading spokesmen of the free world have begun to employ the term without sufficient attempt to analyze it and purify it of the corruption which infects it. Since for the free world peace is a matter of principle and for the Kremlin a calculated maneuver, surely our spokesmen should be able to express our desire for peace in some warmer and less tarnished language. It is up to us to remember that the Kremlin's tactical maneuvers can be most flexible because these are severely disciplined by an overall strategy and unshakeable objective of world conquest. But we can get lost in these tactical zigzags if our own overall objective is lost sight of. I cannot believe that that objective is merely to survive while peace is steadily eroded and the more vulnerable parts of the free world picked off one by one. Our idea of peace is wrapped up with justice and with freedom and is ultimately secure only to the extent that freedom can defend itself and that peoples everywhere gain control of their governmental policies. To take these corrupt words and artful maneuvers at face value is but to add to the confusion and moral disarming which is their real objective.

"Peaceful coexistence" has a long history now. In the words of Santayana, "those who will not learn from the past are condemned to repeat it."

CONTINUING THE REVOLUTION FROM ABOVE: THE NEW LANDS

In Stalin's last and most significant theoretical work, *Economic Problems of Socialism in the USSR*, published late in 1952,[8] he lays down the prerequisites for the transformation of the present "socialist" Russia into "complete communism." In this work is to be found literally the whole stock of formulae on which Khrushchev and company are now proceeding. Here is to be found the proposal rapidly to increase the satisfaction of consumer demand on the basis of "primacy in the production of means of production." Here is the outline of the drive to increase labor discipline on the basis of "the control over the amount of labor and the amount of

8. The style of the work makes it clear that it was ghost-written for him. There is reason to believe that Suslov was the principal author both of Stalin's last work and of Khrushchev's program of the Communist party unanimously adopted by the Twenty-second Party Congress.

consumption" until labor discipline is transformed into spontaneous self-discipline, from an "obligation into a prime necessity of life." Here, too, is the line on isolating America and promoting differences in the capitalist camp that we have already examined. The work is scrappy and fragmentary but bears internal evidence of summing up in algebraic formulae all the trains of thought that were then actuating Stalin and his close associates.

In it Stalin distinguishes between two kinds of property in the present-day Soviet Union: "State- or publicly owned production and collective farm production, which cannot be said to be publicly owned." The main task of the transition to communism, which is now beginning, is to "raise the level" of collective farm property to that of state- or publicly owned property, and to create thus a "single and united" system. How "the formation of a single and united sector" is to be brought about, "whether simply by the swallowing up of the collective farm sector by the state sector . . . or by the setting up of a single national economic body," Stalin refuses to say. But he is emphatic that it can be done by the pressure of the "superstructure," the state, "upon the relations of production," that it can be done "without upheavals," that is represents a revolution from above, and that it must be undertaken gradually but without delay, that "it is of paramount importance for us," that in the process "the new" will not "simply destroy the old, but infiltrates into it, changes its nature and function without smashing its form." Until it is accomplished, the state has not as complete control of agriculture as of industry and is hampered in its precise planning and calculation.

It would be unpardonable not to see that these factors are already beginning to fetter the powerful development of our productive forces since they create obstacles to the full extension of government planning to the whole of the national economy, especially agriculture. . . . The task therefore is to eliminate these contradictions by gradually converting collective-farm property into public [state] property. . . .

To this subject Stalin devoted more space and attention than to any other and returned again and again. And in this, I think, we can find the theoretical foundation and the emotional force behind the Khrushchev drive for a revolution in agriculture. What was the drive to uproot the collective farms and combine them into agrogorods, begun in Stalin's lifetime, but an attempt to "raise collective farm property to the level of public property . . . infiltrate it, change its nature and function without smashing its form"? Does their opposition to what they thought only a personal project of Khrushchev explain why Beria fell into disfavor during Stalin's last days and help explain why the agrogorod critics, Arutiunian and Bagirov, fell with Beria? And what is the new plowing up of steppe, pasture, marginal, and abandoned lands in Kazakhstan, Siberia, and other distant parts of the empire, with "volunteers" from the cities, but a new mass flank attack upon the recalcitrant collective farm?

Like any flanking movement, it has been presented with dissimulation as a fresh attempt to solve the problem of the shortage of grain and meat (cattle) created by the earlier revolution from above, the collectivization drive of the 1930s. Like that drive it suffers from gigantism, recklessness, and lack of preparation. Like the earlier drive its shock troops come not from the farms but from the cities. These young men and women may have no preparation for farming, but neither have they any loyalty to the collective and the private parcel or any memory of the days of individual farming. What is this mass displacement of young men and women and tractors and seeds to virgin or untilled lands but a gigantic step on the road that bypasses the *kolkhoz* and presents it with a rival in a new congeries of giant *sovkhozes* or state farms?

Of the 32 million acres of virgin soil to be brought under cultivation during 1954-1955, 15.8 million acres are located in Kazakhstan. Without a word being said of it, the over 140,000 workers who have been "volunteered" into the new regions represent one more invasion in the long war against the Asiatic steppe and its nomadic, cattle-raising, Turkic peoples. This war was not begun by the bolsheviks but by the tsars. But the drive for forced collectivization of the early 1930s hit hardest in individual-farming Ukrainia and in cattle-raising Kazakhstan. In the latter, where the nomads follow the grass on the range, the wholesale slaughter of stock reached catastrophic proportions from which, as Khrushchev's reports show, Russia has not yet recovered in more than two decades. According to Khrushchev, the number of cattle in the Soviet Union in 1953 was below that of 1916 (last year of the tsars and in the midst of world war) and less than 1928 (before the collectivization drive began). But since 1928 there has been an enormous increase in population and in area, so that the amount of meat, butter, milk, hides, as well as grain, per capita has greatly diminished.

There is already a serious labor shortage on the old collective farms and a serious shortage of machines, but as in the earlier experiments in gigantism and revolution from above, everything is being thrown into the battle of the moment so that the old areas are being stripped of machines and seed and technicians and hands while the new areas lack drinking water, irrigation, housing, sanitation, food, tractors, and seed. Lands are being plowed up that are marginal. If the rains are good, the lands will yield. When bad years come—and it is their semiaridity that makes them range rather than farm areas—they are likely to become dust bowls. There are deep inconsistencies in the promise of more meat on the one hand and the planned figures for increased cattle breeding on the other and between both of these and the plowing up of the range. But as in the collectivization drive of the early 1930s, Khrushchev in the best Stalinist tradition is counting that there is "no fortress the bolshevik determination cannot conquer," that the "superstructure" (the state) can "without upheavals" force changes in "productive relations." While they are at it, they hope to solve the nationalities problem in the Turkic areas by mass Russification and present the incompletely calculable and incompletely plannable *kolkhoz* sector with a completely controlled sector of new state farms.

STALINISM AFTER STALIN

To sum up. The "new men" who have succeeded to Stalin's power are not so new as they look to the uninquisitive eye, for they are Stalin's men. And a good look at the "new look" suggests that it is not so new either, for—more than Stalin would admit or they dared to claim, while he was alive—they worked out the Stalinist policies with him. Now that he is dead they have been able to cut the losses of some of the minor errors with which his stubbornness or prestige had become involved, but all their major policies from "peaceful coexistence" to the sensational plowing up of the virgin lands are in accord with plans elaborated and drives initiated while Stalin was alive. They do but give "arithmetical values" to "algebraic formulae" already worked out in the decisions of the Nineteenth Congress and in Stalin's so-called testament: *Economic Problems of Socialism in the USSR.* What the "new" men bring to their drives is the fresh vigor of younger men and a fresh flexibility in maneuver. But they are manifestly continuing the war on their own people —"the revolution from above"—and the war for the control of the world.

—January 1955

PART IV

Proletarian Dictatorship as a Higher Form of Democracy

* The title of this section comes from Lenin. He developed the cover terms, Soviet Government and Proletarian Dictatorship, for his own dictatorship and that of his party, then declared that it represented a "higher" and "the highest" form of democracy, "a million times more democratic than the most democratic parliamentary republic or the Constituent Assembly." These ideas are elaborated in his pamphlet, *The Proletarian Revolution and the Renegade Kautsky*, and his *Theses and Report on Bourgeois Democracy and the Dictatorship of the Proletariat* presented on March 4, 1919, to the First Congress of the Communist International.

I PROMETHEUS BOUND *

Ivan Ivanovich, sovereign member of the Russian ruling class, fretted at the snail-slow pace of the trolley car that carried him, sardine-fashion, along with eighty-eight co-rulers of the Russian land, to their respective places of work. It was Thursday morning, June 27, 1940. Ivan had got up early because twenty minutes' lateness meant obligatory dismissal and the entry of his dereliction in his workbook, which he must show wherever he applied for a new job.

Ivan stopped trying to peer out of the grimy window round the too broad back of the woman worker just in front of him and struggled to insert his folded *Pravda* between his nose and her hair. He didn't mind being squeezed against her softness, but one's eyes ached trying to read at such close range.

"UKAZ," he read in big, comfortable type, "OF THE PRESIDIUM OF THE SUPREME SOVIET OF THE USSR." Then his eyes came into sudden incredulous focus on the rest of the lengthy headline: "CONCERNING THE CHANGE TO THE EIGHT-HOUR DAY AND THE SEVEN-DAY WEEK, AND THE PROHIBITION OF SELF-WILLED DEPARTURE BY WORKERS AND EMPLOYEES FROM ENTERPRISES AND INSTITUTIONS."

But could this be today's paper? The seven-hour day had been the law of the land since 1927! Likewise the five-day week! They had even incorporated it into the Stalinist constitution of 1936, as a permanent conquest, under the head of the "right to leisure and rest." The constitution, he knew, could be amended—that was in Article 146—only "by decision of the Supreme Soviet of the USSR, approved by a majority of not less than two-thirds of the votes cast in each of its chambers." Yet the Supreme Soviet was not even in session. Then it could not be a ukaz but some sort of project for discussion.

No, there was no mistake. This was *Pravda* all right; and Thursday, June 27; and it was a decree with the usual signatures. At midnight, while he was snoring on his pillow, his terms of employment had

* Reprinted from *Harper's Magazine*, June, 1941, copyright 1941 by Bertram D. Wolfe. Original title, "Silent Soviet Revolution."

changed. Without discussion or referendum, without negotiation or collective bargaining, thirteen more hours had been added to his working week.

Would there be more pay for the additional hours? Just below the ukaz was a brief supplementary "decision" of the Council of People's Commissars: to keep the old daily wage without change and to reduce piecework and hourly rates so that the longer day would yield no more than the shorter. And there was an explanation by Comrade Shvernik, head of the Trade Unions. "If increase of wages were admitted," it said, "then there would not be any question of sacrifice. . . ."

The reader must not imagine that Ivan ceased to care whether he arrived on time. Nor did his mind dwell long on the lengthened day and the wage cut. The second part of the lengthy title of the ukaz drew his interest more than the first. He ran through the legal and technical terms of the decree until he reached Article 5:

> . . . workers and employees who, of their own will, leave state, cooperative and/or public enterprises, shall be handed over to the courts and, by sentence of the People's Judges, condemned to imprisonment. . . .

"Imprisonment"? The prisons were bursting already. Where would they find jails or concentration camps for all who tried to change their jobs in quest of a better dining hall, a friendlier foreman, a factory barracks or apartment house closer to the place of work, a more agreeable task? And what would they do now about lateness and absence, if these were no longer punishable by dismissal, no longer a recourse for discontent with one's job? The very next sentence suggested the answer to his questions:

> . . . for idleness (staying away from work, without acceptable cause, workers and employees of state, cooperative, and public enterprises and/or institutions shall be handed over to the courts and, by sentence of the People's Judges, condemned to forced penal labor at their place of employment, up to a term of six months, and to have withheld up to twenty-five per cent of their wages.

At their place of employment! So that was it. His own factory would be his "prison"; labor under penal discipline at the very job he had tried to leave would be his punishment; the deduction of twenty-five per cent from his wages would provide for him—and for his family—their prison fare of bread and water.

A SILENT SOVIET REVOLUTION

The ukaz which took Ivan Ivanovich by surprise that fine June morning of 1940 was but the culmination of a whole series of changes that had been taking place over a two-year period. Taken all together, they amounted to a silent social revolution—or counterrevolution, as you prefer—in the Soviet way of life.

To a degree unknown in history (even in the history of old Russia), these far-reaching social changes introduce fixity and absence of individual will or individual right. On the land, they attach the peasant permanently, from birth to death, to his *kolkhoz* or collective farm, and they introduce collective responsibility to the state for its yield. The worker in the city they attach permanently, from late childhood to death, to his particular factory and particular task. No one is to change his position or status except on the order of his superiors and as the interests of the state, interpreted by those superiors, may dictate.

Concomitant decrees prescribe fixity for the children of the working class by abolishing free secondary and higher education, thereby laying down the foundations of a new caste system in which only the children of well-paid bureaucrats and intellectuals can possibly prepare themselves to become officials or members of the intelligentsia. They establish a system of labor conscription and apprenticeship for boys and girls from fourteen years onward, attaching them to particular occupations and branches of industry which they may never leave for the rest of their lives unless it should please their superiors. And the decree we have quoted above makes the attempt to change one's job literally a criminal offense and by the provision for punitive "forced labor at their place of employment" converts factory labor into a form of prison labor.

The decrees of which we are speaking were given but little publicity abroad. The *Daily Worker* and *Soviet Russia Today*, journals which specialize in telling the world what life is like in the land of the Soviets, were silent on the letter and the spirit of this transformation. These decrees made the good Dean of Canterbury's book, dealing with the Soviet setup of 1937, seem to describe another world. The non-Communist press also let most of these changes and their cumulative import pass unnoticed. After the great trials of 1936-1937 and the quieter, more ruthless and more continuous purge which followed, silence settled down on the Soviet sixth of the earth. Pilgrimages, labor delegations, tourist travel were reduced to a thin trickle, then choked off altogether. Even loyal Communist party members, even party officials designated for official missions, were denied visas if they were of Russian birth, could speak the

Russian tongue, had relatives living in the Soviet Union.[1] After the invasion of Poland and Finland, the Kremlin clamped down a censorship on foreign press correspondents more absolute than any that had ever prevailed before in Russia's long history of censorship.

The "new order" thus shaping up in the Soviet Union has little in common with the socialism that was envisaged by the thinkers who founded the socialist movement. (Lenin came to power fully believing that the state, the apparatus of prisons, police, compulsions, dictation, and coercion, was shortly to "wither away" as useless in a free, socialist society.) But there is much of that old Russia which, despite three revolutions, has never altogether vanished. *Krepost* and *nevolya*—fixity and absence of individual will or individual freedom—were the outstanding characteristics of the old Russian life until they were modified by the *Razkreposhchenie*, the emancipation of the serfs, and the general "loosening of the bonds" in the closing decades of tsarist rule. Today they are the outstanding characteristics of the "new order" in the Soviet Union.

Other people, it has been mockingly said, consist of two parts, a body and a soul, but the Russians consist of three: a body, a soul, and a passport. The internal passport, abolished by the revolution, has been revived once more, and a Russian can go nowhere within his vast land—not to speak of crossing the frontier—without the special order (*komandirovka*) of some superior and without showing innumerable officials his workbook, his passport, his *propusk* or pass to the particular office, factory, public building, or institution he is visiting, and various other documents.

The fixity of the peasant in old Russia was not created, as was the case of the serf under Western feudalism, by a shortage of land, for always in Russia there was the boundless steppe. Immobility had to be created by law, or rather by ukaz. So too Peter the Great, Russia's most important industrializer before Stalin, filled his newly decreed factories by the simple expedient of assigning serfs from the state farms to the state factories. Long before socialism was so much as thought of, the Russian state was the largest landowner, the largest employer of peasant bondmen, the largest owner of factories and capital and the largest employer of industrial labor in Russia and in the world. Theoretically too, all of old Russia was one vast patriarchal family with a single, all-powerful, divinely inspired, all-knowing, all-wise, and infallible head. The totalitarian state of the new Russia has not learned its essentials, as some have charged, from Hitler, but has its roots deep in the ancient ways of the Russian land.

1. For example, M. J. Olgin, Russian-born member of the Central Committee of the American Communist Party, was named as its delegate to the Comintern but was never able to take up his post because the Russian authorities refused him a visa.

POLICING THE PEASANT LEADS TO POLICING THE CITIZEN

Despite its truly impressive industrialization, the Soviet Union is still predominantly an agrarian land. As in the past, the changes in industry we are discussing were preceded by changes in agriculture. When, in the early 1930s, Stalin swept the individual peasants into the giant state collective farms—not by convincing them of the advantages of collectivism, but by police measures—freedom of movement became increasingly impossible on the Russian land. Those advanced Russian workers who acquiesced in this wholesale employment of coercion in place of persuasion and even approved of it, unwittingly helped to prepare the conditions which would extend coercion to every phase of Soviet life. The powers needed to make the officials into police overseers of farming and harvest inevitably made them into police overseers over factory, trade union, and soviet. Rural coercion started earlier but because of the slowness and vastness of the countryside ripened more slowly so that in 1940, at almost the same instant in which the Russian worker was reading of his permanent attachment to his factory, his country cousin was digesting the ukazes of the spring of 1940, which represented the climax of the system of collective responsibility to the state for the yield of the collective farms. According to these decrees, the quantities of meat, milk, wool, eggs which the farm must deliver to the government were no longer based on the actual number of livestock possessed by the given *kolkhoz* but on the acreage of the estate. And the obligatory quanties of grain, potatoes, rice, and so on were based not on the area sown or the size of the actual crop but on the acreage of land, good, bad, and indifferent, which is included in the given farm. (Ukazes of April 1, 6, 11 and 16, 1940.[2])

With fatal inevitability, the fixing of the population on the land dried up the labor reserves from which new industrial workers might be recruited. As new factories opened, as aging workers wore out, as the armies of soldiers and the armies of officials, technicians, and office workers and police took on ever-increasing dimensions, a labor shortage began to

2. As late as 1969, despite all the loosening of the bonds to permit movement of potential labor from farm to factory, the heirs of Joseph Stalin were still wrestling with this problem of fixity. On Jan. 15, 1969, *Selskaia Zhizn* (Village Life) proposed that each farm boy upon reaching the age of 16 be formally enlisted into the ranks of the collective farmers at a special ceremony in which he would take a solemn oath of allegiance to the kolkhoz and receive a labor booklet just as city children at 16 received their internal passport and labor booklet. At the ceremony, the young kolkhoz recruit would take the following oath:

Entering upon the honorable ranks of tillers of the soil of the USSR, I solemnly promise to love labor, which is the source of plenty and happiness; to cherish and honor my collective farm; to live and work in a Communist way; to remember always that land is the greatest national resource.

develop. In despite of edicts, factories began to bid silently against one another. Thus the tendency of Soviet workers to move about from job to job was augmented. With the trade unions gutted, it was the one freedom left to them, the one outlet for discontent. They changed jobs in hope of advancement, to get away from an ingrown antagonism, an intolerable overseer, or because, in Russia as elsewhere, the grass is likely to appear greener farther off. There was a silent, prohibited, but nonetheless inevitable tendency of wages to rise.

A second force that operated to deplete the labor reserves was the state-caused famine attendant upon the wholesale, forced collectivization of agriculture. Still more unexpected to the authorities was the fall in the birth rate in the cities, where the five-day week with a different day off for each member of the family and intolerably crowded living quarters, made for a silent strike in parenthood, increasing numbers of Soviet workingmen and women deciding to forgo having children. That decision was strengthened by the decreasing purchasing power of the ruble, the shortage of consumers' goods, the impossibility of getting a bottle of milk, a rubber nipple, a yard of diaper cloth unless you were a member of the privileged bureaucracy entitled by a card to shop in special "closed" stores.

But the labor shortage really became acute when the huge forced-labor armies recruited by the GPU began to wear out, and there was no great "unliquidated" social layer from which to renew the supply. All during the early 1930s, the GPU had recruited such labor armies from the "former people," what was left of the old upper and middle classes and recalcitrant peasants and kulaks. The GPU thus became the largest employer of labor in Russia by the simple expedient of herding whole families into concentration camps for the harvesting of timber, draining of swamps, construction of canals, railroads, highways, and other public works. These great labor armies died off rapidly, and some portion of the remnant was released as "socially rehabilitated." But when the regime had completed the "liquidation of the kulaks as a class," there was suddenly no new social layer from which the catastrophic losses could be made good.

The main answer of the Kremlin to the problems of labor shortage, labor turnover, and pressure for rising wages was a series of decrees tying the worker by force to his job, culminating in the ukaz of June 1940. But such measures were not enough.

The next answer was to seek new labor reserves among the youth of the rising generation. The party chief sought to stimulate the birth rate by all the means known to organized governments (except the production of sufficient housing and an ample supply of diapers, baby clothes, milk bottles, milk, and rubber nipples, which the plans keep postponing for some indefinite and millennial future).

WOMAN WORKER OR HEROINE OF MOTHERHOOD?

On March 8, 1940, the Government reported that the number of women workers had more than trebled in the preceding decade—from 3 million to almost 11 million in 1939. Obviously, this represents a broadening of the horizon of Soviet women and increasing relief from economic dependence on men.[3] It further reflects the inadequacy of the wages of the head of a household from the standpoint of a "family wage." But when the report boasts, as it does, that in the Soviet Union women work as coal miners in the underground shafts and as furnace workers in steel mills, once more we come to a state of affairs so bitterly denounced in Marx's *Capital*. In the England of which he wrote the employment of women in steel mills and underground pits has long since disappeared; the same is true throughout Western Europe.

But there comes a time when the use of women to augment the labor supply conflicts with another aim of the Kremlin: a rapid rise in the birth rate. In the middle 1930s Stalin boasted of an annual population increase of three million; for the census of 1937 he made a series of glowing predictions which added up to an estimate of 180 million people. When the long-heralded census revealed the catastrophic effects of the famine of 1932-1933 and the forced collectivization of agriculture, and the even more alarming and unexpected fact of a decline of the birth rate in the cities, Stalin's answer was characteristic of his rough and ready methods of "genial" solution of all problems. He denounced the census figures as a product of foreign sabotage, purged the entire census staff, and ordered a new and more favorable count. About the same time he began to "hold that grin," which I had so rarely seen on his face in public, let himself be photographed kissing babies, patting the prolific mother on the back, handing out premiums and decorations for fecundity. Divorce was made difficult, the marriage tie was glorified, responsibility of the father for the support of the children was made more stringent, and abortion was decreed a penal offense for both mother and doctor. All this overnight in a land which had been boasting for a decade and a half of Lenin's achievement in making divorce simple and easy, giving woman the freedom to dispose of her own body and countenancing abortion!

3. And adds industrial labor to waiting on queues, waiting for a burner in the communal kitchen, and other household cares.

There are certain contradictions that cannot be resolved by ukaz, one of them being the conflict between the desire to have women as producers in the factories and simultaneously as producers of endless streams of babies. The eight weeks' leave of absence before and after childbirth which, so far as it was actually carried out, represented one of the great achievements of Soviet law, was another victim of the new dispensation. New ukazes reduced the maternity leave from sixteen weeks to nine, and decreed that women who changed their jobs after they were two months pregnant (even though they were dismissed by one factory and hired immediately by another!) should receive no leave of absence with pay at all. Needless to state, the birth rate continued unsatisfactory.

CONSCRIPTION OF YOUTH

The authorities next turned to the Soviet youth as a potential source of fresh labor supply. Here too, early Soviet legislation had been offered as a model for the world. The laws prohibiting child labor could be matched elsewhere, but not the provisions for free, universal education from top to bottom nor the payment of wages to students of the higher schools while their studies continued. If these laws remained mostly so much paper, they nevertheless proclaimed noble intentions as soon as the poverty and universal breakdown could be overcome; and they were, in some small measure, carried out. Where there was a shortage of facilities, moreover, it was the children of the poor, of the erstwhile underprivileged, who received preference over the children of the former rich. Though this worked gross injustice in countless cases and introduced a new class discrimination into the school system instead of providing education for all with the desire and the capacity, yet there seemed a certain poetic justice in its reversing of roles. But on October 3, 1940, the Soviet system of free, universal education and stipends for higher education, was summarily abolished by ukaz.[4]

Once more the Supreme Soviet was not even in session to amend the constitution, which in Article 121 of the "Fundamental Rights of Citizens" declares:

Citizens of the USSR have the right to education. This right is ensured by universal, compulsory elementary education; by education, including higher education, being free of charge; by the system of state stipends for the overwhelming majority of students in the universities and colleges.

4. The *ukaz* was quietly rescinded by Khrushchev shortly after Stalin's death.

Once more the new decrees came as a shock to Ivan Ivanovich, and his young son Vanya. They were actually made retroactive to the beginning of the school term that had started on the first of September, and no one knows how many thousands of Vanyas were abruptly thrown out of school because they could not pay their tuition fee. By the new ukaz, students in the eighth, ninth, and tenth grades were obliged to pay a tuition of 200 rubles yearly in towns and 150 rubles in villages—that is, roughly an entire month's wages of their workingmen fathers—while students in high schools and colleges were required to pay 400 rubles in the cities and 300 in the towns and those in art, music, and drama schools 500 rubles annually. When it is borne in mind that the average wage of a Soviet worker (excluding foremen, technicians and government officials) at the time of this new decree was less than 200 rubles a month—most of which vanished in the mere hunt for food, with even serviceable clothing and shoes outside their grasp—it is clear that this decree did not "go back to the bourgeois world" but to the last monarch of nineteenth-century Russia, Alexander III, and his Minister of Education Delyanov, who issued the celebrated ukaz which read: "The children of coachmen, servants, cooks, laundresses, small shopkeepers, and suchlike persons should not be encouraged to rise above the sphere in which they were born."

THE NEW CLASS SOCIETY

The significance of this amazing decree is twofold: on the one hand it was the pinnacle of a long-mounting trend toward the creation of a new ruling class or privileged caste in the Soviet Union, that of the well-paid, well-housed, well-provided-for Soviet officialdom, technicians, foremen, and overseers, workgang bosses (Stakhanovists), artists, and writers; on the other, it was a means of getting millions of the sons of workingmen and peasants to the farms and factories at an earlier age than heretofore (at the age of fourteen instead of seventeen).

All Soviet observers have noted the tendency toward the creation of a new ruling and privileged layer of the population, and the Trotskyites, leftist critics of the Stalin regime, have waged fearful polemical battle in their own ranks as to whether this privileged layer should be designated as "stratum," "caste," or "class," or whether some new term should be invented. In these discussions much has been made of the fact that the privileged had no way of bequeathing their privileges to their children. To be sure, there was always the silent force of influence or pull: a simple telephone call, a mere hint or a courtierlike anticipation thereof could secure for the better-clothed, better-fed, better-schooled, better-served son or daughter of the high-placed official a better position when he began to earn his own living. But these new decrees, which abolish free education and payment to the students for their upkeep, result automatically in a sort of wholesale or collective system of inheritance whereby only the children of well-paid officials, artists, and writers (these last being among the best paid in the Soviet Union) can possibly aspire to the training that will create the next generation of officials, technicians, artists, and writers. Thus is equality of opportunity abolished at a single stroke of the pen, and the Communist party decision is completely realized which condemned Soviet education for its "chase after quantity" and warned that party education also had until now "concentrated too much on the workers and neglected the cadres of command." (Central Committee resolution of November 14, 1938.)

But the primary motive for this "cultural exploitation of the youth" is to be found in another decree on child or youth labor published in *Pravda* on the same day as the decree abolishing free education.

"The old sources," commented *Pravda*, "which assured a spontaneous influx of labor (from the villages) have been cut off, disappeared. . . . We haven't got people who would be compelled to knock at factory gates and beg admission into the factories, thus spontaneously forming a constant reserve of labor power for industry." But if higher schooling is closed to the children of the poor, then automatically a new class of millions is created who are obliged to beg admission to the factories. However, Soviet planners leave nothing to chance, which brings me to the second decree, to which I referred above.

The ukaz of October 3, 1940, provided for the conscription of approximately a million young people between the ages of fourteen to seventeen for "industrial training." [5] The first batch was "called up" before the end of the year, with a million or more scheduled each year thereafter. They were assigned to specific industries for a period of four years of "training" combined with practical work, after which they were to be permanently attached as full-fledged workers to the industries in which they had been conscripted. The young industrial draftees were to be exempt from military conscription, and were to receive during the four-year period as wages roughly one-third of the estimated value of the product of their labor.[6]

---

5. This decree was partially repealed under Khrushchev and rendered inoperative under Brezhnev.

6. Later decrees show that actual schooling, when any is given, does not run above nine months of part-time teaching during the draft period of four years. In some places night classes are provided and in others only propaganda meetings—with no formal education at all.

THE ARMY REFLECTS THE NEW ORDER

The military terminology and procedure employed in the youth "mobilization" ukaz brings us to the heart of what has happened in Russia, the total militarization of the daily life and labor of an entire people.

"Every army," to quote a Soviet commentator on military history, "reflects the political constitution and the whole order of society prevailing in the land to which it belongs." Inevitably, the militarization of industry and civil life was bound to react in turn upon the structure of the Red Army. In the crucial years we are discussing (indeed, since the purge of the old General Staff inherited from civil war days), the authorities were busy restoring tsarist military titles and traditions and eliminating from the Soviet army and navy their last vestiges of democracy, initiative from below, egalitarianism, comradely relations between officers and men—all the things that gave the Red Army its specifically "revolutionary" or "socialist" coloring. Taken together, the decrees in this field added up to an extreme remilitarization of military life, and made the Red Army, from the standpoint of hierarchical structure, absolute command, and internal discipline, the most rigidly organized large-scale army in the entire world.

The first thing to go was the celebrated Red Army oath. The old oath, which I have heard impressively intoned phrase by phrase by tens of thousands of deep masculine voices on the great Red Square, began: "I, a son of the toiling people," and ended with a pledge to "direct every act and thought to the grand aim of the emancipation of the toilers throughout the world." On January 3, 1939, a new oath was introduced. It substituted "citizen" for "son of the toiling people," and, for the emancipation of the toilers of the world, the pledge "to defend the fatherland . . . without sparing blood or life itself in order to win complete victory over the enemy."

On May 8, 1940, was announced the restoration of tsarist military titles in place of the simple "commander." The "reform," wrote *Pravda* next day, "aims to raise the authority of our commanders and strengthen military discipline. The entire mighty organization of the modern army must unqualifiedly be subordinated to the will of the plenipotentiary commander and execute all his orders." Between that date and the date of the ukaz discussed at the beginning of this chapter, *Pravda*, *Izvestia*, and other Soviet papers were filled with entire pages of photographs of newly created generals and admirals of various categories—all in all, 953 new generals and 100 new admirals.

On June 23, an order of the day from Marshal Timoshenko made the saluting of an officer mandatory off duty, thus abolishing the last vestige of the famous Order No. 1 adopted by the soldiers section of the Soviet in March 1917. Officers were warned that they must insist on strict fulfillment or themselves be punished; "unscrupulous playing up to the Red Army masses and efforts of the commander to show his democratic feelings" were branded as "an offense against the service regulations."

On June 28, a new order provided greater severity for arrested soldiers, stipulating that in "strict arrest" no work was to be permitted, no sleeping during the daytime, sleeping only on a wooden cot at night without mattress and for no more than six hours, and hot food no more frequently than every other day. Again officers were warned that they themselves would be punished for insufficient severity. The same order introduced the eight-hour day and Sunday rest for all industries under the defense commissariat—the first public acknowledgment I could find of a rapidly accelerating process of putting industry after industry directly under military orders as "essential war industries."

The climax came on October 12, 1940. The old army regulations were scrapped and new ones substituted. The most amazing provision of the new code gave officers the right in cases of insubordination "to apply all measures of coercion up to and including the application of force and firearms," without consulting others or resorting to court-martial. He is to "bear no responsibility" for injury or death thus inflicted but is held responsible if he does not in all cases of insubordination "evince firmness and apply all necessary measures." (*Red Star*, October 15, 1940.) Under Article 7 of the old army regulations, which were replaced by this order, officers had been forbidden to apply such armed compulsion "except in a military situation and only in the execution of actual battle orders." So far as I know, this makes the Red Army the only modern military force in which the officers have the right to apply the death penalty without trial for insubordination in peacetime or when not in actual battle. Thus, from one of the least militarized and most democratic armies in the world, the Red Army has become the most military and the most hierarchical. In September 1946 the *Red* Army was renamed the *Soviet* Army.

MILITARIZATION OF THE WHOLE OF LIFE

With these decrees the Red Army necessarily lost what was left of its value as a "propaganda" army intended to set by its example the men of opposing armies against their officers. Its power of dissolving the armies sent against it, rather than its discipline, equipment, or military might, was one of the secrets of its success against White armies and detachments of foreign troops in the days of the civil war. It remained to be seen how much it had gained by way of compensation. In comparison, even the German Wehrmacht seemed to be based upon the conception that in modern mechanized and parachute warfare considerable initiative must be fostered in the individual soldier. The experience in Finland, though indecisive, did not seem to indicate that the gains overbalanced the losses. But then the invasion of Finland was incompatible with the spirit of the early Red Army.

The remilitarization of the army in turn reacted upon industry. As "war industries" were increasingly placed directly under the army, the Soviet Union was increasingly turned into one vast military encampment. The Soviet "experiment" became the vastest experiment in total militarization of a people, its life, labor, and thought known to the history of man. One looks in vain through the reaches of history for a basis of comparison. This "new order," which surely can have little attraction for other peoples, has yet to prove its efficiency in regimenting its own. The Soviet regime has become a vast testing ground where mankind can determine whether in the long run it is really possible to operate modern large-scale industry, to foster modern science and technology, or to conduct modern warfare efficiently, by something approaching a combination of the old-fashioned army discipline with a prison regime and universal labor conscription, whether the unsettling problems arising from modern invention and technical change—not to mention the traditions and aspirations of political and economic democracy—can really be frozen permanently into this mold.

—June 1941

II THE DARK SIDE
OF THE MOON *

"The Middle Ages left Russia with a heritage of torture, knout, and exile. The eighteenth century abolished torture, in the nineteenth the knout was done away with, and the first day of the twentieth will be the last day of the penal system based on exile."

With these words the Russian delegate to the International Congress of Prison Officials held in Brussels in 1900 gave expression to a dream which had been animating all the best public servants of tsarist Russia during the closing decades of the nineteenth century. Russia, they knew, had been the last stronghold of slavery (along with the United States and certain colonial lands) in the modern world. Forced penal labor for the profit of the state they considered to be the reflection in prison of serfdom or slavery in the outside world. But in 1861, Alexander II had emancipated the serfs, even endowing them with some land, and in 1863 Lincoln had freed the Negro slaves.

Thus Russia was putting an end to the fixity or bondage (*krepost'*) which had been decreed by the enlightened autocrats, Peter and Catherine and their successors. That bondage had been primarily a military device to fix every man to his post, where the tax-gatherer and the recruiting sergeant could find him. With bondage had come the internal passport, the universal obligation of service to the state, the conscription of capital and labor for military industrialization. Peter the Great, Russia's foremost industrializer before the bolsheviks, had begun by ordering "the gathering of a few thousand thieves from all over the provinces and cities" to aid in the building of his capital. Then he and his successors had added debtors, vagabonds, and political malcontents. Thus the institution of penal forced labor on public works had arisen as the state's industrial counterpart of agricultural serfdom: to build ports, fortresses, and roads, to work salt mines and metal mines, to clear forests, to populate the frozen north and the otherwise almost uninhabitable wastes on the marches of the empire.

But two centuries had elapsed since then, and Russia had defeated

* First published in *The American Mercury*, November 1947.

Charles XII, Frederick the Great, and Napoleon. Secure against attack
and expanded to her "natural frontiers," could she not now turn her
resources inward for the welfare of her people, and begin the "loosening
of the bonds"? Russia's conscience and the world's had been aroused by
the antislavery societies and new humanitarian penal concepts. The last
strongholds of serfdom and slavery were being broken up. Torture and
conviction by confession and corporal punishment were abolished. It remained only to put an end to the anachronistic vestiges of penal servitude
and forced labor in exile. Such was the basis of the optimism of the
Russian delegate to the 1900 Congress of Prison Officials.

But after the revolution of 1905 there was a slight relapse. According
to Andrei Vyshinsky, whose services as prosecutor and purger were to
make him perhaps the world's leading expert on forced labor, *katorga*
(heavy penal labor) began to increase once more. By January 1, 1906, the
number sentenced to *katorga* had climbed back to nearly 6,000, by January 1, 1914 to almost 30,000. How enormous, how monstrous those figures
seemed then: how idyllically exiguous they seem now!

The 1917 revolution came, bearing with it a heritage of humane
traditions and dreams of equality and freedom. "Educational institutions
are to be substituted for prisons," begins a 1918 decree of the People's
Commissariat of Justice. The words *guilt, punishment, vengeance*, were
deleted from the official vocabulary. The terms *prison* and *exile* were "forever abolished." Society was responsible for the criminal's criminality—
poverty for his theft; illness, or chaotic social arrangements and lack of
proper education and opportunity, for his acts of violence. He was to be
treated as a victim in need of help, a sick man to be healed, a misfit to
be redeemed and fitted into society by being taught a trade. Labor, under
wholesome therapeutic conditions and with trade-union rates of pay, was
to be used to support him and to redeem him.

To safeguard the rights and "human dignity" of those unfortunates
who had to be placed for a while in "places of social detention and rehabilitation," various rights were guaranteed to them: the right to smoke,
to read, to write, and receive letters, to interview relatives without the
humiliation of bars between visitor and detainee, to be addressed civilly
by the warders, to be fully compensated for useful labor. Chains, handcuffs, solitary confinement, torture, punishment by hunger were abolished.
Whatever the grim realities of a land in revolutionary travail, no one
could deny the nobility of this new code:

> Bourgeois penal policy aims at moral and physical maiming and physical
> destruction, achieved by means of organized torture and violation of the
> human dignity of prisoners. . . . The exploitation of prison labor [production
> for the profit of the state rather than the use of the prisoner], the system
> of squeezing "golden sweat" out of them, the organization of production in

places of confinement which, while profitable from a commercial point of view, is fundamentally lacking in corrective significance, are entirely inadmissible in Soviet places of confinement.

Even the dread Cheka (the secret political police that has since been transformed successively into the GPU, NKVD, MVD, and MGB) was originally conceived only as a temporary emergency device, and was therefore named Extraordinary [i.e., Emergency] Commission to Combat Active Counterrevolution. It, too, was to disappear, as soon as the counterrevolutionary armies were defeated or driven off Soviet soil. *Mais n'est-ce que la provisoire qui dure.*

All through the 1920s and early 1930s, a series of political choices were made that bit by bit with tragic fatality were to lead to the miscarriage of that noble dream. There was a gradual change from labor for the prisoner's use and redemption to labor for the state's profit and the prisoner's destruction: the development of a system of "squeezing golden sweat out of them" on a scale hitherto undreamed of in the entire history of mankind, under any social system whatsoever.

DECISIONS THAT LAID THE FOUNDATIONS OF TOTALITARIANISM

Here are a few of those fatal political choices, and the reader can add to them others of a like nature:

The decision to retain the "Extraordinary Commission to Combat Active Counterrevolution" after the counterrevolution had been beaten.

The decision to outlaw all political parties, including democratic and socialist parties, except the Communist party.

The decision to outlaw all dissent within the Communist pary.

The decision to reduce the Soviets from parliaments of labor, to which all working-class parties might send candidates, to mouthpieces and transmission belts of the Communist party.

The decision to determine the plowing, seeding, planting, harvesting, and disposal of the crop of the peasants not by the inducements of industrial goods but by police methods, which required the swelling of the police apparatus into a monstrous ubiquity for coercing the overwhelming majority of the population. Inevitably, such an omnipresent police spilled over into the Soviets, the trade unions, the Communist party, into the very Central Committee of the party.

The decision to treat the state as coextensive and identical with the whole of society, denying all autonomy to nonstate organizations and to individual conscience, intellect, judgment, and will.

The decision to police all expressions of thought, opinion, emotion, personal life, art, science, beliefs, dreams.

The decision to "collectivize" the peasants at a single stroke, not by persuasion and the offering of superior inducements but by police methods, and to "liquidate" as "kulaks" all who were reluctant to surrender their bit of land or cattle and all nomads who were reluctant to settle down.

The decision to industrialize the land at a tempo that would take no account of consumers' goods or strain or sacrifice, procuring the necessary "capital" by increasing the speed-up and exploitation of labor and by keeping wages at a low minimum even after the reserve army of unemployed had disappeared. The alternative to attracting workers by suitable inducements was to fix them in their jobs by force, and to decree lateness, absence from work, or voluntary change of employment, a crime against the state. Thus even "free" labor became, in effect, a form of state forced labor.

The decision to treat all proposers of a different tempo or method or approach as subhuman beasts, "mad dogs," "wrecker-diversionist-spy-scum-riffraff-fascist beasts in human form."

What wonder that the monstrous abuse of prisoners in words was accompanied by a monstrous abuse in deeds! All these decisions, and others like them, reduced man once more (to use the words Marx used in his indictment of capitalism) to "subordination to the products of his own labor, the machines." With the tying of even "free" laborers to their jobs, there came the inevitable increasing enslavement of those others who had lost even this shadowy freedom. Thus, bit by bit, one of humanity's noblest dreams was converted into one of its most fearful nightmares until the Soviet state became the greatest and most ruthless employer of slave labor that the world has ever known.

"A prison is a prison," Soviet officials now wrote:

Why such finicalness? "Measures of social protection" is a ridiculous term. We must overcome this sugary liberalism, this compassionate attitude toward the offender. . . . The Five Year Plan requires tasks involving a great demand for unskilled labor. . . . It is here that the places of confinement can come to the assistance of those economic enterprises which experience a shortage of labor. . . . Incorporate the work performed by those deprived of liberty into the planned economy of the country, and into the Five Year Plan. . . . Bring about the realization of a series of economic projects with great savings in expenditures . . . by means of the widespread use of labor of sentenced individuals. . . . The following are objects of mass labor best fitted for the realization of the purposes of corrective labor: large-scale industrial construction (factories, dams, dikes, blast furnaces, railroads, etc.) . . . irrigation works; highway construction. . . .

Only one problem remained to be solved. Historically, slave labor was one of the most inefficient forms of labor and scarcely yielded more than enough to sustain the slave. But, as Stalin more than once observed, "nothing is impossible to bolshevik determination." The solution lay along two lines. First there was the fact that unlike private chattel slaves, who cost their owners money, state slaves can be recruited without cost, and it does not matter how soon they are worked to death. The second line of solution was that which had been worked out in regard to "free" labor: the norm, the wage insufficient to sustain life for those who cannot or will not reach the norm, and the incentive system of extra rations or extra compensation for those model or speed-up workers who exceed the norm. In the prison camps and places of exile, the compelling argument of the club, the dog, and the gun was supplemented by a system of regulated starvation and feeding according to norms, fixed neither by the feeble health nor the feeble zeal of the prisoner but by the will and plans of the state.

The change was made only gradually and, to do the Soviet leaders justice, at first only with reluctance. The outside world, even as it was so long unwilling to believe that the Nazis could set up genocidal crematoria in the "enlightened twentieth century" and in the land of "German culture," has been reluctant to believe that slave labor could become an essential part of the economic structure of a land that "has abolished all exploitation of man by man." Still less would admirers of a "planned economy in a planless world" believe that planned recruiting of prisoners and planned forcing of their labor was an essential part of the plan. Or an essential political foundation stone in "Soviet economic democracy."

WHO SPEAKS FOR THE SILENT?

The Soviet Union is the only great nation in the world which does not publish penal statistics. It ceased publication of these figures in 1931, the year that the Anti-Slavery Society in England began an inquiry into the conditions of the Soviet camps. The results of this investigation, which was undertaken in a careful and objective manner by Allan Pim and Edward Bateson, were published as the *Report on the Russian Timber Camps*. Unfortunately a number of timber and manganese companies and certain boards of trade attempted to take advantage of the report by advocating embargoes on Soviet imports. As a result, the numerous "friends of the Soviet Union," as well as the millions who refused to open their minds to the possibility that such horrors existed, were enabled to dismiss the report as the contrived invention of vested economic interests.

In 1935, Vladimir Tchernavin's moving personal record of his servitude and escape, *I Speak for the Silent*, was published. By this time American intellectuals had been so shocked by our depression that many longed to believe that somewhere in an imperfect world there was rational planning, real security, and a special organization capable of producing abundance. Tchernavin's cry fell on deaf ears.

During World War II, the more sensitive were occasionally shocked for moments by casual side remarks in the most ardently pro-Soviet books: remarks like Quentin Reynolds' in *Only the Stars Are Neutral*, in which he described a ragged, hopeless battalion of 800 convict women he had witnessed marching to forced labor; like Walter Kerr's in *Russia's Red Army*, concerning the apathetic reception of lend-lease goods in Murmansk by the slave laborers functioning as longshoremen; like Wendell Willkie's declaration in the prepublication serialization of *One World*: "Between the airfield and the town of Yakutsk we looked for the usual concentration camp, but there was none or at least we never came across it." (Significantly, this telltale sentence was omitted when *One World* was published in book form, for there was the will to believe that all concentration camps, torture systems, police state, and totalitarian features were in the opposing camp and not in the camp of our own "United Nations.")

RETURN FROM THE DARK SIDE OF THE MOON

It remained for the citizens of another united nation, Poland, to make the fearful journey "to the dark side of the moon" and, unexpectedly, by a turn of fate, return with reports on the fate of the submerged and the damned. When the Stalin-Hitler pact partitioned Poland in 1939, from Russia's portion over a million men, women, and children, including all possible bearers of the idea of a free Poland, were driven, in sealed freight cars or on foot, into distant places of exile and concentration camps in Siberia's wastes and frozen north.

There they found that they were being punished not as Poles but as people who did not fit into the reasons and plans of the Soviet state, for they found there Russians as well as members of all nationalities in the great family of Soviet nations. Their wet clothes turned to rags as they worked in the snow and ice; bodies and spirits were broken; ulcers, scurvy, pneumonia, tuberculosis, hunger, exhaustion, despair, took a frightful toll as they worked to exhaustion and early death under brutalized guards, fierce trained dogs, lash, and gun. Why waste them? the state reasoned, even as it had already learned to reason concerning its own peasants resisting collectivization, nomads resisting a planned sedentary existence, officials convicted of inefficiency, or corruption, or heresy, or mere friend-ship with other convicted officials. Why waste them, when it saves powder and lead and yields a profit to the state to keep their skin and bones to-gether until they are worked to exhaustion? Why use the wasteful death penalty when in a few years they will be worked to death anyhow?

But then a miracle happened. The partners who in 1939 had formed their partnership over the prostrate body of Poland fell out with each other in June, 1941. Now Stalin, needing Polish military manpower and above all needing the support of Britain, which had gone to war precisely over the invasion and partition of Poland, agreed to let General Sikorski and a British parliamentary commission recruit an army among the ragged, vermin-ridden, ulcerated, and pallid ghosts who still eked out their exist-ence in the land of the damned. How frightful the toll had been was proved by the pitiful remnant, numbering a few hundred thousand that could be nursed back to health out of the more than a million which the International Labor Office statistical report had recorded as having gone into deportation.

Now the harrowing record was made available in countless documents, personal narratives, and piteous tales. They told not only of themselves but of the other shadows that would never return to the land of the living. Through the account distilled from innumerable narratives and set down with painful restraint in such books as the *The Dark Side of the Moon* (written anonymously) and *La Justice Soviétique* (by Sylvester Mora and Peter Zwierniak), we got some conception of the number of concentration camps, their geographical distribution and activities, the conditions obtaining in them. It would take a new Dante to do real justice to this modern inferno, yet this collective account, derived from thousands of letters, diaries, conversations, documents, and reports is the distillation of the anguish and agony of an entire people.

An intolerably painful book for us to read, *The Dark Side of the Moon* must be read, every word of it, by any who would attempt to understand the history of our time. For, as the brief and sober preface of T. S. Eliot points out:

This is not merely the story of what happened to Poland and to in-numerable Poles between 1939 and 1945. . . . It is also a book about the USSR, about the Europe in which we now live, about the world in which we now live.

Forced Labor in Soviet Russia, by David Dallin and Boris Nicolaevsky, is a more illuminating, less emotionally shattering study of the same sub-ject in all its ramifications. It is the first systematic and scholarly examination of all the documents available, all the eyewitness accounts, all the meaningful fragments of Soviet comment, of the history and social signifi-cance of that "peculiar institution" which had become a cornerstone of Soviet polity and economic life. Here the reader will find the carefully reasoned and documented answers to his shocked and incredulous "Why?" He will find the historical background from which I have drawn in part for the opening paragraphs of this discussion. He will find a map locating all known concentration camps; a careful breakdown of the various indus-tries in which they are engaged; an economic analysis of why human flesh is substituted for machinery in certain types of construction and produc-tion; a careful collation, erring only on the side of understatement, of the statistical evidence on the numbers of millions involved; a digest of all eyewitness reports and accounts of participants from Tchernavin to the Poles and the latest returning Russian war prisoners and displaced persons; a study of the fabulous rise of Magadan, capital of a slave empire; pen portraits of the principal architects of the system—in short, an analysis of all available material, fitted into a systematic exposition.

With admirable patience and skill the authors slowly put together, over a period of more than a decade, the tiny bits of evidence from Soviet sources, put them together like fragments of an ancient mosaic of which many parts may still be missing but of which all the outlines are already clear. They have preferred to let Soviet records and Soviet spokesmen speak for themselves, citing date and page and verifiable source. The book contains thirty-two photostats of actual documents of GULAG (the chief administration of corrective labor camps, prisons, labor and special settle-ments of the NKVD), and the photostat of a page of instructions for the seizure and deportation of all Lithuanian leaders (trade union, socialist, democratic, economic, political, and cultural), the originals of which are on file with the International Red Cross at Geneva and microfilm copies of which are in the New York Public Library.

Dallin and Nicolaevsky have thus produced the first definitive study of slave labor as a cornerstone of Soviet economy and the first general theoretical analysis of its social, political, and economic meanings. It is the Soviet government's own fault if the authors have had to guess at the total figures involved. Their figures, advanced with excessive caution, re-veal a slave class running well above the ten-million mark, more than three times as numerous as the total number of workers under tsarism who were to be emancipated in 1917—more numerous, too, than the total number of male "free" workers in Russian industry.

THE CLASS AT THE BOTTOM OF THE PYRAMID

As Dallin earlier made clear in his *The Real Soviet Russia*, this class of slaves is today the largest productive class in Soviet society, situated at the bottom of the social pyramid, unreached even by the shadowy paper constitution and bill of rights, devoid of all rights whatsoever, planfully exploited to the point of exhaustion and annihilation. Yet—a significant and essential part of this peculiar planned economy—this class is in need of being continuously replaced by the creation and "recruiting" of new groups and classes of heretics, dissenters, criminals, "class-alien" or "national-alien" or "enemy-alien" bodies of men.

As has been the case wherever a numerous class of slaves, private or state, exists alongside of poor freemen, the latter inevitably begin to feel the pressure of the slave system in lowered remuneration and lessened freedom. It was the existence of this growing class of slaves throughout the 1930s that made it possible for the Russian state to reintroduce the internal passport, fixity in factory and farm, the conscription of youth for labor, the conversion of trade unions from protective agencies to speed-up agencies, and the gradual blurring of the uncertain boundaries between the various degrees of unfreedom.

If *I Speak for the Silent* and *The Dark Side of the Moon* correspond to the *Uncle Tom's Cabin* of the new antislavery movement that is bound to develop in our time, then Dallin and Nicolaevsky have produced the study of the Bradleys, the Wilberforces, and the Hinton Helpers.

And they have provided a touchstone to test every new book and reporter and lecturer on Russia: if he has nothing to say on this essential foundation stone in the Soviet structure, then his book is either ignorant or dishonest. Henceforward one can no more talk about the Russian working class without discussing the millions of its slave producers than one could talk about production in the Old South without mentioning chattel slavery or about labor in the New South without mentioning Jim Crow. And anyone who has nothing to say about this dehumanization of millions of human beings can henceforth be regarded neither as a liberal, a democrat, a humanitarian, nor a socialist.

These books and reports are a must for everyone who would understand Russia and the history of our time. They teach us what the regime of "economic democracy" is like. They provide the missing key to many enigmas, such as the unwillingness of the Russian rulers to permit observers to travel freely through their land; their refusal to accept America's proposal of international control of atomic energy. (How, indeed, could they accept a control that is tied up with freedom of movement and freedom of inspection in a land that is dotted with scores of concentration camps?

From the first antislavery societies and reports of the eighteenth century to the abolition of the slave trade and Lincoln's Emancipation Proclamation took the better part of a century. Now these books and investigations and reports force into our consciousness and consciences an awareness of the new total slavery inseparable from the totalitarian system.

—November 1947

III THE FORCED LABOR REFORM AFTER STALIN'S DEATH *

During the course of the years 1953-1956, a number of things contributed to a reform of the slave labor system. Chief of these was the pressure of world opinion upon the Soviet Government as a result of a two-year-long investigation of forced labor by an Ad Hoc Committee set up by the United Nations and the International Labor Office. Appointed in 1951, the Commission finished and published its report in Geneva in 1953, the year of Stalin's death. The report differed from previous ones in the great volume of materials unearthed, in the official sponsorship of the United Nations and the ILO, and, most strikingly, in the fact that the resulting study contained hundreds of documents bearing the official seal of the Gulags (Concentration Camps) and thus authenticated by the Soviet Government itself, which this time could not deny the truth of the reports.

I had suspected the existence of such documents ever since I learned in 1950 that there were papers of General Anders under seal for twenty-five years at the Hoover Institution. In 1951 I persuaded General Anders, in exile in London, to lift the seal and make available to me all documents throwing light on the existence of forced labor camps.

The circumstances that had produced these documents and put them in General Anders' papers were the following. In 1939, when the German Wehrmacht invaded Poland, the Polish army fought a rearguard action as it retreated toward supposedly friendly Russia. But Stalin's armies struck at the Poles from the rear. The prisoners taken were not treated as prisoners of war but put into concentration camps all over Russia. Some 14,500 of their officers were murdered in the course of March, April, and May, 1940, in a mass murder made public after the unearthing of the first four thousand bodies in the Katyn Forest.[1]

In 1941, when Hitler attacked Russia, Stalin gave permission to the Polish Commander-in-Chief, General Anders, to visit the concentration

---

* Written for the present work, April 1969.
1. On this see *The Crime of Katyn: Facts and Documents,* with a foreword by General Wladyslaw Anders, London, 1965.

camps of Russia and recruit those Polish soldiers who after two years of prison camp labor were still regarded as battle-worthy. As was characteristic of a country in which no one could travel without a passport or other certification of identity and right to travel, each Polish recruit was given a document certifying to his identity and the purpose of his journey. Each such document was rubberstamped with a circular seal bearing the name and location of his forced labor camp together with the telltale word *Gulag* (initials of the State Administration of Forced Labor).

With the help of Professor Witold Sworakowski, then Curator of Slavic Documents at the Hoover Institution, and various other devoted people, I selected, translated, and photostated all documents bearing the Soviet Government's Gulag seal and put them into the hands of Toni Sender, Representative of the International Free Trade Union Committee to the Twelfth Session of the Economic and Social Council of the United Nations meeting in Santiago, Chile. The session was a long one, from February 20 to March 21, 1951. Miss Sender presented the material so effectively, and the documents themselves complete with government seals and certifications were so eloquent, that the Ad Hoc Committee was set up by the United Nations and the International Labor Office. Its full report, printed in Geneva in 1953, aroused world opinion as no less official document had been able to and put tremendous pressure upon the Soviet Government to reform or eliminate its forced labor camps.

The pressure of an aroused public opinion was reinforced by calculations of self-interest among the still unconfident heirs of Joseph Stalin. A labor shortage on both farm and factory had begun, for the "hollowed out years" of forced collectivization, blood purges, and war had caused a great deficit in births. There was a shortage now of maturing men of the classes born during that succession of frightful days. The drastic drop in infantry recruits caused the government to announce a "voluntary reduction" in the size of its infantry and to substitute superior weapons for the drop in manpower. But this in turn caused a further shortage in factory labor, only partially compensated by shortening the schooling and bringing young men from the farms to the factories. Under these circumstances slave labor became obviously uneconomic. The population in the camps was permitted to decline by releases, neglect to "renew" the term of commitment when it ended, shorter sentences for new "offenders," and the amelioration of camp conditions by a restoration of wage incentives, decently stocked canteens in which to spend the "wages," and a reestablishment of the eight-hour day.

A typical measure, which had existed prior to 1937 but had been abolished during the fury of the purges, was to give two or three days credit on the serving of his term for each working day in which the penal laborer actually fulfills or exceeds his norm. Thus a strong and productive prisoner might complete a five-year term in four years or even three. In practice this did not mean that he was restored to the normal "free" civilian population, for either by administrative measures or by the handicaps of his passport and poverty he was obliged to live and work only in the same area in which he had served, under police supervision. In demographic statistics these were now added to the "free" population, but they were either kept in the region or allowed to choose a distant place similar to the one from which they had been released: Kolyma, Vorkuta, Karaganda, the lead mines of Kazakhstan, and the like. Yet they could live outside the camp free from the surveillance of guards and dogs, send for their families or found new ones, prepare their own food as far as scarcities allowed, know the privacy of their own living quarters, and the joy of free labor. In any case their lot was improved by this transition from forced labor to forced residence.

The "reform"—if we can give it so large a name—was thus the result of a number of compelling factors, among which we can distinguish:

1. The power crisis that followed upon Stalin's death.

2. The pressure of the United Nations' unchallengeable report.

3. The shortage of manpower in factory, farm, and army.

4. The great strikes in Vorkuta and other camps following Stalin's death, which were broken by a combination of amelioration of conditions and execution of leaders.

5. The transfer of jurisdiction over many of these industries of remote areas from the MVD to their respective industry sectors when the party leaders decided to weaken the power of the secret police at the time of Beria's execution.

6. The fact that the heads of industries were more interested in production figures than in punitive terror and could not fulfill their plan targets when they were charged with a huge labor force of unproductive, weak, and apathetic forced labor.

7. The growing influence of "destalinization" and rehabilitation of numbers of the condemned.

The reform still left the pressure of some millions of slave laborers hanging over the free labor of the Soviet Union. But there were fewer sentences to forced labor, and the numbers diminished even as their conditions were somewhat improved. It was recognized that forced labor and even forced penal residence were economically unsound under conditions of labor shortage, yet the men in power were unwilling to give up the system altogther.

In the late sixties, forced labor was still being used for Poles, Czechs, Hungarians, Germans, Ukrainians, Kalmuks, Kirghiz, Latvians, Lithuanians, and Estonians in the mining of precious and nonprecious metals and coal, in road and railroad construction, drilling of oil wells, machine manufacturing, airfield construction, stone quarrying, metallurgy, building of factories and power plants. It is noteworthy that these required greater skill and presumably more incentive than earlier forms of simply working the condemned to death. Once more the whole thing is shrouded in silence, but some complete their terms and others escape to tell their stories. When the poet Brodsky was sentenced to forced labor in the Arctic Circle as a "social parasite" who refused to perform "socially useful labor" and was set to shoveling manure in place of writing and translating, the resultant agitation by writers and scientists made the world aware of the fact that a new punitive function was being attached to the forced labor sentence even as its economic importance dwindled. In April 1968, the *AFL-CIO Free Trade Union News* published a new study on the present state of forced labor, pinpointing the existence and location of fifty-six forced labor camps, the national composition of the inmates (comparatively few were Russians, but one camp was exclusively populated by army officers and another by unstated military personnel), and giving the types of work being done in most of these camps as well as a map of their location.[2]

Under the decree of July 1966 against "hooliganism" so many persons were deported to forced residence and "rehabilitating labor" in remote regions where there were no jobs for them that within a year the protests began pouring in from the remoter regions of the empire. Thus the Komi-Perm Autonomous Okrug whose tribal population lives entirely by hunting fur-bearing animals protested that there were more "hooligans" than tribal population and since the only enterprise in being was a Fur-bearing Hunters Kolkhoz and since hooligans could not be trusted with guns, they were all idle and a source of crime.

To meet the problems of forced residence in remote areas for youthful "hooligans," in the summer of 1968 the Presidium of the Supreme Soviet of the U.S.S.R. created an entire new complex of forced labor camps for minors. These new camps grew up silently without system until they became part of the way of life for rebellious and delinquent youth. On June 5, 1968, the official bulletin for the publication of decrees of the Supreme Soviet carried a new ukaz for the following purposes:

1. To ratify the Statute on Labor Colonies for Minors under the Ministry for Safeguarding Public Order [MGB]. . . .

2. To promulgate the Statute on Labor Colonies for Minors under the Ministry for Safeguarding Public Order on August 1, 1968.

3. To permit the Ministry to keep convicted persons who are serving sentences in labor colonies for minors as of August 1, 1968, in the same colonies

2. *AFL-CIO Free Trade Union News,* Vol. 23, No. 4, April, 1968, pp. 4-5.

until they have finished their terms, unless released or paroled ahead of schedule or until transferred to a corrective labor colony [for adults]. . . .[3]

Article 7 of this new code provides that "labor colonies for minors are divided into two types: standard-regime labor colonies and strict-regime labor colonies." First offenders and female minors are kept under the more generous regime. The list of offenses to which the strict regime applies is staggering in its length and inclusiveness. It includes "the theft of state and public property under aggravating circumstances or from which serious consequences arise," " an attempt on the life of a member of the militia or a people's volunteer while in the performance of his duty," "malicious or specially malicious hooliganism," and the bearing of arms while "stealing firearms, munitions, or explosives," as well as acts of minors who "systematically or maliciously violate the penal conditions." It is obvious from the decree that under the MGB there already exists an entire complex of strict-regime camps for adults and another of standard-regime camps since "a convicted person who reaches 18 years of age while serving sentence is transferred from a labor colony for minors to a corrective labor colony for adults . . . from a standard-regime labor colony for minors to a standard-regime labor colony for adults, and from a strict-regime labor colony for minors to a strict-regime labor colony for adults."

However, the differences between the generous "standard-regime camp" and the "strict-regime camp" are not too great. Article 28 provides that "Inmates of a standard-regime labor colony for minors are entitled to have one visit every two months, receive one package or parcel every two months, spend seven rubles a month," while the inmate of a strict-regime labor colony for minors is entitled to have one visit every three months, receive one package or parcel every four months, and spend up to five rubles a month. After spending at least one-fourth of his term in the first case and one-third in the second, model prisoners who have manifested good behavior and a conscientious attitude toward the allotted labor quota may be transferred to "privileged conditions." If this good behavior and fulfillment of labor quotas has been manifested by an inmate of a standard-regime camp, the privileges consist in the right to receive one visit a month, receive one package every two months, and spend up to ten rubles, where as privileges for well-behaved and labor-norm-fulfilling inmates of a strict-regime camp consist in having one visit every two months, receiving one package or parcel every two months, and spending up to seven rubles a month. If one remembers how Lenin in forced deportation to Siberia could receive all the mail and all the books he wanted, visit other prisoners or be visited by them, play chess, write books, hunt and

3. Text in *Vedomosti Verkhovnovo Soveta SSSR,* No. 23, June 5, Item 189, p. 312. Translation in *The Current Digest of the Soviet Press,* July 3, 1968, pp. 3-7.

fish, and do no labor, one gets a perspective on the generosity and humaneness of the present penal regime.

Although in practice the head of a forced labor camp is within his little realm an absolute dictator, the new code for juvenile offenders spells out for him a whole catalogue of permissible measures of punishment 'for violation of the requirements of the penal regime. These include a dressing down ("oral warning"); "reprimand or strong reprimand; out-of-turn detail for cleaning up the colony's buildings and premises . . . ; forfeit of the right to receive the next parcel; complete or partial forfeit of the right to spend money; revocation of the privileges [described above]; confinement in a disciplinary isolation cell . . . for up to five days in standard and for up to ten days in strict-regime camps; handcuffs if they display physical resistance to the colony's officials," and other similar measures.

Clearly the system of forced labor camps is growing again, no longer for "economic" purposes but for punitive and political purposes, and taking in everything from rebellious youth and juvenile delinquents to adult criminals and politicals including "parasite poets" who refuse to perform "socially useful labor" or who seek to exercise the rights of freedom of press and speech guaranteed to them under the Soviet Constitution. The attitude that Brezhnev and Company have been displaying toward the partial relaxation of the totalitarian dictatorship in a fraternal neighbor country like Czechoslovakia speaks volumes concerning the nature of the Soviet regime and the attitude of its rulers toward the guarantees in their own Constitution.

Until some unexpected spin of the wheel of fortune may perhaps again make available another mass of documents like the Anders papers, it is with such fragmentary bits of information that we must leave the question of the scope and limitations of the forced labor reform under Stalin's successors.

—April 1969

IV ELECTIONS UNDER
THE DICTATORSHIP*

1. "The Most Democratic Elections in the World"

In its franker days, bolshevism openly avowed its contempt for democracy and democratic process. "Communism rejects parliamentarism," the Second Congress of the Communist International proclaimed in theses drafted by Lenin. "Its fixed aim is to destroy parliamentarism. . . . There can be no question of utilizing [such] bourgeois institutions except with the object of destroying them." By force of arms Lenin dispersed the Constituent Assembly that was to express the democratic will of the Russian people and draft a constitution by democratic procedure. It was the only legislative body ever chosen in the whole history of Russia, tsarist or Soviet, by universal, direct, free, and equal suffrage; but the bolsheviks showed their contempt for democratic process by surrounding it, barring its freely elected deputies from assembling, having a sailor with cocked pistol adjourn its only session, and by firing on the unarmed procession of workingmen that demonstrated on its behalf.

DICTATORSHIP'S TRIBUTE TO DEMOCRACY

Yet the Communist dictatorship has felt compelled to imitate many of the processes and the very terms that have emerged from centuries of struggle for democracy: nominations, candidates, mass meetings, elections, universal suffrage, secret ballot, budget report, discussion and approval by elected representatives, report of the deputies to their constituents—and all the rest of it. The totalitarian dictator may preach the necessity and superiority of dictatorship, but in his heart he knows that man today is everywhere filled with the longing to have a voice in the settlement of his own affairs, to be represented by delegates of his own choosing, to have

* First written for and published in *Six Keys to the Soviet System,* 1956.

the right to control, instruct, replace, or recall them, to reject policies of which he does not approve, to turn out of office arrogant, dictatorial, or blundering or unpopular officials.

More important still, a totalitarian dictatorship is deeply aware of its perpetual illegitimacy. Its minority seizure of power by force represents a rupture of the fabric of legitimacy. Nowhere, in any country of the world, whether Russia or a subjugated satellite, has communism ever won power in a free election.[1] In Italy, where the political tutelage and political illiteracy and inexperience of two decades under Mussolini joined with the secret infiltration and capture of the Socialist party (Nenni wing) by the Communists to constitute a real threat of a legal rise of communism to power, the other parties saved the day with a simple and truthful warning: "Vote this time, or you may never vote again." If any other party wins power it can be turned out of office again; if a totalitarian party wins power it will never permit another election.

Because it has ruptured the whole fabric of consensus and consent and continuity by which men are led to give free obedience to their government, because it is aware of its own rupture of legitimacy, totalitarianism therefore feels the perpetual need for some sort of show of approval of its rule and deeds by its victims. This quest for legitimacy and the outward show of legality explains alike the rubber stamp Soviet, the plebiscites in which one may only say yes, the elections in which there is no choice of whom to elect, the publicly staged trials and confessions of those whom it is intended to destroy.

And everyone has to participate in the show. Not only is there no right of opposition, of real choice, of control from below, but there is not even the right of abstention—not even the right of silence.

It was none other than Stalin, in his speech on the draft constitution—which was proclaimed "the most democratic constitution in the world"—who declared: "It may be said that silence is not criticism. But that is not true. The method of keeping silence, as a special method of ignoring things, is also a form of criticism."

A TYPICAL ELECTION CAMPAIGN

On March 14, 1954, as on so many other occasions, the Soviet Union went through one of these typical ritual election campaigns. The details of

---

1. With the exception of San Marino, which has an area of thirty-eight square miles and a population of 15,000. Here the Communist party, backed by a Communist-infiltrated Socialist party, won by 743 votes in a "country" which had previously "voted" Fascist by the same procedure of importing votes from Italy. They did not succeed in establishing a dictatorship and have since been voted out of office.

this ritual, and the energy consumed by it, are some measure of its significance for students of the totalitarian system.

From the beginning of January, the Soviet press had been full of news of nominating meetings, naming of committees to bring out and count the votes, names of candidates, times and places of election rallies, transcripts of campaign speeches which were endlessly pronounced and reprinted—though they endlessly said the same thing.

Newsprint in the USSR is scarce. Important papers like *Pravda* and *Izvestia* regularly appear in only 4–6 pages. Yet front pages and inside pages, and sometimes extra two-page or four-page supplements, were filled with lists of election committees from Kamchatka to Kalinin, and from Murmansk to Erivan, and of all the details of their activities. And all this despite the fact that there were no competing views, no alternative policies to choose from, no rival platforms, no contending parties, no right of question or challenge, no possible change or difference to be made by voting and no possible doubt about the results except whether the single list of candidates would receive the votes of 99.2 per cent or 99.8 per cent of the total of eligible voters.

In a land where there is a perpetual shortage of consumers' goods of all sorts, the entire country was blanketed with hundreds of millions of pamphlets, leaflets, posters, pictures, at an enormous cost of hundreds of millions of dollars to the state and its subjects. Though there is a perpetual shortage of manpower, millions of political agitators gave their full time to grinding out the spoken and written word to inform Soviet citizens that they must vote and for whom. Every home was visited and checked on, every citizen told why he must choose the candidate that had been chosen for him and why he must go to the polls. Though factory workers need nothing so much as rest after a hard day's work, they were kept in after hours to listen to agitators and campaign speeches. Though there is nothing more boring than to have to pretend that there are issues when there aren't any, that there is an election when the single candidates have already been designated elsewhere, though there is nothing more humiliating than that officials in power should mock men's natural longing to choose their own representatives and decide in some measure their own fate, millions of tired and bored workingmen and peasants, and millions of no less bored intellectuals and officials, were compelled to go through this strange simulacrum of an election campaign for two full months of days and nights and Sundays and holidays.

On January 12, 1954, *Pravda* gave instructions: "In making the preparations for the elections to the Supreme Soviet, the party organizations must thoroughly explain the tasks facing the country . . ." (the same tasks that are explained in the same way, day in and day out, when there are no elections).

Unctuously *Pravda* continued,

. . . the great principles of the Constitution of the USSR, the rights and obligations of Soviet citizens, the Soviet election system, the world's most democratic election system, must also be explained. This explanatory work will help raise the political activity and socialist consciousness of the workers and solidify the peoples of the USSR even more in their struggle for the successful fulfillment of the great creative tasks given to them by the party and the government: it will help raise the vigilance of the Soviet people and strengthen and widen the international links between our people and all peace-loving peoples.

Another strange feature of this strange electoral process, a feature unheard of in any democratic country—was that *Pravda* instructed the citizens that they were to speed up even more and work even harder to show their gratitude for this "election." All during the campaign, workingmen were apprised that they must joyfully double or triple their norms in gratitude for being given the right to vote for the candidates selected for them.

"It is essential," said *Pravda*, "to insure a powerful drive in the nationwide socialist competition in industry, transport, and agriculture for the fulfillment and over-fulfillment of the national economic plans by every enterprise."

Said the Crimean *Pravda* one day later: "Deputies to the Supreme Soviet are elected on the basis of the most democratic electoral system in the world by means of general, equal, and secret balloting."

The balloting was certainly "general," since every citizen over eighteen, except those in prison, concentration camps, or insane asylums, was eligible to go—or was accompanied, marshaled, or driven—to the polls and since the sick were dragged from their sickbeds or polled in the hospitals. And the balloting was "equal," for all alike had to go through this performance. Only children, madmen, and criminals were exempt.

But one wonders what the authorities meant when they said the vote was "secret." Since there was only one candidate, it was no secret if you voted for him. To vote against him, the voter had to go openly to a special booth where pencils were provided and had to cross out the only name. He was not allowed to insert another. The only thing secret about it was how many people actually went through this brave, defiant, mortally dangerous and—so far as direct results are concerned—futile gesture. The counting of the ballots was indeed secret, and the government which reappointed itself and forced the populace to endorse its acts decided in secret whether it wished to report the magic 99.2 per cent or 99.8 per cent. As early as January 13, one day after *Pravda* issued the election orders, the youth paper *Komsomolskaya Pravda* confidently predicted: "There is no doubt at all that the Communist party and nonparty bloc will win a new and brilliant victory at the forthcoming elections." [2]

The results in this particular election turned out to be closer to 99.8 per cent than the 99.2 per cent of some previous elections; but the victory was not as sweeping as the dictatorship professed to believe. For the real "secret ballot" in the midst of this mockery is deep in the heart of a man where no agitator or *agitpunkt* [3] can altogether reach.

2. The Other Election: Men Stake Their Lives

In the same Soviet empire there is another type of election which takes place in the mind of each citizen who finds himself faced with, or seeks out, the opportunity to cross the line that separates the known from the unknown, the Communist world from the uncertain world outside.

The most dramatic instance of the exercise of this franchise has occurred in East Germany, where Berlin itself is divided and where opportunities for making a physical break are greatest and the chance to choose therefore becomes a real one. This election, too, has its statistical record. [4]

Choosing the closest comparable date to the election which we have just been following, let us examine the report of the government of West Germany on the number of East Germans who, in the year 1953, "voted with their feet." During that year alone, 340,000 East Germans abandoned their native scenes and homes of a lifetime, left behind their friends and relatives and worldly goods (even a suitcase would arouse suspicion), and chose the uncertainties of an uprooted refugee's existence in preference to remaining in the Communist paradise of the East.

Each of the 340,000 had an individual tale to tell; but personal sufferings, personal stories, personal motives, are submerged when the numbers run into hundreds of thousands. Nor can statistics show the number who were caught by the police, snagged in barbed wire, or shot crossing the wasteland belt.

Strangest of all the statistics in the cold report was the news that 4,700

2. The party nominates not only open Communists but also obedient, nonmember followers of the Party line on its ticket. This is known as "the Communist party and nonparty bloc."

3. The headquarters from which election materials, agitators or party speakers, etc., are sent out is called an *agitpunkt*.

4. This was written before the wall was begun on the night of August 12–13, 1961. Until Berlin was thus divided to keep workers and intellectuals in the East German socialist paradise, well over 4 million had fled to the West.

members of the East German people's police were among those who escaped to freedom. This helps to explain why barbed wire, watchtowers, guns, dogs, check points, and border guards are not enough to keep people imprisoned in the vast prison that Soviet troops and German puppets have made of East Germany. How often have the police looked the other way, felt a glow of sympathy, thought of the time when they too might flee from their supposedly privileged positions? How many joined the police in order to provide themselves with an opportunity for escape?

All around the vast perimeter of the Soviet empire, each day this same type of election takes place. In no other place has it been as easy as in Germany. Around all the Soviet empire, the Soviet and satellite police have created an artificial wasteland—a belt of soil from which all inhabitants have been ousted, all trees uprooted, the soil plowed up fresh so that every footprint will show, the whole surrounded by barbed wire entanglements; at fixed intervals, watchtower redoubts; in some places land mines, in others electrified wire; and, all along the frontier, guards, guns, fierce dogs.

Thus the whole Soviet empire is converted into one vast concentration camp from which none may leave except on an official mission. Yet somehow, between the mines and the wires, men crawl. Under the earth men tunnel. Through the road blocks they break with trucks going at full speed. Locomotives, with throttle wide, have smashed through the barriers at the end of the line. Men tunnel under, fly over. Men put out to sea in tiny skiffs, leap from ships into the waters of foreign harbors. Every known means of locomotion, and every feat of human ingenuity and human daring, have been put to use in this effort to escape.

Thus there are two kinds of elections in the Soviet empire. There is the rigged mockery in which there is only one party and everyone is driven to the polls to "vote" though there is nothing to vote about. And there is this other election, real, dangerous, illegal, punishable by concentration camp or instant death. This is the election in which men can sometimes choose between communism and the uncertain freedom of the refugee and wanderer. In every Communist land, men have made this choice. "They have voted," as Lenin so well said of the Russian peasant soldiers in World War I, "they have voted with their feet."

On November 6, 1946, Andrei Vyshinsky told the United Nations that his government was demanding the return of more than 1.2 million refugees and displaced persons. Since that date, over 6 million additional persons have escaped from iron curtain countries. Some 5 million have escaped from East Germany, where the chance to "vote" is greatest; over 760,000 from the other subjugated countries; over 1.3 million from Communist China through Shanghai and Hong Kong. From North Korea since the Communist armies split Korea in two and erected their paradise there, more than 2 million have escaped to South Korea. From North Vietnam over a million fled south before armies closed the frontier. Is this not a plebiscite which tells what kind of government people prefer?

ELECTION IN A PRISON CAMP

While the vote by flight to freedom from East Germany is dramatic because of the annual numbers involved and because it is here that escape is easier (though hardly easy!), it was in Korea, after the Korean War, that the most significant election took place.

In all previous wars, until the middle of the twentieth century, it was always taken for granted that, once hostilities ended, every war prisoner would automatically wish to return to his own country. There is no precedent in history to the situation in which thousands of prisoners have not wanted to return to their native lands.

Only in World War II did this strange phenomenon appear for the first time. And the numbers that did not then want to return to their homelands ran into millions. On November 6, 1946, Vyshinsky told a committee of the General Assembly of the United Nations that his government claimed the right to have returned "more than 1.2 million refugees and displaced persons." The Allied governments, and notably the United States to its eternal shame, assisted in the forced repatriation of untold numbers—hundreds of thousands—of persons who did not want to return to their Communist homelands.[5]

But after the Korean armistice a decision was made which, although insufficient significance is attached to it today, will one day be noted by historians as a turning point in the war for freedom. Many North Korean soldiers, who might conceivably feel at home in South Korea, refused repatriation to the North. But even among the so-called "volunteers" from Communist China, of whom 24,440 had been captured, over 14,200— many with families on the Chinese mainland—refused to be repatriated. *About two out of every three Chinese "volunteers" refused to go home!*

Could it have been the attraction of new scenes? But the new scene was nothing but barbed wire around a prison camp. Did the outside world offer such wonderful inducements? The world promises very little to a refugee or a displaced person. He must find himself a land, a home, a job, friends, must sink new roots, must accustom himself to an alien tongue and way of life.

---

5. On this see the forthcoming book by Julius Epstein, *Operation Keelhaul: The Story of Forced Repatriation*. "Operation Keelhaul" was the Army's code name for the deportation to certain concentration camp or death.

TURNING POINT IN THE COLD WAR

Why did the Chinese "volunteers" elect to stay? Why did the East Germans elect to leave? And the East Europeans, and the Balts, and more than a million Russians who managed to escape?

Under the circumstances of totalitarianism, the ordinary man does his best to adjust himself to the demands of the state. He cheers when he is ordered to cheer, boos when he is ordered to boo, tries to fulfill the norms set by the speed-up system. He does his best to serve his country, work with his neighbors, adjust himself to the inevitable, remain a useful member of society. But deep in the secret recesses of his heart he preserves the natural human will to think for himself, to follow his faith and his conscience, to give trust to his friends and loved ones. Always there is that little ineradicable spark of humanity longing for its freedom.

And when, suddenly, the dweller under the Soviet system finds the screws released, the frontier open, a chance to escape, a haven in the outside world, and even if that haven be no more than a prison camp followed by the uncertainties of a refugee's fate, he seizes the opportunity.

Thus the phenomenon arose of the million who, after World War II, would not return to the Soviet Union and its satellites. Thus the prisoner issue arose in Panmunjon over the tens of thousands of Chinese and North Koreans who refused to return to Communist China and Communist North Korea.

Bewildered at first by this phenomenon of war prisoners who do not want to go home when hostilities cease, the free world has gradually come to understand it. The United Nations, at a cost of many thousands of lives in the additional fighting, refused to reach an armistice agreement with the Communists until it had succeeded in pushing through its new principle of nonforcible repatriation. This moral triumph was a signal to the captive peoples that, when an opportunity presents itself, a real election will be theirs. And to the men in the Kremlin it was a signal that in war they would expose themselves to the risk of mass desertion. A single decision—to give our North Korean and Chinese "enemy" prisoners the right of refuge—immeasurably shifted the balance between the free world and the world of totalitarian communism. It told the victims of totalitarian oppression that at last we recognized them as our potential allies and knew how to make a distinction between the government that oppresses them and its first and chief victims.

That decision on the part of the United Nations did more than all its other acts, save only its defense of Korea, to make general war less likely. For it made the men in the Kremlin more uncertain than ever of the reliability of the armies it would have to launch across the frontiers.

And if, nevertheless, they should some day force what they call "the final conflict" upon the world, it gives promise of shortening that war and assuring the victory of freedom. For these prisoners of war to whom we did not even give the right of asylum,[6] but merely the right not to be repatriated by force, have demonstrated what a man's choice will be when he is free to choose, after having had the direct experience of living under the totalitarian Communist system.

—Boston, 1956-1960

---

6. I distinguish between the "right of refuge," *i.e.*, the right of a refugee not to be returned by force, and the "right of asylum," *i.e.*, the right of a man who has staked his life on freedom to find a real welcome in a new home. I realize that hitherto the terms "refuge" and "asylum" have generally been used interchangeably, but recent experience has taught us that the right to flee (refuge) and the right to find a real home are by no means synonymous. Some of the short-sighted and ungenerous provisions of our immigration laws and their narrow construction by uncomprehending officials have meant that too often those who thought they were escaping to freedom have found only a refuge in a displaced-persons camp.

PART V

The Conditioning of Culture

I OPERATION REWRITE: THE AGONY OF THE SOVIET HISTORIAN *

For over two decades, Soviet historiography has been in steadily deepening crisis. Histories succeed each other as if they were being consumed by a giant chain smoker who lights the first volume of the new work with the last of the old. Historians appear, disappear, and reappear; others vanish without a trace.

Originally, only party history was subject to rigid prescription. Then Soviet history was added. Latterly, the area of command performance and commanded conclusions has spread outward to America and Asia and the wastes of Antarctica, backward to the Middle Ages, to Byzantium, to the shadowy origins of the Slavs and the predawn of the Kievan state, to China's earliest culture. One day a given statement of events or interpretation is obligatory. The next it is condemned in words which seem to portend the doom of the historian who faithfully carried out his instructions.

UNPERSONS, UNPEOPLES, UNOBJECTS

Often the central personages of an event become "unpersons," as if they had never existed. The Soviet civil war must now be rewritten as if there never had been a war commissar named Leon Trotsky. The Soviet theater, once the subject of so many histories, is historyless once more, until somebody contrives to write a new version without a trace of the great innovator-director, Vsevolod Meyerhold. On February 15, 1951, *Pravda* accomplished the feat of "commemorating" the tenth anniversary of the Eighteenth Party Conference, in which Voznesensky had delivered the main report, without so much as mentioning the name of the reporter!

Today the Balkarians are missing from volume B of the new edition of the *Great Encyclopedia*; the Volga Germans have become an "un-

* Prepared for the State Department. First published in *Foreign Affairs*, October, 1952, copyright by The Council of Foreign Relations, Inc.

people"; and the Crimean Tartars, having been expelled from their centuries-old home to a region under the Arctic Circle, have had the place names of their former habitations extirpated and are being subjected to the shrinking of their historical role in the Crimea to the point where they are gradually becoming an "unpeople," too.[1]

During the spring of 1952 even objects began to become "unobjects" as *Pravda* and the regional press from February to May reported a grim and thoroughgoing purge of scores of local and national museums all the way from Lithuania to Kazakhstan. The Lithuanian museums were rebuked for failing to show the influence of Great Russian culture and the struggles and longings of their people for the extinction of their independence while the Kazakh museums were condemned for the nostalgic splendor of their daggers, guns, harnesses, bridal costumes, and for failing to display any objects showing Great Russia's civilizing influence and the "progressive" character of her annexation of Kazakhstan.

It would require many volumes to give an account of this continual retroactive rewriting of history. The present study aims to give some notion of the scope of this vast Operation Palimpsest, to seek the "line," or rather some of the fragmentary and frequently contradictory lines, discernible in the revisions; to look for the reasons, or a rationale, for what seems to contain an element of the personal and irrational as well; and to ask what these tamperings with the historical record portend concerning the present and immediate future intentions of the regime. History has become a "weapon," an arm of propaganda, the essential function of which is the justification of the changing policies of the Soviet government through reference to the "facts" and "documents" of the past. The penchant for making every change in foreign relations or domestic policy historically retroactive serves as a vast though distorting glass through which the observer may see these policy changes magnified. It is that which makes V*oprosy istorii* (Questions of History) undoubtedly the most interesting and revealing of all present-day Soviet publications.

Macaulay once said that his idea of hell would be to have to listen to fiends endlessly misquoting history and be unable to correct them. But in the Soviet Union the historian himself must do the misquoting. His own point of view is neither consulted nor, except by the accident of coincidence with the line of the moment, ever likely to find expression. The textbook writers and lecturers under the limited absolutism of the last tsars could easily be identified as liberal and democratic, as in the case of a Platonov, or as conservative and monarchical, as in the case of an Ilovaisky, or as Marxist, as in the case of a Pokrovsky. But

1. See *Pravda* and *Izvestia,* June 4, 1952. Recently Tartars and Germans were "rehabilitated," but the Tartars still denied their home in the Crimea.

under total state absolutism, history, as all of culture, has been "nationalized," and there are no individual viewpoints or private judgments or pluralistic approaches. Tarlé, specialist on Napoleon, is ordered to rewrite his principal work in such fashion as to "prove" that Napoleon himself burned Moscow (no doubt to make it untenable as his winter quarters!). The liberal-democratic Vipper, who first wrote on Ivan the Terrible in the early years of the century, is charged with bringing his book of 1922 "up-to-date" and glorifying the protagonist. S. V. Utechin writes:

> From my experience as a student at Moscow University in 1939-41, I know that the late Professors K. V. Bazilevich and S. V. Bakhrushkin held a negative attitude towards the present regime. Yet in their volumes we find no traces of views different from those professed by Stalin. Thus the personal political opinions of the authors do not necessarily coincide with, and may even be contrary to, the views expressed in their books. These reflect not their political biases . . . but their understanding of the party line.[2]

As the great editing process embraces more and more of the remote corners of the earth and earliest past, there are no longer safe and neutral topics. Nor does the historian enjoy the right to pick his period and theme, nor the right of silence where he cannot in good conscience speak. As in music the politician-critic or the supreme critic in the Politburo tells the composers what and how and in what style to compose, so in history. *Voprosy istorii* bristles with menacing strictures upon historians for picking remote, neutral, sharply delimited, or apolitical subjects; for neglecting fields which have been given priority in party directives and the Five Year Plan for Soviet historians; for drawing their own conclusions or failing to find in the materials the conclusions predetermined for them.

It is suggestive both of the hazards in the field and of the real feelings of the historians that, despite urgings, dangled prizes and repeated threats, no one has yet been found to complete a single volume or even a single serious article in the field of the history of the party and regime, though Stalin himself first suggested it in 1931, ordered it at regular intervals thereafter, and forced it into the place of top priority in the Five Year Plan for Soviet historians adopted in 1946. Fifteen years after the task was first assigned by the dictator, the lead editorial in *Voprosy istorii* (No. 8, 1949) warned that the failure to produce the ordered works created a "completely impermissible situation" which it "would be completely wrong to look for objective circumstances to explain." This stubborn silence constitutes the most eloquent page in present-day Soviet historiography.

2. S. V. Utechin, "Textbooks on History," *Soviet Studies,* Glasgow, Vol. IV, No. 1.

FALL OF THE POKROVSKY SCHOOL

In the 1920s, not a politician but a professional Marxist historian, M. N. Pokrovsky, was the virtual dictator in Soviet historiography. He represented a consistent general line ("history is politics projected into the past") and made life difficult for fellow historians who did not accept it. But he held to professional standards, had regard for documents and evidence, though at times he wrestled mightily with them to compel them to yield what he sought. And as a historian he had enormous prestige, which was further enhanced by Lenin's preface to his *Short History of Russia*, which praised it warmly and insisted that it be used as a textbook and translated into other European languages.

But in 1931, Pokrovsky's excessive respect for the facts of party history and his Marxist denigration of much of Russia's prerevolutionary past came under Stalin's personal scrutiny. In 1934, he was posthumously purged—he had had the luck to die in time—along with all his works and disciples. At about the same time, Ryazanov, Russia's outstanding Marxicologist, whose headstrong, self-directed devotion to Marxist documentary scholarship closely resembled Pokrovsky's attitude toward history, suffered a similar posthumous fate.

Pokrovsky was accused of being antinational and antipatriotic (he shared Lenin's internationalism and disliked tsarist wars); of neglecting actual events, dates, facts, periods, and personages in favor of generalized sociological schemata (until then considered a hallmark of Marxist historical interpretation); of being "antiscientific" and "anti-Marxist"; of "underestimating" Lenin (he wrote: "Whenever Lenin differs from me I blindly accept his view; he can see ten feet deeper into the earth than any of the rest of us"); and of underestimating Stalin (which was undoubtedly true and the immediate though not the only explanation of his downfall).

At first it seemed to historians that a new line might emerge which would put pluses where Pokrovsky put minuses and offer them considerably more freedom for examination of sources without regard to Marxist interpretive schemata. But alas, life was not to be that simple. Though Pokrovsky had been condemned for neglect of concrete historical facts, before long V*oprosy istorii* (No. 12, 1948) was to give warning that "the proper historian" must be free from "objectivism" and from "an exaggerated attachment to facts" and at home in the citation and application of the "theoretical generalizations" and dictates of the party line. Now it was not a single, simplicist, recognizable line like Pokrovsky's but a continuous bombardment by *ad hoc* fragments of lines, changing with each political shift or change in mood, frequently internally contradictory, constantly being altered and even suddenly reversed.

Apparently these fragments issued from Stalin's latest pronouncement or some earlier one exhumed from context after four decades or from the quotations from Lenin or Marx or Engels which adorn their promulgation. But study of such texts will not help the historian, nor is there any real defense for him in an umbrella of quotations, for in any vast and historically evolved sacred scripture you can find quotations for any side of anything. To quote yesterday's Stalin may today be "talmudism and scholasticism." The historian must divine the dictator's coming pronouncement, for his latest word is always the last word in history even though Marx, Engels, Lenin, and yesterday's Stalin all be united against it. A sudden reversal in Stalin's relations with Germany or England or America is pushed backward retroactively so that the present enemy is absolute evil and, though yesterday an ally, must always have been an enemy. All books, articles, and documents that testify to the contrary must be consigned to the Orwellian "memory hole" to be consumed in flames or must be "rectified" and brought up to date without any mention of the fact that there was ever an earlier version.

Not only changes in relationships, strategy, and tactics, but even changes in the dictator's awareness of the nature of his own regime, or his subjective identification with some deed of a figure of the past—say an Ivan IV or a Marshal Kutuzov—can require a complete retroactive revision of the figure thus honored. Such revaluations cannot be deduced by the historian from a study of sources, but only by sensing the reactions of the dictator whose attitude toward history has been summed up by Orwell in the formula: "Who controls the present, controls the past."

THE CREATOR OF SOVIET HISTORICAL SCIENCE

Stalin first entered historiography through the field of personal and party history. In January 1924, one week after the death of Lenin, he chose the occasion of a memorial address to predate by some four years the beginning of their personal acquaintance.[3] At the time it might have seemed merely a faintly ghoulish example of the natural human inclination to reshape the past nearer to the heart's desire. But when one remembers that Lenin had just called for the removal of Stalin as General Secretary and when one contemplates the subsequent revisions that car-

---

3. For the evidence, see Bertram D. Wolfe, *Three Who Made a Revolution,* New York: The Dial Press, 1948; Delta Paperback, 1964, pp. 424-427. For the Stalin-directed predating of Gorky's first meeting with Lenin, see *The Bridge and the Abyss,* New York, 1967, pp. 27-31.

ried Stalin from "loyal disciple" to "best disciple," and then "the only loyal disciple," and on to "faithful companion-in-arms" (*soratnik*) and "wise guide and counsellor" and more-than-equal partner, one cannot but be struck by the meticulous attention to detail and long-range planning implied in this first little retouching of history.

A Napoleon, a Trotsky, a Thucydides, a Xenophon, or a Josephus may wait to turn his energies into the writing of history until defeat has deprived him of the opportunity of making it. But Stalin engaged in writing history as one of the means by which he climbed to power. That explains the ruthless political utilitarianism, the pugnacious factionalism or *partiinost* that he has impressed upon it. That is why first "rotten liberalism" and then "objectivism" were to become the gravest of historiographical crimes. History was one of the "weapons" with which he fought his way to power, and he enlarged the scope of his revisions with every increase in the actual power drawn into his hands.

There was much to revise. First there was that personal symbol of the revolution and the regime: the duality-unity, *Lenin-Trotsky*. Mountains of books, newspapers, pamphlets, decrees, and documents had to be consigned to the "memory hole," mashed to pulp or brought out in "corrected" editions, in order to substitute for *Lenin-Trotsky* a new duality-unity, *Lenin-Stalin*.

Then there were the other close associates of Lenin, glorified as "old bolshevism" in the struggle with Trotsky, and then themselves destroyed. To obscure all traces of their actual deeds and substitute nameless and monstrous evils that would justify their murder is another task that Stalinist historiography never ceased to concern itself with. With notable impartiality Stalin barred foreign and domestic accounts, pre-Stalinist bolshevik historics, Stalinist histories written to order by Knorin, Popov, and Yaroslavsky, the footnotes to the second and third editions of Lenin's *Works*, the *Great Encyclopedia*, and all the telltale passages in the letters, writings, and speeches of Lenin and of Stalin himself. There is a mass of Lenin-Trotsky correspondence at Harvard that can never be published in the Soviet Union. There is Lenin's testament. And typical of Stalin's self-censorship, was his omission from his *Collected Works* of his tribute to Trotsky published in *Pravda* of November 6, 1918, on the occasion of the first anniversary of the Bolshevik Revolution.

For the foreign observer, the most important document that Stalin omitted from the corresponding volume of his *Works* is a letter he wrote Lenin in 1920, criticizing the latter's "Theses on the National and Colonial Question" because they failed to provide an intermediate or transitional form of the annexation of new Soviet states, like a "Soviet Germany, Hungary, Poland, Rumania," which had never formed part of the old tsarist empire and therefore might object to immediate incorporation in the Soviet Union. This early foreshadowing of the future "People's Democracies" can be found, however, as a footnote to Lenin's "Theses" in the second and third Russian editions of his *Works* (Vol. XXV, p. 624).

I was in Moscow during the first six months of 1929 when, on central command, every periodical and paper in the Soviet Union broke out with a picture of Stalin on the front page. This was the beginning of the Stalin cult. At first it seemed to me wholly "rational." Having just eliminated Bukharin, the last of the close comrades of Lenin, Stalin had now to become "old bolshevism." But a number of circumstances later caused me to conclude that there was an irrational element as well.

First, there was the fury of the purges, with the arrest, execution, or reduction to unskilled slave labor of millions: the neutral, the indifferent, the innocent, the loyal, including entire technical, bureaucratic, and military layers desperately needed for the enhancement of the very power of the state. It may be urged that such random terror was "needed" on the principle that "if you want to make your enemies afraid, begin by cutting off the heads of your friends," and that total state power in a populous state can spend a few million lives on the process of completely atomizing society so that every particularized atom depends absolutely on the state and no man can depend upon any other. Still, it is hard to believe that so many millions were required or that the state had so greatly to weaken itself technically and militarily in the process.

Second, there was the insatiable and unappeasable appetite of the dictator for the enlargement of the incense, the trembling obedience, the worship, to the point where in his last years Stalin became the coryphaeus of all the arts and sciences (history of course among them) and was increasingly endowed with the attributes of a living god.

Third, there was my unexpected discovery while going through the pages of *Zhizn natsionalnostei* (*Life of the Nationalities*—Stalin's personal organ when he was Commissar of Nationalities) that Stalin had retroactively inserted two minor "prophecies" into one of his articles when he included it in his *Collected Works*. And, more startling still, the discovery of an item headed "Greetings to Comrade Stalin," with the following (slightly abbreviated) text:

The Conference of National Sections . . . sends you its greetings and declares its conviction that by following firmly along the path pointed out by you for the solution of the national question . . . we will create throughout the world a united, brotherly Communist family which we will teach to appreciate those great merits which belong to you—the leader of the oppressed peoples.

Here was the beginning of that *potok privetstvii* (flood of greetings) which filled the columns of all the Soviet papers and journals for many years. But the date was December 24, 1920! Lenin was still alive and in leadership, and, by general consent, it was Lenin who had pointed out the solution of the national question and who was the leader of the oppressed peoples of the world. Stalin was still outranked by five or six of Lenin's associates and had neither expropriated their deeds nor executed them. Thus the craving for flattery and the need that "the world appreciate his great merits" preceded by almost a decade the "rational" motivation of the Stalin cult.

In 1931, Stalin issued his first public directive on the spirit of the new historiography in the form of an angry open letter to the editors of *Proletarskaia Revoliutsia (Proletarian Revolution)*. He charged them with "rotten liberalism" for having printed a "discussion article" on the problem of why Lenin had continued to admire Kautsky and the Orthodox-Marxist majority of the German Social Democracy until he was shocked by their stand on the war of 1914. *Bolshevik* (No. 22, 1931) published Stalin's open letter with its own appropriate editorial gloss, headed: "Give the Study of the History of Our Party a Scientific Bolshevik Footing!" All the earlier histories, from Shlyapnikov's to Yaroslavsky's and Popov's, were attacked. "There must be a thorough housecleaning in all book, textbook, and journalistic literature dealing with the history of the Party. . . . The ruthless struggle against every manifestation of rotten liberalism must be intensified. . . . The significance of Stalin's letter far transcends the gateposts of history. . . ."

The dictator next turned his attention to a close supervision of a new history of the civil war which was to eliminate all trace of Trotsky—except as a secret agent of the other side. Then Stalin began to dictate all the details of the now renowned *History of the Communist Party: Short Course*. On January 20, 1946, *Pravda* reported that Stalin was himself the author of this strange work of historical falsification, endless self-quotation and self-glorification, and that it would appear as volume XV of his *Collected Works*.

But even Stalin's mighty name has not protected the *Short Course* from the ravages of retroactive obsolescence. Thus the first edition had substituted for a number of "unpersons" the new chief purger, Yezhov, as the "preparer of an uprising of the soldiers on the Western Front in Byelorussia." [4] It soon developed that Yezhov was but twenty-one at the time and, moreover, that the chief purger must himself be purged. Stalin's *Short Course* kept appearing in revised editions as the greatest, dullest, and most mendacious best-seller in the history of literature. But he himself streamlined the Great October Revolution further and further

4. New York: International Publishers, 1939, p. 206.

until the latest version to appear (in the chronology in the back of the corresponding volume of his own *Collected Works*) actually read:

Oct. 24 (Nov. 6, New Style)—Lenin arrives at Smolny in the evening. Stalin briefs him on the course of political events.
Oct. 24-25—Lenin and Stalin lead the October uprising.

Whether it be wholly "rational'" in terms of the rationale of the total state and the absolute ruler or whether there be also an irrational element, it should be clear that we are dealing with the most striking example in all history of a man who has succeeded in inventing himself. It takes total organization and total power—not propaganda skill but the union of pen and sword in a single hand—to do so complete a job. Once the total state has concentrated in its control not only all the means of production of material but no less of spiritual goods—all the modes of expression, communication, criticism, thought, feeling, all cheers and boos, all love and hate, all paper, ink, type, loudspeakers, microphones, cameras, cinemas, montage and cutting rooms, theaters, walls, schools, churches, street corners, all books, magazines, newspapers, leaflets, caricatures, pulpits, chairs, lecterns, meeting halls, all import and export of and traffic in ideas—it becomes possible to reshape the public past nearer to the heart's desire. Having worked so efficiently in personal and party history, the spirit and this method were next applied to general historiography.

From the beginning of the 1930s, Stalin's policies determined with steadily increasing rigor and detail the character of Soviet historiography. His letter of 1931 on "rotten liberalism," his brief dogmatic remarks of 1934 on what a Soviet history text and a modern history text should be, the successive liquidations of the two professional journals that preceded *Voprosy istorii*, the spiritual trauma of the purges—all serve as urgent reminders to the historian that "Stalin Is the Creator of Soviet Historical Science" (title of article in No. 2, 1949). Yet, if we except his claim to have written the *History of the Communist Party*, all his historical writings, directives, and *obiter dicta* which are supposed to serve as guides to historiography would not together make a single chapter. How, then, does the Soviet historian divine what is expected of him? And how shall the observer deduce from the twists and turns of the hisoriographical line what the real policies and intentions of the Kremlin are?

CRISIS IN THE IDEOLOGICAL FOUNDATIONS OF THE REGIME

An especially revealing moment for the examining of these questions is the end of World War II. Dictatorship thrives on war, and total dictatorship lives by total war on two fronts: against its own people and against the outside world. Hitherto the Soviet regime had offered three justifications for the cruelty, ubiquity, and perpetual strain: (1) the terror regime was necessary to crush the enemy within; (2) it was necessary to protect the land of socialism from a completely hostile world; and (3) it was justified by the fact that it was already producing an incomparably more glorious life than that beyond its borders. Now all three justifications were suddenly called in question, and the regime was faced with an acute, all-embracing crisis:

(1) The internal enemy had been officially liquidated some time ago, in the late 1930s, when it was proclaimed that classes had been abolished, that socialism had been achieved, that everyone loved the government and the leader. The Stalinist constitution was supposed to have institutionalized this new state of affairs.

(2) The theory that the Soviet Union was surrounded by a completely hostile world in which it could find neither friends nor allies but only enemies collapsed the day Hitler attacked and—no doubt contrary to Hitler's expectation and Stalin's—Churchill and Roosevelt called upon their peoples to give unstinting support to the Soviet Union. The Soviet people noted with warmth that they had friends and allies. They heard Stalin himself, on the anniversary of the October Revolution in 1941, proclaim that "England and the United States of America possess elementary democratic liberties . . . trade unions . . . parties . . . parliaments." They saw that the Kremlin was summoning them to defend not the dictatorship but the Fatherland and democratic freedoms. Confidently they looked forward to the dawn of a new day in return for their unstinting sacrifices.

(3) As in 1813, once more the many-peopled Russian armies entered the outside world and felt its impact. The whole fictional world of evil and misery without, and of superiority and perfection within, fell to pieces. Either the dictatorship had to relax, or new enemies and new superiorities had to be synthetically created.

Out of this crisis came Stalin's address to his electors on the inseparability of war and capitalism and on the need to continue the strain-and-storm tempo to prepare for future wars; Zhdanov's attacks on permeation of the "world's most advanced" music, painting, literature, and philosophy by "servility to everything foreign," "rootless cosmopolitanism," "kowtowing to the West," lack of *partiinost* and *ideinost* (party spirit and high level of ideas, literally "partyness" and "ideaness"); the "revival" of the Comintern; the rejection of Marshall Plan aid by Molotov who, while his regime hesitated, took eighty-nine advisers to Paris, in the end only to advise him on how to say *niet*.

In June 1945, exactly one month after V-E Day, *Istoricheskii zhurnal*

(*Historical Journal*), which had naturally been edited in the spirit of the Grand Alliance, was informed that it had been unequal to its tasks and had lowered the level of historical scholarship and was forthwith liquidated in favor of a new journal to be called V*oprosy istorii*, or *Questions of History*. The "questions" or "problems" it has had to handle were those of this spiritual reconversion and rearmament.

MEANING OF THE HATE-AMERICA CAMPAIGN

The first problem was to make the Soviet people forget their most recent and greatest experience. They must forget, or press down into the unverbalized, unthought, unfelt unconscious, the memory of the fact that their leader had joined in a pact with Hitler which touched off the war. Since the V*ozhd* had made one of the greatest mistakes in history, the extravagant cult of his infallibility and wisdom must now reach new and unheard-of heights. The memory of lend-lease, the memory of the titanic joint effort and the embrace on the Elbe, of England's valiant holding out alone during the period of the Stalin-Hitler pact—so many memories had to be forgotten or, rather, transformed into their opposites.

A sample will serve. The collective history text on the *History of the USSR*, edited by Pankratova, in its 1945 edition quotes Joseph Stalin on the Normandy landing: "A brilliant achievement. . . . The history of war knows no other enterprise like it for breadth of purpose, grandiose skill, and masterful execution."

One year later the book had been replaced by a new edition in which the passage reads: "On June 6, 1944, Allied forces accomplished a landing in Northern France."

And the latest approved history text, that of the textbook prizewinner Shestakov, describes the Normandy landing in these terms:

England and the United States, in the course of three years of war, dragged out in every way the opening of a second front. . . . But when, after the gigantic victories of the Soviet Army, it became clear that the Soviet Union might alone defeat the enemy, occupy the territory of Germany, and liberate all Western Europe, including France . . . in June 1944, the English and American armies left England and landed on the coast of Northern France.[5]

Every such revision of history has its *resonance effect*, spilling over into a score of unexpected places, reverberating backward into the past, so that the enemy of the moment must always have been the enemy. Especially must the high points of alliance and friendship be turned into

5. Moscow, 1951, pp. 277-278.

sinister and hateful acts. And every such revision is the product of *multiple determination*. Thus the Russia-won-the-war-alone-against-a-Hitler-Anglo-American-Imperialist-conspiracy version of World War II inevitably reverberated into the hate-America campaign. But the latter campaign had many additional causes and implications.

It was the United States that had contributed the greatest help and evoked the greatest warmth. It represented the greatest power. Its productivity was the envy and admiration of the materialistic, technocratic official Soviet culture. Its conduct in the Philippines and Latin America, above all in war-ruined Europe (like that of Great Britain in India) was the startling refutation of the Lenin-Stalin dogmas of "monopoly capitalist imperialism" and of "capitalist encirclement." And the United States was a living refutation, no less, of the dogma that total statism was the most productive system. America represented the possibility of social reform without revolution ("reformism"), a land of plenty and freedom, visibly achieving an expanding economy and an ever greater measure of social justice and labor-farmer welfare, without the liquidation of entire classes.

The war ended with the Soviet Union as the only great power astride the Eurasian land mass, with a power vacuum to the west and a power vacuum to the east of it. The United States represented the only possible obstacle to the rapid expansion of the Soviet Empire into both vacuums. America sought to restore a balance of power by restoring Europe and—a little more hesitantly and uncertainly—by reconstrucing and restoring a free Asia. Not only was its postwar use of its unprecedented power a reproach and a refutation. Increasingly, it was the main obstacle to the march of Soviet power to world conquest as America moved from the blind illusions of the Grand Alliance to the sadder and wiser policy of "containment"; from containment to "defense of the free world from positions of strength"; and then to collective defense of Korea as a victim of aggression. The Truman Doctrine stood between the Soviet Union and the Dardanelles; the Marshall Plan and the North Atlantic Pact blocked the road to Western Europe; American troops formed the backbone of the United Nations armies holding the narrow waist of Korea.

The slow development of America's postwar policies began to inspire hope in all those who dreamed of ultimate liberation. It offered refuge (a little too niggardly) to escaping fighters for freedom. And when it decided that it would not be a party to the forced repatriation of those who had escaped or been taken prisoner, it adopted—almost unwittingly—a policy which makes the Soviet armies and all auxiliary armies potentially unreliable.

All of these elements, and others like them, enter into the calculations of the Soviet regime, but none of them can be so much as mentioned in overt expression. The vocabulary of *newspeak* and the "researches" and "documentation" of Soviet historians must be employed to make each of these look like its opposite and to envelop the whole concept of America in hatred. It is sufficient to look at the list of books that have been praised and awarded Stalin prizes, to see the volume and the titles of the articles in *Voprosy istorii*, or to note that the articles vilifying the United States are criticized only because they do not go far enough.

If it were an individual instead of the head of a great state and its passive members that was making these statements—ranging from assertions regarding bacteriological warfare to those about castration of colored peoples—we would regard it as pure pathology; loss of memory of recent events, loss of the reality principle, persecutory delusions. But there is "method in his madness," as proved by the fact that while Stalin's ministry of hate has filled all the earth with its roars, his ministry of love has cooed in a tiny whisper in the *Moscow News*—in English.

THE NEW IMPERIAL HISTORIOGRAPHY

No field of historiography is now exempt from this inexorable process of retroactive re-editing. The early Middle Ages must be revised to pre-date by three or four centuries the origins of a high Great Russian culture and of a centralized state. The Varangian theory has to be rejected, not on the basis of the evidence, but because it implies that the Great Russians did not know how to set up a powerful centralized state of their own, except by conquest from without. The new total state is very sensitive about this matter of a "centralized, powerful state." That which the democratic and earlier Marxist historians regarded as oppressive has now become "progressive." It is no longer permitted to suggest that this great state arose in the course of the defense of the Eurasian plain against outside invasion, or that bondage in its wide and sparsely settled lands arose through political imposition, so that the recruiting sergeant and tax collector might know where to find the peasant. Ivan the Terrible must become a progressive and heroic tsar because he enlarged the Russian lands, strove to take the Baltic, set up the *Oprichnina* which Stalin recognized as an analogue of the GPU, purged his opponents and even faithful servitors and son in ways which in his heart Stalin also recognized, and because he completed the centralization of the state and the absolute power of its ruler.

Soviet Byzantine scholarship has to break with Western scholarship in order to refute the idea that the declining empire was "rigid, static, and obscurantist," in order to show that the countries of southeast Europe, "which have embarked on the path of the People's Democracies," had an early, "progressive and original culture." Soviet historians must discover "the influence of the Slavs on the history of Byzantium." They must "expose" the Ottoman conquest of Byzantium in 1453 and show that "the Turkish assimilators are the most brutal of all assimilators who tortured and maimed the Balkan nations for hundreds of years." Indeed, "the very fact that the 1953 Congress of Byzantine scholars (on the five hundredth anniversay of 1453) was being held in the capital of Marshallized Turkey" was evidence enough that it would serve "American imperialist and Pan-Turkish aims." After all, Istanbul is but another name for Constantinople, and that for Byzantium, always the Tsargrad of imperial dreams, and for the Soviet empire the gateway to the Mediterranean and the Near East.

If Turkey or Iran is slated as victim of the next forward move in the Near East, then Lenin's friendship with the new Turkey and denunciation of tsarist aspirations in Iran must be buried seven fathoms under the ground. The influence of the high Iranian civilization upon the Tadjiks must be denied or, as has actually been done, reversed. So must the influence of the Turks upon the Turkic peoples of the Soviet Union. Only Great Russian influence remains, even if it has to be invented. Adding to the multiple determination of the process, there is the restlessness of these Soviet Iranian and Turkic Mohammedan peoples, the growth of their national feelings, the specter of Pan-Turanianism and Pan-Iranianism as possible counterfoils to Pan-Slavism.

The history of the Balkans and other "People's Democracies" is also being rewritten in the Soviet Historical Section of the Academy of Sciences, and particularly in the Slavic Studies Section. Bulgaria is getting a new look. Non-Slavic Albania has "longed for centuries for liberation from the Turkish yoke and has long sought the friendship which now binds it to the Soviet peoples." Rumania's animus toward old Russia is being retroactively transformed and her language being considered for honorary Slavic citizenship. Tito became the eternal traitor and in 1941 was simultaneously serving Hitler and the Anglo-American imperialists.[6]

Two successive editings of Czechoslovak history have been scrapped, and a third was already under fire after it had been out only a year. The Polish historians are in continuous torment. Poland's culture must of course be decisively influenced by the Great Russian, but not by Rome or the West, while all trace of Polish influence upon Great Russian culture is being deleted or equipped with a minus sign. "The task of scientific history is to relate events truthfully," the Poles were admonished by Voprosy istorii (No. 4, 1949) "and to show that the responsibility for the policy of hostility toward Russia in the past rests not with the Polish

6. Now the whole history of Titoism is destined to be rewritten again.

people but with the governing classes." In all the partitions, the seizure of the Russian share of Poland was justified.

MARX TO THE "MEMORY HOLE"

To the "memory hole" have been consigned all the works of Marx and Engels on the menace of Russian absolutism, imperial expansion, Pan-Slavism, in favor of the restoration of Poland "with the boundaries of 1772," in favor of Shamil and Georgian independence. After fifteen years of suppression, Stalin published his secret attack of 1934 on Engels' article "On Russian Foreign Policy." But Marxism is still needed as an ostensibly invariant philosophy to refer to in vindicating changing policies; so for the most part this censorship proceeds in absolute silence. With the retroactive purging of Ryazanov, no Marxist scholar has ventured to continue the publication of these articles in the *Gesamtausgabe*.[7]

In 1934, Stalin could still rebuke a textbook for failing to brand "the annexationist-colonializing role of tsarism . . . the Prison-House of Peoples" and its "counterrevolutionary role in foreign policy . . . as the international gendarme"; and for failing to show the influence of western thought upon the democratic and socialist revolutionary movements in Russia. To quote the 1934 Stalin in Russia two decades later was to take one's life into one's hands.

Now Great Russian nationalism is inextricably blended with "Soviet patriotism." Internationalism is for use abroad and was defined by Stalin as "unconditional loyalty to the Soviet Union." At home it is "cosmopolitanism" and "servility to all things foreign." Nationalism of any other variety than Great Russian is "bourgeois nationalism" and is fatal. A Sosyura may not "love the Ukraine" unless he remember to love above all its yearning for annexation and the Great Russian imprint upon its culture. (Sosyura was brutally rebuked for his poetic *Love the Ukraine*, and no one has publicly expressed such love since.)

Each of the "autonomous republics" is rewriting its history, revising its poetry, remaking its memories. Heroes become antiheroes (Shamil, Kenessary); insurrections against tsarism, until yesterday celebrated, are today execrated; epics become antiepics (*Dede Korkut*), or the versions that have lived so long in oral tradition and are the very national memory of illiterate peoples are purged and reissued in "new authentic texts."

---

7. For the writings of Marx and Engels that are now suppressed in the Soviet Union, see Karl Marx and Friendrich Engels, *The Russian Menace in Europe*, edited by Blackstock and Hoselitz, Glencoe, Ill.: Free Press, 1952.

The expurgation of the epic [*Manas*] should be strictly scientific and principled. It should take into account all the historical circumstances in the life of the people. This demands a suitable selection of variants, songs, and episodes, a selection of which the fundamental principle must be the preservation in the epic of all the best elements inherent in the past of the Kirghiz people.[8]

Even so did Orwell picture a functionary in his ministry of truth whose task was to "produce garbled versions—definitive texts they were called—of poems which had become ideologically offensive but which, for one reason or another, were to be retained in the anthologies."

THE AIMS OF "OPERATION REWRITE"

Thus the great Operation Rewrite which began with Stalin's obliteration of his contemporary political and personal history and the invention of a new past for himself has spread outward through the boundaries of the old Russian and the new Soviet empires, and backward to the beginning of recorded time. The process is vast and all-embracing, even as the total state is total. But the immediate aims are simple enough:

To strengthen the power of the state over the minds of men and make it ever more complete and absolute.

To enlarge the power of the leader and the cult of his infallibility and grandeur by identifying him with every mighty tsar and military leader, with every hero of thought and deed, with the deepest historical memories of the people over whom he rules; for his omniscience, omnipotence, omnicompetence, and infallibility are the very fulcrum of all the levers of totalitarian organization and power.

To destroy the critical sense, the historical perspective, the possibility of objective check or comparison from outside the system.

To "justify" the global ambitions and "demonstrate" the inevitable global triumph of the total state regime as well as its inexorably intensifying total organization within its own borders and its empire.

To strengthen its centralization by the increasing Russification and Stalinization of the "autonomous" units of the "federation" and the "sovereign People's Democracies" of the empire.

To root out all memories of comradeship with recent allies and as far as possible all friendliness and all common human fellow-feeling for the peoples who have been selected as the next victims and for those selected as the long-range enemy.

To counteract the war-weariness and the weariness with the unending

8. *Literaturnaya Gazeta*, May 27, 1952.

internal war on the part of a people who have been kept unremittingly on the stretch for over a third of a century.

To provide, in the form of a synthetic national glory and glory of the party, the state, and the system, ersatz satisfactions as a substitute for any real fulfillment of the revolution's promise.

To close the eyes of Soviet citizens and conquered subject peoples to the shabby and cruel realities that the regime inflicts upon them and to close their ears to the peaceful, friendly, and attractive message of the outside, nontotalitarian world.

To prepare the next steps in the long-range aim: the total conquest of the world.

By an examination of each sudden historical revision or reversal, one can deduce what the next tactical objectives of the Kremlin are, even though not the tempo of its moves—for into the actual moves themselves enter other calculations of power and of relations of forces that reside in the nontotalitarian world.

We can, however, deduce from the spirit and sweep of the new Soviet historiography that there will be no relaxation in the cold and not-so-cold war of the total state on its own people, on its neighbors and on all the peoples of the earth. The unending war of nerves, of which the rewriting of all history is a significant segment, grows sharper not gentler, more reckless not more cautious, more inclusive not less.

As long as all the more spacious cities of the world have not been reduced to slums and rubble, Stalin's 1947 address proclaiming the 800-year-old Moscow the only city of the world free of slums is in danger of objective refutation. As long as anywhere in the world there is more freedom, more happiness, more comradeship and love, or simply a higher standard of living and higher productive power, the men in the Kremlin cannot make good their boast that the Soviet system and way of life are superior.

Indeed, as long as anywhere in the world there is a lone surviving copy of any document which has been consigned to the "memory hole" or a single historian writing and pursuing research in freedom from the "guidance and control" of the total state, there is always the danger that world history, Russian history, Soviet history, party history, and the personal history of Joseph Stalin and his comrades-in-arms may once more be reconstructed, and that history itself, embodiment of the human memory and consciousness of self, may revive out of the ashes of its works.

TOTALITARIANISM AND HISTORY

In the new historiography there is a startling reversal in the roles of history-maker and historian. In the pretotalitarian epoch or in the free world, men make their history as best they can, and then the historians try to determine the relations between what they thought they were doing, what they said they were doing, and what they have really done. But the new rulers know what they are doing. They possess in their ideology and in their charismatic attributes a prophetic insight and an absolute key to the future. They are history-makers in a new sense, having banished all uncertainty and contingency from human affairs. They no longer need nor can permit critical interpreters and assayers of their intentions, their words, their deeds, and the consequences of their deeds.

Furthermore, there is a reversal in the roles of history or experience and ideology or theory. The experimental thinker likes to believe that he derives his ideas concerning society and history from the facts of history as they have developed. But for the totalitarian his ideology is unquestionable and absolute, and history must conform with it, or rather, derive from it. "Who controls the future, controls the present. Who controls the present, controls the past."

The totalitarian movement begins by being its own historian. It is a movement that, before it takes power, already aims at a total rupture with the past. It rejects the idea of organic growth, mocks at all traditional and inherited and evolving institutions and ideas and all their living representatives. Even the mighty dead must be made "usable" (i.e., made to conform), or they must be mocked, diminished, and retroactively purged.

The leaders of the totalitarian movements are essentially autodidacts who in their hearts have contempt for history. They are assured and certain men who have no place for uncertainty, contingency, tentativeness, no humility before the vastness of the unknown and the refractoriness and impermeability of the given, no sense of the precariousness and fragility of the accumulated heritage of culture and civilization. They are the "terrible simplifiers" whom Burckhardt foretold: monists who have no toleration for pluralism in theory or in life. Before they are in power they ignore, after they are in power they burn the documents that might testify against their overriding ideology or call in question their version of any event, however remote. They are driven by a compulsion to ferret out and destroy or "edit" any document that might sow the slightest seedcorn of doubt. Doubt—the tiniest shadow of doubt—is for the totalitarian intolerable. More, it is menacing. Still more, it is treason. "So-and-so has since been revealed to be an enemy of the people."

The totalitarian leader, as Hannah Arendt has pointed out, finds his chief recruiting ground among untutored and inexperienced masses that have hitherto been inert and passive and have had no experience with programs or history. Life has recently roused them from their historyless limbo by inexplicably casting them out of a society that was at best inexplicable. There is real satisfaction in finding someone who can assure them that all the organic and traditional is as meaningless as it has seemed to them, that all the dignitaries are undignified and fraudulent deceivers carrying on a meaningless show which will stop the minute the sailor with a pistol dissolves the parliament or the half-wit with the torch sets fire to the Reichstag building. Then "their" meaningless history will stop, and "our" meaningful historyless history will begin.

Totalitariansm is painfully, morbidly distrustful and susceptible to suggestion from even the most remote analogy. Its cruelty and resolute thoroughness are based on its own inner unsureness, whence the astounding energy and hatred with which it may attack the tiniest and most neutral-seeming observation.

Thus, a morbid awareness of Russia's own backwardness in 1917 (making it, from a Marxist view, inappropriate for a socialist revolution) and a morbid awareness of Russia's backwardness in many spheres today, compels the totalitarian historian to revise the history of the steppe tribes and their backwardness in relation to Byzantium, to make Tadjikia more advanced than ancient Persia, and Kazakhstan than Arabia and Turkey. How Soviet historiography is wrestling with the problem of rooting out the memory of the old Slavic chronicle which told how the Kievan Slavs asked Norsemen to come and rule over them!

Because it is totalistic, totalitarianism assumes that every event, every interpretation, every symbolical person or act, every thought or institution, every element of the social system and our vision of it, no matter how remote or significant, has implications for society as a whole and for the ideology that rules it. This ideology saturates life as water does a swamp. All politics, all institutions, all feelings, are now "nationalized" and, what is more important, stylized to agree with the overall style that characterizes the regime.

Hence the tribute which the official historian Pankratova paid to the supreme architect of history and lord of life is literally true: "Stalin has extended the limits of *Soviet* history by 1500 to 2000 years." The latest textbooks on "The History of the USSR" actually extend Soviet history through the shadowy origins of the Slavs into the Balkans; through the intercourse of the Slavs with Byzantium, through the Transcaucasian kingdoms; and because the Tigris and Euphrates rivers take their rise in the farther slopes of the Caucasus, into Babylonia, Assyria, Greece, the

Middle East and even Egypt; through the Mongols and the Central Asian peoples into the history of Asia; through the Yakuts and their relations with Bronze Age China into Chinese prehistory; through the Russian and Russian-hired explorers of Alaska, California, and the Antarctic, into every continent but Australia.

Thus totalitarianism, which begins by being so sure of the future that in its name it declares war on all the existing conditions of the present, ends by making war on the entire past. Yet the past will not be mocked and takes its own peculiar revenge. It is wiser to approach the past with the "revolutionary" principle of the Apostle Paul, "Prove all things, and hold on to that which is good," than with all the slogans of Marx, Engels, Lenin, and Stalin. The past shapes the present and nourishes it and he who tries to throw it out indiscriminately will find the worst elements of his country's past reasserting themselves and enlarging their evil while all that is best tends to be lost or destroyed. For what is the new order which tried to break once and for all with autocracy and bondage and the tsarist Okhrana but a monstrous enlargement of police and autocracy and bondage into totality? And the great love of humanity in nineteenth-century Russia that moved generous spirits everywhere has been lost or rather driven underground by this cruel indiscriminating war on the present and the past in the name of the future.

History may be but a feeble rushlight to illuminate the mists of the present and the obscurity of the future, but without a sense of history man cannot make a single step forward at all or even hold his precarious footing in the stream of time. That is why the hero of Orwell's *1984* feared that he was going mad when all the objective landmarks by which he might get his bearings began to shift and crack and change into undependable and unrecognizable shapes.

—October 1952

II PARTY HISTORIES FROM LENIN TO KHRUSHCHEV *

"The laws of history are irreversible," wrote Academician G. Aleksandrov reassuringly in Stalin's last year.[1] But neither Stalin nor his disciples and successors are disposed to take any chances. Hence the archives have been for a long period, as the most touchy still are, in the scholarly care of the secret police; a fitting symbol is the pen fastened down by ball and chain. Hence, too, the frequent reminders to historians that history must not be expounded in an objective spirit, for that would be a departure from the Leninist principle of *partiinost* in science.[2]

Out of this flow the admonitions that "the sharp ideological struggle in the workers' movement is accompanied by no less ferocious battles in historiography";[3] the instructions for dealing with the future no less than the past ("It's a poor sort of memory that only works backwards," the Queen said to Alice in Wonderland); the proclamations that "historical science has been and remains an arena of sharp ideological struggle, has been and remains a class, party science," that "the struggle against bourgeois ideology has been and continues to be the foremost task of our historians," that "the historian of the party is not a dispassionate recorder of the events of the past but a scholar-fighter," and that "the science of the history of the party occupies an outstanding place in the ideological struggle of the communist party for the revolutionary transformation of society."[4]

The same considerations dictate the stern commands of the central committee, the presidium, or the leader, to the practitioners of the historian's craft; the steady hail of precise formulations which must be "verified" by history; the sudden changes in the editorial boards of the leading historical journals; and the emergence in due course of the single

---

* Lecture delivered in July 1961 at the Institut de Hautes Etudes Internationales in Geneva. First published in *Contemporary History in the Soviet Mirror,* John Keep and Liliana Brisby, Editors, New York and London, 1964.

1. *Literaturnaya Gazeta,* January 1, 1952; *Kommunist* No. 3, February, 1969, p. 67, calls this "bourgeois objectivism."
2. *Pravda,* July 1960, No. 17.
3. *Voprosy Istorii KPSS,* 1960, No. 5, p. 172.
4. *Voprosy Istorii,* 1960, No. 5, p. 157; No. 8, editorial.

official history, besides which there shall be no other. It is the development of this sultry atmosphere in which historians must carry on their
work and the emergence, amid storms and alarms, of the single official
history so suited to the single-party, dictatorial state, that form the central
theme of the present essay.

Each of the leaders of the Communist Party of the Soviet Union in
turn, and each of the contenders for such leadership, has perforce been
a historian of sorts. It was Lenin who set the example of harnessing Clio
to his chariot every time he changed his tactics, got into a fight within
his own movement or in the Russian revolutionary movement as a whole,
started another split, or celebrated the anniversary of one of those innumerable schisms in his life and that of his movement. Historicism,
authoritarianism, pedantry, Marxist and historical learning or pseudo-
learning, and *Rechthaberei* were all so strong in him, so charged was he
with passion for theoretical battle, that he never tired of enlisting for each
ideological fray, faction squabble, or tactical maneuver the entire panoply
of the history of Marxism, the history of Russia, the history of its social
movements, the history of his own faction and that of his opponents, and
—not infrequently—the history of mankind.

To the socialist-revolutionaries, when he was telling them that they
could never be "socialists but merely revolutionary democrats," albeit
"devoted and honest revolutionary democrats," and graciously allowing
that they had the right to a place in the Petersburg Soviet of 1905 since
"we are at this moment making precisely a democratic revolution," he
explained that with their "inconsistencies and vacillations we can easily
get along, for history itself supports our views, at every step reality
supports us." [5]

Lenin felt he could not give battle to populism without setting down
his own propositions concerning that movement's history and the past,
present, and inevitable future of Russia. He analyzed the brighter pages
of populism's history in such fashion that his own movement became
the "legitimate heir" of all that was admirable in it, leaving for latter-day
populism only the dregs of "vulgar, philistine radicalism." [6] His volume
on *The Development of Capitalism in Russia*, his "What are the
'Friends of the People'?" and "What Heritage do we Reject?" are on
varying levels typical of his use or abuse of history in his war with
populism.

In the same fashion, his battles with the "economists" prompted him

5. Lenin, X, p. 7. How literally Lenin took history's support is suggested by the style
of this *obiter dictum:* for history itself supports our views, reality supports it at every
step.
6. The Russian reads "poshlyi, meshchanskii radikalizm." This analysis first occurs in
Lenin, I, p. 246, but recurs again and again whenever Lenin returns to the subject.

to review the history of Marxism and social movements while his war on the Kadets and zemstvo liberals called for similar excursions into the history of liberalism, socialism, and Russia. When *Iskra* fought the other socialist movements and journals and again when the Iskrists themselves split and Lenin joined battle with the other five *Iskra* editors, one of his main weapons was a thumbnail history of Marxism and of Russian and non-Russian social movements. Just as he had sought to outflank populism by claiming all he thought good in its heritage and identifying the residue with petit-bourgeois radicalism, so now he claimed to be the heir of Marxism and of all that was good in *Iskra* tradition while he sought to identify the other editors with economism and with the Kadets. All this was done in the guise of historiography.

Nor did his technique vary essentially when his battle was with Bolshevik disciples who were deviating to left or right, or being "conciliatory" at moments when he wanted a split, or holding to Lenin's earlier formulas and historiography against today's. The moment a fight began, he was ready with an *ad hoc* and *ad hominem* historical sketch of how his opponents got that way, of the various stages in their degeneration, of their "essential identity" with some movement he and they had previously denounced, and of the inevitable path of their further decline.

One of the peculiarities of Soviet historiography is its obsession with "periodization." In part this can be traced to a vulgarization of Marx's famous 1859 listing of diverse stages in the history of society, which were stages according to some Marxists successive, and to others inevitable-progressive. With Marx the listing was ambivalently typological *and* "progressive" or "inevitable." But when pressed he was ready to declare that the listing of ancient, feudal, capitalist, and socialist was typology rather than inevitable succession and at most applicable to western Europe at a certain stage of its development. For Soviet historiography, however, every land has its unilinear path marked out for it: feudalism, capitalism, socialism, communism. For every society such periodization is obligatory. This is a marvelous device for ensuring feudalism where there is no trace of it and socialism where there is neither capitalist industry nor a working class.

The author of the habit of "periodization" in Communist Party history is Lenin. He is tireless in his use of it as a device for demonstrating the progressive rise and magnification of his own movement and the progressive decline of opposing movements. His periodization is rarely twice the same, but it always serves the same ends. In his conclusion to *What is to be Done?* the history of the socialist movement in Russia is divided into three periods, one of "intrauterine" existence without workers, a second of "birth" as a political party looking to the working class but separated from its spontaneous movement, a third of decline and confusion (coinciding in time with the period when Lenin was in Siberia and unable to keep the movement on the right course), and a fourth triumphant age of true socialism fusing with the spontaneous movement of the working class and embodying itself in *Iskra*.

In a report prepared under Lenin's direction for the Amsterdam congress of the International (1904), there are four historical periods: pre-*Iskra*; *Iskra* period; second congress with its split; post-congress period with the triumphant development of Bolshevism into the true movement. New variants appear in his introduction to the collection *After Twelve Years* (1907); "The Historical Meaning of Inner Party Struggles in Russia" (1910); "On some Peculiarities in the Historical Development of Marxism in Russia" (1910); "The Ideological Struggle in the Workers' Movement" (1914); and in his "Result of Three Decades of Development of Social-Democracy in Russia," as given in *Socialism and War* (1917). When Lenin begins to lecture left communists in other parties of the Communist International in his *Infantile Sickness of Left Communism*, he gives a new periodization of the main stages in the history of Bolshevism. These periodizations may differ in periods (dating) and in summation (names and meanings assigned to the periods), and in this sense the periodization is *ad hoc* and history as flexible as a rubber band. But they all have one single, overall meaning, which may be summed up in Lenin's remark, already cited, to the sʀs in the 1905 Soviet: "History supports our views, at every step reality supports us."

Soviet historians of the Communist Party have all made use of one or another of Lenin's formulations. Cut off now from the living, nutrient medium of contemporaneity, they are imbedded like fossils in every subsequent party history.

No one has yet compiled a collection of all Lenin's historical excursions, which would serve as a "Guide to the Perplexed" for party historiography; but there is evidence that such a treatise is in preparation, to be called *Lenin as Historian of the Party*. In the meanwhile, the following quotations from *Voprosy Istorii KPSS* (1960, No. 5) can give us some notion of the general conclusions and approach to this theme:

1. Together with the rise of the Marxist party of the working class arose its historiography.
2. There is scarcely a single work of Lenin in which the history of the revolutionary movement is not illuminated from a Marxist standpoint.
3. The science of the history of the Party occupies an outstanding place in the ideological struggle of the Communist Party for the revolutionary transformation of society. There exists a definite relationship between historical investigations and the political activity of the Party, between historical problematics and the political tasks of the Party.

4. The development of the science of Party history can be understood only in its general connection with the entire ideological work of the Party, in connection with that struggle which the Party waged at its various stages against the multifarious enemies of Marxism.

Though every polemical work of Lenin was thus equipped with an "offensive" history of the Party and other historical weapons, Lenin himself was too busy to write a systematic textbook on the subject. This he left to faithful followers like Liadov, whose *History of the Russian Social-Democratic Labour Party*, published in 1906, was republished three times under the Soviet regime. But in 1909 Liadov fell into sin, or deviation from Lenin, and never brought his work up to date.[7] After the Bolshevik seizure of power everybody was too busy making history to write it. Lenin continued to clothe each polemic in the armor of history, his disciples echoing him as best they could. Minuscule works like Bubnov's *The Chief Moments in the Development of the Communist Party of Russia*, no bigger than a single long-winded talk, were of little interest then and are of less interest now.

The year 1923 marks a watershed in party historiography, for in that year Zinoviev delivered six lectures on "The History of the Communist Party of Russia (Bolsheviks)" and Trotsky poured fat into a smoldering fire with his *Lesson of October 1917*. These two had turned their hand to history, not as a weapon of struggle against other parties but as a weapon of struggle for the succession in the Communist Party itself. From 1923 until the end of the 1930s, when Stalin ordered and edited the *Short Course*, intraparty warfare was the main function of party history. The lesser lights who engaged in the perilous craft, Bubnov, Nevsky, Kardashev, Volosevich, Yaroslavsky, Popov, Kerzhentsev, and Knorin, all had to weigh every line not merely as a justification of the Bolsheviks against the world but, with still greater care, as a justification of the "true" Bolsheviks against the deviator Bolsheviks, who in due course would turn out to be anti-Bolshevik enemies within the party.[8]

7. There was also a *Sketch of the History of Social-Democracy in Russia*, by N. N. Baturin (N. N. Zamiatin), who in 1912 was a member of the editorial board of *Pravda*. Though it was reprinted eleven times after 1917, I have been unable to learn the date of original issue, or to secure a copy.

8. *Voprosy Istorii KPSS*, in its editorial, "Toward a New Upsurge of the Science of Party History" (1960, No. 5), recognizes the following as "scientific works and systematized textbooks of party history" which in their time represented "significant material . . . but contained many methodological and theoretical errors." Liadov and Baturin for the pre-1917 period; A. S. Bubnov, *Fundamental Problems of the History of the RKP*, 1924; V. I. Nevsky, *Outlines of the History of the Russian Communist Party*, Part I, 1923; N. N. Popov, *Outlines of the History of the All-Union Communist Party* (from 1925 to 1935—sixteen editions); V. I. Nevsky, *History of the RKP (b), Short Outline*, 1925 and 1926; Em. Yaroslavsky, *Short Outlines of the History of the VKP (b)*, Part I, 1926; a collective work under the editorship of Yaroslavsky, *History of the All-Union Communist Party*, I, 1926, II-IV, 1929-30; P. M. Kerzhentsev, *Pages of the History of the RKP (b)*, 1925; D. I. Kardashev, *Fundamental Historic Stages and Development*

For the next decade, party historiography was in a steadily deepening crisis. Histories succeeded one another at a faster and faster rate, as if they were being consumed by a more and more irritable gigantic chain smoker who lit the first page of each new work with the last page of the old. Histories, and, a little later, historians, disappeared without trace. Nevsky published the first part of a two-part history of the party in 1923, but there was no second part. The published part was scrapped, and in 1925 he started over again. Yaroslavsky did the same. Indeed, Yaroslavsky kept writing histories which kept disappearing in favor of new histories by the same Yaroslavsky, so that by now no bibliographer can decipher how many Yaroslvsky histories there really were and what happened to them.[9] In 1926 he assembled a team, or *kollektiv*, of historians and issued a four-volume work (Vol. I, 1926; Vols. II-IV, 1929-30). But the fourth volume was obsolete within a year of its appearance. In 1933 he issued a new two-volume work which had a longer life, being reissued at various times until 1938 when it disappeared. At that time Nevsky and Bubnov disappeared too, their histories having disappeared earlier.

To the outsider the bewildering thing is that each of these histories and cycles of histories had been entrusted to its respective authors by Stalin as weapons in his struggles with Trotsky, Zinoviev, Bukharin, and, finally, with his own followers. Each was designed to belittle Stalin's opponents, or annihilate them, and to glorify his name. But the heroes of one work became the dubious weaklings of the next and the villains and traitors of the third; persons of one work became unpersons in the next; the stature and single-handed achievements of Stalin became so much larger from one year to the next that each earlier version had to disappear, lest, rising from oblivion, it might bear witness against its successor.

In despair at the transitoriness of all these efforts of his faithful servitors, Stalin ordered a political lieutenant who was not even on speaking terms with Clio, V. Knorin, to assemble a *kollektiv* of pliable Red Professors to write the definitive Party history. Knorin was an Old Bolshevik of Lettish origin, who had joined Lenin's party around 1912, perhaps a

---

of the VKP, 1927; *History of the VKP* (*b*) *in Congresses*, ed. P. N. Lepeshinsky, 1927; A. S. Bubnov, *VKP* (*b*), in two volumes; Em. Yaroslavsky, *History of the VKP* (*b*), Parts I-II, 1933 (reissued until 1938); *Short History of the VKP* (*b*), ed. V. Knorin, 1934; *History of the VKP* (*b*), *Short Course*, under the editorship of a commission of the CC of the VKP (b), 1938 and a series of other editions. The rather chaotic chronological order is theirs. The fact that a historian starts a two-volume work and publishes only the first part, then starts a new one, is a sign of the high mortality rate in these histories. There are other editions of works by Yaroslavsky and Bubnov which *Voprosy Istorii KPSS* has chosen to ignore, as they have such histories as Zinoviev's. The last work mentioned in the list is, of course, the one known as Stalin's *Short Course*.

9. I have seen a number of Yaroslavsky efforts which are not mentioned in *Voprosy Istorii KPSS*'s bibliographical note. In *Kommunist* (1962, No. 4), Yaroslavsky is described as a "renowned historian" whose errors had been criticized not by Stalin but by the now rehabilitated Pokrovsky.

little earlier. He had been in the Comintern as Stalin's overseer of the German Communist Party in those fateful years when Stalin compelled it to "direct its main fire" against the socialists and the Weimar Republic while Hitler rose to power. This seemed to be a suitable qualification for supervising a group of the Red Professors' Institute of Party History, with B. Ponomarev as group leader (*rukovoditel*). Published in 1935, Knorin's history proved to be as mortal as its predecessors. In 1937, its editor was arrested, accused of "nationalist deviation," tortured, forced to confess that he had been a Tsarist agent first, then an agent of the Gestapo. He was shot within a year.[10]

This high mortality rate among Soviet party histories and historians has compelled western writers to resort to a kind of archaeological method, as if they were dealing with a long-buried institution in a long-buried civilization. They must dig through the mutually contradictory, successive layers of relative truth and calculated falsehood in an effort to determine which of the many layers represents the true Homeric Troy. It is possible to reconstruct the course of events by tracing the successive versions of some tender or touchy point—for example, why the Bolsheviks played no significant role in the 1905 Soviet, or in the February revolution of 1917; or what Trotsky's role was in the 1905 Soviet, in the 1917 seizure of power, in the Red Army and the civil war. Every tender spot, and these works abound in them, offers some hope that probing will establish the cause of the tenderness.

Or the historical detective may ask himself why a certain fact or a certain history has disappeared altogether. Thus we may well ask: Why is it that the most important party leader to engage in the direct writing of a party history (if we except Trotsky, who did most of his historical writing after he was no longer in a position to make history), namely Gregory Zinoviev, does not get into the canon of works which in their time represented "significant contributions but contained methodological and theoretical errors"?

Zinoviev's history, which unfortunately stops at February 1917, was the reprint of a series of six carefully prepared and interminably long lectures, which he delivered early in 1923, when Lenin was already ill but still able to dictate a few articles. His disciples were sizing each other up and maneuvering for position, but the struggle for the succession had not yet flared up, nor were the disciples sure that the master might not recover enough strength to reprove them. Moreover, Zinoviev was closer to the past and more intimately acquainted with it than any of the later historians. We can therefore learn many things from Zinoviev's history that we cannot find in any subsequent account.

The Bolsheviks, we can see from his history, were in 1923 only begin-

10. See *Survey*, April-June 1960, pp. 112-3.

ning to get used to the one-party system. Hence the first of these six lectures is taken up with the question of what a party is and why the Bolshevik Party is arrogating to itself a monopoly of power. Zinoviev grapples with various sociological definitions of a party; he tries to explain why a party is not a voluntary organization of like-minded individuals who agree upon a common program; he rejects this view for the one that a party is the fighting organization of a class. He is troubled by the existence of a number of parties of the working class, and the consequent implications that there may be "classes" and a "class struggle" inside the working class. He is troubled, too, by worker and peasant support for the SRs. We learn that the SRs claim to represent "in the first instance the working class, in the second the peasantry, and in the third the working intelligentsia." This, he insists, cannot be so; the "true class party" can represent only one class. Thereby we are reminded that today the Soviet Communist Party claims to represent and be made up of the self-same three clases that the SRs once claimed.

The lecture on "What is a Party?" is full of evasions. There are "many parties of the working class" but "only one party of the *proletariat*." The bourgeoisie has many parties, liberal, conservative, etc., but they are really all "factions of one bourgeois party." Zinoviev realizes that this rule may also be applied to the many parties of the working class, making them really all factions of one party. His answer is that the other working-class parties must also be reckoned as "only factions of the bourgeois party."

We find names, and even currents of thought, that today are ignored. We learn that the Bund "in the darkest night of Tsarist reaction was the first to rise in struggle." We learn of the SRs that "as long as it was a matter of victory over tsarism, these revolutionists had élan, energy, enthusiasm, and zeal . . . knew what they were fighting for . . . what they were sacrificing themselves for, and from their ranks came such great men as Gershuni." There is praise for Plekhanov in really moving language. We are told that from Martov's "instructive" *History of Russian Social-Democracy* we can learn much "despite its errors." We learn that Prince Obolensky was a member of the Party at the beginning of the century and a contributor to *Iskra*. We will search in vain in all subsequent histories for such nuggets of information. But by using the archaeological method of ranging the various versions of an event side by side, and by probing for the tender spots, we can learn something from even the worst of them.

At last, after the blood purges had re-edited the age of Lenin by turning all his close associates into traitors, save only one, the survivor determined to fix the past himself.

Thus was born the first party history that lived long enough to grow up and circumnavigate the globe, "the book that," according to *Pravda*, "has sold more copies than any other in modern times, the work of a genius, *The Short History of the Communist Party of the Soviet Union*, by Joseph Stalin." [11]

At this point Party history was stabilized. No new history appeared for fifteen years. All works in the field, and in many other fields of political, economic, and philosophical writing, became glosses and exegeses derived in whole or part from the *Short Course*. There was even a secret Politburo decision that no one was to be permitted to publish anything new about Lenin, while countless already published memoirs were burned or pulped.[12]

Stalin's *Short Course*, though virtually unreadable, could be memorized by the faithful, and indeed, as a life insurance policy, had to be. It performed the function of ensuring that no communist "need ever be at a loss for the official answer to every problem. No one understood better than Stalin that the true object of propaganda is neither to convince nor even to persuade, but to produce a uniform pattern of public utterance in which the first trace of unorthodox thought immediately reveals itself as a jarring dissonance." [13] By 1953, fifteen years after its publication, it was still the definitive "work of genius" and had been printed in editions of more than fifty million copies in the Soviet Union and in all the important languages of the world.

In March 1953 the author died. In July, some still duller writers calling themselves Agitprop issued 7,500 leaden words of "Theses on Fifty Years of the Communist Party of the Soviet Union." They were published in *Pravda* on July 26, 1953. Now the millions who had toiled to learn by heart every formulation in the *Short Course* realized that their "insurance policy" had been canceled. For, in the "Theses," they perceived that Stalin, who until then had been up in front at the right hand of Lenin— the two of them alone remaking the world—was now no longer Leader, no longer cofounder of the Party, nor mastermind of the seizure of power, nor creator of the Red Army, nor winner of the civil war.

Indeed, where was he? Lenin was mentioned eighty-three times in the 7,500 words, Stalin only four. Still worse, the "Theses" gave no clue as to the current order of precedence. Apart from those of Lenin and Stalin, the only name mentioned was Plekhanov. All safely dead! To the initiated,

---

11. The book was published in 1938. The *Pravda* quote was published twelve years later. Whether Stalin wrote it, or wrote only parts of it, it bears the unmistakable imprint of his unique temperament. It will hereafter be referred to as Stalin's *Short Course*.

12. The Politburo decision was adopted on August 5, 1938, but kept secret for twenty years. See *Spravochnik partiinogo rabotnika*, 1957, p. 364.

13. Leonard Schapiro, *The Communist Party of the Soviet Union*, London and New York, 1960, pp. 471-2.

this was a sign that a new time of uncertainty had begun and that no living name was mentioned because no successor had yet emerged. The only thing that was certain in this new time of uncertainty was that the *Short Course*, all fifty million copies of it, had to be scrapped, and with it all the works of gloss and exegesis.

From the summer of 1953 to the summer of 1959, the much-chronicled Soviet Communist Party was without any approved history, except for the 7,500 words put out by the Department of Agitation and Propaganda.

Before a new history could be published, Stalin's ghost had to be wrestled with and its size at least tentatively determined. The dictatorship had to beget its new dictator; infallible doctrine its infallible expounder; authoritarianism its authority. The "collective leadership," so unnatural in a dictatorial society where there are no checks on the flow of power to the top, had to be disposed of, one by one or in batches, until one only should emerge as the embodiment of the party. Furthermore, the emergent authority had to have time to lay down the line on the problems, persons, and events likely to find their way into history. Only then could a new official history be written. For the present to be projected into the past, the present has to be authoritatively determined. So it was that on June 17, 1959, a new manuscript was given to the press, with instructions to print a first edition of 750,000 copies. This was the history according to Khrushchev.

Not that he claims personal authorship. Khrushchev is free from that pathological greed for credit that made Stalin claim credit for everything. The new history was prepared, like Knorin's in 1935, by an "authors' collective"—eleven academicians, doctors or masters of "the historical, economic, and philosophical sciences."

Where so many histories have perished so swiftly, it was pleasant to find that the *rukovoditel* or leader for the Knorin history, B. N. Ponomarev, has survived the death of his earlier work and appears as *rukovoditel* once more. And I. I. Mints, who has written so many legendary pages (*legend* is to be taken in its literal not its poetic sense) in histories of the civil war, is alive and present, too, though Stalin once denounced his work. If Ponomarev is once more *rukovoditel*, there is no longer a general editor to replace Knorin. Rather, there are signs on many pages that Khrushchev and his Agitprop secretary, Suslov, themselves took on the political overseer's task. For what we now have is quite manifestly intended to be the official history for the age of Khrushchev.

The history of Russia in the twentieth century has been a turbulent one: conspiracy, party strife, war, general strike and uprising in 1905, world war, fall of the Tsar, seizure of power by the Bolsheviks, civil war and intervention, Kronstadt and NEP, liquidation of the private peasant as a class, purge of all Lenin's closest lieutenants by one of them, Stalin-

Hitler Pact, Second World War, struggle for the succession, emergence of Khrushchev. What material for the historian! But if the *Short Course* seemed dull and devoid of actual personages, motives, and events, it had at least a kind of fascination by virtue of the malevolence, the pathological boasting, the touch of the demonic on every page. Though in Khrushchev's *History*, as we shall now call it, whole pages are lifted from the *Short Course*, what was demonic in Stalin's history is only dogmatic in the latest work.

The Khrushchev *History* calls itself a "concise account." "Concise" must be more extensive than "short," for it is more than twice as long; nor is the additional flood of words altogether accounted for by the fact that an additional twenty years have had to be chronicled. Where formulas of boasting or denigration have not been copied verbatim, the new book is likely to use many more words to recount an episode than the old. Yet its pages seem strangely empty—empty of men, empty of events. In the place of men, there are the Party, the government, the masses, and Lenin. In the place of events, there are theses and formulas.

No need to be surprised if the great Bolshevik hold-ups of 1905-1907 are missing; no Party historian has spoken of them. But where are the Moscow Trials which formed the closing section of the *Short Course*, like the baleful hell-fire which lights up the last scene of Mozart's *Don Juan*? All of Lenin's close associates save one were tried, confessed, liquidated—surely a chapter in Party history by almost any test. But not one word. Twice the Party purges of the thirties, in which Nikita Khrushchev played a substantial role, are obscurely hinted at, obscurely justified, and as obscurely called in question. On page 463 we learn that the Party was strengthened by purges but "mistakes were made in the unfounded expulsion of so-called passive elements." Yet, after the purges, "two-faced and enemy elements remained in the party," and Kirov's murder "showed that a party card may be used as the cover for abominable anti-Soviet acts." Twenty-one pages later we learn that "many honest communists and nonparty people underwent repressions, being guilty of nothing." But the villians now are Beria and Yezhov. Inexplicably, Yagoda, their predecessor as "flaming sword of the revolution," is missing, both as the first great purger and as victim and confessed traitor. Just as inexplicably, for time is slippery in this history without a fixed chronological framework, Beria, whom Stalin appointed to call off the fury of the Yezhov purges, here precedes Yezhov.[14]

14. Even the delicate allusions and sporadic rehabilitations permitted during the "thaw" are not to be found. As archives were published and memoirs, long suppressed, were re-published with excisions, footnotes were permitted. The climax of refinement came in the formula used in the brief biographical notes on twelve purged memorialists in Volume II of *Reminiscences of Lenin* (1957), of whom it was said: "In 1937, he became a victim of enemy slander; later rehabilitated." Only after the 22nd CPSU congress did rehabilitation become more public; but a large number of hapless souls still remain in limbo.

It is the disappearance of such large events and of so many persons which makes the pages of this thick history seem so interminable and so empty. A standard feature of earlier histories was a list of Central Committee members elected by each Congress, a list of rapporteurs at each Congress, and many other such accounts of persons and their posts or their proposals or their deeds. Too bureaucratic to be exciting, it yet peopled the pages of the text. But with each successive history the lists became shorter. More and more men were shifted to the anonymous "and others." Now many of those who still found a place in Stalin's *Short Course*, if only to be denounced, have dissolved in the acid of oblivion. Moreover, Khrushchev has names to eliminate from honorific lists whom Stalin delighted to honor as extensions of himself. The inde-structible-seeming Molotov, the able and ruthless Kaganovich, who did what he could to forward Khrushchev's advancement, the rotund Malen-kov, once Stalin's chief of cadres, a party secretary, a member of the supreme military council during the war, main rapporteur at the Nine-teenth Congress, after Stalin's death both General Secretary and Premier —at least for nine days—have ended up without a past, rubbish for the "antiparty" dustbin.

It is now largely depeopled and faceless Party which is the protagonist, the Party as the instrument of history, carrying out history's mandates and intentions. Its outstanding leader and master may in his last years have been grievously, even monstrously wrong, but the Party which did not stay his hand was never wrong, never ceased to carry out history's will. In such a disembodied, uneventful, bureaucratic history, a Party con-gress is an epoch-making event. At the Nineteenth Congress, shortly be-fore Stalin's death, Molotov made the opening address, Malenkov de-livered the main political report, Beria the report on the nationalities problem, Saburov on the fifth five-year plan, Khrushchev, Bulganin, and Mikoyan on the revision of the party statutes, and Kaganovich on the revision of its program. Dealing now with the Congress, the *History* mentions reports, but neither their contents nor the rapporteurs. Only N. S. Khrushchev remains as the sole rapporteur on the party statutes, from which a seven-line quotation rates inclusion in the pages of history.

Even those whom Stalin execrated have suffered further diminution. Stalin still had need of Trotsky as the Antagonist in the drama of good and evil. He had to paint Trotsky as saboteur of each of Trotsky's own chief actions since one of the aims of the *Short Course* was to replace in men's minds that unity in duality, Lenin-Trotsky, by a new unity in duality, Lenin-Stalin. Thus Trotsky's name was still bound to large events, if only by a minus sign. Though Khrushchev's *History* copies some of these pages from the *Short Course*, he does not have the same need of Trotsky to play Antichrist to his Savior; hence the baleful glare that lengthened his shadow throughout the *Short Course* is subdued here to a dingy light. The October Revolution takes place without the Chairman of the Petrograd Soviet and Military Revolutionary Committee, who directed the operations of the seizure of power and conceived its strategy. The civil war is fought and the Red Army built without him. The Kronstadt mutiny is gloriously crushed without either his or Tukhachevsky's intervention. Voroshilov has retroactively been appointed director of the attack on Kronstadt while Marshal Tukhachevsky, who seemed on the way to rehabilitation until Zhukov fell, disappeared once more from history, to be yet again disinterred at the Twenty-second Congress.

If the climax of Stalin's *Short Course* was the "Liquidation of the Remnants of the Bukharin-Trotsky Gang of Spies, Wreckers, and Traitors to the Country," which is the actual title of the closing section of its last chapter, the new Khrushchev *History* has no climax. It just stops because when it was issued the Twenty-first (extraordinary) Congress was over and the Twenty-Second had not yet been convened. It was obvious that it would not last the fifteen years of its predecessor, for history would keep adding to its bureaucratic sum, and had already subtracted several of the leaders designated by the Twenty-first Congress, such as Beliaev and Kirichenko.

Further evidence that the *Concise Account* is already becoming obsolete, and for really serious purposes unsatisfactory, is to be found in the plan for a new "many-volumed" history of the Party (actually six volumes, the first of which was reported at the end of 1960 as having already gone to press and the rest as being prepared "at high speed"). For these both the archives and many of the earlier histories are being treated as "useful material." Most interesting is the partial rehabilitation of Stalin's *Short Course*, which Khrushchev had damned so thoroughly in his 1956 speech. After listing the other histories which enter into the canon of those which in their time "contained a large amount of factual material . . . but [also] many methodological and theoretical errors," *Voprosy Istorii KPSS* (1960, No. 5), continues:

From these errors the *Short Course of the History of the* VKP (*b*) was not free either although it was also for its time a mighty stride forward in the development of party-history science. The fact that this book served for a long time as a peculiar standard for party-historical investigations significantly held back the further scientific working out of problems of the history of the Party. Of course, this does not in any degree whatsoever justify the position of those historians who, incorrectly interpreting the decisions of the Twentieth Congress of the CPSU, tried, under the flag of a struggle against the cult of personality and its consequences, to re-examine some of the fundamental propositions of party theory and policy laid down in the *Short Course*. . . . Characteristic of this insignificant number of historians was a nihilistic attitude toward the entire party-historical literature of the late thirties and the forties. They called loudly for a return to the textbooks of the twenties and thirties which contain innumerable theoretical and political errors.

The "high speed" with which Voprosy Istorii promised that its Party History Section would produce the six-volume history has since met with the usual traffic jam caused by conflicting red and green lights. In June 1962 a flurry of new directives descended on the heads of the historians. In Pravda (June 22 and 24) a long article appeared "On the Forthcoming Many-Volumed History of the CPSU." From it we learn that the six volumes are to consist of nine parts and to appear by 1967, in time for the fiftieth anniversary of the seizure of power.

The history must continue to reflect the "irreconcilable struggle" of Lenin and Stalin against the Trotskyists, Left Communists, Democratic Centralists, Workers' Oppositionists, Right Capitulators, National Deviationists. Khrushchev's period is to be given enormously more space and importance:

> The entire content of the many-volumed history must be permeated with the spirit of Leninist ideas, base itself on the Marxist-Leninist scientific method, the decisions of the Party, especially of the Twentieth and Twenty-second Congresses, must be permeated with the spirit of the new Program of the CPSU, the Communist Manifesto of our time.

In short, it is to be a Khrushchevist history. It is to contain formulas resolving, at least bureaucratically, the new problems facing Khrushchev. Thus:

> One of the most important tasks of the work is to reveal the role of the CPSU in the world communist movement, the international significance of the experience of the CPSU at all stages of its activity, the influence of this experience on the successful construction of socialism in a number of lands of Europe and Asia, on the development of the international labor and communist movements, and also on the development of the national-liberation struggles of the peoples of the oppressed lands. . . . In it will be shown the continuous and consistent struggle of the CPSU against splitters, revisionists, petit-bourgeois adventurers, dogmatists, sectarians, for the unity of the international labor and communist movement on the basis of Marxism-Leninism and proletarian solidarity.

There is a new and greatly extended check list of Stalin's errors to be noted and developed, but once more the critique will be within the familiar limits and his services, considerably diminished, are once more to be noted. Once more, also, it must be shown that while these grievous errors were being committed by the Party under Stalin's orders, the Party remained sound and its actions correct. Thus the authors will be called upon to perform an exercise in apologetic ingenuity unparalleled outside the field of church history and exegesis.

The directives end, as was to be expected, with a glorification of the Congresses led by Khrushchev. The Twentieth, for instance, "laid the foundations of a new epoch in the world communist movement" and "showed that the Party, its Leninist Central Committee with N. S. Khrushchev at its head . . . revealed itself as the center of the development of Marxist theoretical thought," and the Twenty-first and Twenty-second Congresses continue the wonders, accompanied by a spate of rather banal quotations from none other than N. S. Khrushchev.

Thus Khrushchev is still wrestling with the size of Stalin's ghost. In a historiography in which everything is made to order according to party needs, various sizes and patterns have been tried in an effort to determine Stalin's place in history. To convince ourselves of that we need only compare the Stalin of the secret speech at the Twentieth Congress with the Stalin of the 1959 *History* and with the grimly enlarged but still far from complete list of Stalin's "errors" in the directives on the projected many-volumed history as given in *Pravda*, June 22 and 24, 1962. At present the trend is toward Stalin's further diminution, but his legacy is zealously preserved and built upon. It is instructive to close this examination with some consideration of the "cult of personality," the formula which seems to have been the biggest event in Party history since the publication and scrapping of the *Short Course*.

On the one hand, there was need to write Stalin smaller than in the *Short Course*, lest all his successors remain too dwarfed for any of them to succeed him. Moreover, his lieutenants, not without cause, so feared each other, and the party so feared the inevitable struggle among them, that it was necessary to give assurances "that henceforth such occurrences should never again take place in the Party and the country." This was promised by a resolution of the Twentieth Congress and is repeated in the *History*. Insofar as it implies the rejection of the pathological extremes of Stalin's vengeful reign and seeks to put on him and his purged disciples all the burden of Khrushchev and company's coresponsibility, it may be taken seriously.

On the other hand, Stalin's successor could obscure but not destroy the link which puts him in the line of apostolic succession. For what else but the apostolic succession from Lenin, who seized power, to Stalin, who usurped it by taking over and perfecting Lenin's machine, has the present First Secretary? What other legitimacy and claim to rule over a great empire?

The inheritance includes many things for which the 1959 *History* gives Stalin great credit:

1. The annihilation of all rival parties, such as Mensheviks and So-

cialist-Revolutionaries and Kadets. (Hence the *History* repeats the absurdities of the frame-up trials of the Mensheviks, the Industrial party, the Toiling Peasant party.)

2. The annihilation of all anti-Stalinist communist groups (Trotskyists, Zinovievites, Bukharinites, for whose views there can be no rehabilitation).

3. Forced industrialization and the primacy of heavy industry over production for consumption.

4. The annihilation of millions of peasants and the forced collectivization of agriculture.

5. Party penetration and control of all organizations and the atomization of the individual. (This is a heritage from Lenin perfected by Stalin and is inseparable from totalitarianism.)

6. Stalin's conquests of the Baltic Republics, half of Poland, part of East Prussia, Finland, and Rumania, and Tannu Tuva.

7. The "liberation" of the rest of Poland, of Hungary (two "liberations"), of East Germany *and* Berlin, of the Balkan lands including Yugoslavia, of China, North Korea, and North Vietnam.

8. The "struggle for peace" and the enlargement of the "peace camp" which permits of, nay requires, the "liberation" of further parts of the noncommunist world but not the "re-enslavement" of any part that has been liberated.

This is a large balance sheet. In it Stalin's crimes against the Russian people, against the Russian peasants, against allies and neighbors and occupied countries, are all transformed into virtues listed on the credit side of the ledger. His crimes against other socialist and democratic parties and opposition Communists are listed as virtues, too, with the sole reservation that he dealt too harshly with "good Communists" (which seems to mean Stalinists) when he liquidated them. Even then, when the guillotine falls on loyal Stalinists, the *History* does not cry "Crime!" but mumbles "Error" or "Harmful consequences of the cult of personality."

Its final verdict reads: "Under the leadership of the Communist Party and its Central Committee, in which J. V. Stalin played a leading role, the Soviet Union has achieved enormous, world-wide successes. J. V. Stalin did much that was beneficial to the Soviet Union, to the CPSU, and to the whole international workers' movement."

Thus Khrushchev's tremendous indictment of Stalin's cruelty and paranoia in his secret speech dwindles into a bureaucratic formula for a little praise and much self-serving blame, now that Khrushchev himself is secure in the possession of his heritage.

What, then, is hapening to the size of the "personality" of Nikita Sergeyevich Khrushchev?

To get a perspective, we must bear in mind that this is not the final masterpiece of Khrushchev historiography but only a first attempt, analogous rather to the early efforts of a Yaroslavsky than to Stalin's *chef d'oeuvre*—the *Short Course*. Moreover, Khrushchev has difficulties that Stalin did not have. It is not possible for a man who joined the Party only after it had won power to picture himself as one of the Party's cofounders. Hence the book's only living hero (the dead heroes being Lenin and Stalin) does not enter into its 745 pages until page 314, then modestly enough as one of a list of Lenin's "comrades-in-arms and disciples hardened in the civil war . . . on whose backs lay the burden of liquidating the consequences of the war and constructing a socialist society." The list contains twenty-three names, in discreet alphabetical order, Stalinists all, and the impartial Russian alphabet puts Khrushchev in the twentieth place and Stalin himself in the eighteenth.

Not until page 608, with the Nineteenth Congress, does Khrushchev begin seriously to employ the technique of self-enlargement. Here, as we have seen, Molotov who delivered the opening address, Malenkov who delivered the main report, Beria, Kaganovich, and Saburov who reported too, all become unpersons, while Khrushchev holds the vast stage alone.

By the Twentieth Congress, Khrushchev had such a grip on the Party machine that he did in fact hold the stage alone and make all the reports. The order of business was: opening address, Khrushchev; report of the Presidium and Central Committee (covering everything), Khrushchev; chairman of the committee to draw up a resolution on the report, Khrushchev; chairman of the new Bureau on Party Affairs of the Russian Republic, Khrushchev; secret report on the cult of personality, Khrushchev. Only Bulganin was permitted a sub-report, a gloss on the First Secretary's remarks on the sixth five-year plan, and Bulganin has of course since disappeared from public view.

As for the Twenty-first Congress, which makes up the final chapter of this book, it had only one order of business: a report on the control figures for the seven-year plan, by Khrushchev. Such is the fitting bureaucratic climax, or anticlimax, to the strange transformation of so many clashes of arms and deeds of blood into bureaucratic formulas. Stalin's closing chapter ends with a quote from Stalin; Khrushchev's with a quote from Khrushchev. The First Secretary and former "best disciple of Joseph Stalin" has learned his trade,

In each case the closing chapter is followed by a brief coda called "Conclusion." In the *Short Course*, Stalin jostles Lenin for first place. Whether it be good sense or greater need, in the conclusion to the new history Lenin and the Party are given first place.[15] Yet even here Khrush-

---

15. The final section of the directives for the six-volume history quotes only Khrushchev; Lenin gets in only when he appears in one of these Khrushchev quotations.

chev is quoted four times. In the *Short Course* the last words are a quote from Stalin. In the new history Khrushchev bows out three pages before the end while the last two sentences are eight words from Lenin on the Party as "the intelligence, honor, and conscience of our country" followed by twelve from Marx on communism's promise: "From each according to his means, to each according to his needs."

Such is the nature of the Party history in which the two new features, lacking in the *Short Course*, are the "liquidation of the harmful consequences of the cult of personality" and the recording of the substantial beginnings of a new cult.

Of the various learned societies which are beginning to send messages of admiration and appreciation to "Nikita Sergeyevich personally," the most interesting to us is, of course, that of the historians. On October 20, 1960, the Section of Historical Sciences of the Academy of Sciences of the USSR held a general meeting to discuss the eleventh International Congress of Historical Sciences in Stockholm. The report on this discussion in *Voprosy Istorii* reaches its climactic end with these words, so obviously relevant to the order of business:

At the close of the General Meeting of the Section of Historical Sciences of the Academy, Academician N. M. Druzhinin read a letter addressed to the First Secretary of the Central Committee of the Communist Party of the Soviet Union, the Chairman of the Council of Ministers of the USSR, N. S. Khrushchev:
Dear Nikita Sergeyevich!
The General Meeting of the Section . . . warmly congratulates you, dear Nikita Sergeyevich, on the great and important successes achieved by you at the Fifteenth Session of the General Assembly of the UN [the session in which Khrushchev took his shoe off]. . . . You displayed such many-sided and fruitful activity in the interests of the happiness and progressive development of the whole of humanity.
Your passionate and untiring struggle for peace . . . for general disarmament, for immediate liquidation of colonialism, has won for you the deepest gratitude of all honest people. Your amazing capacity for clearly and simply explaining the high humanist principles of our advanced Marxist-Leninist ideology exercises the most powerful influence on the widest masses of people on our planet.
We historians, specializing as we do in the study of the great events of the past, can easily distinguish in the contemporaneity of present events also those which have a transcendent historical significance.
We do not doubt that your activity at the Fifteenth Session of the General Assembly of the UN will go down in the annals of history as a most valuable contribution to the cause of the struggle for peace, as a bold and far-sighted act worthy of an outstanding statesman of the Leninist type. Proud of the fact that at the head of the Soviet Government stands a man who so well understands the basic needs and demands of our epoch, we, from

the bottom of our hearts, wish you good health and the continuance for long years of your inexhaustible energy in the pursuit of the goals of the fastest resolution of the gigantic historical tasks placed on the order of the day— the freeing of mankind from wars and the evils connected with them, and disarmament.

The resolution was adopted unanimously by all who attended the meeting.[16]

After this conclusion to the discussion of the 21st Party Congress, there could be no doubt that the *Concise History* issued in 1959 was already out of date, and that a drastic revision was needed, particularly of its closing sections. Small wonder that *Voprosy Istorii KPSS* (1960, No. 5), found editorially that the *History of the Communist Party of the Soviet Union*, issued in 1959, though it "gives a Marxist-Leninist illumination of the basic stages of the historical road traveled by the CPSU up to our days, nevertheless is only a short textbook, in which, naturally, the many-sided activity of our Party in its fullness and concreteness cannot be given." And, indeed, in 1962 a new revised edition of the *History* was published, making the appropriate changes in the light of the Twenty-second Congress of the CPSU. No sooner had it appeared than there were indications that it was already out of date and that further revisions were necessary to bring past history in line with the ever-changing present requirements.

16. *Voprosy Istorii,* 1960, No. 12, p. 113.

III SCIENCE JOINS THE PARTY*

If the man from Mars, or from that scarcely less remote planet, the western world, had wandered into the 1948 Summer Congress of the Lenin All-Russian Academy of Agricultural Sciences to listen to the "discussion" on genetics, he would never have imagined that he was at a scientific congress at all. There was only one report, "On the Situation in Biological Science," [1] and only one reporter, who chaired the sessions, had the first word and the last. The "sessions" had the air of a political mass meeting with a touch of Roman gladiatorial circus. The forty-six members of the academy present were submerged in a turbulent sea of over "seven hundred practical workers from the agricultural research institutes, biology teachers, agronomists, zootechnicians, economists," political commissars and "dialectical materialist philosophers." The members of the Academy were not there to discuss experiments, present papers, submit difficult and subtle specialties to the judgment of their peers. Indeed, there were no papers presented, no breaking up of the general sessions into special subsections for the consideration of specialties—only eight days of target practice, with Trofim D. Lysenko as the number one sharpshooter, and all of Russia's most distinguished geneticists as targets.

Throughout this singular "genetics discussion" there were outbursts of stormy applause, raucous laughter, hoots, catcalls, sinister threats and a constant hail of abuse for the more important members of the academy. Geneticists who tried to remain silent were provoked and taunted for their "cowardice." Those who tried to speak on their difficult technical specialties—genes, chromosomes, diploids, polyploids, pure strains, and hybrids—before an unprepared audience, were heckled, interrupted, silenced by a storm of ignorant jests and coarse epithets. Those who, faces white with fear, sought to "confess their errors" were mocked for the "belated" and "inadequate" nature of their confessions. As they heard the work of a lifetime ridiculed and called in question, a few attempted

* First published in the *Antioch Review* in March 1950.
1. *The Situation in Biological Science: Proceedings of the Lenin Academy of Agricultural Sciences of the USSR*. Complete Stenographic Report, New York, International Publishers, 1949.

310

to justify some fragment or save some remnant. They were heckled more cruelly than the others. The epithets might not all seem like insults to the man from Mars, but they were genuine cusswords in the murky twilight world in which Soviet science was fighting a losing battle for scientific freedom. These scientists, many of them convinced Communists and dialectical materialists, whose only ambition had been to excel in their field, to serve science and their people, heard themselves called "idealists" (which, in the land where dialectical materialism has been made the state faith, is not a compliment but the master cussword). They were called "metaphysicians," "adherents of clerical reaction," [2] "Mendelist-Weissmannist-Morganist scholastics," "men alien to the world outlook of the Soviet people," "unpatriotic fly-breeders," "formal geneticists, cognitively effete and practically sterile," "wagers of an unseemly struggle against Soviet science," "Menshevik idealists in philosophy and science," "rotten liberals," "corrupters of the scientific student youth," "adherents of reactionary-bourgeois racist theories," "debasers of Darwinism," "propagators of the harmful, hostile myth of the international unity of science," "servile worshipers of alien, hostile, enemy, reactionary bourgeois science," "enemies of the progress of Soviet science and the Soviet people."

PORTRAIT OF TROFIM LYSENKO

The director of this orchestration of abuse was Trofim D. Lysenko, a thin, broad-shouldered man of peasant origin, with the Order of Lenin on his breast, a protruding, active Adam's apple, blazing, slightly asymmetrical eyes lit with a faantical gleam of triumph. He stood there supremely confident, for as he repeatedly hinted to his appreciative claque and to the cringing veteran scientists, behind his assault stood "the party of Lenin-Stalin and Comrade Stalin personally." If they doubted it, there was the Order of Lenin on his breast, the two Stalin First Prizes for Achievement in Science, and the pages of *Pravda*, which reported these speeches and epithets as if genetics had become a popular sporting event or *Pravda* a scientific journal for genetical specialists.

Moreover, the Party had been moving Lysenko steadily upward into positions of power: Vice Chairman of the Supreme Soviet; since 1938 President of the Lenin Academy of Agricultural Sciences; since 1940 Director of the Institute of Genetics of the Academy of Sciences; and thenceforth, wielder of the unseeing shears that can cut a lifetime scientist off from scientific work, or cut the thread of life itself.

2. Unfortunately for the reputation of genetics in the Soviet Union, two clerics, Malthus and Mendel, played important parts in developing its theoretical ideas.

This singular figure first appeared in Soviet biology in the early 1930s. We get revealing close-ups of Lysenko in that stage of his career from the fact that he was interviewed and his work investigated by two foreign scientists, both so sympathetic to the Soviet Union and so impressed by its work in the field of genetics that one visited its laboratories and the other went to live and work in them.

Dr. S. C. Harland, aging and highly esteemed British geneticist, has this to say of his interview:

I found him completely ignorant of the elementary principles of genetics and plant physiology. Having worked on genetics and plant-breeding for some thirty-five years, I can honestly say that to talk to Lysenko was like trying to explain the differential calculus to a man who did not know his twelve times table.[3]

Dr. H. J. Muller, Nobel Prize winner in genetics for his ground-breaking work in producing mutations in the genes of fruit flies by X-ray irradiation, honored by the Soviet Union by an appointment as senior geneticist at the Institute of Genetics of Moscow where he served for four years (1933-1937) and by membership in the Soviet Academy of Sciences, has this to say of Lysenko:

In 1935 genetics had reached a very high state of advancement in the U.S.S.R., and many eminent scientists were working in it. The Soviet Communist Party, unable to find a single reputable scientist willing to take part in its attack on genetics, began systematically to build up in that year the reputation of an alleged "geneticist," a peasant-turned-plant-breeder named Trofim Lysenko, who had achieved some dubious success in applying, by trial-and-error proceedings, an early American discovery about pretreating of seeds in order to influence the time of maturation of certain crops. Lysenko's writings on theoretical lines are the merest drivel. He obviously fails to comprehend either what a controlled experiment is or the established principles of genetics.[4]

The interpreter at the interview between Dr. Harland and the future dictator in Russian biology was Nikolai Ivanovich Vavilov, at that time head of the Academy of Agricultural Sciences and of the Genetics Institute, and famous throughout the world for his researches on the geographical centers of origin and the genetical evolution of the most important cultivated grains. Dr. Harland, finally throwing up his hands in despair, said to Vavilov: "Will you ask Citizen Lysenko to answer my question

3. John Langdon-Davies, *Russia Puts the Clock Back*, with a foreword by Sir Henry Dale, London, 1949.

4. "The Destruction of Science in the U.S.S.R.," *Saturday Review of Literature*, Dec. 4 and 11, 1948; *Bulletin of Atomic Scientists*, December, 1948.

with a 'yes' or a 'no,' if such a fine distinction is possible in the language he speaks." Vavilov smiled protectively, shook his head, and said:

"Lysenko is one of the 'angry species.' All progress in this world has been made by angry men, so let him go on working. He may find out how to grow bananas in Moscow. He does no harm, and some day may do some good."

There are still no bananas growing in Moscow, but Lysenko has hounded Vavilov out of genetics. He has displaced Vavilov as director of the Genetics Institute and as president of the Academy of Agricultural Sciences. In 1939 he made Vavilov chief target of his attacks. In answer, Vavilov praised, as well he might, the practical and theoretical achievements of Soviet experimental biology; but he urged also the international interdependence and unity of world science and pleaded that Soviet biology should not deny itself the privilege of learning from other lands. This brave defense of the internationalism of science (once a basic belief of communism, and indeed of all civilized men) sealed Vavilov's fate. He was befouled in the press. His posts were taken from him. Before the Nazi-Soviet pact he was pronounced "a propagator of Nazi racist theories," and after the Stalin-Hitler pact he was sent to the Siberian Arctic as a "British spy" (he was an honorary member of the British Royal Academy of Sciences), where he died under circumstances that the Soviet government refused to clarify on inquiry from his foreign colleagues. To Vavilov's own brother, Sergei, has been given the deeply humiliating task of delivering lyrical public addresses praising the "thoughtful care which the Soviet Government and Comrade Stalin personally show for Soviet science and Soviet scientists."[5] No less interesting is it to note that Lysenko's brother, Pavel D. Lysenko, leading fuel and coke chemist, has fled from the "sheltering care of the Soviet government" and now resides (since the summer of 1949) in America.

The purpose of Lysenko's address at the 1948 Summer Congress was to put an end to a theoretical controversy that had been raging for more than a decade, and to consummate a purge of all remaining experimental geneticists. Ever since 1931, when scientists had been ordered to give up their long-range investigations in favor of "work of immediate practical application," and to coordinate all their work into the framework of the Five Year Plans, all of Russia's leading geneticists—and they were among the world's best—have been under steadily increasing fire. In 1933, the geneticists Chetverikov, Ferry, Ephroimson and Levitsky disappeared from their laboratories, to turn up later in forced-labor camps. In 1936, Agol followed, and the impressive Medico-Genetical Institute was dissolved.

5. After hounding Nikolai Vavilov out of genetics and then out of life itself, Stalin characteristically had his brother, Sergei Vavilov, a physicist, "elected" president of the Soviet Academy of Sciences.

All through the following decade, the casualty rate among Russian geneticists and, along with that, the moral casualty rate (renunciation of doctrines, abandonment of experiments, forced confessions of "scientific and philosophical guilt") remained high. Yet, as a body, these devoted scientists continued their dedication to their difficult and complicated experiments and to scientific truth as they found it in their laboratories. And the Soviet Government, a little distrustful of anything which could not readily be comprehended by the "greatest genius, scholar-scientist of all lands and all times" and could not readily be settled by ukaz or Politburo resolution, nevertheless saw how much the world esteemed these men and their work, and continued to "tolerate" it and to recognize by that tolerance that truth is a modest and elusive maiden that cannot always be taken by shock troops or storm attacks.

Not until 1939 did the geneticists of the entire world become aware of the fateful drama that was being enacted in Soviet science. In 1936, they had chosen Vavilov to preside over a congress of the geneticists of the world, which was to have been held in Moscow. But Moscow had suddenly canceled the invitations without explanation. After repeated postponements of the congress, it was set at last for Edinburgh for the summer of 1939. Papers by Vavilov and fifty other Russion scientists were received; yet, at the last moment, they did not appear. Vavilov's chair, as president, remained dramatically vacant throughout the sessions. Along with the fifty Rusians, six out of twelve German experts had been "unable to attend."

Even from his new vantage point as president of the Academy of Agricultural Sciences, Lysenko proved unable to convince the serious scientists who made up the majority of the Academy members. The party began to pack the Academy with a whole detachment of new members to outvote the old, if they could not outtalk them. Yet the real leaders of Soviet genetical experiment, though they could be bullied and outvoted, still felt that no quotation from Marx or Engels or Michurin or Stalin could quite take the place of experimental evidence and theoretical reasoning. No mere vote could convince them that Lysenko understood the genetical experiments he so brashly attacked. Nor convince them that, in experiments involving artificial pollinization of a castrated plant (to cite one instance), in place of their careful conveying of a single pollen grain of a single pure strain, and their washing of hand and glove and apparatus with alcohol before the next pollen grain was handled, one could substitute a mass of mixed and unpedigreed pollen grains, letting the female organ of the plant or its ovule "select" by "love marriage" (*brak po liubvi*) "the best spermatazoid from the mixture which will produce the best adapted offspring." Nor that heredity could be usefully or scientifically defined as "the property of a living body to require definite conditions for its life and development and to respond in a definite way to definite conditions." Nor that variation or mutation could be induced in offspring of a plant or animal at will by subjecting it "to external conditions which, to one extent or another, do not correspond to the natural requirements of the given form." [6]

The science of genetics, they knew, was very young, no older than the years of the present century. But they were not disposed to deprive their laboratories or their land of its growing body of important and verifiable conclusions concerning the chromosome and gene in determining heredity, and mutations in the genes and chromosomes as the primary cause of variation from heredity. Nor to accept the dogma that the will of a fanatical plant-breeder, or the enactment of "laws of Nature" by an ignorant Politburo, could automatically make it possible to control heredity by ukaz and plan and "bolshevik-tempo" in any desired direction, by some uncontrolled, undefined and scientifically unverifiable changes in the environment, or random mixtures of impure strains, depending on the passion and wisdom of the ovum or spermatazoon to take the place of the intelligence and planful care of the experimenter.

LAWS OF HEREDITY PASSED BY THE POLITBURO

It is impossible in a brief space to do more than suggest some of the differences that have arisen in a field as technical as that of genetics; but the above examples, crude and strange as they sound, are actually taken from Lysenko's propositions and are not unrepresentative of the "theories" and methods which Lysenko had been advancing to replace the whole body of careful experiment and close reasoning by the geneticists of many lands, including those of the Soviet Union—a body of experiment and reasoning which has been growing steadily since Darwin first tried to put the rule-of-thumb methods and superstitions of plant- and animal-breeders on a scientific basis, since Mendel first made his experiments with the hereditary results of mating round and wrinkled peas, since Weismann first postulated the useful division into soma and chromosome and since Morgan and others first began their famous experiments on the heredity of such swiftly producing organisms as fruit flies.

Some other of Lysenko's views which are rejected by the geneticists of all lands may be schematically stated as follows:

(1) Lamarck was right as against Darwin.

(2) There is no special hereditary substance (chromosomes with their genes); but it is the whole plant or animal which, by "assimilation and dissimilation" of its "external and internal environment," determines the

6. T. D. Lysenko and others, *The Situation in Biological Science,* pp. 35-37, 122.

character of the offspring. The breeder has only to change the environment or assimilation slightly, and he can produce variations or new species at will.

(3) Hereditary changes in plants can be determined at will by grafting, the graft being able to change the heredity of the stocks or the stock the heredity of the graft, according to which is made the "mentor."

(4) At the present stage of genetical knowledge, "chance" and "fortuity" can be completely expelled from mutation or variation, and hereditary changes can be introduced, decreed, "planned," or "directed" in any direction desired by the breeder. Whoever does not recognize this is "asking favors from nature" instead of giving her orders. He is a bourgeois, reactionary, fascist, metaphysical, scholastic, foreign-minded element, agent of the enemies of the Soviet Union, saboteur and wrecker of Soviet agriculture. Whoever wants to work on slow and difficult and painstaking genetical experiments is by that fact committing treason to Soviet agriculture and the Soviet people.

(5) Statistics and mathematical reasoning are inapplicable in biological problems. This last is particularly interesting since England's leading mathematical genetical expert, J. B. S. Haldane, as a scientist has helped develop the refining techniques of mathematics for the analysis of genetical experiments; but as chairman of the editorial board of the *Daily Worker* he tries to defend Lysenko and deceive the British public as to the issues in the pogrom against Soviet science. In England he could still thus serve the Communist Party and the *Daily Worker* without giving up his mathematical genetics, but in Russia he would long ago have disappeared in the purges. (Some time later Haldane quietly resigned, so quietly that I did not learn about it until his biography was published four years after his death, a quiet that did nothing to embarrass his party nor help Russian genetics in its struggle to survive.)

(6) The heredity of a plant or animal is but the accumulated assimilation of its past environment through many generations. The "conservatism" of the plant or animal (Lysenko's word for the tendency of offspring to resemble their parents) can easily be "shattered" by changes in the environment, and the new characters thus inculcated will breed true. "It is possible to *force* any form of plant or animal to *change more quickly and in the direction desirable to man*." (Emphasis by Lysenko.)

There is not one of the above assumptions—and Lysenko makes many more like them—that would be accepted by the geneticists of other lands, or was freely accepted by those of Russia. All of them require precise definition and could easily be tested under conditions of scientific freedom, by the devising of a critical or crucial experiment with proper controls; and all of them could easily be proved, indeed have been proved, to be: (a) too sweeping; (b) meaningless for both theory and practice;

or (c) arrant nonsense—or all three at once. The interested reader can further study the issues involved, insofar as they are biological and not political, by reading the balanced scientific summary of Lysenko's views in Hudson and Rich, *The New Genetics in the Soviet Union,* or more polemical statements of the controversy for laymen in Langdon-Davies' *Russia Puts the Clock Back;* Julian Huxley, *Heredity East and West;* Conway Zirkle, editor, *The Death of a Science in Russia.* A comprehensive bibliography on the subject is Morris C. Leikind, *The Genetics Controversy in the USSR* (American Genetic Association).

A BOMB IN A SCIENTIFIC CONGRESS

The Summer Congress of 1948 was the hour of Lysenko's triumph. For in his possession that July day was a secret weapon, more powerful in Russia than the atomic bomb. In his opening address he hinted at it ominously:

So far, I as president of the Lenin Academy of Agricultural Sciences have been wanting in the strength and ability to make proper use of my official position to create the conditions for the more extensive development of the Michurinite trend . . . and to restrict the scholastics and metaphysics of the opposite trend. . . . We Michurinites must frankly admit that we have hitherto proved unable to make the most of the splendid possibilities created in our country by our Party and the government for the complete exposure of Morganist metaphysics in its entirety, an importation from foreign reactionary enemy biology. It is now up to the Academy, to which a large number of Michurinites have just been appointed, to tackle this task. . . .

Now that genetics had joined the Party, as the reader will note, it had developed its "ites" and its "isms," its unexaminable dogmas, its orthodoxy and its heresy, its loyalties and its treasons, its political promotions and purges. Even as Stalin professed to inherit the mantle of Marx, Engels, and Lenin, so Lysenko professes an apostolic succession from Timiryazev, Williams, and Michurin—whence the term, "Michurinites." (Michurin was the "Soviet Luther Burbank," another man with a "green thumb," an ardent plant-breeder who, like our own Burbank, had his hits and misses without ever getting to understand very much of the theoretical problems of the new science of genetics, which is just beginning to reduce the thousand-year-old rule-of-thumb plant- and animal-breeding to a systematic, experimental science.) And just as Stalin made hate words out of the names of his opponents—"Trotskyite-Zinovievite-Bukharinite-diversionist-wrecker-agent-spy"—so the Michurinite-Lysenko-ites now speak with "class hatred" and "nationalistic indignation" of the "unpatriotic fly-breeder, hostile, alien, reactionary, capitalist, Mendelite-Morganite-Weissmannite genetics."

But it was not this abuse that was new or sent the chill of fear down the spines of the Russian scientists. It was the dread hint contained in the word "Party, government, and Comrade Stalin personally." Yet the majority of the geneticists still held their tongues or tried to avoid head-on collision or moral suicide, still believing that surely the government which they had served so loyally would not altogether abandon its uneasy neutrality before the issues of the laboratory.

Still cheated of his public triumph, Lysenko began his closing speech by hurling his secret weapon:

Before I pass to my concluding remarks, I consider it my duty to state the following. The question is asked in one of the notes handed up to me, What is the attitude of the Central Committee of the Party toward my report? I answer: *The Central Committee of the Party has examined my report and approved it.*

At this point, *Pravda* reported:

With one impulse, all present rose to their feet and gave a stormy, prolonged ovation in honor of the Central Committee of the Party of Lenin-Stalin, in honor of the wise leader and teacher of the Soviet people, the greatest scientist of our epoch, Comrade Stalin.

And among those who had perforce to rise to their feet and cheer with all their might were those who had just heard their sentence of doom and knew that their work had ended and all the issues of all the genetics experiments in all the laboratories of the world had been settled by a simple vote of a group of tough, ignorant politicians.

Now began the surrenders and desertions and self-humiliations, for now there was no longer any crevice in which science might hide in this totally coordinated society. Yet, as sometimes a dying bull rises to its forelegs and makes one more desperate thrust at the triumphant matador, so there was one more thrill reserved for these spectators of the gladiatorial death pangs. Old Nemchinov, director of the Timiryazev Agricultural Academy, rose to his feet:

"Comrades, not being a biologist, I did not intend to speak. . . . I observe that there is no unity among our scientists on certain questions, and I personally as director of the Timiryazev Academy see nothing bad in this." (*Commotion in the hall.*)

"Both tendencies are allowed to teach at my Academy. . . . I have said, and I repeat it now that the chromosome theory of heredity has become part of the golden treasury of human knowledge, and I continue to hold that view."

A *voice:* "But you are not a biologist; how can you judge?"

"I am not a biologist, but I am in a position to verify this theory from the viewpoint of the science in which I do my research, namely, statistics." *(Commotion.)*

"And it also conforms to my ideas, but that is not the point."

Voice: "How is it not the point?"

"Let it be the point. I must then declare that I do not share the viewpoint of the comrades who assert that chromosomes have nothing to do with the mechanisms of heredity." *(Commotion.)*

Voice: "There are no such mechanisms."

"You think there are no mechanisms. But this mechanism cannot only be seen, it can be stained, and defined."

Voice: "Stains and statistics!"

". . . I bear the moral and political responsibility for the line of the Timiryazev Academy. . . . I consider it right, and as long as I am director I will continue to pursue it. . . . It is impermissible, in my opinion, to dismiss Professor Zhebrak, who is a serious scientist. . . . The course on genetics should present the views of Academician Lysenko, *and* the principles of the chromosome theory of heredity should likewise not be kept from the students. . . ."

Thus in the nine pages of the stenogram devoted to the remarks of the venerable Nemchinov, every other paragraph is devoted to taunts, commotion, laughter, "a voice," known or unknown, of bullies sure they are playing the winning side. *Pravda* grimly commented:

The declarations of Comrades Zhukovsky, Alikhanyan, and Polyakov [three who "repented"] showed that in the minds of a number of yesterday's adherents of the Mendelite-Morganite tendency, a deep transformation was beginning. . . . On such a background the position of such participants as V. S. Nemchinov exhibited themselves as especially unseemly *(nepriglyadni).*

THE CHAIN REACTION: PURGE IN THE OTHER SCIENCES

Purges in the Soviet Union invariably have the character of a chain reaction. Slowly the purge spread in an ever-widening wave, to the Institute of Cytology, Histology, and Embryology, to the Institute of Evolutionary Morphology, to the Institute of Plant Physiology, to the Direction of the Botanical Gardens—then to medicine. Then to the general Academy of Sciences, and each of the national academies. After that physicists came under fire, then economists, statisticians, mathematicians. Then the purge widened into a general onslaught on the very idea that there is an international community of science until this land of erstwhile internationalism proclaimed the parochial nationalism of the human spirit and a mad isolationist chauvinism in every field: in culture and thought, in music and art, in drama and movies and circus and criticism and philology.

And each field, each group, each academy, as it began to suffer a purge, was forced at that very moment to write a hymn of thanksgiving and praise to the source of the evil, such as is unparalleled in the whole history of sycophancy, whether in the tsarist empire or that of the mad Emperor Caligula.

> The Academy of Sciences turns to you, our beloved leader, with heartfelt gratitude for the attention and help which you are daily showing to Soviet science and the Soviet scientist. . . .
>
> Glory to the leader of the Soviet people, the coryphaeus of advanced science, the great Stalin! . . .
>
> We promise you, our beloved leader, to correct in the shortest time the errors we have permitted, to reconstruct the whole of our scientific work . . . to struggle for bolshevik partyness (*partiinost*) in medicine, to root out the enemy, bourgeois ideology and blind servility before foreignness (*inostran-shchina*) in our midst. . . .[7]

These two strange words, "partyness" and "foreignness," bring us to the heart of the attack by Soviet politicians on Soviet and on human thought. Modern science has been made possible by (1) freedom of inquiry; (2) the agreed use of terms and of a general logical language capable of being tested anywhere by critical experiment, rather than being settled by appeal to authority, *argumentum ad hominem* or *opinionem* or *creditum* or nonlogical emotion; (3) the unity of science as a world-wide body of knowledge, based on international interchange and the recognition that every achievement is a cumulative growth built upon countless contributions by men in many lands. All three foundations have here been dynamited. Even if Lysenko were correct in all his biological claims and fantasies, still the decision of the issues by the Polit-buro or "Comrade Stalin personally" would be fatal to the further flourishing of science, for the dispute does not concern genes and chromosomes but the very functioning of the human spirit.

GIANT OF BRASS WITH FEET OF CLAY

Twice in our generation have we watched an authoritarian state making this effort to "coordinate" all science into its totalitarian politics. In both cases there was a demand that science abandon its objectivity and specialized methods and "join the party," suiting methods, investigations and

7. The three paragraphs above are taken respectively from addresses of the All-Union Academy, the Lithuanian Academy and the All-Union Academy of Medical Sciences. Their basic formulae were repeated in all the addresses.

conclusions to the requirements and dogmas of a police state. Both states set party commissars over scientists, or made cranks and pliable scientific politicians into the directors of scientific institutions. Both showed a profound incomprehension and suspicion of pure theoretical science, of the pursuit of truth for its own sake, wherever it might lead. Genetics, too, was a particular target of the Nazis because its free pursuit was incompatible with the state dogma of the master race. In Russia it became a target because a Lysenko had convinced the all-powerful, all-directing, and all-meddling, but not therefore all-wise Politburo and Comrade Stalin personally, that the "conservatism" of plant and animal heredity could be "shattered" according to plan or command, by quick, easy, simple, and random changes in the environment.

Both Hitler and Stalin made the mistake of believing that pure theoretical science has no great practical significance in the immediate power struggles that were their central preoccupation. Yet even this scientific pursuit of truth for its own sake, and not for the state's or the leader's, sometimes has startling practical results. It was the banished Albert Einstein with his mass-energy conversion formula who called the attention of Franklin Delano Roosevelt to what had been done in Germany and elsewhere in atomic research. And this country "happened" at the moment to have most of the world's best theoretical physicists in that remote and speculative field, among them Bohr, Fermi, Bethe, Szilard, von Neumann, victims of the totalitarian persecution. Thus did the most "pure and remote," the most lonely "metaphysical and alien-Jewish" pursuit of truth for its own sake prove to have the most decisive "practical results."

So, too, when the Politburo and Stalin personally discovered "alien, hostile, diversionist wrecking in astronomy" (*Izvestia*, December 16, 1937), the galactic systems may have seemed infinitely remote from practical consequences for the total state and its power plans. Yet science itself was delivered a staggering blow in those purges.

Biology, because its by-products are vegetable and animal and industrial materials, obviously touches practical matters more closely. Stalin was convinced that Lysenko's get-rich-quick methods would deliver the goods. In vain did Vavilov, in 1939, warn that American genetics had produced a superior corn hybrid which enabled the American corn farmer to lead the world and which the Soviet Union would do well to imitate.[8] That patriotic defense of American genetics for Russia's sake was the very heart of his crime.

Under such circumstances, the talents of the thinker must yield to those of the parrot, science wither into dogma and die of lack of intel-

---

8. Later, the Soviet government did send delegations of "farmers" (actually political and managerial directors of Soviet agriculture) to study American corn-growing and buy hybrid seed.

lectual freedom and theoretical courage. The new authoritarian religion of untouchable dogmas which are prior to investigation; the official state philosophy-religion to which all research must conform; the intuitive infallibility in all fields he cares to turn to on the part of *Vozhd* or leader; the decision of subtle and difficult questions by a group of bureaucrat-politicians or a single absolute ruler; the purge of all those who would learn from, teach to, communicate with the scientists of other lands— these things in the long run must corrode the giant of brass until its feet crumble into dust. For in our modern world, even the power purposes of great states cannot in the long run be served except where the the state knows enough to limit its interference and leave the human spirit free to seek the truth.

—March 1950

POSTSCRIPT: GENETICS UNDER STALIN'S SUCCESSORS

Seven years later, the men in the Kremlin, whose absolute power makes them absolute experts on all things, completed a re-examination of the havoc they had worked in the biological sciences by their decree supporting Lysenko. In *Botanichesky Zhurnal* (Botanical Journal) for March-April, 1955, the re-examination was summed up in the following fashion:

> . . . It has now been conclusively demonstrated that the entire concept [advanced in Lysenko's *New Developments in the Science of Biological Species*] is factually unsound and theoretically and methodically erroneous and that it is not of practical value. . . .
>
> Not a single halfway convincing experiment was conducted in 1954 nor a single strictly scientific argument advanced in support of T. D. Lysenko's views. . . . The "Dilizhan hornbeam hazelnut" [one of Lysenko's alleged forced changes of species] was conclusively dethroned. . . . Investigation of the pine with fir branches growing near Riga . . . led to the firm conclusion that this phenomenon was a grafting. . . .
>
> . . . the transformation of spring forms into winter forms of wheat and vice versa . . . was put in doubt . . . compelling a re-examination of many prematurely canonized views.
>
> P. A. Baranov has again drawn the attention of Soviet scientists to the problem of polyploids and shown its great practical importance, which is denied by T. D. Lysenko and his supporters. . . . This denial has resulted in a cessation of work on polyploids in our country . . . definitely detrimental to our agriculture. . . .
>
> . . . Cluster planting of trees has caused tremendous losses to the state and threatened to discredit the idea of erosion-control in forestation.
>
> T. D. Lysenko is resurrecting in our science . . . the naïve transformist

beliefs that were widespread in the biology of antiquity and the Middle Ages that survived to some extent up to the middle of the nineteenth century. . . .

Lysenko . . . assigns to trees in a forest the property of knowing when they should die off so that they will not be crowded in the future. The clearly theological nature of T. D. Lysenko's explanation of the process of self-thinning has never before been stressed. . . . A new species . . . always arises as a result of the historical process, the chief moving force of which is natural selection. . . .

The scientific level of discussion was lowered by a weakening in the last few years of serious research on problems of evolutionary theory. . . . In the field of botany almost no research was done on the evolution of any group of plants, genus or family. . . .

In 1954 Soviet biologists saw with great satisfaction that our journals . . . *finally* allowed the opponents of the teaching of the "engendering" of species to appear on their pages. . . . In serving the people, in struggling for an understanding *in terms of the Marxist dialectic* of the laws that govern the development of the organic world, scientists see the essence of a profound Michurinist orientation in biology.

At this point one would like to say, All's well that ends well. But genetics was still in the power of men who, because they have power over everything and possess an infallible key to everything, therefore have knowledge of everything. Not the scientists but the men of power had decided that the ruin of forestry and the continued stagnation of agriculture required a reversal of Lysenko's "laws." The new decree did not bring back the vanished men, the dispersed collections, the working teams of researchers, the broken laboratories. And in the partial restoration as in the crushing of genetics, the principle still prevailed—the party knows best.

The state giveth, the state taketh away, blessed is the name of the state. Before long, the state was synonymous in agriculture with the rule of Nikita Sergeyevich Khrushchev. And there was something in Lysenko's haphazard experiments, large promises, and truculent boasts that was congenial to the style and beliefs of Khrushchev. Once more Lysenko received new support and credence. His stock rose again though not to the old level of a biological dictator armed with a Party pruning hook. He continued to write on the wonders of "our Michurinite biology that had developed Darwinism further to the point of demonstrating that under appropriate conditions some biological species can quite rapidly engender other species, for example, wheat engender rye." [9] He was allowed to bemuse inexperienced volunteer farmers on their way to the virgin lands with his accounts of wondrous successes in changing one

9. *Pravda,* August 5, 1960.

species into another. His critics were rebuked or silenced though no longer eradicated from the fields of their specialties.

The former science of genetics, once so promising in Russia, remained a vacant wasteland: no laboratories, no experimenters, no journals, no new Vavilov. In August of 1964, the distinguished physicist, Andrei Dmitrievich Sakharov, was publicly rebuked by Khrushchev for criticizing the "scientific methods" employed by Lysenko. But two months after this episode, Khrushchev was dethroned by a conspiracy of his "best disciples," and Lysenko deflated along with his protector.

Then a miracle occurred: not the rehabilitation of the dead Vavilov, but the sudden and miraculous-seeming resurrection of the science of genetics from out of the tomb. For the seed had not been utterly destroyed as Lysenko and Stalin had intended but hidden in a safe shelter to be brought forth and made to sprout again now that conditions were favorable. The safe shelter had been provided by another branch of science, a branch so important for power and war and so complex that the omniscient and omnipotent men in power had not ventured to disturb it, namely the field of atomic energy. Here brave and understanding scientists, Kapitsa, Kurchatov, Landau, Sakharov, and associates, set up a special division for the study of the influence of atomic radiation upon hereditary and cell life. They supplied funds and equipment and took over bodily an entire staff of the men who had been driven out of genetics. Thus, Nikolai Dubinin, once slated to head the Institute of Genetics before Lysenko reduced it to a shambles, emerged with a trained staff of geneticists who had been keeping their hand in by working in that interdisciplinary place where radiation studies and genetics meet. He was installed, twenty years late, as the head of a new Institute of Genetics not unlike the one envisioned for him by the Academy of Sciences two decades earlier. Not all of the twenty years were lost, for a significant body of men and a significant corpus of studies were ready almost at once to come out in the open. A new professional journal, *Genetika*, began to appear as a monthly in 1965. Ten new laboratories sprouted in the Institute of Biological Sciences in Moscow. In Minsk, the Byelorussian Academy of Sciences set up under Turbin an institute to work on hybrids of corn and wheat. In Kiev, the Ukrainian Academy set up a department of genetical studies on the genesis of mutations by radiation and radiation chemistry. Papers appeared as if by magic in the fields of evolutionary genetics, viral genetics, immunogenetics, beneficial mutations, studies of plant and animal diploids and tetraploids, and a host of other fields that required years of work yet appeared within a few months of the emergence of the science that had thus been living its underground life in the shelter of physics and chemistry. This heartening story tells us something of the toughness of the human spirit even under unfavorable circumstances, the solidarity that exists among men of science working in different fields, and the reasons for the new found courage and determination among Russian scientists that has prompted them to speak out boldly for freedom in the arts as well.[10]

—Postscript dated April 1969

10. On the resurrection of genetics see the article by Walter Sullivan in *The New York Times* of October 17, 1967, entitled "Soviet Genetics Reborn," subsequently included in *The Soviet Union: The Fifty Years*, by Harrison Salisbury and the Staff of *The New York Times*, New York, 1968.

IV CULTURE AND COMMUNIST CRITICISM *

The man of good will who cannot comprehend the depths of an evil of which he is himself incapable, the liberal who has wanted to be anti-fascist without being anti-totalitarian, the apostle of the double standard who looks unseeing on any wrong so long as it be committed in the name of "progress," the poet or painter who longs for state patronage as a way out of free-lance insecurity—all are prone to certain errors in their estimation of the fate of culture in the Soviet Union.

—They comfort themselves with the hope that terror is a by-product of danger to the state and will diminish as the regime becomes more secure.

—They comfort themselves with the formula that "the state will wither away" upon the attainment of socialism.

—As the juggernaut crushes artists, writers, historians, they identify themselves with the accusers and not with the accused. For are they not themselves "forward-looking and progressive"? Are they not all that the Soviet state demands of its intellectuals, and are they not free of guilt for all the crimes of which the victims are accused?

It is my purpose to examine each of these three misconceptions.

TERROR AND THE SAFETY OF THE STATE

In the early days of civil war, intervention, and famine when the state was most in danger art was most free. All that was asked of the artist then was that he be in favor of the regime, or at least not actively conspiring against it. It was a time of hunger and of hope, of pluralistic

---

* This was an address delivered on March 29, 1952, to a gathering of writers and artists under the auspices of the American Committee for Cultural Freedom. The Committee's conference was held simultaneously with a conference at the Waldorf arranged by Communist Front organizations and led by a delegation from the Soviet Union whose chief spokesman was the writer A. A. Fadeyev, General Secretary of the Soviet Writers' Union. Fadeyev had been a member of the Communist Party since 1918, and was a member of its Central Committee. He committed suicide in 1956 after Khrushchev's denunciation of Stalin at the XXth Congress of the C.P.S.U.

schools and movements, of overflowing experimental life. The state did not begin to dictate in detail until the danger had passed, just as the Menshevik party was not finally outlawed until the civil war and the Polish war were safely over. So only after all opposition parties had vanished and the last opposition within the Communist party had been destroyed, only then was the peasant driven into state serfdom, the worker chained to his job, the scientist ordered to stop "daydreaming" and take his directions from the Politburo planners, and the artist appointed an "engineer of the soul" and mustered into line on the "literary front."

In the war years of 1939-1945, when the state was once more in danger and its very survival was in question, there was a new era of comparative liberalism. Then censorship relaxed and poets like the gentle Akhmatova, silenced for more than twenty years, were encouraged to write again and given a chance to be published. But no sooner was the danger safely past than the Soviet dictators began a renewed war on their own people and a new war on other peoples. The year 1946 saw Zhdanov delivering not only his declaration of war on the rest of the world at the newly revived Cominform but also his declaration of war on Soviet artists, writers, and musicians in Leningrad.

Thus the relation between danger to the state and total terror is just the opposite of what is generally imagined. Unending terror or the threat of terror is inherent in totalitarianism. Total power is not sobered by responsibility nor softened by submission. While opposition is alive or danger is great, these are hindrances to total terror. When they no longer exist, then they can safely be invented. Then terror rages unchecked, and the state treats its victims as "rebels" precisely when they are most helpless, most atomized and most submissive.

WITHER AWAY—OR SWELL TO TOTALITY?

Nor is there any comfort in the pretotalitarian formula that "the state will wither away" as soon as there is complete socialism. The year 1937 saw the completion of the Second Five Year Plan and Stalin's official announcement that it had brought "complete socialism." Life was decreed happier, the enemy classes had officially disappeared, everyone was declared to love the leader and the system. But precisely at that moment the blood purge broke out in all its unparalleled fury.

The excuse offered was "capitalist encirclement." But if that were the cause, then, although the army might have remained strong, at least the secret police should have withered away. The internal censorship should have ceased, and artists who had given their lifetime to the service of the government and the party should have been left ever freer and more unmolested. Just the opposite occurred.

In 1946, when the war danger was at an end, came the new decrees on "formalism," "internationalism," "cosmopolitanism," "servility to the West." Taste became a monopoly of the great critics in the Politburo, who began telling artists what to paint and in what style, telling poets what mood to feel and with what formulae to express it, telling composers what subjects to choose and in what styles to treat them. With "complete socialism," the state, far from withering away, then swells to totality, embracing every aspect of life in its all-encompassing, steadily more constricting grasp. For total domination does not allow for free activity or free initiative in any field of life. In the total state, no task exists for its own sake. As Robert Ley once wrote, "The only person who is still a private individual in Germany is somebody who is asleep." And Huxley, as we know, worked out a way for the boss even to reach the sleeping by a whispering machine built into his pillow.

BUT IT CANNOT HAPPEN TO ME

At this point, I want to address myself to the artists and writers and scientists of good will who are serving the monster by embellishing it and forming part of its front organizations. In their hearts these well-intentioned persons say that those who have been tortured and silenced must surely have been "guilty of something." And in their hearts they think: "It cannot happen to me or those I esteem, for we are progressive, forward-looking, on the side of the people—surely not enemies of the people."

I want you to consider a few case histories of "honored artists of the Soviet Union" so that you may judge whether it would be good for your art or your science to have such a regime spread here or to any part of the world.

THE CASE OF DMITRI SHOSTAKOVICH

Shostakovich is an "honored artist." He has won more than one Stalin Prize. As early as 1930 he was widely hailed as a composer of talent. Had he developed freely, by now we might well have had to say "a composer of genius."

As late as January 20, 1936, *Izvestia* wrote that his *Lady Macbeth* was "the most brilliant Soviet production in music" and "had conquered the love of the mass spectator."

Exactly eight days later, on January 28, 1936, *Pravda* spilled a bucket of ugly epithets upon the composer's head: "enemy of melody and harmony in music, sympathizer with his bourgeois heroine, inaccessible to the masses, leftist emphasizer of ugliness!"

Shostakovich bowed his head and submitted his spirit to the dictates of the musical commissar-policeman and the taste and wisdom of the supreme critic. He learned to curb his muse and worked his way back into favor.

But the total state requires that no citizen should feel too secure. On February 11, 1948, *Pravda* opened a new attack on "the formalist trend in Soviet music," and even a decade of submission and praise did not save Shostakovich. Compositions of his which the party had praised and showered with awards were now retroactively banned. A number of critics —Belza, Zhitomirsky, Veinkop, Shleifstein, Ogolovets, Martynov—were condemned in 1948 for having liked Shostakovich's Ninth Symphony in 1940. Shostakovich responded by writing music to Stalin, to his great irrigation works, his power plants, his "transformation of nature." The composer became an accomplice to injustice by condoning the punishment of his colleagues and of the critics who had committed the crime of praising his work.

Once more Shostakovich is in favor. Some of his works remain banned; others, including those whose very title is a humiliation, are praised and performed. His leash is lengthened a bit. He is permitted to go abroad to a Congress of "Peace and Culture"—of course, with all his loved ones left behind as hostages.

Do you, fellow-traveling composer, identify yourself in your heart with Shostakovich or with his tormentors?

PRIZE ON A STRING

Perhaps in your secret life you dream of yourself as a Stalin Prize winner. Then let me tell you about *From the Depths of the Heart*. On March 15, 1951, it received a Stalin Prize. A few days later, the great man went to see the opera which his name had honored. On May 13, the Council of Ministers revoked the prize—an event unheard of in the history of prizes in any land. But in a bureaucratic state, as Marx once wrote, "the bureaucracy possesses the state as its private property." And in a total state, the dictator possesses the state as his private and total possession. The prizes are his prizes, the poets and singers his minstrels, the philosophers and scientists his philosophers and scientists; his taste is the "taste of the people," and to be against it or displease it is to be "an enemy of the people." Not only was the prize revoked, but the composer was condemned and forced to confess his error, the director of the theater was discharged, the head of the All-Union Arts Committee removed. Even the mediocre policeman-censor, General Secretary Khrennikov of the Composers' Union, who had risen to his post by attacking Shostakovich, Prokofiev, and Khatchaturyan, got a rap over the knuckles.

In the same way, the mighty boss in literature, Fadeyev, found that a Stalin Prize is given on a string, and can be snatched away again. In 1945, his novel *Young Guard* was crowned with the laurel and 150,000 rubles. For two years it was a best-seller; then, the line shifting ever so slightly, it was found that he had "overestimated" the Communist youth and "underestimated" the Party. He repented, withdrew the work, wrote it to the new specifications, venting his pent-up anger on those more helpless than he: critics with Jewish names and too great a knowledge of comparative literature. He called them "homeless, rootless, passportless cosmopolitans . . . without ancestors and without offspring . . . incarnations of traitorous, foul-smelling groveling before the culture of the West." [3] In 1951 he was compelled to withdraw *Young Guard* a second time and revise it once more. Even overseers must not feel too secure or they will lack energy in their tasks as overseers.

THE CASE OF THE OLD BOLSHEVIK

Perhaps you have held a party card since earliest manhood and feel secure in your party loyalty and long years of faithful following of the party line? Then hearken to the case of Bezymensky.

For years he was regarded as Russia's "best political poet." He could take any party line and put it into verse. In February 1937, he was held up as a model to Pasternak, whose lyrical poetry was considered "intimate" to the point of criminality. On February 28, *Pravda* put him at the top of a list of the twenty "best political poets." On June 8, he published satirical verses mocking the newly fallen Afinogenev. On June 12, a poem celebrating the execution of Tukhachevsky. Fourteen days later, he was himself being pressed to confess, and the same newspapers that had just sung his praises now wrote: "Bezymensky's silence is the more intolerable since among the people who have given him unstinted praise are the most evil enemies of the people, Lelevich, Gorbachev, Vardin, led by the chief bandit, Trotsky."

"Is not the main thing what I have written and not what they have written about me?" he pleaded. But no one listened. On August 11, he

---

1. In justice to Fadeyev, it should be said that he did not invent the campaign against "cosmopolitanism" but merely distinguished himself by his zeal in conducting it.

was expelled from the Communist Party of which he had been a member since 1916—a year before the revolution.

DO I HAVE TO WRITE?

Perhaps you think: If they will not let me write, or compose, or paint, or experiment as my head and heart bid me, I can still serve the people by going into a factory. Listen to the case of the critic Rabinovich. His crime? He praised Shostakovich, sincerely, when it would have been unsafe not to praise him. When Shostakovich fell from grace in May, 1936, Rabinovich was grilled.

"The critic, too," he pleaded, "has the right to demand thoughtful treatment for himself. He, too, is a living being, with convictions which it is not so simple to break and reset. . . . I see only two possibilities. Either I must discover the mistakes in my views and bring them into harmony with the directions issued by *Pravda*. Or, if I cannot see those mistakes, I must change my profession."

But one does not resign from the secret police—and one does not resign from the spiritual police either. Rabinovich was condemned as "an anti-Soviet preacher of militant formalism." He did not change his profession—they changed it for him.

THE END OF MEYERHOLD

It may strike you as strange that in the 1920s there were so many books on Soviet drama, and then suddenly they were all burned and now there is no official history of the theater in the Soviet Union. Though they have found a way of writing a history of the civil war without mentioning there ever having been a War Commissar named Leon Trotsky, they have not yet found a way of writing a history of the Soviet theater without mentioning its greatest innovator, Meyerhold. And Meyerhold can no longer be mentioned because he has become an unperson. In June, 1939, he was invited to confess his "formalistic errors" before the First Congress of Soviet Theater Directors. Instead he manfully defended his lifelong devotion to the art of the theater and to the service of his people. Next day he was arrested and vanished from the face of the earth. A few weeks later his wife, the actress Zinaida Raikh, was brutally murdered in her apartment. Anyone who visited the Soviet Union in the 1920s, as I did, will know what a brilliant artist was taken from the

Soviet people by their conquerors when a bullet pierced the mighty brain of Vsevolod Meyerhold.[2]

THE FATE OF EISENSTEIN

Even greater perhaps, a world innovator in the young art of the motion picture, was Sergei Eisenstein. Can even loyal fellow travelers doubt the worth of the man who created *Potemkin* and *Ten Days That Shook the World?* Did he not possess greater skill as a creator than all the motion picture critics of the world put together, including the peerless critics in the Politburo? But in the 1930s four of Eisenstein's pictures were successively banned by Stalin's censors. He did a miserable film called *The General Line*—but the line changed and that was banned. Then he was ordered to undertake the revision of history in *Ivan the Terrible*. He had a heart attack when the second part was banned. Recovering a little, he wrote a curious and humiliating confession, with a touch of Aesopian language which got by the censors; he compared himself to a "sentry who gets so lost in the contemplation of the stars that he forgets his post." (But the duties of sentries and poets are not identical.)

He had remembered the terror and the madness of Ivan the Terrible, forgetting that Stalin identified himself with Ivan.

"Is it not so," his confession continues, "that the center of our attention is and must be Ivan the builder, Ivan the creator of a new, powerful, united Russian power, Ivan the inexorable destroyer of everything that resisted his progressive undertakings? The sense of historical truth betrayed me."

That confession was published in the Soviet journal *Culture and Life*. Eisenstein earned thereby a few more months of life, but in 1948, when he read the second attack on Shostakovich, he suffered a new heart attack and died the same evening.

I have selected but a handful of names from the long and tragic list of the heroes of culture that the total state has martyred. I could list hundreds more who have been tortured into becoming incarnations of Ananias the false artist, hundreds who have been artistically maimed and crippled, silenced, sent to concentration camps, driven to suicide, murdered. Many of these were apolitical. Many more were loyal to socialism, to the people, to the ideals once proclaimed by bolshevism. The best sought to be loyal to the vision that was in them.

But no system that aims to dominate, coordinate, and prescribe

2. Today Meyerhold is being cautiously rehabilitated.

everything, no system that claims to know everything, to be infallible and omnipotent, that claims to be able to explain by a single formula the entire past, control the entire present and determine the entire future, can tolerate the unpredictability that springs from difference, creativeness, spontaneity, uniqueness. How can totalitarianism endure the fact that men are creative and can produce from that unique tension between their inner selves and the outer world something new that nobody can foresee, command, predict, or interdict? Wherever the Politburo senses that it cannot direct and control, there it polices. And for the artist who is irremediably, ineradicably an artist, its only means of controlling is to silence with exile or a bullet in the base of the uncontrollable brain.

But, because man is human, this "great experiment" in total organization, permeation and automatization will not succeed. Man, being man, will continue to engender under the most unfavorable conditions a unique personality. Man, being man, will continue to suffer, to dream, to surprise, to create, to stake his life on his conscience and his vision.

And to those men of good will who have served the monster while dreaming that they were serving man, I plead that they re-examine the fate of their prototypes in the Soviet Union. If they re-examine this record, if they do elementary justice to the Shostakoviches, the Meyerholds, the Eisensteins, the Besymenskys, surely they will join in the struggle to keep culture free at home and to help it wherever it is threatened or gasping for the right to continue to exist.

—March 29, 1952

V SOME WONDERS OF
THE RUSSIAN TONGUE *

I am one of those hapless mortals who are condemned to read what Turgeniev once called "the great, powerful, truthful and free Russian tongue" with the aid of a dictionary. Next to the telephone book there would appear to be no more dismal consecutive reading than a dictionary. Gone are the days when a crotchety lexicographer could indulge his feelings as Dr. Johnson did when he defined *oats* as "food for horses, and, in Scotland, for humans." Modern dictionaries are collective, cumulative, standardized compilations, informative but uninspired and uninspiring. At least, so I thought until I began to consult the highly useful abridged *Russko-Angliiski Slovar*, published by Ogiz-Gis, the State Publishing House for Foreign and National Dictionaries.

Naturally, I did not set out to read the dictionary from *abazhur* to *yashchik* as consecutive reading. I perused Russian books and papers, and, in moments of confusion, turned to this little compendium for help and enlightenment. It is a good dictionary for its size—none better—and it rarely failed me. Only gradually did I become aware of the fact that other words on the page might be more interesting than the one I was seeking.

For most words there was the Russian, and then, without more ado, a single English equivalent, e.g., "*ventilyator*, ventilator" or "*verblyud*, camel." No less natural was it to find occasional words like "*velikii*, great," first defined and then illustrated by the expression, "*velikie derzhavy*, great powers," or even to find that "*vera*, faith," was illustrated with the expression "faith in the revolutionary cause," without any hint that there might also be a faith denominated as religious.

It was when I stumbled across the word "*piad*, span or inch," that I first began to note the unexpected qualities of this usually so laconic book. For after the word "inch" I found, "*Ni odnoi pyadi chuzhoi zemli ne khotim; no i svoei zemli ne otdadim nikomu (Stalin)*" and after that, in English: "We do not want a single foot of foreign territory; but we will not surrender a single inch of our territory to any one (Stalin)." Thus not only was foreign territory inexplicably measured in feet and

* First published in *The Modern Review*, November 1947.

domestic in inches, but the tiny, simple-seeming word "inch" occupied not one line but eight in this tightly abridged dictionary.

Anxiously I glanced at the date of publication (1942) and wondered how, after the annexation of half of Poland, part of Finland, and all of Bessarabia, Lithuania, Latvia, and Estonia, a dictionary published in Moscow could still be renouncing every single foot of foreign territory. I hastily turned to the letter *L* and on page 111 found "*Litovskaya Sovetskaia Sotsialisticheskaia Respublika,* the Lithuanian Soviet Socialist Republic," whence I concluded that this particular foot of ground had not been rejected. Still I felt an inexplicable conflict between the definition of *piad* and that of *Litovskaia* until I noted that besides the publication date 1942 (which accounts for the second) there was also the note "printed from plates of 1939," which accounted for the retention of the first. I breathed easier, but somebody may yet get purged for this failure to keep up-to-date in definitions.

WORDS THAT MAKE YOU THINK

After that, I could never resist the temptation to stray from the word I was seeking, usually so coldly and briefly defined, to any other on the page that happened to have a lot of type after it. My habit of straying from the straight and narrow path was surprisingly rewarded, for this proved to be a dictionary in which some select words gave you not only definitions but something to think about.

Thus if "*voina,* war" on page 30 was followed by "imperialist war" and "civil war" but not by "Great Patriotic War," you could blame it on the "plates of 1939" and ponder on the change of fashions in the meanings and affective overtones of words and the mutability of pacts and attitudes toward war. Or, if "*smertnost,* mortality" was bloodily illustrated by "*smertnaya kasn,* capital punishment" and "*smertnyi prigovor,* death sentence," it inspired reflections on what progress has been made since the Soviet Union abolished the death penalty in 1947, in order to lessen the opposition of other countries to returning Russian refugees.[1] And reflections, no less, on the superior economic uses to the state of working prisoners to death in concentration camps rather than wasting a bullet on them along with their potential labor power.

But it is time to let the dictionary speak for its inimitable self, in words culled at random, since I have still not started to read it from *abazhur* to *yashchik.* On page 79 under "*znamya,* banner" the reader will find in both languages "to hold aloft the banner of Lenin and Stalin," which surely should help him to use the word properly. Under

1. The death penalty has since been restored.

"*nezavisimo*, independently" on page 140, there is a lengthy aid to proper use: "the equality of the rights of the citizens of the USSR, independently or irrespective of their nationality or race, is an indefeasible law," which mouthful gives *nezavisimo* ten lines instead of one. This business of "rights" moreover seems to have bothered the lexicographers, for on page 136 under "*natsionalnost*, nationality," we again find the same statement about the "indefeasible law" in all its amplitude. And on page 209 under "*podlinnyi*, genuine" we find the genuine exemplification in the sentence: "genuine democracy is carried out in the USSR." I wondered about the English words "carried out" until I was brought up short by the added expression, "*s podlinnym verno*, checked and found correct." And, unexpectedly, under "*neprelozhnyi*, immutable," there is the illustration: "the equality of rights of the citizens of the USSR is an immutable law." To silence doubt, follow the words, "*neprelozhnaya istina*, indisputable truth."

Perhaps the climax in lengthy illustration of the definition of a short word comes with "*pravo*, right." No Soviet dictionary could let it go at that. There are twenty-two lines of exemplification, including such rights as "the right to vote" (but not to choose between candidates or tickets), "the right of self-determination," "the right of asylum," "the right to work in the USSR is ensured by the Socialist organization of national economy," and "citizens of the USSR have the right to rest and leisure which is ensured by the institution of annual vacations with pay." How touching to have so many exemplifications of the word "right" on a page where other and more difficult words must go badly defined and unexemplified!

But not every word; for on the self-same page, as if the alphabet itself or the paging were the work of a diversionist or wrecker, is the word which droppeth as the gentle rain from heaven, "*poshchada*, mercy" with the truly startling exemplification by the sentence "no mercy for the enemies of the people!" (exclamation point in the original). And when it began to seem to me in my simplicity that that was a poor exemplification of the word "mercy" I found my answer under the simple word *tot*, meaning "that," which was followed by the disconcerting "*tem samym vy prisnaete svoyu oshibku*, by that you confess your mistake." Lest I demur further, the dictionary added severely "*tem khuzhe*, so much the worse for you."

—November 1947

VI THE GREAT BLACKOUT *

What are the real population figures of the Soviet Union? Since 1939, they have been a state secret.

What is the birth rate? The death rate? The infant-mortality rate? The number of hospital beds? The number of married and unmarried adults? Since 1938, these vital statistics have been state secrets.

What is the number of insane? Of sick? Of invalided? Of blind? Since 1927, these figures have been state secrets.

What is the relation between wages and the cost of living? What is the real wage of a Soviet worker? What is the standard of living of the average Soviet family? How do grain prices compare with the prices of industrial products? What is the *kolkhoznik's* real income? What is the purchasing power of the peasant's ruble in terms of the town products he needs to buy?

In every modern country, the trade unions demand such information. The farmers' organizations demand such information. The government and nongovernmental bodies vie with each other in supplying wage indexes, cost-of-living indexes, production indexes.

That is, in every modern state except one. For many years, the Soviet government has refused to let the workers and peasants know such facts. And governments like the Czechoslovak, East German, and Polish— governments which for years published such statistics—have ceased to report to their people since their subjugation by the Kremlin.

Every new state that calls itself a "people's democracy" now keeps such facts secret from its people. Every state under the hammer and sickle instantly slips back into the dark ages when its government does not feel obligated to report to its people. In every one of them, the government rules arbitrarily and secretly and makes it a crime for any official to report these facts to the public. In every one of them, there is a blackout of statistics.

Even worse, instead of the simple truth, instead of figures that do not lie, now there is false propaganda. In place of figures, the people are

* First published in the *New Leader*, November 30, 1953.

given percentages—but percentages of what real figures? These, too, are a state secret. So the percentages mean nothing. They mean worse than nothing, since they are one more propaganda device for keeping the real truth from the people.

DEMOCRACY AS ACCOUNTING TO THE PEOPLE

Democracy began when governments started to make public their budgets, how they gathered their money and how they spent it. Parliaments arose when those who had to pay the taxes began demanding the right to approve or disapprove a given tax, its size, its purpose, how it was raised, how it was spent. "Democracy is publicity," Unamuno wrote to Joaquin Maurin.

"The Russian tsarist government," Lenin wrote in 1903, "only survives by living in the dark, and that is why complete and truthful information about the life of the people in the whole country is rarely collected in our country." Yet, at that time the tsar's government was printing innumerable statistical reports, giving out all kinds of economic and demographic information, permitting, even encouraging, nongovernmental organizations to publish all kinds of statistics. The tsar's government, like every civilized modern state, felt it a duty and a necessity to publish population statistics, vital statistics, penal statistics, economic statistics, to inform its people and the world.

There can be no modern economic and political science without such statistics. Lenin could never have written his *Development of Capitalism in Russia* in 1899 without such statistics. By actual count, Lenin's book makes use of 299 theoretical and statistical works in Russian published in tsarist Russia and, with the permission of tsarist officials, sent to him by his wife, Krupskaya, while he was in prison and exile in Siberia.

We know how many men the tsar's government sent to prison and exile. The Soviet government, too, published penal statistics after the bolsheviks took power. There were 6,000 political prisoners in Soviet prisons in 1926; 30,000 in 1928; and 662,257 on May 1, 1930. Then came the forced collectivization, the great speedup, the purges. The figures for political prisoners shot up into the millions, and the Soviet government no longer dared to publish penal statistics.

No other government publishes no penal statistics. No other government sends millions and tens of millions to concentration camps and prisons. Only as long as the figures were relatively small were they published.

In the first years of the Soviet regime, more statistical information was published than in tsarist Russia. Soviet statistical agencies ranked with those of the advanced countries.

In 1924, Joseph Stalin said to the Thirteenth Congress of the Communist Party:

In bourgeois states, a statistician has a certain minimum amount of professional honor. He cannot lie. He can be of any political conviction and inclination, but wherever facts and figures are concerned, he will submit to torture but will not tell a lie. If only we had more such bourgeois statisticians, people who respect themselves and possess a certain minimum of professional honor!

If that does not sound to you like the words of the Stalin of later years, look at page 215 of volume VI of his *Collected Works* or at the organization report he delivered to the Thirteenth Congress, and there you will find these honest words about "bourgeois" statistics and about the honor of a statistician.

But in 1928, Stalin suppressed the *Economic Bulletin* of the Moscow Business Cycle Institute, and in 1930 its head, Professor N. D. Kondratiev, was tortured by Stalin's police, and, because he would not join in the new statistical lies, he was liquidated. In 1930, all the great Russian statisticians (Bazarov, Groman, Kafenhaus, Makarov, Minz, Chaianov, Ginsburg, Chelintsev, Weinstein, and many, many others) were arrested. The great blackout, the great conspiracy against the Soviet people by the Soviet government, became total and all-embracing. No longer would the government account to its people even as to the facts concerning their own labor and what was done with the fruits of it. No more statistics on the cost of living, real wages, real price indexes, agricultural, and industrial prices. The *Economic Review* was killed in 1930. The *Monthly Statistical Bulletin* died in 1930. The *Paths of Agricultural Economy* was discontinued in October 1929, with the beginning of the great war on the peasants. *Socialist Economy* was discontinued in 1930, *Labor Statistics* in 1930, *Statistical Survey* in 1930, *Statistical Herald* in 1930, *Financial Herald* in 1930, *Problems of Trade* in 1930. It was as if a plague had hit the economics institutes and publications, the economists and statisticians.

And each year since 1930 the blackout has become darker. The first Five Year Plan contained 1747 pages; the second, 1262 pages; the third, only 238 pages; the fourth was published as a mere six pages in *Pravda* and the fifth in three and a half pages, containing nothing but propaganda slogans and fraudulent percentages.

In June 1947, the government issued the State Secrets Decree, forbidding any economist or official to follow his conscience and inform the citizens of anything. Today, an economist, statistician, or official can get from eight to twelve years' imprisonment for disclosing statistical information on industry, agriculture, trade, means of communication, monetary reserves, balances of payments, deposits and plans for financial operations, the real purchasing power of the ruble, the gold backing of the ruble, plans relating to imports and exports, and countless other subjects which are published as a matter of course by every government which has the slightest claim to being regarded as democratic.

THE IRON CURTAIN WITHIN

This great blackout is part of the oppressive design of totalitarianism. It is part of the iron curtain that imprisons every citizen of a Communist state. The iron curtain governments will not let their people travel freely abroad to find out about the economy of other lands. They will not permit the statistics of free governments, United Nations economic institutions, or universities of other nations to circulate freely in the Soviet Union. Nor will they let their own people know, or other people know, the real state of the economy, the health, the prisons, the concentration camps of the countries they rule.[1]

1. Concealment of the facts of the "political economy" of the country has gone so far that it begins to handicap even the bureaucracy itself. Thus the August 1955 issue of *Kommunist*, top theoretical organ of the Communist Party, complains: "Party and Government decrees are no longer published systematically. . . . In recent years we have actually had no collections of statistics on the USSR, union republics, and capitalist countries, or on individual branches of the national economy and culture. . . . *Scientific, party, and soviet officials, unable to find primary sources, are frequently forced to work with unverified data* from popular magazines and newspaper articles. . . . We do not publish any biographical-bibliographical dictionaries such as . . . were published before the revolution." (Emphasis added.)

In 1956, some attempt was made to remedy this defect by publishing a Statistical Reference Book on the National Economy of the USSR. It contained a good deal of statistical material, but vast areas of Soviet life were covered with a blanket of silence. And the published statistics themselves were immediately demonstrated to be false in many and fundamental respects. Not only did foreign experts demonstrate this, but a few of the more courageous and independent Soviet statisticians and economists have done the same. Thus in *Kommunist*, No. 9, of that same year, Vasilii Sergeevich Nemchinov (the eminent economist-statistician who lost his job as Director of the Timiryazev Academy of Agriculture because he refused to give Lysenko's ideas on genetics and on the uselessness of genetical statistics a monopoly in that school) published a cautiously critical article on the new Statistical Handbook. The editors reproduced as genuine some of the falsified statistics, but his article did not refer to the "accompanying" table. He complained that "the material presented in the Handbook is entirely inadequate for scientific research." He regretted the absence of much essential data, including such key statistics as "the aggregate balance of material production, balance of the national economy, balance of money incomes, balance of the labor force, balance of production and consumption, balance of money incomes and expenditures of the population." He showed quiet contempt for Khrushchev's propaganda concerning surpassing the United States in bread consumption per capita by observing that the small consumption of bread in the United States is due to the large consumption of meat and milk.

One thing is clear: where the people have no control of taxation and government expenditure, there is no democracy. Where there is no recognized right to demand an acounting, to turn out of office, to change government policies in taxation, planning or spending, there is no democracy. Where there is no accounting by public officials to the citizens on all public matters, the officials are not public servants but masters, and the people are not citizens but subjects or slaves.

Man has spent centuries fighting for parliamentary institutions, for the legalization of opposition, for control of taxes, government budgets, government plans and policies. In three and a half decades, the Soviet government has wiped out all of these achievements. It calls itself a democracy—which means rule of the people, for the people, by the people. It even calls itself a people's democracy—which presumably means a people's rule of the people. But it does not inform its people. It does not consult its people. It does not account for its stewardship. Everything it does is done in secret. Secrecy is the breeding ground of tyranny. Secrecy is the opposite of democracy. Secrecy in government means that every Communist government is neither more nor less than a conspiracy against its own people. *Communism everywhere always begins as a conspiracy against existing government, and, wherever it manages to seize power, it continues as a governmental conspiracy against the people.*

—November 1953

And in a hitherto unpublished collection of essays, issued in September 1960, the dean of Soviet economists, Stanislav Gustavovich Strumilin (the quondam author of the illusions and the very slogan Stalin used in the first Five Year Plan: "There is no fortress that Bolshevik determination cannot conquer"), emboldened by his eighty-three years and his sense that he had lived his life, published an admission that Soviet production growth statistics are hopelessly inflated by "double counting." Thus sheet steel is counted first when it is pig iron, then when it leaves the mill as steel, then when it goes into a truck or automobile as part of its construction, in short, over and over again. "Growth of gross output purposely exaggerates the real rate of growth," he writes. And the procedure has been increasing with the passing years. He gave a much lower rate of growth than Soviet propaganda has been claiming, but it is still vastly inflated. Strumilin figures the rate of growth to be roughly three-fourths of what the Soviet government has been claiming, while the Rand Corporation, using such items of the jigsaw puzzle of Soviet statistics as it can lay hold of by collation and mathematical detective work, puts the figure as less than half that which Strumilin has estimated. Not only are the world's experts handicapped, but the Soviet officials responsible for alternative investment of scarce capital, labor, and resources, all matters requiring accurate statistics, will never be able to engage in real planning as long as the blackout and statistical juggling continue.

PART VI

Problems of Foreign Policy

I COMMUNIST IDEOLOGY AND SOVIET FOREIGN POLICY *

> It was only toward the middle of the twentieth century that the inhabitants of many European countries came, in general unpleasantly, to realize that their fate could be influenced directly by intricate and abstruse books of philosophy.—Czeslaw Milosz

For four and one-half decades we have waited for the Soviet Union to mellow. Repeatedly, we have thought we were witnessing the longed-for change of dynamism, direction or heart, which would make Communist totalitarianism in power just "one state among many"—different of course, but a member of the comprehensive genus of orderly, constituted governments, content to tolerate orderly neighbors and act according to the not-too-generous rule of live and let live by which governments, reluctantly, indifferently or a little contemptuously, suffer each other's presence on the same earth.

A review of the judgments of statesmen and analysts over these 45 years makes melancholy reading. From the notion that Lenin's regime would last but a few weeks or months (Lenin shared this view for a while) to the certitude that power and responsibility always sober; from Lenin's N.E.P. to Stalin's "socialism in one country" and Khrushchev's "thaw"; from the celebration of Russia's entry into the League of Nations through the shock of the Molotov-Ribbentrop Pact to the Grand Alliance that was to build "one world"; from Stalin's "peaceful coexistence" to Khrushchev's "peaceful competition"; from the "collective leadership" following Lenin's death to that following Stalin's, to the personal rule of Khrushchev—at every zig we have proclaimed, "At last it has come," at every zag muttered, "Surely it cannot last!"

In London I chanced some time ago on the diary of a deceased noble lady, one entry of which noted that Fridtjof Nansen had come to tea, bringing glad tidings: "Our troubles with Russia are over: Lenin is returning to capitalism." The entry was made in 1922, the lady's informant being one of the most knowing of Soviet experts in his generation.

* First published in *Foreign Affairs*, October 1962.

Four decades after that entry, I read in a work of an American political scientist a rejection of the very conception that "totalitarianism is a radically new social form," which, while it exists as such, will continue to maintain "its combative posture vis-à-vis democratic societies."

Even on a simpler intuitive basis, [the writer continues] one can question the basic assumption of the theory—namely, that society becomes completely atomized and rule is anomic and direct. In a *crisis* situation, a state can fragment all social life, and through terror, perhaps, mold a people to its will. But can a society live in permanent crisis? Can it hold such a rigid posture without either exploding into war or relaxing? The basis of all social life requires not only a minimum of personal security but the reasonable expectation by parents that their children will be educated, develop careers, and so forth. To that extent, a tendency towards "normalization" is at work in any crisis state.[1]

Leaving aside the assumptions which our theme prevents us from considering (*viz.* that rule by secretaries, cells and transmission belts is "direct rule;" that totalitarianism is "anomic," *i.e.*, either unstructured or without a value system, merely because these are given from above; and that militant totalitarianism is incompatible with giving children "education and careers"), the passage cited touches on the heart of the questions that will concern us in this article.

How can a regime that arose through a crisis (in Russia and our civilization) endure for 45 years? How does it differ from the usual "crisis regime?" How has it been able to prolong its "crisis" for close to a half-century? Is there a built-in eroding factor which will compel it before too long to "explode into war or relax into 'normalization'?" Is the "simple, intuitive basis" of Western thought a proper tool for understanding a society so different from the one in which that intuition was formed? Or is its concept of "normalization" applicable to the ideology and structure of militant totalitarianism?

Conversely, is the opposite extreme tenable? Can we deduce the twists and turns of Soviet policy by simple transposition from its ideology and totalitarian structure?

Or, as this article will seek to suggest, is not Soviet conduct a composite of disparate and conflicting forces, namely: (1) the influence of the traditional situation of the nation upon those who usurped power there; (2) the alterations forced upon them by recalcitrant reality; and (3) the drives and preconceptions of the intensely held ideology which they possess, and which possesses them?

Forty-five years, it goes without saying, have brought important changes—cumulative changes which come from expanding power, length-

1. Daniel Bell, *The End of Ideology*, New York, 1960, p. 308-9.

ening experience in power, defeats and deterrence, and changes in the outside world. Hence a central question of this analysis must be: Are there discernible, amidst these changes, fundamental features of the ideology and institutional framework which have endured, which are decisive for the shaping of foreign policy, and with which we are likely to have to continue to reckon for the foreseeable future? [2]

II

Let us begin with the easiest part of the problem: the influence on Bolshevik policy of the imperial heritage.

Lenin seized power, not in a land "ripe for socialism," but in a land ripe for seizing power. "It was as easy," he wrote, "as lifting up a feather." His coup was supposed to touch off a European socialist revolution; but while the revolution "matured," the opportunity presenting itself was to seize power in the Great Russian Empire. "The point of the uprising," he chided those who hesitated about Russia's "ripeness" for his blueprint, "is the seizure of power. Afterward, we will see what we can do with it."

Many of the things Lenin and his successors had to do were those which any new tsar would have attempted after an interregnum, a ruinous war, and a shrinkage of empire: namely, to re-establish order (their kind of order); to identify Russia's interests in the minds of their subjects with their rule; to subdue and reconquer seceding provinces and peoples;[3] to end the war as best they could, re-establish Russia's frontiers, and resume under new forms and for new purposes Russia's secular expansion.

Insofar as there appears to be identity between the policy of the stronger tsars and that of Lenin, Stalin, and Khrushchev, this springs from the fact that, more often than not, the same territories constitute the objectives of reincorporation or conquest. Georgia, Poland, Finland, the Ukraine, Byelorussia, the Baltic States, Bessarabia, the Balkans, the Dardanelles, the Near East, Persia, the Turkic Empires, Sinkiang, Mongolia, Manchuria, Korea—all these have appeared in the pages of Russian history before.

2. This last phrase, by implication, tells all that I shall have to say in the present article concerning our own foreign policy in dealing with the Communist powers. As to the enduring elements of the institutional framework, I have discussed them in my paper, "The Durability of Despotism in the Soviet System." The present article deals only with the enduring elements of the ideology.

3. Twenty-eight years ago in *Foreign Affairs*, Karl Radek wrote: "The attempt to represent the foreign policy of the Soviet Union as a continuation of Tsarist policy is ridiculous. . . . Tsarism, or any other bourgeois régime in Russia, would necessarily resume the struggle for the conquest of Poland and the Baltic states. . . . The Soviet Union, on the contrary, . . . [considers] their achievement of independence a positive and progressive historical factor." (*Foreign Affairs*, January 1934, p. 194.)
Alas, poor Radek . . .

The same geographical situation gives the same neighbors. The Soviet Empire is still the Eurasian heartland, subject to pressure from East or West or both at once, capable of exerting pressure on East and West— on one at a time under the tsars with their limited aims—on both at once under the Bolsheviks with their unlimited ones. As before, Russia is the great land power, many of whose policies are conditioned by the traditional contests between land power and sea power. As before, in moments of strength, this land power still strives for control of its bordering seas.

If the dream of controlling the Pacific proved a wild chimera and Alaska and California had to be abandoned, the Caspian proved easy. With a little luck—and the Dardanelles!—the Black Sea would prove easy, too. And the Mediterranean has been entered before.

The conquest of the Baltic Provinces and Finland had started Russia's way around the Baltic. Stalin's desperate effort to seize Hamburg, his annexations in East Prussia, his claim to fortify Bornholm, would have startled us less had we borne this inherited appetite in mind. Certainly it explains more concerning Russia's "geopolitical" attitude toward her bordering seas than does the journalistic cliché of "hunger for a warm-water port." Not as exporter or importer but as the great land power blocked in its secular ambitions by surrounding sea powers does Russia look on her bordering seas.

The military advantage of the land power is its interior lines of communication (providing its transport and logistics are adequate). But one disadvantage is that the sea powers are more mobile and can strike at any of its many frontiers, or several at once, compelling Russia to keep large armies in reserve at all her borders. This is further complicated now by airpower; by the radar, plane, and missile bases all around the empire; by the missile-launching submarine.

Another preoccupation of the power sprawling across the open Eurasian plain is the "rectification" of its frontiers to get more defensible lines. The Pripet Marshes was one such to the west, which was too bad for Poland since a more defensible line for one meant a less defensible for the other. The Carpathians played a similar role to the southwest. To the historian there was no novelty in Stalin's partition of Poland with Hitler, reconfirmed by default by the Grand Alliance. The novelty was the military ignorance (or was it faith in Hitler?) that led Stalin to station his main armies *in front* of the river and swamps, so that these served to hinder not the Wehrmacht's advance, but the Soviet armies' retreat.

The "rectifying" of borders is, of course, a traditional objective. Kutusov, between 1812 and 1815, urged his sovereign to take advantage of Russia's advance on Paris to "rectify" Russia's borders along the Carpathians and the shortest line along the Oder to the Sea and "compensate" the Prussian King—as Stalin was to "compensate" Poland—by lands to the west. Actually, Alexander I had too much consideration for his brother sovereign, the King of Prussia, and for the diplomatic practices of his day. His forbearance arose out of the code of personal conduct of nineteenth-century sovereigns, "cousins" all, and the generally limited nature of the aims that characterized the European system from 1815, when Napoleon fell, until 1914, when peace fell.

Despite a certain archaism carried over from the days of Russia's isolation, the foreign policy of the tsars was the customary policy of a great national state. Its vague ideological overtones were no different from those of other nations. The belief that the tsar's power and duty came from God is analogous to the divine right of kings. The idea of the Third Rome" played no larger role, indeed not as large as the doctrine of the Holy Roman Empire played over the long period from Charlemagne and Barbarossa to Napoleon. France, like Russia, concerned itself with the "protection of the Holy Places" in Palestine while St. Petersburg's fluctuating interest in the Ottoman Slavs was less intense than Austria-Hungary's absorption with Slav stirrings inside and below its Empire. Panslavism and Slavophilism remained feverish fantasies of isolated intellectuals, suspect at court, analogous to, and not as influential as, Pan-Germanism in the German Empire.

Though the diplomacy of the tsars resembled that of Stalin and Khrushchev in its freedom from the overt and organized pressure of public opinion and the natural inclination of autocrats to engage in summitry and personal settlements, Russia's diplomacy as a whole was conventional, employing professional diplomats, following the practices of a world-wide diplomatic tradition which has almost vanished from memory now that conferences and negotiations are habitually put to the uses of a revolutionary power. Foreign policy aims were limited, pursued on the whole circumspectly and in a certain sequence, expressed in the prevailing terms of national interest, balance of power, concert of Europe, spheres of influence, rectification of frontiers, protection against incursions, respect for engagements and alliances, readiness to take into account the opinions and pressures of the other great powers (as in the various settlements with Turkey).

Just as autocracy, though it claimed absolute power, did not dream of totalist power within its own realm, so it had no global aims in foreign policy, no all-embracing plan for the world, no over-all unifying idea. Neither an ideocracy, nor insurrectionary, its generals brought no plans for revolution in their baggage. It had no fifth column as its servant, no world to bury, and no world to win. Though it might prefer autocracy in its neighbors, it did not feel impelled to set up a replica of its own regime wherever its armies entered; nor did it feel "insecure" and "provoked" unless all the world should consist of autocracies.

Alexander I marched into Paris at the head of the most powerful armies in the world, then withdrew leaving no permanent traces of his occupation and the essential France much as before. The same was true of the other countries he occupied en route. If Stalin could have possessed such overriding military power and led his armies to Paris in 1945, the result would have been startlingly different, for he would have brought with him a set of rulers for each occupied country and a set of rules, an ideology covering the whole of life, a totalitarian structure, and single-party rule.

III

It should be clear, then, that the men who make policy in the Soviet Union think and act differently from the tsars and that we neglect their ideology to our peril.[4] Once this is recognized, it might perhaps seem that all we need do is study their ideology to discover their "operative code" and foresee their every move. But ideology is not a set of Euclidean theorems.

Even for Communists there is no automatically "correct translation," no one-to-one correspondence, between any segment of ideology and any particular act. Their doctrine combines a religion and eschatology of salvation; a vast accumulation (from pre-1848 to the present) of political commentary and judgments, most of them out of date if they were ever valid; an economics now irrelevant; a historical sociology and critique of economic and social institutions, some of which is still suggestive; a philosophy which is little more than verbal casuistry. To make matters worse, every assertion in the voluminous, contradictory writings of Marx, Engels, and Lenin is held to be part of a single science, a canon in which any sentence may be treated as having probative value. Hence the application of the doctrine to any given situation is subject to argument, and it is not always easy for the Communist leaders themselves to deduce from it the appropriate conclusion or action.

If it is hard for them (they solve their problem by forbidding factional controversy and developing the institution of the infallible leader as sole authorized interpreter at any given moment), how much harder is it for us!

"What matters," Sir Lewis Namier once wrote of political ideas, "is

4. See Donald MacRae, "The Appeal of Communist Ideology," in Inkeles and Geiger, *Soviet Society: A Book of Readings*, New York, 1961, p. 104-13.

the underlying emotions, the music to which ideas are the mere libretto." All we can master is the words; to their music we are tone-deaf.

Though the doctrine operates persistently and powerfully to shape their vision, passions, thoughts, and actions, it does not operate in a vacuum. It must be applied, in fragments and contradictions, to a real world of which even the doctrinaire, and particularly the adepts of this doctrine, take account. The masters of the doctrine have inherited from Lenin—and continued to develop—a distinctive Bolshevik blend of dogmatism and empiricism.

Nothing could be more deceptive than the inclination to answer from within ourselves the questions: "What would I believe if I accepted this proposition which they accept? How would I act in the situation facing them if I held their beliefs?" The illusion that we can easily "put ourselves in their place" contains a built-in trap, that of tending to put them in our place and tending to think that they think and feel as we do.

When we do pay attention to their ideology and its emotional context, we tend to be so impressed by its dogmatic character that we forget that it is dogma applied to reality. It is true that this application has its ambiguities. When they study the world for "theoretical" purposes, dogma has priority over reality, which has orders to confirm and reinforce their faith—"confirm the truth of our science." Thus filtered, it does. Still it is their contention that their dogmas are derived from the empirical study of society and the universe. And it is their pride that the science enables them to appraise reality, react properly to it, judge the exact extent to which the "concrete, objective situation" and "real relations of power" permit them to advance on the path marked out for them by it.

Moreover, we do them wrong to imagine that they will abandon this path and choose rather to blow up the world when given no other choice than open retreat. This *Götterdämmerung* frenzy or petulance was a constituent of Hitler's spirit but not of Lenin's. Lenin was as proud of knowing "when to retreat" and "how to retreat in good order" as he was of knowing when to advance and push to the limit. For him, offensive and defensive, retreat and simulated withdrawals and outflanking maneuvers were all precious elements of a strategy of protracted conflict which was to last until final victory. For every battle, his favorite adage was taken from Napoleon: *On s'engage, et puis—on voit!*

Within rather strict limits, contact with refractory reality has forced upon these men adaptations ("creative extensions") of their doctrine. "Facts are stubborn things," Lenin would say. They could not, of course, refute "science." But they could show him that a particular tactic or plan of a given moment had to be abandoned or a particular proposition reinterpreted.

Lenin and his successors are always at pains to show that their "creative extensions" do not constitute a "revision." This is more than mere casuistry, for it corresponds to a genuine psychological and political need and possesses an underlying meaning.

Though Marx's views of his last years were different from those of 1848, there was an enduring framework of dogma and continuity of spirit which made it not unwarranted for disciples to make of his teachings an "ism" and an orthodoxy. More fearful of "revisionism" than the founding fathers, the "orthodox" sought to turn every possible aspect into a dogma. Yet, most dogmatic of Marxists though he was, Lenin found it needful, consciously and unconsciously, to transform what he adopted, give it a Russian cast, put on it the stamp of his own temperament.

Repeatedly he "creatively developed" the doctrine, so that the Leninism of the foundation period (1902-14) was profoundly different from the Leninism of the First World War (1914-16). In 1917, he made even more drastic changes, so that he had to fight all the old leaders of his party—they quoting the Lenin of the foundation period against the living Lenin. Still more startling was the next transformation: from the pronouncements of the six months from spring to autumn of 1917 (anarchistic, decentralist, spontaneous mass-actionist, syndicalist, equalitarian) to the Leninism of firmly established power. Each of these stages represents a significant break in strategy and tactics against the background of an even more important and fundamental continuity of dogma, spirit, and long-range aim. Moreover, all these variform pronouncements of Lenin, like those of Marx, are now held to represent a single sacred canon. Yet each of these "creative extensions" in its day caused not only opponents but often devout disciples to believe that Lenin was "abandoning Leninism."

With these complexities in mind, let us enter the thicket of Communist doctrine, to see what trails we can find leading from dogma to policy.

IV

Marxism-Leninism is a "science," indeed a superscience of the laws of motion of both nature and society. It makes a science of history, politics, sociology, social and individual psychology, and all the subtle realms of the spirit.

Its God is personified History, the Future His Word and His Kingdom. Its mythology, as Herbert Lüthy has observed, has an astonishing "conceptual realism," which puts on the stage of history as living, thinking, and acting personages such abstract concepts as Capitalism, Imperialism, Socialism, as in the morality plays of the Middle Ages Jealousy, Slander or Avarice were accustomed to appear. Those who can juggle with these puppets and possess this conceptual wisdom are masters of the plot, bearers of History's will, beneficiaries of History's guarantees, executors of History's judgments.

A predictive science, it works to fulfill and is intended to fulfill its prophecies. As it includes its own verification, so it includes its own morality—what history intends being at once scientifically and morally right. Whoever and whatever hastens the coming of the future is thus doubly sanctioned; whoever or whatever gets in the way is both un-scientific and immoral.

The final victory of history's millennial intentions will usher in a state of absolute grace in which history-as-conflict ceases and loses its impera-tives of harsh struggle; man can at last become human and humane, love can replace hatred, and all be made whole. This exempts "correct," *i.e.*, scientific and moral, action from the possibility of wrongdoing.

Weltgeschichte ist Weltgericht, but in this court justice is not blind, for judge's bench, jury box, attorney's stands, courtroom public, and executioner are provided by the Party. Only the accused is an outsider, known in advance to be guilty as charged, undeserving of mercy. Mastery of the law carries with it the ability to penetrate subjective disguises and recognize the "objective meaning" of the assertions, acts, illusions, and the very existence of the accused. Doubt, question, deviation, uncertainty, opposition, indifference, or willful attempts to escape the judgment, absent one's self from the spectacle, or any impulse of sympathy with the accused, are impermissible. "If we do not allow freethinking in chemistry," as Comte once wrote, "why should we allow it in morals or politics?" Why indeed if morals and politics are science?

The chief significance which the infallibility of the ideology and its adepts has for foreign policy is the combination of strength *and* inflexibility which comes from knowing that you have History on your side. This goes far to explain the unresponsiveness to argument, the stubbornness and repetitiveness of Communist negotiators, the lack of communication in dialogues which are only ostensible dialogues. How can there be genuine dialogue without some consensus? How can there be give-and-take be-tween that which is self-evidently and totally right and that which is self-evidently wrong, both scientifically and morally? [5]

5. "They say," Khrushchev declared in Albania on the eve of the Foreign Ministers' Conference of 1959, "that 'with the U.S.S.R. you must negotiate in the following fashion: concession for concession!' But that is a huckster's approach! . . . We do not have any concessions to make, because our proposals have not been made for bartering. . . . [Their] proposals do not contain a single element for negotiation. . . . They are not based on a desire to find a correct solution."

V

Marxism-Leninism is a combative ideology. At the core of things, it finds conflict, antagonism, clash. Progress (development) comes only through struggle. In this development the most important moments are those when accumulated tension and clash go into open struggle, the highest point of all being apocolyptic, chiliastic, and eschatological. Toward this all history moves. With it history as "the history of class struggles" will come to an end.

Until then, in the unending war, there can be frequent pauses, indeed must be pauses. The ideology gives its possessors the wisdom to know when pauses are necessary, the pride to "crawl in the mud on your belly" without a sense of humiliation, the skill to "keep a clear line for maneuvering," for "retreating when possible and necessary" lest you lose all you have gained, for "renewing the attack" when that becomes possible, for "using treaties as a means of gaining strength," bringing up "fresh forces," obtaining a "better rather than a worse peace as a respite for another war," a "breathing spell." [6]

Even the Apocalypse is divided into stages. That is the meaning of the discussions on the possibility of "victory at first in several countries, or one country taken separately," of "socialism in one country," and of the scholastic distinctions between stages in "the construction of socialism," "the extended construction of Communism," and the "attainment of compete Communism." [7]

Ebbs and "compromises" are "necessary" then, but necessary only in an evil and wretched sense because the enemy is tough and strong and man is refractory material for the great experiment. The long war is made up of many campaigns and armistices before "final victory;" the road to revolution is "not as straight and smooth as the Nevsky Prospekt."

But Lenin trained his disciples to hate compromise for compromise's sake. His Hell is full of "compromisers," "opportunists" who do not seize opportunities to advance, conciliators, procrastinators—"Verily, procrastination is like unto death." The lowest circle of Hell is reserved for

6. All the expressions quoted are from Vol. VII of Lenin's Collected Works (London: Lawrence, 1962), where he discusses the Brest-Litovsk Treaty. Similar views are found throughout his works. Analysts who become aware of the apocalyptic element in Communism are apt to overlook this realistic, calculating, pragmatic element. This is one of the main sources of our continual misunderstanding of Communist peace maneuvers, retreats, and "agreements." Lenin taught his disciples: "If you are not able to adapt yourself, if you are not ready to crawl in the mud on your belly, you are not a revolutionist but a chatterbox." Neither Lenin nor Stalin was a chatterbox. Khrushchev, despite his unending chatter, analogous to a state magician's line of patter, is not a chatterbox either.

7. The first formula in quotes is Lenin's, the second Stalin's, and the others have been used by Stalin and Khrushchev.

those who would compromise in order to come to real agreement, settle matters, or call off the struggle in favor of permanent and enduring peace. They would not succeed, for history decrees otherwise, but they must be cut off as dead limbs lest they spread rot.

Clearly, in our relations with the Soviet Union we are not dealing with a "crisis" regime that will settle down to "normalcy" as soon as it has solved the crisis which brought it to power. Lenin managed to seize power because of a crisis in another regime. His purpose was not to resolve the crisis but to use the new-won power as a mighty base for waging the war to which he was committed—a twofold war: on his own people, until he had remade them according to his blueprint (the New Soviet Man in the New Communist Society); and a struggle for the world, until that too is reconstructed to the same blueprint. That is the meaning of all the gentle little homilies with which Nikita Sergeyevich assures us that "Your grandchildren will live under Communism" and "Do whatever you will, we shall bury you." This is not a "crisis regime" seeking to end the chaos caused by total war and economic breakdown (that crisis has long been ended) but a state-of-siege regime seeking to conduct its own total twofold war until it achieves that total victory promised by its ideology.

In this war, though armistices and temporary agreements are necessary, the essence of any agreement is that it is temporary, not that it is an agreement. The struggle may have to be continued "by other means" for a "shorter or longer period." But war itself is only the continuance of the politics of peace, and peace the continuance of the politics of war, "by other means." This is the wisdom which Lenin has distilled from Clausewitz.

To continue an undeclared war or to launch an open war, no *casus belli* is needed, only fresh breath and favorable circumstances. The war itself has been decreed by history and was declared by Marx once and for all in 1848 when he wrote: "The Communists scorn to conceal their aims . . . the forcible overthrow of all existing conditions . . , a world to win."

Between irreconcilable opponents, one of whom is destined by history to be destroyed, the other to conquer, agreement—like dialogue—can be only ostensible. It cannot form the basis of an enduring peace, for it aims only at respite and advantage, or the limiting of disadvantage, in a continuing and scientifically and morally correct struggle.

The implications of these views are manifold and too all-pervasive even to be listed here. At the least, however, they suggest that in every encounter we remind ourselves that "negotiate" and "agree" have different meanings for them than for us. To them lulls cannot conceivably or decently be preliminaries to all-out peace. Nor are separate issues really separate, except in the sense that they have been separated out for strategical or tactical convenience from the general context of struggle. Every negotiation, every issue, even every day's session they regard primarily as a move in that irreconcilable conflict. While we doubtless must, acording to our aims, treat each negotiation and issue on its own terms, we will be lost if we forget what it means in their aims, and what "negotiation" and "settlement" mean to them.

Only if we bear this in mind will we be less likely to be caught off guard by broken treaties (how many our government has noted in the past decade!); by agreements which, on the day after adoption, prove to be disagreements on what was agreed; by the helplessness of "neutral" "enforcement" commissions; by the "irregular" or "volunteer" or "guerrilla" detachments, officially disowned but quite openly recruited and supplied, which continue the efforts to unsettle what has been "settled." Only then can we remind ourselves that all "agreements" must be defined with more than "Byzantine" rigor, and be self-enforcing—which, generally speaking, means that they must contain arrangements for ourselves and our allies to have the forces at key places to defend our interests.

Finally, this awareness should enable us to avoid the trap which we have set for ourselves by the practice of conventional diplomacy: to call off actual combat when negotiations are on, "in order to create an atmosphere favorable to peace." Theirs has been the revolutionary practice: to step up hostilities when negotiations begin, prolong them if the battle is going favorably, seek to gain by combat the most favorable position for a possible "settlement," and the best jumping-off place for the eventual renewal of the conflict.

VI

In all politics, Lenin taught his followers, there is one central question. This he expressed in lapidary form: "Kto kogo?—Who whom?" In Russian no verb is needed; here the first word is subject, the second object. But besides the compact form, Lenin's works supply various verbs in different contexts: Who beats whom? Who takes advantage of whom? Who uses whom? As long as the question "Who whom?" has not been finally decided by the victory of Communism on a world scale, tension is the breath of life. "Peaceful coexistence does not mean ideological coexistence." Truce is not détente.

Even the atom bomb and intercontinental missile do not permit of the conflict's being called off although they require more care than ever in preventing it from going over into all-out war. Early in 1961, Khrushchev said:

Liberation wars will continue to exist as long as imperialism exists. . . . These are revolutionary wars. Such wars are not only admissible but inevitable . . . the peoples can attain their freedom and independence only through struggle, including armed struggle. . . . We recognize such wars and will help the peoples striving for their independence. . . . Can such wars flare up in the future? They can. . . . But these are wars which are national uprisings. . . . What is the attitude of the Marxists toward such uprisings? . . . The Communists fully support such just wars and march in the front rank with peoples waging liberation struggles.[8]

Like Lenin and Stalin, there are two things that Khrushchev tries with all his might and skill to avoid: all-out war and all-out peace. Because time is "on their side" and because they set the highest value on power and their possession of a great power base from which to accelerate history and fulfill their mission, they will not voluntarily jeopardize its possession. Hence all-out war is a risk to be avoided. Fission and fusion bombs and missiles have only served to further strengthen this determination. But they have not persuaded the Soviet leaders to tolerate all-out peace.

For a movement whose essence is struggle, the most dangerous periods are those of comparative relaxation, entailing as they do the perils of loss of vigilance, acceptance of peace as natural, passivity, complacency, letdown, the danger of being "influenced" by the too "friendly" and persuasively powerful enemy—in short, the menace of spiritual demobilization and ideological disarming. "Revolutionary Social Democracy," Lenin wrote in mid-1906 when the high tide of the previous year seemed to be receding, "must be the first to enter on the path of the most decisive and relentless struggle, and the last to have recourse 'to methods that are more roundabout.' "

Methods that are more roundabout—Lenin abounds in instructions for going roundabout toward the unabandoned goal when it is clear that, for the moment, you cannot break through. Far from "losing face," a Bolshevik is tested above all by his ability to retreat in good order and show skill in methods of struggle that are more roundabout.

To carry on a war for the overthrow of the international bourgeoisie [Lenin admonished the Communist International], a war which is a hundred times more difficult, prolonged, and complicated than the most stubborn of ordinary wars between states, and to refuse beforehand to maneuver, to utilize the conflict of interests (even though temporary) among one's enemies, to refuse to temporize and compromise with possible (even though transient, unstable, vacillating and conditional) allies—is not this ridiculous in the extreme? Is

8. Speech of Jan. 6, 1961, "For New Victories of the World Communist Movement." It was originally delivered at a closed meeting in the Kremlin and released for publication abroad some ten days later. Khrushchev and his successors have returned to the same thought a number of times since.

it not as though, in the difficult ascent of an unexplored and heretofore inaccessible mountain, we were to renounce beforehand the idea that at times we might have to go in zigzags, sometimes retracing our steps, sometimes abandoning the course already selected and trying out various others? [9]

It is these "retracings of steps" and "zigzags" that have been the undoing of so many of our analysts. At each retreat, we have been told: "This is for good; now relaxation has set in." At each zig, there have not been lacking those who saw in it the longed-for permanent change. They extrapolated the zig, prolonged it in a straight line out toward the horizon. Caught in outer space by the zag, they have rushed back to the turning point, only to prolong the zag on a straight line toward the other horizon. Perhaps this explains, as Leonard Schapiro once observed, the noiseless and not unwelcome obsolescence of so much of our Sovietology.

An awareness that the ascent of the mountain is tougher than they thought carries with it no reassurance that they have abandoned the ascent. Lenin's retreats and zigzags were meant to circumvent impassable ravines, not renounce the climb. Flexible tactics can be undertaken without misgiving precisely because Bolsheviks are inflexible (certain) about their goal and have history's guarantee that they must reach it. The peculiar Bolshevik blend of dogmatism and empiricism, tactical flexibility and goal-seeking inflexibility, action-affirming myth and pragmatic ability to take account of the "real relations of power," are all part of, and reinforced by, a peculiar blend of rationality with what can only be described as a paranoiac vision of self and "enemy" and reality, that is not subject to rational refutation. And all these "blends" are at the heart of their movement and ideology, having been there from the beginning and having been reinforced by their long war.

In the past forty-five years has history not encouraged them to believe that they are the future and we the decaying past? At the outset—unless it should be saved by World Revolution—Lenin barely ventured to hope that his rule would "last longer than the Paris Commune." It is rounding out four-and-a-half decades secure in its might, the second power on earth straining to be first, the stronghold of a "socialist camp."

What reason does a man looking with Khrushchev's eyes have for abandoning the view that "capitalist-imperialism" is decadent when it is losing all its colonies, did not show the resolution to protect Hungary's freedom or complete the unification of Korea, failed to make the military moves to prepare its sort of peace during World War II, thereby letting maimed and bleeding Russia pick up all of Eastern Europe, half of Germany, win powerful allies and partners in Asia, expand the "camp of Communism" from one-sixth of the earth to one-fourth, with one-third

9. *Lenin*, Vol. XXXI, p. 51.

of the earth's population? We may offer our explanations of all this. None of them would seem to him to refute his simple explanation of "decadence" and "progress."

VII

Khrushchev and his lieutenants were born in the ambience of their ideology, like a fish in water, and educated in that ideology's tenets and techniques. This ideology-technique guided his upward path from *rabfak* graduate and local student secretary to a place as one of Stalin's most vociferous and active claque-leaders, to wheel horse of the post-Stalin machine, to sole authorized interpreter of the doctrine. In a world where power is knowledge, his power to interpret the ideology—after consultation or off-the-cuff—has given him knowledge of all things from breeding sows and raising corn to directing poets and philosophers and space-probers.

The monopoly power of the machine he heads, and the institutional framework through which it operates, are given legitimacy (in so far as the word is applicable) by the ideology which is the wellspring of the Party's power and its image of the world. The Party is the word made flesh: Khrushchev cannot permit its wellspring to be polluted; it is the source of his emotions, his sense of the meaning of life, his insight into it, his vision of himself, his power and worth. What would give him the claim to rule over a great and ancient people and have his voice heard with awe in the councils of the mighty if not his mastery of the remarkable machine rooted in this ideology?

VIII

The vagueness of the ideology should not blind us to the definiteness of its myth-affirmed will to action or the intensity of the passion it evokes. It nourishes not so much love of the future, which is vague, as hatred of the present, which is clear and visible. Until the millennium, the god of history is a god of wrath. Only after Judgment Day's dreadful work has been completed will there be room for love among the saved. "Class hatred," wrote Lenin, "is the prime mover of revolution." Since hatred for "the oppressor" predominates over hatred of oppression as such or love for the oppressed, the movement finds no obstacle to sweeping away all existing restraints on power and developing a tyranny of its own, more systematically, pedantically, profoundly and all-embracingly ambitious in its oppression than history has hitherto known. Since there cannot be evil in this system, the paranoid mechanism of projection attributes all evils, and evil itself, to capitalism-imperialism. Domestic shortcomings can be but "vestiges" and "survivals" of the enemy that has not yet been totally rooted out, or the work of conscious or unconscious agents.

But the mechanism of projection is notoriously invulnerable to fact and argument. The doctrine teaches that the enemy must be conspired against, subverted, overthrown: therefore the enemy must surely be conspiring, subverting, striving to overthrow the system which spells his death. In that field the dogma is not shaded by the ambiguities of self-doubt or self-understanding. When the enemy offers gifts, fear him; when he offers kindness, then is he most susject.

If the principle of reality could have penetrated this paranoid barrier, the Grand Alliance of wartime would have done it. "Experience" should then have said: "After all, there is not a single enemy; the imperialists have not formed a 'single, hostile camp;' they did not gang up to put an end to us, their mortal foe; instead, the best and mightiest have offered alliance and friendship." When the Axis should be obviously beaten, it might look as if Communism were at last without an enemy!

But the ideology was equal to this, potentially the gravest crisis in its history. Even before the tide turned, as General Deane, Churchill, Djilas, and others have testified in their reminiscences, the men in the Kremlin were determined to keep it what it was to them: a "strange alliance." They could hardly wait until the tide had in effect securely turned at Casablanca and Stalingrad to begin the "cold war" within the United Nations before the dying hot war was over. Even in 1943 they began to subjugate where their armies had liberated, to create by their acts, or recreate, the enemy whom even as "ally" they had so carefully kept out of their citadel. The Zhdanov campaigns completed the rearming of those who had yielded to the illusion that Communism was now without a mortal enemy whom even as "ally" they had so carefully kept out of eheir citadel. man's-land, the infallible interpreters of the infallible doctrine felt comfortable again in their totalist power at home and their total aspirations abroad.

Khrushchev's main accomplishments in this have been two: domestically, to re-establish the clear lines of party control of all transmission belts (including police, managers, officials, and army) which Stalin's "many hats" and manias had somewhat blurred; externally, to apply Lenin's and Stalin's teachings about "depriving the enemy of even the weakest allies," in a new world of neutralist infant nations.

IX

Finally, there is one aspect of the Communist ideology which distinguishes Leninism from all other varieties of Marxism and it is central to our problem: namely, Lenin's absorption not with the dream of socialism but with the mechanics and dynamics of organization and power. In a world where most intellectuals were in love with ideas and accustomed to the gap between dream and deed, Lenin's idea was organization. He was an organization man, *the* organization man of whatever movement he participated in. An enemy alike to the dawn-to-dusk discussions of the intelligentsia and the "unreliable," "spontaneous" flareups and subsidings of the masses, he was all his life at work on a machine to control untidy, unreckonable, detestable "spontaneity." [10]

Organization, control and centralism were the sacred tripod of power. "*Now* we have become an organized party," he early wrote, "and that means the creation of power, the transformation of the authority of ideas into the authority of power, the subordination of the lower party organs to the higher ones."

It was on these issues that Lenin split the Social Democratic Party at its "unification Congress." They are the unifying thread running through all he has said and written, down to the occasional scraps. The party he created was made in this image: a party of *apparatchiki*—men of the machine—concerned with seizing power, holding power, extending power over all the spontaneous, free, and uncontrollable aspects of life, power to crush what must be crushed, to confine, direct and control the rest. "We must organize everything," Lenin said in 1918 after he had power, "we must take everything in our hands." To the authoritarian trend inherent in an infallible doctrine, he added the further dream of an *apparat*, a machine with "transmission belts," penetrating and using all organizations to "organize everything, take everything into our hands," make wayward, refractory life totally malleable and totally controllable. Out of this totalitarianism was born. Totally organized power over everything is the real core of its ideology.

In place of seeking to close our eyes to this, I am afraid we must learn to keep it in the center of our thinking for the foreseeable future. For of all the appetites of man, the appetite for power is the one most known to grow by what it feeds on, the least likely by its exercise to diminish, be sated, or "erode."

---

10. Lenin even created heresies of his own such as *khvostism* ("tailism")—"dragging at the tail of the spontaneous mass movement," and "slavish kowtowing before spontaneity." In 1920 he wrote: "Petit-bourgeois spontaneity is more terrible than all the Denikins, Kolchaks, and Yudeniches put together!"

II POLAND:

THE ACID TEST OF

A PEOPLE'S PEACE*

The decision handed down to the Polish people from the Crimea conference is ominous for Poland's fate and for the peace. At Teheran secretly, at Yalta openly, Europe was divided into spheres of power, and the three biggest states decided the fate of the lesser ones in the absence of the lesser powers.

The Polish government, which has carried on for five and a half years against the Germans, is put in this position: it must commit suicide by signing away nearly one-half its territory without consulting its people, or else England, which went to war supposedly to defend Poland's integrity, threatens it with disrecognition. The United States, father of the Atlantic Charter violated by this annexation, does likewise. And Russia, which has annexed this territory by unilateral force and set up a puppet government to sanction it, holds over their heads the threat of continued purge of the Polish democrats and socialists who support the Government-in-Exile. Whoever among them is willing to sign away this territory will be permitted to name a few members on the "reorganized" and "broadened" Lublin government formed in Russia by Poles who had renounced their Polish citizenship.

Roughly the Yalta formula for "reorganizing on a broader democratic basis" seems to be: one-third Lublinites; one-third people from inside Poland, where the Lublinites already ruled and where a purge of Polish patriots was raging; and one-third members of the legitimate government, who would have lost their legitimacy and democratic character as soon as they signed away nearly one-half their land without a people's mandate.

The background of the Crimea formula is Teheran and beyond.

Here is what former Polish Premier Mikolajczyk told Anne O'Hare McCormick of *The New York Times* in December 1944, after he returned from one of his fruitless efforts to reach an agreement with Stalin on Polish independence:

---

* Written in 1944. First published in the March 1945 issue of *Common Sense*. The first discussion in English of the responsibility of the Russian government for the Katyn forest murders.

He [Mikolajczyk] went to Moscow prepared to negotiate on the basis of the Curzon line but found no opportunity for discussion. Stalin told him flatly that everything had been settled at Teheran, and nothing remained but for him to sign the agreement already made and cooperate with the Lublin Committee.[1]

And here is what Raymond Daniell of the *Times* cabled:

Premier Stalin sat as judge and jury, and Mr. Churchill had the role of public prosecutor. It was Mr. Churchill who did all the arguing for Premier Stalin at the latest Moscow discussion about Poland's future boundaries. . . . When Mr. Mikolajczyk pleaded for mercy by asking that Vilna and Lwow be included within Poland's frontiers, Mr. Molotov interrupted him by saying: "There is no use discussing that, it was all settled at Teheran." [2]

The Teheran agreement was "one of those great historic partition treaties," according to the *London Observer* of December 18. Not only Poland, but the Balkans, the Baltic, and all Europe were divided into two spheres.

SICKNESS AT THE HEART OF EUROPE

Poland lies in an open plain between Germany and Russia. Russia-Poland-Germany: that triangle of relationships is the heart of Europe. When there is sickness there, Europe is sick, and the peace and order existing are a false order and a false peace.

When Catherine, Frederick, and Maria Theresa began the first partition of Poland in 1772, they laid the basis for the *Dreikaiserbund*—an unholy alliance of guilty accomplices, forced to work together for the crushing of every movement for national independence in Europe, lest it prove contagious and Poland arise from the ashes of partition. It was that partition which made the Romanovs into the watchdogs of reaction in Europe and turned their once fairly tolerant conglomerate of nationalities into a prison house of peoples.

Only when Russia and Germany finally parted company over conflicts in other areas and when, paradoxically—both of them suffered defeat in World War I, did Poland arise phoenixlike from the ashes of its desolation.

With its history of a century and a half of suppressed struggle the new Poland suffered inevitably from an exacerbated nationalism which made things hard for the minorities under its rule. It was tortured, too, by fear of renascent German and renascent Russian might. All through

1. Dec. 20, 1944.
2. Dec. 12, 1944.

the 1930s it went to great lengths to keep peace with its two powerful neighbors. And this was, it must be noted, while Poland was under the rule of the reactionary, dictatorial, nationalist "Colonels' government" of Pilsudski and Beck. Beneath the surface, the democratic, progressive, socialist, and agrarian forces gained steadily in strength and cohesion so that they alone were able to form a government commanding mass support when Poland was attacked, and they alone were able to carry on the resistance underground. That was the origin of the four-party agreement (Socialist, Peasant, Christian Democratic, and National Democratic [3]) which secretly governed underground Poland and whose public expression was the Government-in-Exile in London.

On February 10, 1935, Marshal Goering suggested to Polish Foreign Minister Beck "an anti-Russian alliance and a joint attack on Russia . . . the Ukraine would become a Polish sphere of influence, and North Western Russia would be Germany's." Again on February 16, 1937, Goering renewed the proposal.[4] The offer was made again by Von Ribbentrop on September 29, 1938, and, for the last time, on March 21, 1939.[5] On each occasion the Polish government declined to entertain the proposal. Thereupon, Hitler decided to punish Poland for its "impudence" and to make it the next area of German expansion.

At this point, alarmed at the results of their appeasement in connection with the German minority areas of Czechoslovakia, the British and French governments decided that it was time to call a halt to German expansion. They decided to urge Poland, a second-rate power, to run the risk of war with the German military machine. To that end they offered Poland a guarantee. Since the question of Poland's independence and frontiers is now under dispute, the language of the public statement of the British prime minister to Parliament (March 31, 1939) is of interest:

I now have to inform the House that . . . in the event of any action which clearly threatened Polish independence, *and which the Polish Government accordingly considered it vital to resist,* His Majesty's Government would feel themselves bound to lend the Polish Government all support in their power. . . . I may add that the French Government authorized me to make it plain that they stand in the same position. . . .[6]

3. The National Democrats were a conservative party opposed to the prewar "Colonels' dictatorship."

4. Texts in *Polish Facts and Figures*, No. 8, Sept. 1, 1944.

5. Dallin, *Soviet Russia's Foreign Policy* (Yale, 1943), pp. 6, 15.

6. Text in British Blue Book; italics added.

MOLOTOV-RIBBENTROP PACT UNLEASHES WORLD WAR II

Now Hitler's problem became what it has always been when Germany engages in war with the West: to safeguard the rear in the east—to avoid, at any cost, a two-front war. He bethought himself of the possibility "of restoring the classic relationship between Germany and Russia" by a new partition of Poland.[7] That partition, Poland's fourth, was the real foundation of the Russo-German nonaggression and friendship pact of August 23, 1939, which assured the German rear and thus unleashed the Second World War. Such was Poland's reward for having refused a pact with Germany against Russia.

Two days after the Molotov-Ribbentrop pact was made public, Great Britain renewed her guarantee to Poland, in still more sweeping terms. Again Poland was made the judge of which territorial demand it considered "vital to resist." The guarantee was extended to include "any European power" and even "any attempt to undermine independence by processes of economic penetration or in any other way."[8]

For seventeen days the Polish army fought against the fresh might of the Wehrmacht (a longer time by far than the much mightier Red Army was able to hold its portion of the Polish plain in 1941). Badly hurt, but unbroken, the Polish armies retreated and converged toward the east and south, with the aim of a last-stand fight in the protective terrain of the Pripet marshes and the Carpathians and the hope of seeking refuge in Russia if all were lost. Then, on September 17, the Red Army struck from the rear. Not Germany but Poland was forced to fight a two-front war.[9]

The precision with which Red Army and Wehrmacht moved to their appointed demarcation line showed how carefully this joint operation had been worked out in advance.[10] Russia got 77,620 square miles, Germany 72,806. But Germany's portion held twenty-two million people and Russia's only thirteen million. However, to Russia that area was of prime importance because it contained in its multi-national population most of the Ukrainians not already in the Soviet Union. Thus it promised to put an end to the six-century struggle for the control of the Ukraine, originally part of the Polish kingdom. And only with all the Ukrainians in one state

7. See Von Ribbentrop's statement as quoted in the French Yellow Book, *Documents Politiques 1938-9*, Document 123; and Hitler's address on the seventh anniversary of his seizure of power. The relevant citations are also available in Dallin, *Soviet Russia's Foreign Poicy*, pp. 27ff.

8. Full text in Government Blue Book (London, 1939).

9. Despite the heartbreaking news, Warsaw, largely under socialist leadership, held out for three weeks, from September 8 to September 29.

10. See *Dienst aus Deutschland*, Sept. 23, 1939, and text of Molotov-Ribbentrop "Treaty of Mutual Friendship and Agreement on Frontiers."

would it be easy to keep in check tendencies for an independent, united Ukraine.

"Both countries recognize this division as final," read the Molotov-Ribbentrop declaration to the world, "and will resist any interference on the part of the other powers." England and France, the declaration continued, which had gone to war to safeguard the integrity of Poland, should recognize that the very country had ceased forever to exist. Both the German and Russian governments ". . . will pool their efforts to liquidate the war . . . Should the efforts of both governments fail, then the fact will be established that England and France are responsible for the continuation of the war, and the governments of Germany and Soviet Russia will consult as to necessary measures."

The high point of this astonishing "friendship" was reached that December 21, when Ribbentrop telegraphed to Stalin:

Remembering those historic hours in the Kremlin which laid the foundation for the decisive turn in the relationship between our two great peoples and thus created the basis for a long and lasting friendship, I beg you to accept on your sixtieth birthday my warmest congratulations.

And Stalin replied: "The friendship of the peoples of Germany and the Soviet Union, cemented by blood, will long remain firm."

The blood was Polish blood.[11]

Fortunately for Poland, and for the honor and ultimate destiny of Russia and of the world, the cement did not prove firm. Hitler was ideologically more uncomfortable about the alliance than Stalin. Drunk with easy victories over Poland, Holland, Belgium, Denmark, and France— with only England to "finish off"—Hitler broke the pact and attacked Russia in June 1941. The Russians, who had determined to Russianize the half of Poland which they had gotten from the pact with Hitler, had been engaged in wholesale arrests, deportations and executions of the élite. Their aim had been nothing less than to eliminate all possible leadership of resistance and nationhood. The first batch of exiles were army officers. The next were "members of the Polish intelligentsia, state and local government officials, teachers, judges, lawyers, and the professional classes generally, together with a number of Jews and Ukrainians of the same classes and other middle-class people." Then deportation was extended to Polish and Jewish labor leaders and leaders of the socialist party, the Jewish socialist bund, and all other Polish parties, democratic as well as reactionary. Thereafter, deportation was extended "to Polish and Ukrainian farmers."

11. The Red Army lost 737 killed and 1862 wounded. The Polish losses are unknown; but *Red Star* reported that 191,000 Polish military prisoners were taken in the brief campaign.

The main movement from Soviet-occupied Poland to the East began in June, 1941, immediately before the German invasion, and increased in volume after the German invasion had begun. Hundreds of thousands of people were either forcibly removed or evacuated to inner and Asiatic Russia. . . . According to a statement issued by the Polish Foreign Minister on May 7, 1942, one and a half million persons were transferred. The [Jewish] Joint Distribution Committee estimates the total number of evacuees from Soviet-occupied Polish territory at two million, of whom 600,000 were Jews, these figures including those who were transferred in 1939-1940.

This quotation and all words in quotation marks in the paragraph preceding are from Eugene M. Kulischer's study of *The Displacement of Population in Europe*.[12] He also includes a breakdown of 1.2 million of the total, by regions of Russia and Siberia to which they were sent, a breakdown "on the basis of information collected locally." Most interesting are the large numbers of Jews. Some of these were refugees from German-occupied western Poland who did not wish to become Soviet citizens. Others were Polish-speaking and Yiddish-speaking Jews from eastern Poland, including Jewish socialists and trade unionists. Others, it should be noted, were evacuated only after the German armies began their advance and were glad to be sent to Russian concentration camps as preferable to German. Professor Kulischer points out that the figure of 600,000 Jews is accepted by the Institute of Jewish Affairs, whereas the American Jewish Yearbook [13] gives it as 500,000. The lowest estimate was made from Moscow itself by the Russian correspondent of the Jewish Telegraph Agency, Wolkowicz, who sets the figure at 350,000.[14] The most probable figure is that of the Joint Distribution Committee, which handles relief. In any case, several hundred thousand Jews, many Ukrainian farmers, political leaders, and leaders of the Ukrainian Uniate Catholic Church, and many White Russians—figures not available—were deported during the period of the friendship pact with Germany. These facts dispose completely of the argument to the effect that only "ethnic Poles" failed to welcome the seizure of eastern Poland.

EXTIRPATION OF A NATION'S LEADERSHIP

So thorough was this seizure of all possible persons of leadership in eastern Poland that, when the Russians decided to set up the Lublin puppet government, they had to use a number of ex-Poles who had become Soviet citizens (for example a Communist, Bierut, Chairman of the

---

12. *The Displacement of Population in Europe*, Montreal, International Labor Office of the League of Nations, 1943, pp. 58-59.

13. Vol. 44, p. 239.

14. *Contemporary Jewish Record*, April, 1943.

Council) and had to take others out of Soviet jails or concentration camps. For instance, the former Commander-in-Chief of the Lublin Polish auxiliary troops of the Red Army, General Berling, was in a Soviet prison camp until Sikorski negotiated his release in 1941. Unique is the case of Dr. Sommerstein, until recently the Jewish representative in the Lublin Council, who was both prisoner and Soviet citizen in turn. He came from the extreme right of Polish Jewry, belonging to the right wing of Zionism. At a time when all other Jewish groups boycotted the vote on the constitution of 1935, as a deputy in the Polish Sejm he voted yes.[15] While in a Soviet jail after 1939, he was pressed to accept Soviet citizenship and became a Soviet agent for the purposes of forming the Lublin Council. He did and soon after blossomed out from jailbird to Lublin leader. He was even named as delegate "from Polish Jewry" to the World Jewish Congress in Atlantic City. But he was incautious enough to ask for a visa for his daughter also. His own visa was canceled, and he has disappeared from the Lublin Provisional Government.

Such thumbnail biographies give some idea of the conditions under which the Lublin government was formed. We need only add the detail that some of the members of the London government are also ex-residents of Soviet prisons. One good example is the venerable Polish historian Stanislaw Grabski, president of the National Council of Poland. Another example is Jan Kwapinski, socialist metal worker, who was in a tsarist prison from 1906 to 1917 and then became first chairman of the Orel Soviet. He returned to Poland to lead the Farm Laborers Union and in 1939 was elected mayor of Lodz. The NKVD deported him to Siberia once more when the Red Army attacked Poland in 1939. Freed by the Stalin-Sikorski agreement of 1941, he went to London and became Minister of Industry in the Government-in-Exile.

If the Poles were generous in forgiving all these outrages, the Russian government, in the first blush of its new agreements with the United Nations against the invading Germans, was generous, too. The first sentence of the Polish-Soviet agreement of July 30, 1941, reads: "The Government of the Union of Soviet Socialist Republics recognizes the Soviet-German treaties of 1939 as to territorial changes in Poland as having lost their validity."

To make this historic sentence doubly clear, the British Foreign Office, the same day, quoted an official note of Eden to Sikorski:

---

15. The frequently raised political issue of the 1935 constitution versus the 1921 constitution is a false issue. The London government is made up of parties and individuals who fought the 1935 constitution and the Pilsudski-Beck government; most of them were in jail under the latter regime. They long ago voted to call a Constituent Assembly, not to return to the constitution of 1921, but to adopt a new democratic constitution as soon as the country should be free to express its will.

On the occasion of the signature of the Polish-Soviet agreement of today . . . I desire to assure you that His Majesty's Government do not recognize any territorial changes which have been effected in Poland since August 1939.

And the British communiqué continued:

General Sikorski handed Mr. Eden the following reply: "This corresponds with the view of the Polish Government, which . . . has never recognized any territorial changes effected in Poland since the outbreak of the war."

These notes of Stalin, Eden, and Sikorski leave no shadow of a doubt that the intention, like the original British guarantee, was to restore the frontiers of Poland, to defend which war had been declared.

MURDERS IN THE KATYN FOREST

On September 17, 1940, the first anniversary of the invasion of Poland by the Red Army, that army's official organ, *Krasnaya Zvezda* (*Red Star*), boasted that in the brief attack 191,000 Polish prisoners had been taken, including 10,000 officers. These officers had been kept in three large prison camps—at Kozielsk, at Starobielsk, at Ostashkoff—and a small group, near 400, at Griazovec. But on April 5, 1940, the Soviet government had begun "transferring them to some unknown destination." All communication with their families ceased.

Now the Polish government desperately needed these officers to form new armies of the hundreds of thousands of prisoners in the Soviet Union. However, only the small group of officers who had been interned at Griazovec put in appearance at the mobilization centers, while not one officer showed up from those who had been in the major camps. Gravely concerned, the Polish government repeatedly asked for information. They were told by Molotov, by Vyshinsky, and by Stalin himself, that these officers had all been released and would appear in time. Sometimes the excuse was given that they had been transferred to a far-northern camp and could not come until winter was over, that they were making their way on foot. In December 1941, General Sikorski, visiting Stalin in the Kremlin, gave him a partial list (3,843 army officers). Once more Stalin answered that they had been set free.

In April 1943, the German press and radio announced that they had found the bodies of thousands of executed Polish officers buried in the forest of Katyn, near Smolensk. Only then (April 16, 1943) did the Soviet news agency, Tass, declare that the Polish officers had never been transferred inland but had been "captured by the Germans in the summer of 1941."

To make matters worse, the Polish underground was still reeling from the shock of Litvinov's letters to the presidents of the American Federation of Labor and of the Congress of Industrial Organizations, admitting that Henryk Ehrlich and Victor Alter had been executed by the NKVD. These two outstanding leaders of the Polish socialist movement and the Polish Jewish labor movement had been heroes of socialist and antifascist struggle all their lives. Imprisoned by the Russians in 1939, they had been released by the agreement of July 1941 and were engaged in the task of building a world Jewish antifascist movement. Then they were arrested again at midnight on December 4, 1941. Because of their prominence in the Labor and Socialist International, labor leaders and leaders of American public opinion, including Eleanor Roosevelt, signed petitions for their release. For more than a year no answer; then—though it seems they had been shot on December 5, 1941—in February 1943, Maxim Litvinov officially informed William Green and Philip Murray that they had been executed. The news that these beloved Jewish antifascist leaders had been killed by the Russian government had barely filtered into the Polish underground when the German radio began its series of gruesome broadcasts on the murdered officers in the Katyn forest.

The Polish government would have been unworthy of its people's trust if it had not attempted to clarify this terrible state of affairs. It had recourse to the only neutral agency in wartime, the International Red Cross at Geneva. The answer of the Russian government was to refuse the Red Cross permission to investigate and to break off relations with the Polish government. The Russians charged the Polish government which had been conducting an effective underground resistance to Germany since 1939, with being "pro-German."

Even after April 1943, if the Russians had permitted a Red Cross inquiry or invited United Nations representatives to be present when they exhumed the bodies and investigated—their first duty was to invite the Poles to be present!—doubts might have been resolved. But these bodies were dug up, a report and exhibit prepared by Russian authorities and then a few representatives of the foreign press were called in.

Here are some passages from W. H. Lawrence's account from Smolensk, to *The New York Times* of January 27, 1944:

The Russian authorities showed us hundreds of bodies, each with a bullet hole in the base of the skull . . . each execution seemed to have been individual. The reporters said that the experiences of the German atrocity investigations at Kiev and Kharlov were mass executions carried out with machine guns. . . .

Some wore heavy field overcoats lined with fur. Later we asked the commission why some prisoners were so warmly dressed if they had been shot by the Germans in August or September. Mr. Tolstoi answered that the prisoners were wearing the clothing they had when they were captured by the Red Army in 1939. [That would mean that for a year and a half they had been wearing furs summer and winter.]

However this terrible question will eventually be solved, the perfectly proper request for a Red Cross investigation was only the pretext for breaking off relations with the Polish government and subsequently setting up the Lublin puppet government. The real reason was that, after it had become clear that the Russian armies would hold in retreat and the tide would eventually turn, Stalin decided to return to his demand for approximately half of Poland, as based on the Molotov-Ribbentrop line of 1939.

THE MOLOTOV-RIBBENTROP-CURZON LINE

The Molotov-Ribbentrop line for the partition of Poland has been tactfully rebaptized the "Curzon line." But, with the exception of a small sector around Bialystok, which the Russians were willing to permit the Poles to keep, it is the Molotov-Ribbentrop line of 1939. The part that Russia now [16] wishes to annex, without negotiation and without waiting till the war's end, is slightly more than forty-five per cent of prewar Poland, instead of slightly more than fifty per cent, as in 1939.

To call it the "Curzon line" is but a face-saving device to make it easier for Churchill to bring pressure on the Polish government in London and to obscure from world public opinion the fact that it is essentially the Molotov-Ribbentrop line. Actually the line antedates Churchill's countryman, Lord Curzon, for it is substantially the same line arrived at when Catherine divided the spoils of Poland with Frederick.

Lord Curzon's name got attached to this old historic frontier between Germany's share of partitioned Poland and Russia's, briefly and quite by accident, in 1919. Poland had just been reborn during World War I and, under Marshal Pilsudski, had made an effort to recover all of its old territory, or set up buffer states between Poland and the Soviet Union. But the young Polish state was too weak and war-ravaged to make good its over-ambitious drive. When its armies were repulsed and rolled back, the Soviet forces in turn tried to take all of Poland and Sovietize it. They drove up to the very gates of Warsaw but then proved too weak to finish the job. Both sides became anxious for peace. The Allied powers, who had just reconstituted Poland, proposed a temporary military demarcation line between the two exhausted armies, while peace was being negotiated.

16. *I.e.,* March, 1945.

The note specifically stated: "The rights that Poland may be able to establish over the territories situated to the east of the said line are expressly reserved."

Moreover, a glance at the map of Central Europe will reveal that the "Curzon" armistice line of World War I did not include a single square mile of that part of Poland which had belonged to Austria-Hungary, the area known as Eastern Galicia. The Soviet armies at the time had not entered any part of Eastern Galicia. It is an area which for more than six hundred years was a part of Poland and never in all history belonged to Russia for a single day until Molotov and Ribbentrop carved up Poland in September 1939.

As if to make matters historically still more clear, the Soviet government in 1919 had rejected Lord Curzon's demarcation line as a suggested territorial line which would be "unfair to Poland" and had told the Poles that if they would negotiate directly they would get a territorial line more favorable to their hopes and claims. On March 18, 1921, the two countries signed the Treaty of Riga. The line agreed upon was neither the line of old Poland before the First Partition, nor the line between Catherine's and Frederick's shares in 1772. It was roughly the line of the Second Partition of Poland in 1793, except—and this is most important—*except that the Poles kept all of Eastern Galicia*. On the basis of this line, peace was established between the two countries and maintained in a series of nonaggression and friendship pacts from 1921 to 1939.

During all the period from 1921 to 1939 the Soviet government praised the settlement as fair to Poland and favorable to the Soviet Union. As late as 1941 the *History of the USSR*, published by the Historical Institute of the Academy of Sciences and approved as a secondary-school textbook by the Soviet Commissariat of Education, stated.

In March, 1921, in Riga, a peace treaty was signed between Soviet Russia and Poland. By the Treaty of Riga the Soviet Republic established for itself a more advantageous frontier with Poland since it moved the frontier eighty to one hundred kilometers farther to the west.[17]

Now world and American public opinion is being bewildered by a complex of new arguments about the Molotov-Ribbentrop "Curzon" line. Eastern Poland is ethnologically composite. It contains Poles, Jews, Ukrainians, White Russians, in numbers which make the Poles the largest single ethnic group but not an absolute majority. If an honest plebiscite were taken, it is argued, all but the Poles would vote to become Soviet. To this a democratic-minded American would be moved to answer:

17. *History of the USSR* (Moscow, 1941), p. 252.

"Then why not wait until after the war—surely no honest plebiscite can be taken under the conditions of mass deportations and war—and give the people of the area a chance to vote whether they want to be Polish citizens or Soviet citizens?"

But the "ethnic" argument is less than honest, as proved by the hundreds of thousands of Jews, Ukrainians, and even White Russians whom the Red Army deported from this area. The Ruthenians (Galician Ukrainians) have never been altogether happy under Polish rule; however, what the Ukrainian National Democratic Union of Eastern Poland has always wanted is not to be joined to Russia but to become an independent Ukrainian country. The rather cruel attempt at Polonization of Eastern Galicia by the Poles in 1930 might have made these Ukrainians more pro-Russian had it not been for the forced collectivization and man-made famine in the Soviet Ukraine in 1932. These Ukrainians of Galicia were even more anti-Russian than anti-Polish, and it was among them that Hitler found a few quislings, whereas he could find none among the Poles or Jews of Poland.

If the Russians had permitted a true plebiscite in 1939, when there was no Polish state left and the choice was: to Germany, or to Russia, or a new independent state of eastern Poland—then possibly the Russians would have gotten a sizable majority for incorporation. But they have so long been unaccustomed to permit their own citizens to choose between rival sets of candidates and rival platforms or proposals that they were incapable of holding a true plebiscite. First they deported hundreds of thousands of leaders and active members of all parties and unions; then they rigged up a totalitarian "plebiscite" in which there was only one set of candidates.

How little the Russian authorities took this totalitarian travesty seriously is evidenced by the fact that they ceded Bialystok to the Lublin puppet government although it had an "ethnic" majority of White Russians and Jews and also voted "ninety-nine per cent" for incorporation into White Russia, of which it became the capital.

The fact is that besides "blood brotherhood"—to quote the original Soviet document of annexation—there is the question of democracy and civil liberties versus dictatorship, the question of religion, the question of property forms, and many other issues which would influence voters in a free election. The Ukrainians of eastern Poland, for example, are largely Catholic Uniates and not Russian Orthodox, while the Poles are Roman Catholics.

FREE POLAND OR A REGIME OF BAYONET AND PURGE

The real question is not how much of prewar Poland shall belong to Russia and how much to Poland, which went to war to defend its territory and sovereignty. The real question is whether there is to be an independent Poland at all.

The membership of the Lublin government is not such as to inspire confidence in the type of government it would offer Poland if it were genuinely independent. But the make-up of this "free, strong, and independent" government is less important than the fact that it was made in Moscow and made for the specific purpose of signing away almost half of Poland in the name of a people under the German heel, who could not be consulted.[18] No government made in Moscow, symbol of so many partitions of this unhappy land, and no government which began its life with such an act, can possibly rule over Poland except with the aid of continuous and ruthless purges.

Conscious of its weakness, the Lublin government arrested and purged the leaders of the underground in the territories whose administration had been entrusted to it by the advancing Soviet armies.[19] During Warsaw's heroic sixty-three-day uprising against the Germans, not only did the puppet government try to influence world opinion against giving arms and aid to the insurrection, but General Rola-Zymierski arrested and disarmed underground forces of the Polish Home Army that were going to its relief. Nor can the Lublin government rule except with the aid of Russian bayonets and constant Russian intervention to hold down the people over which it rules. A goverment so constituted violates every principle of democracy. A government resting on foreign bayonets is a perpetual threat of war.

As democrats, we should insist that the Poles be permitted to have a government of their own choosing; that territorial settlements, to be decent, enduring, and safe for peace, should be arrived at by negotiation and agreement; that if there is disagreement—and there is—then the question be postponed till the end of the war and be settled by the impartial arbitration of all the United Nations.

Moreover, the people in the disputed area should have the final voice in settling their own fate. We must not be party to a scheme in which millions of men and women are handed around as if they were bundles of faggots or lumps of coal. Nor can we ask the Polish Government-in-

18. And for the purpose of having a pliable government which would not investigate the Katyn Forest murders.

19. By February there were five permanent and several temporary concentration camps in which members of the Polish Home Army and underground were being imprisoned. See *The New York Times*, Feb. 7, 1945.

Exile and its underground Home Parliament to consent to the loss of nearly one-half of their territory and one-third of their population before they have had a decent opportunity to consult their own people and get a mandate from them.

The Polish government, facing the desperate conditions of a series of ruthless purges and *faits accomplis*, has declared itself willing to negotiate concerning the "Curzon line" as a "temporary demarcation line" until the end of the war, begging only for guarantees of genuine independence in the remaining half of Poland and one or two concessions on the "Curzon line"—particularly the historic, overwhelmingly Polish city of Lwow, which never belonged to Russia in six hundred years of its existence, until 1939. These are pitifully modest requests. It is cruel and false to call these elementary things "perfectionism." If the Polish government goes beyond them, under the pressure of Churchill and Stalin, as part of the trade of Greeks for Poles, then it is forever disgraced in the eyes of its own people. It becomes a puppet, too, bearing the same brand on its forehead as has marked Lublin from the day of its birth.

What kind of peace could the world build on such foundations? A peace that would begin with an open wound once more in the heart of Europe. Resentful Poles would detest the puppet government that had betrayed them and had been the agent of one more partition—the fifth. Russia, too, would be less secure. Generosity would make for a good and grateful neighbor. The opposite policy would be capitalized upon by the first new enemy of Russia that might arise. Worst of all, for the Poles, would be the horrible "compensation" with which they are now being tempted—thousands of square miles of ethnic Germany, more than a truncated Poland could ever digest or hold. That, too, would compel Poland to rest on Russian bayonets.

Who can fail to see in such a "settlement" the fearful outlines of a third world war? Who can fail to see how the moral conditions under which the preesnt war is being waged have deteriorated since this secret trade of Greeks for Poles was hatched at Teheran?

It is a frightful travesty of our "Good Neighbor" policy to compare it to this. Since we proclaimed the policy, when have we ever compelled any government to sign away half its territory, deported a million and a half of its people, murdered the leaders and active members of its democratic and socialist parties? Doubtless, we have made mistakes—but there are no invasions, no deportations, no purges, no annexations by force. Nor would the conscience of America tolerate them. Actually it is just such beginnings of a higher morality in the relations between great powers and their lesser neighbors that is at stake. The kind of Europe and the kind of world which will emerge from this war is being determined now. Poland has become the test for a moral and enduring peace.

—March 1945

III THE CONVERGENCE
THEORY IN
HISTORICAL PERSPECTIVE*

Recently, when John Kenneth Galbraith departed for a trip to the Soviet Union, he sent a message to his friend, Sidney Hook, "Tell Sidney not to worry, I won't come back a Communist." To which Hook retorted, "I'm not worried that he'll come back a Communist; I'm afraid he'll come back saying that *they* aren't Communists." Galbraith returned to add the weight of some four hundred pages of his wit and learning to the already fashionable convergence theory. This is fortunate for the present writer since it excuses me from trying to expound in my own words a theory to which I would find it difficult to do justice. Indeed, Galbraith also supplied a timely five-hundred-word resumé of his viewpoint in the course of an interview with *The New York Times*'s crack reporter, Anthony Lewis, who tape-recorded it and published it in full in the magazine section of Sunday, December 18, 1966. The interview concluded with the following exchange:

GALBRAITH: The nature of technology—the nature of the large organization that sustains technology, and the nature of the planning that technology requires—has an imperative of its own, and this is causing a convergence in all industrial societies. In the Eastern European societies it's leading to a decentralization of power from the state to the firm; in the Western European [and American] industrial societies it's leading to *ad hoc* planning. In fewer years than we imagine this will produce a rather indistinguishable melange of planning and market influences.

The overwhelming fact is that if you have to have a massive technical complex, and there will be a certain similarity in the organization, and in the related social organization, whether that steel complex is in Novosibirsk or in Nova Huta, Poland, or in Gary, Ind.

LEWIS: *Are you suggesting that as the two societies converge, the Communist society will necessarily introduce greater political and cultural freedom?*

GALBRAITH: I'm saying precisely that. The requirements of deep scientific perception and deep technical specialization cannot be reconciled with intel-

* First published in July 1968 in *Sidney Hook and the Contemporary World*.

lectual regimentation. They inevitably lead to intellectual curiosity and to a measure of intellectual liberalism.

And on our side the requirements of large organization impose a measure of discipline, a measure of subordination of the individual to the organization, which is very much less than the individualism that has been popularly identified with the Western economy.[1]

There are fashions in theories as in clothes. Just now it is the fashion among many political scientists, sociologists, sovietologists, and economists to speak of convergence when they write about the Soviet Union or discuss relations between the Russian government and the American. Though it has only now attained to high fashion, in one form or another the theory has been around for some time. Thus in the diary of Lady Kennet of the Deane, made available to me while living in Lord Kennet's home in London, I found this entry for a date in late May 1921: "Nansen was here to tea and gave me the reassuring news that our troubles with Russia are over. Lenin is introducing a New Economic Policy which restores a free market and represents a return to capitalist exchange of goods in Russia." Such wishful thinking is one of the perennial springs that has fed the current of the convergence theory.

In 1932 and 1933 there was a spate of books on technocracy, all assuring us that the United States and the Soviet Union were converging toward a common industrial and political system in which technologists or technocrats would determine policy and set the basic standards for social and economic life. In 1941, James Burnham published his *Managerial Revolution*, extrapolating one of the complex curves in modern industrial life in a tangent into outer space. His book was a confident prophecy that in all advanced industrial lands:

Institutions and beliefs are undergoing a process of rapid transformation. The conclusion of this period of transformation, to be expected in the comparatively near future, will find society organized through a quite different set of major economic, social, and political institutions and exhibiting quite different major social beliefs or ideologies. Within the new social structure a different social group or class—the managers—will be the dominant or ruling class. [These changes] will constitute the transformation of society to a managerial structure. . . . The theory of the managerial revolution is not merely predicting what may happen in a hypothetical future but is an interpretation of what *already* has happened and is now happening. Its prediction is that the process which has started and which has already gone a great distance will continue and reach completion.[2]

1. Emphasis here, as in all quoted passages, is in the original.
2. James Burnham, *The Managerial Revolution*, pp. 74-75. Mr. Burnham has long since abandoned the prophecy, but the notion that managers and technocrats are running, or will soon run, both societies is still a key element in the convergence theory and central to John Kenneth Galbraith's *The New Industrial State*. From Burnham to Galbraith, economic determinists and economists generally have found it hard to believe that politicians and governments keep such specialists on tap, but not on top.

When Hitler "perfidiously," as the Russian textbooks say, double-crossed his ally, Stalin, during World War II forcing him into the camp of the democracies, the convergence theory took on somewhat different forms. There were two new variants, one a popular view, the other a product of the wishful thinking of homesick exiled Russian intellectuals who in the twenties had found refuge in America and made a place for themselves in our academic life.

The popular variant sprang from the naïve crusading nature of American wars with our ingrained tendency to envision our enemies as devils and our allies as knights in shining armor. Hitler's deeds gave plenty of material to justify the devil theory, but we tended to extend it throughout the history of Germany, to every living German, and to generations yet unborn, while we seemed to regard the Japanese people, their leaders, and their sovereigns as villains rather than monsters. The Russian armies fought valiantly as they suffered the brunt of German attack and invasion, which gave us a sense of moral debt, a feeling that was promptly put to use by Stalin and his apologists to obscure the moral issues of the peace. This popular version of the convergence theory said: "The Russians are much like people everywhere and want what we want. [The people of Germany and Japan seemed to be subhuman exceptions, but for various reasons, we were more indulgent toward the Italians]. Since people everywhere want the same things, it will be easy to build 'one world' with a sobered and friendly Joseph Stalin after the war is over. He now knows the value of democracy, who his friends are, and how destructive war is, so the Grand Alliance will continue into the peace; together we will build a world in which the peace-loving countries will become steadily more like each other and come ever closer together." [3]

A more sophisticated theory came from the Russian intellectuals who had been exiled or had fled from Russia in the twenties and become important writers and teachers in sociology or political science in the United States, always retaining a deep emotional attachment to the land of their birth, such men, for instance, as N. S. Timashev and Pitirim Sorokin. Professor Timashev delivered a series of war-time lectures on this theme, then published them as *The Great Retreat* in 1946. Professor Sorokin toured the country lecturing on the convergence theory in 1942 and 1943 and in January 1944 published a book in which all his knowledge of the two lands was brought into play along with his favorite

3. These words in quotation marks are quoted from no one in particular but recurred in a thousand editorials and addresses, and with slight variations were to be heard almost everywhere. I heard them from many platforms on which I debated with Frederick Schuman, Henry Pratt Fairchild, Louis Dollivet, Joseph Barnes, Corliss Lamont, Isaac Deutscher, Vera Micheles Dean, Kirby Page, Sir Bernard Pares, and a wide range of other speakers. It is not my intention to lump these diverse people with diverse motives together in any way beyond the fact that they all advanced in more or less similar language the view expressed in this synthetic, generalized quotation.

sociological, cultural, and ethical generalizations. His *America and Russia* proved enormously popular, running through a number of printings in the first year of its publication, and was reprinted in revised form as late as 1950.

Joseph Stalin did not make things easy for his thesis, for within the next few years, every land that his troops occupied alone was endowed with a "people's democracy" and a purge of democrats, liberals, conservatives, national patriots, and "national Communists" while lands like Germany and Austria that underwent dual or tripartite occupation had a line cut right across them wherever the Russian troops held sway. This seizure of "liberated" lands was followed by the rejection of Marshall Plan aid,[4] the Zhdanov attack on "kowtowing to the West" and "rootless cosmopolitanism" in the arts and sciences, along with other despotic barbarities too blatant to be ignored. But Professor Sorokin was not to be put off in his hopes and creed, for in 1950 he published his revised edition in which he took account of the "Cold War" to minimize and explain away the resultant "incompatibilities." The "seemingly conflicting values [he wrote] . . . are so insignificant that their 'incompatibility' amounts to no more than the 'incompatibility' of the advertisements for this or that brand of cigarettes, each claiming superiority over all others." [5]

Professor Sorokin's study is of special interest because of the broad scope of his analysis of the "spiritual, historical, and socio-cultural compatibilities" of the two nations, because of his influential position as a Professor of Sociology first in Saint Petersburg and then at Harvard, because he is the acknowledged or unacknowledged source of many of the more limited variants of the convergence theory, and because of his deep attachment to both America and Russia and his singular Russian talent to suffer and forgive, and one is tempted to add, to forget.

In Russia Sorokin had been a professor of law and sociology; a secretary of Kerensky's cabinet, editor of the Socialist Revolutionary daily, *Volya Naroda*, which Lenin shut down in February 1918; delegate to the Peasant Soviet, which Lenin submerged in the Soviet of Workers and Soldiers Deputies; delegate to the Constituent Assembly, which Lenin dispersed by force after its first session. On November 22, 1922, Sorokin sent a letter to *Pravda* in which he renounced all political activity and declared his intention to limit himself to teaching and scientfic work. Lenin welcomed his "straightforwardness and sincerity" but, in accordance with the Leninist tendency to politicize everything, added a warning to Sorokin that teaching and scientific work could also be "politically re-

---

4. It seems hard for the new coterie of "revisionist" historians to remember how naïve Roosevelt was about Stalin, how swiftly we withdrew our troops from Europe, and how generous we were in offering massive Marshall Plan aid to Russia and all her neighbors.

5. *Russia and the United States,* London, 1950, p. 176.

actionary." Shortly thereafter the Professor lost his chair and his right to teach when he ventured to publish a study of the breakdown of marriage under the influence of war and revolution and the postcard divorce system. Lenin labeled him a "diplomaed flunkey of clericalism" and announced the intention to "politely dispatch him," i.e., exile him, to "some country with a bourgeois democracy, the proper place for such feudalists." [6] That is how Sorokin found his way, alive, to America and to Harvard. By the time he wrote *America and Russia*, Professor Sorokin had not only forgiven the fact that Lenin stopped him from writing, teaching, engaging in political activity, and living in the land of his birth, but he seemed to forget that Stalin, less "polite," would have taken his life along with his honor. Indeed, Sorokin wrote of the purges as if they were themselves nothing but a great and historically foreordained step forward toward convergence:

> The cycle of the Russian Revolution is clearly demonstrated by the purges of Communist leaders. . . . By whom? Not by counter-revolutionists or anti-Communists. No. They were executed, imprisoned, banished, or excommunicated by Stalin and the Communist Party itself. To these should be awarded the first prize for the mortal blow dealt the Communist phase of the Revolution. . . . Stalin won because he *moved with the current* of history and *not against it*. . . . Those who were purged were purged because they sought to stem the tide of historical destiny. . . . If in the future Stalin and his followers should try to revive Communism as it existed in the first stage of the Revolution, seek to stem the tide of historical destiny, they would be liquidated as inexorably as Trotsky and his adherents. That is why I do not worry about what Stalin or any other leader may think or do. . . .[7]

Sorokin found it possible to speak of the period of the purges as one of the "*restoration of law* and *government by law*," and as the period of the "new Constitution:"

> The profound change which the *structure of the central government* has undergone is marked by the new Soviet Constitution of 1936. In all its essentials the structure of the government under this constitution is explicitly democratic. . . . To be sure, the new Constitution has remained largely a theoretical reform; its provisions have been realized only in part, owing to the short period that has elapsed since its enactment.[8]

"Its provisions have been realized only in part" is a masterpiece of understatement. It is hard to believe it could escape Sorokin's notice

---

6. *Lenin*, Vol. 33, pp. 208-209. Sorokin was first condemned to death, but the death sentence was then commuted on Lenin's order to exile and deprivation of citizenship.

7. *Op. cit.*, pp. 195-196 and 208.

8. *Ibid.*, pp. 195-96.

that the great blood purges began precisely at the moment of the adoption of the new Constitution with all its "guarantees of right" and that one of the victims was the very author of the document, Nikolai Ivanovich Bukharin.

From arguments for convergence in the fields of spiritual, historical, and socio-cultural "compatabilities," Sorokin proceeds to his final clincher, the sphere of economic convergence:

In the economic field we observe the decline of the Communist system [he wrote in 1943]. Regardless of the personal predilections of the Communists and capitalists, there is no impassable gulf between the present economy of Soviet Russia and the United States. Each has evolved a similar system of so-called "planned economy" with supreme control vested in the government, and with a managerial corporation bureaucracy that is progressively driving out the old-fashioned capitalist owners. A like change has taken place in virtually all the other highly industrialized countries. Actually, economically and politically, the two nations have been steadily converging toward a similar type of social organization and economy.[9]

In this thesis it is impossible not to notice the line that leads from the technocrats through Burnham to Galbraith. Sorokin's theory is much wider including all aspects of the life of the two peoples, geopolitics, history, traditions, culture, "socio-cultural creativeness," the life of the spirit and the spirit of life, all of which are presented as having elements of fundamental identity and as converging toward a common character and fate. Hence Sorokin's may be termed the general theory of convergence while the others follow only one line of his thought and may be regarded as special cases of varieties of economic determinism.

Thus Galbraith, the most sophisticated proponent of convergence determined by economic forces, writes:

To consider the future of [our] industrial system would be to fix attention on where it has already arrived. Among the least enchanting words in the business lexicon are planning, government control, state support, and socialism. To consider the likelihood of these in the future would be to drive home the appalling extent to which they are already a fact . . . to emphasize the convergent tendencies of industrial societies, however different their popular or ideological billing . . . Convergence begins with modern, large-scale production, with heavy requirements of capital, sophisticated technology, and elaborate organization. These require control of prices and, so far as possible, of what is bought at those prices. This is to say that planning must replace the market. In the Soviet type economies, the control of prices . . . and the management of demand . . . is a function of the state. With us this management is accomplished less formally by the corporations, their advertising agencies, salesmen, dealers, and retailers. But these obviously are differences

9. *Ibid.,* pp. 205-06.

in method rather than purpose. Large-scale industrialism requires, in both cases, that the market and consumer sovereignty be extensively superseded. Large-scale organization also requires autonomy. The intrusion of an external and uninformed will is damaging. In the non-Soviet system this means excluding the capitalist from effective power. But the same imperative operates in the socialist economy . . . to minimize or exclude control by the bureaucracy. . . . Nothing in our time is more interesting than that the erstwhile capitalist corporation and the erstwhile Communist firm should, under the imperatives of organization, come together as oligarchies of their own members. Ideology is not the relevant force.[10]

Nowhere does Galbraith indicate any awareness of the role played by public opinion, which he portrays as manipulated by the "technostructure" for its purposes, of the role of consumers' choice, which he also portrays as manipulated by the technostructure, of nongovernmental organizations, of a free press, the separation of powers into legislative, executive, and judicial, government regulation, which is also portrayed as an arrangement of the technostructure, of the multiparty system, or any other of the institutional arrangements by which a free society preserves its freedom. He makes one exception to his crude picture of the predominance of the technostructure over every aspect of modern life, and that exception is the "class" to which he belongs and to which he appeals to follow his lead in exposing and reducing this evil dominion, namely, the intellectuals. The industrial system, it seems, needs, demands, and "brings into existence" great numbers of intellectuals. If they listen to him, they can free themselves from the superstitious belief in the system which it inculcates in them, and then they can cut their progenitor down to size. This is his one exception to the assertion that all our institutions and traditions are hollow, outmoded, and manipulated. After all, he is happily aware that he can write this book and get it published, that he can say what he pleases and, if he says it strikingly enough, get it quoted. He is able to criticize the President and strive to prevent his re-election, to oppose the foreign policy of the administration, to make his critique of the technostructure. "None may minimize," he concedes at this point, "the difference made by the First Amendment." But if all this amounts to is a pious declaration made in one or a dozen amendments called the Bill of Rights, wherein are we any better off than intellectuals in Russia? The Soviet Constitution has many more "guaranteed rights" than ours, but since there is no pluralism, no separation of powers, since there are no nongovernmental organizations, no independent press, no parties, in short, no institutional arrangements to guarantee a First or a Tenth Amendment, writers at this moment are being expelled by "their" writers' union, imprisoned, sent to concentration camps in the Arctic circle, committed to

10. Op. cit., concluding chapter "The Future of the Industrial System," pp. 289-90.

insane asylums, denied publication or a chance to state their case, for the crime of taking seriously the rights "guaranteed" under their equivalent of the First Amendment and the other amendments that make up our Bill of Rights.

This appeal to the intellectuals who are created by the industrial system constitutes the one hope Galbraith offers his readers. It is succinctly stated in the final paragraph (three short sentences) of the final chapter of his book. "Our chance for salvation lies," he writes, "in the fact that the industrial system is intellectually demanding. It brings into existence, to serve its intellectual and scientific needs, the community that, hopefully, will reject its monopoly of social purpose."

But it is the essence of his theory of the convergence of the two new industrial states that this self-same type of intellectual community is demanded and required by the intellectual and scientific needs of the Soviet State, for it too is one of *The New Industrial States* that give his book its title. Indeed, this is what his convergence theory and his book are about, and it is toward precisely this that "hopefully" the two great industrial societies are converging. Hence, when Anthony Lewis asks him the crucial question, *"Are you suggesting that as the two societies converge, the Communist society will necessarily introduce greater political and cultural freedom?"* with no ifs and no buts Galbraith answers, "I'm saying precisely that." [11]

Thus the convergence theory both in its simple and its sophisticated variants has as its core the thought that as soon as the Soviet Union approaches the United States as a "mature" industrial society, develops, as it surely has, a large stratum of managers, industrial bureaucrats, engineers, and technologists (and perhaps, as the more exigent may insist, as soon as it goes from words to deeds in producing a decent quantity and quality of dwelling space and consumer goods), then the differences between the two societies will have become minor and may for all practical purposes be abstracted from or ignored. "The future is not discussed [in America]," declares Galbraith, "because to fix attention upon the future would be to bring home the extent to which [its key features] are already a fact." "The theory of the managerial revolution," wrote Burnham "is an interpretation of what *already* has happened and is now happening." "Any sane person pays no attention to the remaining incompatibilities . . . Communism and the destructive period of the Revolution are already corpses, and only political scavengers can be interested in their revival," proclaims Sorokin.[12] In short, the two societies as they approach each other economically or "industrially," are converging as societal systems de-

11. Galbraith, *op. cit.*, p. 399 and interview with Anthony Lewis cited above.
12. Galbraith, *op. cit.*, pp. 388-89; Burnham, *op cit.*, p. 75; Sorokin, *op. cit.*, p. 208.

veloping similar institutions, outlooks, customs, ways of life, becoming mirror images of each other, and only the cultural lag that is natural to ideologically conservative *homo sapiens* prevents the two peoples from realizing how like each other they have become.

II

One examines the history of mankind in vain for confirmation of such simplicities. Thus one can speak loosely of "the Ancient World" or "Ancient Society," but only until one begins to examine the history, culture, and traditions of some "ancient civilization." Then how different does Athens appear from Sparta; how different the lands of the Hellenic peninsula from the Hellenic World of Alexander of Macedonia; how remote all these from the ancient civilizations of Mesopotamia, Persia, Babylonia, Egypt, India, and China; and each of these in turn from the others. Only a "terrible simplifier" like Karl Marx could write such a sentence as, "In broad outlines we can designate the Asiatic, the ancient, the feudal, and the modern bourgeois methods of production as so many epochs in the progress of the economic formation of society." [13]

And in this same book from which this passage was taken by subsequent vulgarizers of Marx to construct simplistic unilinear pictures of economic determination of historical development, one finds an intended introduction, published only posthumously, in which Marx consciously complicates all that he has here appeared to simplify. In the posthumously published "Introduction" he speaks of "accident, *varia*, freedom; . . . certain facts of nature, embodied subjectively and objectively in clans and races," the problem of Roman Law's proving compatible with modern production; the complex and infinitely varied flowering of the human spirit in art:

It is well known that certain periods of highest development of art stand in no direct connection with the general development of society, nor with the material basis and the skeleton structure of its organization. Witness the example of the Greeks, or even Shakespeare. As regards certain forms of art, as e.g. the *epos*, it is admitted that . . . in the domain of art certain important forms are possible only at a low stage of its development. . . . Greek mythology was not only the arsenal of Greek art, but also the very ground from which it sprang. . . . Egyptian mythology could never be the soil or womb which give birth to Greek art. . . . But the difficulty is not in grasping the idea that Greek art and *epos* are bound up with certain forms of social development. It is rather in understanding why they still constitute a source

13. Karl Marx, *A Contribution to the Critique of Political Economy*, New York, 1904, p. 13.

of esthetic enjoyment and in certain respects prevail as the standard and model beyond attainment. . . .[14]

So one can speak, as Marx does, of "the feudal and the modern bourgeois methods of production" and feel comfortable doing so only until one actually approaches the history and institutions of some individual country of "medieval" Europe or Asia or Africa. When medievalists get together to discuss their specialties, the lands break apart like blocks of ice in a spring flood. As we turn to medieval England or France or Germany or Poland or Italy or Russia, we find the most diverse traditions, institutions, attitudes, forms of mutual obligation or lack of mutuality in various latifundial lands, varying degrees of persistence of Roman forms in one land, German customary law in another, Byzantine, plus Mongol plus Slav heritages in a third. How could Italy, for example, develop anything meaningfully called "feudalism" in view of the persistence of the Roman *municipium*, the city states, the ghost of the Roman Empire in the form of the Church, the continued existence of the Mediterranean and the Adriatic as lanes of overseas trade? And which "medieval England" are we talking about, the Anglo-Saxon with its customary common law? The Norman French that attempted to introduce the feudal institutions of Northern France but with the conqueror maintaining a strong monarchy, an institution that is the very antithesis of feudal power dispersion and "immunities"? Or the later medieval England that emerged from the fusion of centralized monarchy with fragments of French feudalism and Anglo-Saxon common law? Or if we take the three centers of the Slav world, Kievan Rus with its Byzantine heritage and its river trade routes; Moscow at the other edge of Russia, borrowing institutions and deriving strength from serving the Tartar conquerors; Poland with its face turned toward Rome and its anarchic *liberum veto*—how varied are the pictures we get. And how far the Russian peasant is from feudal tenure with his allodial and not fief ownership of his land, with his freedom each

14. *Op. cit.*, pp. 266-312. This intended "Introduction to the *Critique of Political Economy*" was left uncompleted by Marx, perhaps because it would have served to complicate the diagrammatic simplicities of the *Critique* as a whole. It was found among Marx's papers after his death and first published by Karl Kautsky in 1903 in the editions of March 7, 14, and 21 of the weekly *Neue Zeit*, then included in English translation as an appendix to the 1904 edition of the *Critique* from which I have been citing. It shows the richness of Marx's mind and his awareness that the history of actual peoples and civilizations was infinitely more complicated than the simple formulae of economic determinism and "inevitable social progression" that his book was intended to advance. No wonder he left it unfinished and unpublished. How else could he get on with the "cause" his writings were intended to serve? As I have suggested elsewhere, a similar awareness that actual social and economic life was more complex than the simplicities he was advancing made Karl Marx leave *Das Kapital* unfinished, or, in the words of Fritz Sternberg, a "mere torso." (See my *Marxism: A Hundred Years in the Life of a Doctrine*, pp. 321-23 and 324-50; "Das Kapital One Hundred Years Later," *Antioch Review*, Winter, 1966-67, pp. 436-37; and Fritz Sternberg, *Ammerkungen zu Marx-Heute*, published posthumously Frankfurt am Main, 1965.)

year on Saint George's Day to change overlords and take his land with him from one patron to another. The feudal system, insofar as there ever was in Northern and Central France something that might be called "a system," was the result of the decline of the central government and the absence of free land. In Muscovite Russia on the other hand there was always free land to escape to, a free peasantry with allodial landownership and both physical and institutional mobility until the later seventeenth century when fixity, serfdom, or bondage, not "feudal mutualism," was decreed by ukaz, so that the recruiting sergeant and the tax collector might find every soul in his place for the great armies required by the Russian Tsar, the first great armies since the decline of the Roman legions. Only in Russia where it is at present obligatory to find "feudalism" everywhere could it occur to the serious medievalist to speak of this as feudalism.

In the late forties of the present century, under the influence of Arnold Toynbee's assumptions concerning repetitive uniformities in history, a group of our sociologists, anthropologists, philosophers, sinologists, orientalists, and historians, with the support of the Rockefeller Foundation and the American Council of Learned Societies, formed a Committee on Uniformities in History, then looked around for some historical theme or field in which there might be some hope of finding uniformities to explore. Feudalism seemed to offer the most hope; so eight specialists in the history of ancient and medieval lands prepared papers on the existence, nonexistence, or pseudoexistence of something that might be called feudalism in the lands they knew best. When the papers were in, the Committee on Uniformities called a Conference on Feudalism at Princeton University.[15]

The reader who turns to the resulting study in the hope of finding a number of patterns repeating themselves, or a single clear pattern he can store in his mind and henceforth call feudalism, is doomed to disappointment. Indeed, he will carry away a far greater uncertainty as to what feudalism "is" and a deeper awareness of the variety, complexity, and disconcertingly multidetermined and contingent nature of human history.

From the "Introductory Essay" by Strayer and Coulbourn he will learn that

feudalism is primarily a method of government, not an economic or a social system . . . a method of government in which the essential relation is not that between ruler and subject, nor state and citizen, but between lord and vassal . . . the performance of political functions depending primarily on personal agreements between a limited number of individuals [in which] political authority is treated as a private possession. . . .

15. The eight papers and the discussion of their meaning were published as *Feudalism in History*, edited by Rushton Coulbourn, Princeton, 1956.

He will learn that great estates (latifundia) can exist without feudalism, that "the existence of private armies in the services of great men" makes feudalism possible, but if "things do not go much beyond this stage," feudalism remains a mere possibility and a "feudal regime more than doubtful."

As for the "idea of feudalism" it is "an abstraction derived from some of the facts of early European history but it is not itself one of those facts." The term itself was invented by scholars of the eighteenth century after most of the institutions and "the system they postulated" were in desuetude or had vanished. The term is derived from the word *feudum* or fief, "but we should remember that the word comes long after the fact and that the emphasis it put on the fief may be misleading." As with private armies and latifundia, "the fact that one man holds land of another does not inevitably create a feudal relation, and the powers of a feudal lord are not a mere extension of the powers of a landlord. . . . On the other hand, the lord-retainer relationship may be of great importance in a society which is not at all feudal. . . . Serfdom was most oppressive when a strong central government controlled lords and peasants alike," a state of affairs such as prevailed in Muscovy that may be described as *servage*, fixity *(krepost)*, serfdom, or bondage, but is lacking in such essential elements as the dispersion of political power and the mutualism that characterized feudal institutions.

All these complications of the simple high-school textbook definition we once so comfortably memorized are in the first seven pages of the "Introductory Essay" by Strayer and Coulbourn. The actual studies of particular countries and epochs (with the exception of the "model" area of Western Europe and in Asia the millennially isolated islands of Japan) serve only to complicate the picture further or to make some progress in proving a negative, namely that the sought-for uniformities do not appear in the lands and times studied and that the term feudalism as thoughtfully defined in the "Introductory Essay" does not apply to the individual histories studied.

Thus Derk Bodde, eager though he is to broaden the definition of feudalism given in the Introductory Essay so that he can find more "feudal features" and semifeudal periods in the long history of China, winds up with a problem of a "managerial society" or a "bureaucratic-gentry form of society" distinct from the nonbureaucratic feudalism of Western Europe.[16] Burr C. Brundage, writing on "Feudalism in Ancient Mesopotamia and Iran" and accepting the definition of feudalism as "essentially a political phenomenon" finds that "on the subject of political relationships the texts are singularly silent. . . . As for the attempt to visualize feudalism in the ancient Near East as a process, our meager

16. *Op. cit.*, pp. 50 and 92.

documentation does not permit us that luxury." [17] The Egyptologist, William F. Edgerton, writes that those of his colleagues who "have applied the term feudal to certain periods of Egyptian history have not had in mind such a substantive concept of feudalism as is put forward in the Introductory Essay. . . . It may be suggested that the institutions described in the body of this essay [on Egypt] were not truly feudal." [18] The paper on "Feudalism in India" by Daniel Thorner ends with these words: "Using feudalism in the sense of a method of government as indicated in the Introductory Essay, we have to conclude that neither the Rajput States nor the Muslim regimes of northern India were feudal." The essay on " 'Feudalism' in the Byzantine Empire," by the late Ernst H. Kantorowicz of Princeton puts the very word *feudalism* in quotes in his title, begins with some elementary semantics for historiographers, then warns the Conference that "nothing comparable to the peculiar conception of the world and the complexity of Western feudal society . . . ever existed in the Byzantine Empire" though after the Frankish conquest of 1204 some features of Western feudal organization were grafted onto favorable rootstocks in the prior Byzantine setup.[19] Finally, Marc Szeftel, the specialist on Russian medieval institutions, finds that in the Kievan period and in the dominion of Novgorod the Great trade with Byzantium, the Near East, and the Northern Baltic gave political predominance to the big cities and the merchant population whereas in the Muscovite period the enormous extent of free land and the competition among princes for tillers of the soil enabled "both military servants and settlers" to change their allegiance without losing their landed property, their property being "an allod not a fief." In the case of land that could not be transferred "the settler had complete freedom to relinquish his tenure and to change his master." Only with the growth of the central imperial power and the requirement of great armies was fixity created by successive ukazes. This bondage was peculiarly Russian so that Professor Szeftel, though he obligingly wrestles with such terms as "semifeudalism, quasifeudalism, parafeudalism and abortive feudalism," finds that "the context being different, the similarity with early feudal development in the West is not more than superficial" and that "all Muscovite institutional changes were results of the action *from above* of a 'liturgical' state, representing not stepping stones in the direction of a feudal system, but as many measures leading from it toward an extreme centralization of all national life." [20]

In short, the fact that men lived for centuries or millennia primarily by

17. *Op. cit.,* p. 93.
18. *Op. cit.,* p. 150.
19. *Op. cit.,* p. 152.
20. *Op. cit.,* pp. 167-181.

tilling the soil supplemented by warfare and plunder does not signify that they developed similar institutions, outlooks, religions, cultures, traditions, or even similar systems of tilling and occupying the soil. Vulgarized Marxist unilinear and determinist simplicities will find scant comfort in this quest of a number of learned men for "uniformities." At most they will find occasional analogies that dissolve into differing contexts as soon as individual regions and periods are examined.

III

If the historian studies the rapid industrialization of Germany, the United States and Russia in the closing decades of the nineteenth century, when they were borrowing their technology from England and, in the case of the United States and Russia, had been getting much of their initial capital for industrialization from England too, he does not find that the growing convergence of technology and gross national product caused their cultural, institutional, and political differences to become nugatory. Indeed, between 1870 and 1914, as Germany pulled abreast of England economically and technologically, the two countries became less like each other politically, culturally, and institutionally. Germany became a unified land empire with an autocratic emperor who had the power to appoint the Chancellor and the high command of the army, possessed twenty votes and decisive power in the Bundesrat, an absolute veto over all proposals to change army, navy, taxes, or the form of government. Prussia dominated the Reich and, by a system of plural voting, the Junkertum, and the Emperor with his absolute powers, dominated Prussia. Heavy industry was tied in ideologically and physically with militarism and a well-drilled, superbly equipped conscript army. England for its part contented itself with a small volunteer army and the self-assurance that Britains never would be slaves so long as Britannia ruled the waves; Englishmen gloried in their ancient charter of liberties wrung by an aristocracy from the monarch, then broadened to universality as every man's house became his castle; they celebrated liberty under law, the supremacy of parliament, and the steady reduction of the powers of the monarch until he became little more than a cherished symbol. The mood of Germany found its expression in "expressionism" in painting, a form that had no analogue in England, or the United States, or Russia, or France, or Italy. In 1914 when they crossed swords with each other, the two greatest industrial powers in Europe were poles apart. The "common" experience of two total wars has made them still more unlike each other. In matters of the history and national character of a country, its traditions, attitudes, philosophy or philosophies, institutions, values, we must hold with the maxim of Aristotle, "Differentiation is the beginning of wisdom." To note the ways in which a given country fits into some generalized pattern is barely to begin the study of that nation. After putting it into a general class, the real work begins of examining the *differentiae* that distinguish it from the other nations in that general class. To note resemblances in some economic or institutional feature is barely to begin the study of a nation. To stop there is to abstract from all the things that give color, flavor, distinction to each people in its life and history.

Even when nations seek to borrow some institution from a "model" country, as nations borrowed the idea of a parliament from England, "the mother of parliaments," they transform what they borrow into something else that fits more nearly into their own heritage and condition. How different are the "parliaments" of England's colonies and ex-colonies from that of the mother country. The American colonies modeled their colonial legislatures, their continental congress, and federal congressional system on England's parliament, but as we examine our division of powers, our cabinet, our president, our constitution, our supreme court, we realize that they are other institutions engendered in another world. If we move from these to the French Chamber of Deputies, the German Reichstag and Bundestag, the Cortes of Alfonso XIII and the Cortes of Franco, the "Soviet Parliament," the "guided democracy" and handpicked parliament of a Nasser or a Sukarno, the What-you-may-call-it of a Hoxha, we realize that they are all quite different institutions. To lump them together as "deliberative bodies" is only to begin, or perhaps to hinder, the work of studying each of them in its own nature. It is one thing to import and copy technical devices, or the names and external forms of institutions, and quite another to import the cultural climate that engendered them.

IV

Joseph Stalin once charged this writer with being "an American exceptionalist." The more I considered his curious charge, the more convinced I became that I was guiltier than his indictment suggested, for I realized that I was an "exceptionalist" not only for America, about which we were then arguing, but for all the lands on earth. I thought, for instance, of India and China and wondered how one could be content to lump them together under the single rubric of "Asiatic lands" without losing all sense of difference in their spiritual and intellectual life, their social structures, literatures, arts, philosophies, faiths, dreams, all the qualities of life that made these two Asiatic lands more different from each other than England from France or Germany. During that wide-ranging debate with Joseph Stalin I became aware of what I had long sensed, that every land moves toward its future in terms of its own past, its own institutions and traditions. To abstract from those differences as Marx sought to, as Lenin did, and as Stalin was trying to persuade me to do, was to miss the essence of each country's life and history. In that moment of challenge to simplifying abstractions, I think a historian was born.

Latterly a new generation of simplifiers has appeared. It employs, perhaps unwittingly, a grossly vulgarized Marxist concept to the effect that economics determines politics and culture, that economics is "the foundation" and all the rest is a "superstructure" that reflects and is determined by the "foundation," or is just "ideology" in the sense of "false consciousness," "cultural lag," or "official myth." This vulgar Marxism I fancy would have made Marx wince and repeat his famous epigram, "If that be Marxism, then I myself am no Marxist."

It is terribly easy to forget that technology is neutral as regards freedom, that it may be used either to liberate or to enslave, to inform or to brainwash.

That was what troubled Alexander Herzen when he contemplated Russia's constant drives for industrialization and "modernization" from above, always "modernizing" Russia's technology and industry for the purposes of power and war, but not permitting development of an autonomous public life. In an open letter to Alexander II Herzen wrote:

If all our progress is to be accomplished only through the government, we should be giving the world a hitherto unheard of example of autocratic rule, armed with everything that freedom has discovered; servility and force supported by everything that science has invented. This would be something in the nature of Genghis Khan with the telegraph, the steamship, the railroad, with Carnot and Mongé in the general staff, with Minié weapons and Congreve rockets, under the command of Batu.[21]

"Some day," Herzen wrote in fear, "Genghis Khan will return with the telegraph." "Hurrah!" cry our convergence theorists, "then he will cease to be Genghis Khan." Can we so soon forget that it was the technologically most advanced country in Europe, with the earliest and best social welfare laws, the highest degree of literacy, the model universities and greatest number of Ph.D.'s, that developed first one of the most extreme forms of militarism and then one of the most rabid forms of totalitarianism?

Are we to believe that when every man can read, it will no longer matter whether he lives under a system that gives him freedom to choose what he will read or under a system that gives him no such choice but

21. *The Bell,* No. 4, London, Oct. 1, 1857.

determines what shall be printed and prescribes that he shall read only a single officially prescribed version of each subject and event, and shall read, see, and hear the same slogan at the same moment in the same controlled press, radio, television, and wall-space in every corner of the land?

Are we to believe that because there are mass circulation journals, a television set in eevry home, and a loudspeaker in every public place, that it no longer matters whether there are many parties or one; rival programs or one incessant iteration of unassailable and unquestionable dogma; rival candidates to choose from or no choice at all; a chance to instruct, rebuke, tame, turn out one's rulers, or no such chance?

Is the presence of heavy industry supposed to make us forget that the central problem of politics is not *Who rules over us?*, but *How do we choose our rulers?* and *How do we tame them?* and *How do we keep some ultimate control over them in our hands?*

Suppose it were true that there is no difference between the way the Russians run a railroad and the Americans; suppose airplanes were just as open to the people of Russia as to the "new class" and any one could ride or fly from one end of Russia to the other without a *komandirovka* or internal passport. There would still be a simple human difference that technological similarities would leave untouched. Here is the difference as stated by two young Russian intellectuals, "B" and "T," interviewed by John Morgan of BBC for the television program *This Week* (one of them consented only to be interviewed in a moving auto with his face covered but both expressed substantially the same thought on the technology and politics of freedom of movement):

—*Who are the privileged classes?*
B: The people who are allowed to go abroad. . . .
—*Are you proud of being a Russian?*
B. Yes, I'm happy to be a Russian. If I had to die for my Russia, I would easily do it, like two uncles of mine. . . .
—*Would you prefer to live somewhere else than in Russia?*
B. Yes, of course. I wouldn't even choose a country if you just offered me one, as long as it wasn't a communist-run country, I would willingly go there. T: In England you may be faced with a hundred political problems, in Russia one single one. "Is it possible to get out of Russia?" No, it is not possible. You cannot imagine what that means. In England you can either solve your problems or not solve them, and leave the country, and say "No" to England. . . . A Russian doesn't have such an opportunity open to him. He is forcefully kept inside this country. It is forbidden to leave it. You are locked in here. Therefore all politics is governed by this simple basic rule. A Russian and an Englishman work from different political axioms. In your conditions parallel lines don't cross, but with us all our lines cross at one point. It is difficult for us to understand each other in this matter. It is a basic condition of being a prisoner, of being surrounded. . . . The whole place is a prison. . . .

P: In spite of the huge territory, everyone here realises that he has 11,000 kilometers one way, and 4,000 kilometers the other, and beyond that just barbed wire.[22]

All the technological similarities imaginable and all the Bills of Rights that paper will put up with will not alter the intellectual barbed wire represented by absolute monopoly of the means of communication and of all the devices, paper, presses, meeting halls, publishing houses, reviews, reviewers, formulations, even vocabularies, by which men communicate with each other and know each other and themselves. The rulers own and control the journals and organizations that might criticize their mistakes, their stupidities, and cruelties. Harvard professor Galbraith could not be a professor in a Soviet University, A.D.A. leader Galbraith could not be a political leader, author Galbraith could not get a book published if it maintained that the two systems are getting to be indistinguishable. If he could steal a bit of paper and use an off-hour mimeograph machine to set down his views, he would be hauled into court for anti-Soviet propaganda, tried by a judge who knew in advance what the verdict was to be and how to make the crime fit the punishment. The courtroom would be packed with secret police masquerading as intellectuals and workingmen, who would testify that his views were intolerable to them, corrupted their children, endangered the public safety. He could not get friends, relatives, or admirers of his wit into the courtroom. The "audience" would drown the words of the accused and his witnesses with jeers and clamor for punishment. If he persisted he would run the danger of going to a sanitarium for the mentally deranged as has been the case with Yessinin-Volpin, Bukovsky, Tarsis, Batashev, Vishnevskaya, and General Grigorenko, whose madness has consisted in taking seriously the Soviet Constitution and its Bill of Rights and trying to act on the basis of the rights guaranteed therein.[23]

To sum up: the convergence theory will not stand up to examination in the light of history nor to an actual examination of the two countries that are supposed to be converging. The likelihood is that they will continue to move each toward its own future under the influence of its own

22. *Encounter*, London, Feb. 1968, pp. 68-75. "P" is a third interviewee.

23. From dependable sources (which will have to be accepted or rejected on faith since I cannot name them), I have learned that there are now two lunatic asylums, one on the outskirts of Moscow and another near Leningrad, given over to "political lunatics" and a third of increasingly political character. In the whole history of Tsarism there was one tsar, Nicholas I, who declared one philosopher, Peter Chaadaiev, insane for critical remarks on Russia's cultural sterility, but he was not committed to an asylum, merely somewhat restricted in his freedom of movement and compelled to accept the indignity of daily visits from a doctor for one year, after which he apparently recovered his sanity. There were no political or literary or philosophical lunatics under Lenin or Stalin but an epidemic of such madness since Khrushchev at the beginning of the sixties declared: "We have no more political criminals in the USSR. The only ones who oppose our system today are madmen." Yet the terms remain inter-

heritage, its traditions, and its institutions, a heritage that will be both conserved and altered more by the actions of men than by the weight of things. Even the technical devices they borrow from each other they will use differently as they assimilate them into their differing ways.

Finally, there are two special matters that carry us beyond the usual framework of academic discussion of a tentatively advanced hypothesis. The first concerns the inner health of American life. If our free institutions, our pluralism, multiparty system, right of dissent, complex of non-governmental organizations, independent press and publishing houses, independent scholarship, freedom of literary and artistic creation, freedom of movement, of dissent, freedom of choice in the market place and the forum, have really been hollowed out and emptied of their meaning by manipulation by the technostructure, or if we are persuaded to this by technocrats, managerial revolutionists, and technostructural determinists, then we lose our perspective on what is worth defending in our society.

Conversely, the advocates of the convergence theory are presuming to speak for the silent in Russia, assuring us, and those struggling for freedom, that technological progress at a certain point brings freedom in its train and the human effort to secure such freedom is pointless or at best an unconscious reflection and epiphenomenon. The words of "B" and "T" to John Morgan, the perils faced by Pavel Litvinov, Yessinin-Volpin, Bukovsky, Chukovskaya, Solzhenitsyn, Sinyavsky, Daniel, Brodsky, and countless other unsung heroes to be true to their vision, to awaken the conscience of the outside world and bring it to bear on their plight, are the best commentary on the notion that freedom comes out of the machine and the requirements of the technostructure and not out of the struggles of men longing to be free. Thus, it seems to me, there is mischief as well as error in the convergence theory.

---

changeable. Yessinin-Volpin, for example, has spent four years in camps and two in asylums, and in February he was again declared insane for his activity on behalf of Sinyavsky and Daniel and his insistence that the Constitution's Bill of Rights be taken seriously by censors, courts, and police. His madness is evidenced in the appropriate fields of philosophy, mathematics, cybernetics, and concern with poetry and freedom. His *Leaf of Spring* was published in English in 1961. The President of the Academy of Sciences, Kaldysh, has more than once secured his release from jail or asylum by insisting on his importance in cybernetics and mathematics. I suppose the use of a madhouse instead of a bullet in the base of the brain may be set down as liberalism, or relaxation, or thaw.

INDEX